Rural Change and Urban Growth 1500–1800

W. G. Hoskins

RURAL CHANGE AND URBAN GROWTH 1500–1800

*Essays in English
Regional History in
Honour of W. G. Hoskins*

Longman

Edited by

C. W. CHALKLIN and M. A. HAVINDEN

Longman
1724-1974

LONGMAN GROUP LIMITED
London
and Longman Inc., New York
Associated companies, branches and representatives
throughout the world

This edition first published 1974

ISBN 0582 50019 2
Library of Congress Catalog Card Number: 74–82566

Printed in Great Britain
by J. W. Arrowsmith Ltd., Winterstoke Road, Bristol BS3 2NT

Contents

List of Plates

List of Figures

Notes on Contributors

P. H. E. BAGENAL, OBE, DCM, FRIBA; Acoustic Consultant, Royal Festival Hall, etc., author, *Theory and Elements of Architecture* (with R. Atkinson, FRIBA) London, 1926); *Planning for Good Acoustics* (with Dr A. Wood) (London, 1931); articles in the Journal of the Royal Institute of British Architects and the Journal of the Architectural Association.

M. W. BERESFORD, MA (Cambridge); Professor of Economic History, University of Leeds; author, *The Lost Villages of England* (London, 1954); *History on the Ground* (London, 1957); *Medieval England: An Aerial Survey* (with J. K. S. St Joseph) (London, 1958); *New Towns of the Middle Ages* (London, 1967); *Leeds and its Region* (edited with G. R. J. Jones) (London, 1967); a chapter in *The History of the Working Class Housing*, edited by S. D. Chapman (Newton Abbot, 1971); *English Medieval Boroughs* (with H. P. R. Finberg), (Newton Abbot, 1973).

C. W. CHALKLIN, BA, BLITT. (Oxford); Lecturer in History at the University of Reading; author, *Seventeenth Century Kent* (London, 1965); *The Provincial Towns of Georgian England* (London, 1974); articles in Agricultural History Review, Urban Studies, etc.

J. C. K. CORNWALL, MA (London), FRHISTS; Senior Lecturer in History at the North East Essex Technical College, Member of the Council of the Essex Archaeological Society; author, *Lay Subsidy Rolls* (Sussex Record Society, 1956); *How to Read Old Title Deeds* (Birmingham, 1964); contributions to a number of historical journals.

A. M. EVERITT, MA (St Andrews), PHD (London); Hatton Professor of English Local History, University of Leicester; author, *Suffolk and the Great Rebellion, 1640–60* (Suffolk Records Society, 1961); *Change in the Provinces: the Seventeenth Century* (Leicester, 1969); *The Local Community and the Great Rebellion* (London, 1969); *Ways and Means in Local History* (London, 1971); *The Pattern of Rural Dissent: the Nineteenth Century* (Leicester, 1972); two chapters in *The Agrarian History of England and Wales Vol. iv, 1500–1640* edited by J. Thirsk (Cambridge, 1967); editor, *Perspectives in English Urban History* (London, 1973).

M. A. HAVINDEN, MA (Cambridge), BLITT (Oxford); Lecturer in Economic History, University of Exeter; Secretary, British Agricultural History Society; author *Estate Villages, a study of the Berkshire Villages of Ardington and Lockinge* (London, 1966); editor, *Household and Farm Inventories in Oxfordshire, 1550–90* (London, 1965); contribution to *People in the Countryside: Studies in Rural Social Development* edited by J. Higgs (London, 1966); *Agriculture and Economic Growth in England, 1650–1815* edited by E. L. Jones (London, 1967); articles in the Economic History Review and the Agricultural History Review.

R. MILLWARD, MA (Cambridge); Reader in Historical Geography, University of Leicester; author, *The Making of the English Landscape Vol. 3: Lancashire* (London, 1955); *Scandinavian Lands* (London, 1964); *The Lake District* (London, 1970); five titles in the *Landscape of Britain* series (London, 1971–2).

R. S. NEALE, BSC.(Econ. London), MA (Bristol); Associate Professor and Head of Department of Economic History, University of New England, Australia; author, *Class and Ideology in the Nineteenth Century* (London, 1972); a number of articles on aspects of the history of Bath in various historical journals.

R. NEWTON, CMG, MA (Cambridge), PHD (Exeter); author, *Tarnished Brocade*, (1937); *Swords of Bronze* (1939), *Victorian Exeter* (Leicester, 1968); *The Northumberland Landscape* (London, 1972). Colonial

Administrative Service, 1931–61, retiring as Colonial Secretary, Mauritius.

D. M. PALLISER, MA, DPHIL. (Oxford); Historical Research Officer, York Archaeological Trust; author, *The Reformation in York 1534–53* (London, 1971); *Chester 1066–1971* (Chester, 1972); contributions to *Crisis and Order in English Towns 1500–1700* edited by P. Clark and P. Slack, (London, 1972); *Perspectives in English Urban History* edited by A. Everitt (London, 1973); *Newcastle-under-Lyme 1173–1973* edited by J. H. Y. Briggs (London, 1973); several articles on local history, especially in the North Staffordshire Journal of Field Studies.

D. PORTMAN, MA, BLITT. (Oxford), PHD (Exeter), MRTPI; Senior Lecturer in Rural Resource and Countryside Planning in the Department of Town Planning, Oxford Polytechnic; author, *Exeter Houses 1400–1700* (Exeter, 1966). Formerly involved in town and country planning in Norfolk and Hampshire.

I. J. THIRSK, BA (London), MA, (Oxford), PHD (London), FRHISTS; Reader in Economic History in the University of Oxford; author, *English Peasant Farming: The Agrarian History of Lincolnshire from Tudor to Recent Times* (London, 1957); *Suffolk Farming in the Nineteenth Century* (Suffolk Records Society, 1958); editor *The Agrarian History of England and Wales IV, 1500–1640* (Cambridge, 1967); *Seventeenth-century Economic Documents* (edited with J. P. Cooper) (Oxford, 1972); contributions to a number of historical journals.

Acknowledgements

We are grateful to the following for permission to reproduce copyright material:

The Trustees of the British Museum for Plates 12 and 13; Exeter City Library for Plate 4; Leeds City Libraries for Plates 15 and 16; Philipson Studios, Newcastle upon Tyne, for Plates 2 and 3; West Air Photography, Weston-super-Mare for Plate 14.

Introduction

The great difficulty in preparing a volume in honour of W. G. Hoskins lay in deciding what subject would best represent his multifarious interests. Clearly the emphasis needed to be on regional history but this in itself was not enough. What was needed was some limitation in time and scope which would give the volume unity and at the same time reflect the variety of approaches which Hoskins has explored over the years. We decided that the economic and social changes which took place in the period of slowly maturing development between the Middle Ages and the Industrial Revolution (roughly from 1500 to 1800) were the most suitable subjects for the book and that detailed local studies were the most appropriate way of emphasising the variable impact of these changes on the diverse regions of England.

Hoskins' role as a path breaker both in rural history (agricultural, social and demographic) as well as urban history (of buildings, social structure and industry) is discussed in the section devoted to him; but because of this dual influence it seemed desirable to divide the book into two parts dealing broadly with two of the most fundamental trends discernible in the period – the slow break-up and transformation of the ancient feudal and localised rural society – and the steady, persistent growth of towns, both old and new. The result is twelve studies contributed by some of Hoskins' former pupils, friends and colleagues, studies which are diverse in subject and setting but are united in a common approach and attitude.

Comprised under the heading of Rural Change are some alterations in social relationships between lords and tenants, changes in local government, population growth (and the diseases and deaths which often so disastrously checked it), agricultural improvements (new crops, new manures and new methods of cultivation) and by no means least important, changes in the standard of living which were reflected in improvements to farmhouses and cottages arising from the growing prosperity which became evident (for farmers at least) after about 1550.

The changes in tenurial relationships and in local government were most obvious in the remote border areas like Northumberland where the military tenures and administration had survived into the sixteenth century nurtured by the ever present Scottish threat. However, Robert Newton's study shows that long before the union of the Crowns in 1603 border tenures were being undermined by the growing commercialisation of agriculture (which placed fat rent rolls before numerous tenants) while the political power of border lords was being sapped by the growth of royal government. All this was reflected in the changing landscape and architecture of the county.

These developments also affected the relationships of classes in society, noticeably that between the feudal nobility and the country gentry about whose rise so much learned ink has been spilt since Professor Tawney first emphasised it in 1941.

It is therefore instructive to have Julian Cornwall's study of a very different aspect of their life in early Tudor time. The squire of Conisholme in Lincolnshire was very poor, lived very simply and his family never rose. But, despite the squire's obscurity, Cornwall's study reveals how dependent Tudor Governments were on such men at times of revolt such as the Pilgrimage of Grace (1536) when their monopoly of armour and weapons often proved crucial against numerous but mostly unarmed peasant mobs. The importance of this in days when there was no standing army and no police force can hardly be overemphasised.

The importance of a growing population as an underlying factor in economic and social change has been emphasised by Hoskins in many of his local studies. A demographic essay in this book is thus particularly apt. David Palliser's study of the mechanics of population change in relation to harvest failures and epidemic diseases in Staffordshire, adds to our still rather sparse knowledge of this important subject.

In the context of a growing population (and of growing urbanisation) an increase in agricultural productivity was an obvious necessity. The discovery of a whole complex of new and productive crops in America (such as maize and potatoes) provided one possible avenue of advance. Joan Thirsk shows how the introduction of such new crops could have a profound influence on agricultural profits and commercial organisation, using the interesting example of tobacco about which hardly anything has previously been written.

New techniques of production were also being introduced and Michael Havinden's study focuses on the spread of lime. The importance of which in neutralising acid soils and enabling them to respond to increased dressings of farmyard manure has not perhaps been fully appreciated. It was particularly important in the upland northern and western counties, of which Devon is a good example (and no study in honour of Hoskins could ignore his native county).

These economic changes were reflected in the standard of living (especially in improved housing) as Hoskins himself demonstrated so well in his study of what he called 'the great rebuilding' after about 1570. Derek Portman's detailed analysis of documents and surviving houses in the Oxford region underlines the reality of this movement and fills in much new detail.

Finally, in the section on rural change, Alan Everitt draws attention to a new aspect of social transformation in the eighteenth and early nineteenth centuries: the rise of a leisured, often professionally based, but non-landed class which he terms the pseudo-gentry. He uses the family of the well known historian of Kent, Edward Hasted, to illustrate the vicissitudes which so often befell families of this kind, families which nevertheless were of growing importance in the English social scene.

Under the heading of Urban Growth attention is drawn to the creation of new towns, the emergence of town planning, the economic basis of urban growth and the rise of the speculative builder to provide cheap housing for the new industrial working class in the late eighteenth century.

Roy Millward's study of the Lake District in some ways mirrors Newton's analysis of Northumberland, but with a different emphasis. Millward shows that in hitherto sparsely urbanised regions like Cumbria, it was still possible to found new market towns such as Ambleside, as well as to expand existing centres, such as Kendal.

Christopher Chalklin pursues a similar theme with examples drawn from a much wider area, showing how changes in fashion and economic needs fostered the growth of a few new towns. For instance Tunbridge Wells developed as a spa, while the expansion of industry and trade led to new ports like Whitehaven in Cumberland for coal exports to Ireland and Portsea (an expansion of Portsmouth) to accommodate the growing navy.

The leisure concept appears again in Ron Neale's examination of the growth and planning of Bath, where large-scale speculative entrepreneurship attained considerable artistic distinction. The growing wealth of the nation in the eighteenth century cried out for new ways of displaying itself, and Bath arose as almost a unique phenomenon – a city devoted to elegant ostentation and pleasure.

In sharp contrast was the work of Richard Paley in Leeds who set out to provide cheap housing for the industrial workers; but as Maurice Beresford shows, although Paley's houses later became notorious slums, they were not inconvenient by the standards of the time, nor were they too densely packed or overcrowded at the time they were built. It was later development which proved their undoing. Finally Hope Bagenal's assessment of the rationale of traditional building draws the two sections together to some extent by spanning the evolution of the distinctively attractive English local architectural styles in both rural and urban areas. He shows how the mundane needs of function were combined with local materials and an aesthetic sense to produce sturdily practical building which is also architecture. As editors (and former research students) we have taken great pleasure in planning the book and watching it take shape as the contributions came in and were related to each other. Our appreciation of the full depth and range of Hoskins' influence grew immeasurably during this process.

CHRISTOPHER CHALKLIN

MICHAEL HAVINDEN

W. G. Hoskins:

An appreciation

Few British historians have been so original in their approach or so influential, both in writing and in the spoken word, as William George Hoskins. The influence has been so many-sided that it is difficult to know where to begin to describe it. Hoskins helped to create a new branch of historical studies, landscape history, when he published *The Making of the English Landscape* in 1955. But before that he had done much to change the study of local history from an amateurish potpourri into a recognised academic discipline as was symbolised by his appointment as head of the first University Department of English Local History (at the University College of Leicester in 1948). This draws attention to the fact that he is the foremost authority on the history of Leicestershire, and yet, as everyone realises who has met him or seen him on television, he is a Devon man to the core. His monumental guidebook and history of Devon (in the New Survey of England series) written in 1954 established his position as the leading authority on his own county beyond any dispute.

All this may lead us to believe that he is a man of limited interests, concentrating on small patches of ground. Nothing could be further from the truth. He has always kept his eye on the crucial relationship between the particular event and its significance for the general understanding of the fundamental movements of economic and social history. Thus, in his hands, specialised studies – such as population growth in Exeter or open-field farming in Leicestershire – are always used to illumine and deepen our understanding of the wider aspects of demographic or agricultural history. He has shown that the more profound and thorough the local study, the more relevance it has for general history. Understanding is built up by a complex appreciation of local variety. His forthcoming book on the economic and social history of England in the sixteenth century entitled *The Age of Plunder* will be the culmination of his many years' original research along these lines.

It is impossible in a brief introduction to do justice to the exceptionally wide range of historical themes which Hoskins has illuminated. One can only draw attention to his most important contributions. The great progress which has been made in our knowledge of agricultural history, especially of the sixteenth and seventeenth centuries, owes much to his pioneer study of the development of agriculture in Leicestershire. His essay on 'The Leicestershire farmer in the sixteenth century' (1950) had a particularly strong impact.[1] Work on the agrarian history of the early modern period was not new: scholars such as R. V. Lennard and Mildred Campbell had already made good use of certain of the available sources in the Public Record Office, but it was undoubtedly the work of his friend Professor R. H. Tawney which inspired him to probe deeply into the agrarian and social aspects of the history of local communities. Tawney's advice and guidance played an important part in the development of Hoskins' outlook. Hence Hoskins was the first to exploit the full range of parochial manuscript material in local and national record offices and particularly the innumerable surviving wills and probate inventories. He made this possible by confining his attention to a single farming region, or contiguous group of regions. His particular emphasis has been not on the gentry, but on the farmers and the farm workers – the 'peasantry' in rural society. These 'yeomen', 'husbandmen' and 'labourers', on whose behalf Hugh Latimer and William Cobbett had belaboured authority, had often farmed the same few acres for generations, and were the backbone of the community in which they dwelt. Hence, in Hoskins' view, they were the key factor in its growth and development.

Urban history also owes much to his inspiration. His first book, *Industry, Trade and People in Exeter, 1688–1800* (1935) was a landmark in historical studies in explaining the history of an urban community in terms of the fortunes of a regional industry. As a leading urban historian has remarked, 'his work ultimately led others to develop a group of studies on industrial towns that are some of the most solid and revealing things to have been done in recent urban history'.

His work on the history of the English landscape has perhaps been his greatest achievement. From boyhood he has been patiently exploring what he has described as 'the history that lies behind the scene of everyday existence'. In early youth he began to explore the pleasant countryside surrounding Exeter, the quiet valleys of Exe and Creedy under the steep hills, the farms and bartons. It is a countryside which, given a receptive mind, nurtures historical imagination and insight. Here in a tranquil landscape a group of barrows, a bramble- and hazel-choked lane (once a Saxon manorial boundary) or a Norman font are records of the long centuries of human settlement which went to the evolution of the modern rural scene. In this area from one of his favourite viewpoints, the Iron Age Cadbury Castle, all Devon between Exmoor and Dartmoor stands revealed; in certain lights its woods and hedgerow trees evoke the shadow of the primeval forest from which the early settlements were cleared. From the wide map spread out by man and nature below Cadbury Hoskins turned to the Ordnance Survey, convinced that it would provide the key to the understanding of what he saw, inspired by Maitland to attempt 'to construe the testimony of our fields and walls and hedges'. Muddy boots, long tramps through the deep Devon lanes, directed in due course by a trained and disciplined curiosity, were to lead to meticulous studies of small corners of English countryside. At length the parts took their place in a larger pattern, and synthesis emerged in *The Making of the English Landscape* (1955).

This use of a combination of documentary and visual evidence is also well exemplified in his paper on 'The rebuilding of rural England, 1570–1640'. Here he showed that there is ample evidence in surviving farmhouses of rebuilding and enlargement in this period, from places as far distant as Cornwall, Lancashire and East Anglia; while documents were used to fill out the picture by revealing the greater privacy and comfort achieved by the types of new rooms provided, as well as illuminating the costs of building, and the economic and social causes and consequences of the physical changes. Hoskins has also shown how the historian can draw on the skills of the archaeologist, the geologist and the botanist, and has suggested that the theory that hedgerows may be dated from the number of different types of trees or shrubs to be found in them, may be a useful working hypothesis (though not every cautious scholar will follow him along this path).

It is perhaps above all as the pioneer historian of the English local community that he is best known. Of local histories Hoskins himself has written that too many have been devoted to pedigrees and the descent of manors, that many local historians were 'too preoccupied with facts and correspondingly unaware of problems'. In seeking to overcome the prevailing antiquarianism, he defined the theme of the local historian as 'the origin and growth of his particular local community or society; the peculiar and individual nature of this society and the way it worked through the centuries – that is, the way it solved certain basic political and economic problems, above all the problem of how to get a living for an increasing number of people from the fixed supply of land and other natural sources'. The study of local history draws together the themes already mentioned, and many others. The history of a country parish is revealed by the farmhouses and field boundaries created over the centuries: by the study of its agricultural system, especially in the sixteenth and seventeenth centuries, when the rural community was reaching the high tide of its prosperity and cohesion; by the development of its trades and crafts, its church and school, the furnishings of its farmhouses and cottages, and not least, by the course of population change and the effect of epidemics.

The study of local history has taken Hoskins far back into the Middle Ages, through the lay subsidies of the fourteenth century to Domesday and the archaeological evidence of Anglo-Saxon England, and even to the Iron Age and the Bronze Age. The nineteenth and twentieth centuries, the period of the collapse of local communities, he has found less sympathetic. All these many interests are outstandingly illustrated in his study of a Leicestershire country parish, Wigston Magna, entitled *The Midland Peasant* (1957), while his insights about the scope and sources of local history have been drawn together for the student in his *Local History in England*, one of the leading textbooks on the subject. This was first published in 1959, and has recently been expanded in a second edition (1973).

In every aspect of his work Hoskins has inspired able colleagues and students. Especially noteworthy have been his successors – Professor H. P. R. Finberg (with whom he jointly wrote *Devonshire Studies* in 1952) and Professor Alan Everitt at the Department of English Local History at Leicester; and Dr Joan Thirsk, an old friend and colleague, who was the first member to join him in the Department of English Local History at Leicester, and who succeeded him as Reader at Oxford. However, there have been a host of others, resulting partly from the expansion of teaching and research in

universities during the course of his career, and by the major growth
in local studies among amateur historians throughout the country.
They have been inspired by the intrinsic interest of the themes he has
explored, and by his literary ability – his aim of writing to be read.
His researches have been published in no less than twenty-three books
and more than thirty articles. It is also the consequence of the
enormous amount of time he has been prepared to give, in advice and
discussion, to anyone with a serious interest in local and regional
history. Generations of students have found his enthusiasm infectious.
A former student of his at Leicester in the later 1940s (Ron Neale)
who has contributed to this volume writes:

> 'He influenced me to look at the English countryside and urban
> landscape in an entirely new light. He urged us to put on our boots to
> walk the ground to which the documents referred. Open field ridge
> and furrow, deserted villages, model villages, country houses and
> country towns – we walked over them and through them with
> Hoskins as a guide.

His kindness to local historians, whether amateurs, colleagues or
research students, is well known and much appreciated. Visits to
seek advice or help are frequently enriched by his generous hospitality, when his appreciation of good food and wine have full play.
In the congenial atmosphere of his home, conversation is stimulated
and encouraged; but though often wise and profound, he is never
heavy or dull and his sparkling wit is always bursting through. For
this serene home background he owes much to his wife, Jane, who
has supported him so loyally and efficiently throughout his career.
Her excellent cuisine is always a delight.

Hoskins' ascent to academic distinction has been a triumph of
talent and determination, for in the early stages of his career he did
not have assistance from a wealthy home, a public school, or an
Oxbridge college – assets which were much more important when
he began his career than they would be today. He was born in
Exeter on 22 May 1908, the eldest son of William George Hoskins of
St David's Hill, Exeter, and of his wife Alice (nee Dymond), who
came from the nearby village of Silverton. Both the Hoskins and
Dymond families have numerous and deep roots in Devon. William
George Hoskins senior ran a bakery and confectionery business in
Exeter which he inherited from his father, and his wife's family were
also bakers in Silverton. Clearly the tradition of appreciating good
food was well established in the family, but the interest in history does

not seem to have been inherited. At least there is no record of any of
his family pursuing this study. The interest in farming is however
strongly reflected in his background for Hoskins is descended
from a long line of yeoman farmers. As he has himself written:

> They had farmed in east Devon since the 1580s, before that in west
> Dorset for many generations. Often they farmed on a considerable
> scale, and accumulated at times a number of leasehold farms besides
> their smallish freeholds. George Hoskins (1773–1839) married well –
> the daughter of a big landowning yeoman at Payhembury – though
> he had no land of his own, and for many years he did well on a large
> farm just outside Sidmouth. Then came the great slump in farm prices
> after 1814. It hit him hard, with twelve children to feed and clothe.
> At last he was forced to give up his farm. In 1827 the parish register
> describes him as 'Labourer' for the first time, and so he remained
> until his death twelve years later. His sons and daughters all dispersed.
> His eldest son, my great-grandfather, walked to Exeter, some time in
> 1825, learnt the baking trade, and set up his own small business in
> 1834 (*Devon*, p. 99).

Hoskins won a scholarship to Hele's grammar school in Exeter in
1919 and then proceeded to his local university (then the University
College of the Southwest) to read economics in 1926. A PhD followed
under the supervision of Professor Joseph Sykes, the subject being
landownership in Devon, 1650–1800; after a spell at Bradford
Technical College Hoskins took up a lectureship in economics at
the University College of Leicester in 1931. Throughout most of the
1930s the teaching of economics and commerce earned his academic
bread and butter; the studies in local history were somehow fitted
into his spare time, and into extramural teaching at Vaughan College
in Leicester.

During the second world war he worked in the Civil Service in
London on the Central Price Regulation Committee, and he has
always said that this experience of governmental administration at
the centre was fruitful in broadening his historical understanding.
The historian gains from knowledge of how decisions are taken in
the contemporary world of affairs. His experience as an Exeter City
councillor in the early 1960s came into the same category, and was
inspired by his lifelong interest in the conservation of historic buildings and by the awareness of a critical mind of the ambiguity of the
word 'progress'.

After the war he returned to Leicester, where his work on local
history increasingly interested the Principal of the University
College, F. L. Attenborough, himself a historian and an expert

photographer, who often accompanied Hoskins on his parochial explorations. Many of the illustrations in Hoskins's books are from Attenborough's plates. In 1948 the Department of English Local History was created at Leicester, to enable Hoskins to pursue his researches more effectively. His star was now in the ascendant and soon after (in 1951) he was invited to succeed R. V. Lennard as Reader in Economic History at Oxford, with rooms in All Souls College. His lecture courses ranged far beyond early modern English economic history to local history and urban topography, and helped to draw many research students to him. His university career culminated in 1965 when he returned to Leicester as Hatton Professor of English History and resumed the headship of his old department as well. Since his retirement in 1968 he has been an emeritus professor there but has returned to his beloved Exeter to live.

Some extracts from a letter written in January 1966 provide a homely glimpse of his domestic life and working environment at this time as well as showing how his perennial historical curiosity could still be stimulated even by the return to a familiar scene.

> We are now comfortably settled in at Melton Mowbray, a busy little town 15 miles from the subtopia of Leicester – a house solidly built in 1923, with Edwardian mantelpieces (an elderly architect, probably) and with half an acre of attractive gardens and many trees. At the moment we merely read the *Amateur Gardener* and wait to see what the garden contains; but then stern action will be required. The house takes all our attention at the moment. As for shelf-room I was in despair until we thought of turning the semi-derelict conservatory (17×12 ft) into a study, with a new roof and a new floor, and with all the staging that once held hideous cacti and tomatoes now cleaned up for my books. I now have a model work-room, which people say resembles a Cornish studio, and here I sit and write while others toil in the garden, clearing up the neglect of a few seasons, shifting stones and other debris, barrowing away sawn-off branches, and so forth. There is much to do. . . . We have found a splendid butcher, a good game merchant, and excellent wine. Also a good reliable builder. Melton is still rather old-fashioned, with several family businesses still in being. The weekly market – on Tuesdays – is most attractive along the streets. I buy all sorts of things because I like the colours and the shapes. It is a good market still, and has been in existence since Saxon times for it is recorded in 1066. I hope they haven't moved the day in the interval. One hates so much chopping and changing. Few things remain as they were before 1066. I should like to think that Melton market is one of them.

From here I shall venture forth soon to work upon the topography of Norfolk, a part of England that draws me like a woman – above all, the cold, austere north coast with its salt marshes, its heathlands behind, and the large gaunt churches smelling of paraffin and old stone.

Hoskins served on the Royal Commission on the Common Lands from 1955 to 1958 and on the Advisory Committee on Buildings of Special Architectural and Historical Interest between 1955 and 1964. He was also a founder member of the British Agricultural History Society (in 1952) and was elected its President in 1971. Additional national recognition included his election as a Fellow of the British Academy (in 1969) and the award of a CBE in 1971 for services to local history, the first time the citation has been used. In 1974 he was awarded an Honorary D.Litt. by the University of Exeter. Though retired from university teaching he is still actively researching and writing and finds time to maintain a vigilant and effective interest in the defence of his native Devon, beleaguered by so many aspects of modern development.

---

1. In *Essays in Leicestershire History*. See the Bibliography for a list of Hoskins' books, articles and papers.

RURAL CHANGE

1   ROBERT NEWTON

The Decay of the Borders: Tudor Northumberland in Transition

A book that awaits the attention of a historian with the requisite time and energy is a social and economic history of Northumberland from the beginning of the sixteenth to the end of the eighteenth century; from the age of the Border Ballads and *Marmion* to that characteristically eighteenth-century moment when the new Assembly Rooms in Newcastle upon Tyne, completed in 1776, were dedicated to 'an age when the polite arts . . . had advanced to a state of perfection unknown in any former period'.[1] For under the more dramatic raiding and lawlessness for which Northumberland in this period is best known can be discerned unmistakable signs of the beginning of a profound transformation of the wild Border landscape and its society. This transformation was at length to reach its climax when the Northumbrian landlords on their orderly estates had established themselves in the van of agricultural progress and Tyneside had become one of the great workshops of the world. E. Hughes's interesting study of the north-east from 1700 to 1750, and the *Short Economic and Social History of the Lake Counties*[2] indicate what is still to be written on Northumberland in a larger work.

The object of this paper is to examine the 'decay' of which Elizabethan administrators so constantly complained, and which they investigated so assiduously. 'Decay' presented itself to the government in the form of a sharp fall in attendance at the musters.

The conclusions are that while 'decay' took several forms, in its most important aspects it was the dissolution of the traditional Border society under political and economic pressures, and the beginning of new growth. Under the troubled surface lay the seeds of new growth which were to reach their maturity only in the sunshine of the Georgian peace after 1745.

In the reign of Henry VIII government policy began to dismantle the framework of society in rural Northumberland by destroying the power of the Percy earls.[3] In the place of the earls governing through their undisputed local eminence, their allies and dependants, the Tudors substituted a new class of administrators dependent on the support of the Crown and with abundant opportunities for prospering at the expense of the old order. This policy in its turn alienated a large section of the gentry and gave a new edge to family feuds and rivalries. The Crown's religious policy created further divisions, it alienated the strong element of the Catholic gentry and also those who, though Protestant, looked back with nostalgia to the past. The government could never wholly rely on the loyalty of the North, where the malcontents were always liable to receive succour and military assistance from kindred spirits across the Border. In 1569 it was touch and go whether Leonard Dacre would be defeated before a strong force of Scottish Borderers came to his aid, and with them the fugitive earls of Northumberland and Westmorland.

Indifference, or open hostility towards the government, must have indirectly removed a barrier to a vital change in the attitude towards land. The Border tenures of the North were intended to ensure the provision of properly equipped armed men for the defence of the Border, and at need to back their landlords with lance and sword. 'There is no lease in that country,' Burghley was informed, 'but with provision to find horse and armour for each tenement, to be held by an able man.'[4] By the second half of the century, in a period of rising prices and conspicuous consumption, there is ample evidence that a holding was regarded more as a source of wheat, sheep or cattle, and less as the maintenance of a horseman. Tenants clung to their customary tenures because they were protected thereby from increased rents, and were given virtually a freehold of their land. Landlords increased fines and gressoms, and rents where possible. Both parties had an interest in the subdivision of tenements. As it was put in contemporary terms, landlords looked more to their profits than to defence, seeking good farmers rather than skilled spearmen; tenants paid more attention to cattle and manure than to the prov-

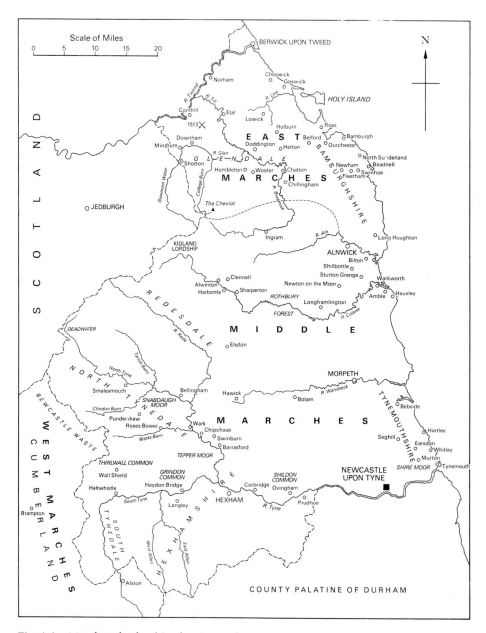

Fig. 1.1   Northumberland in the sixteenth century.

ision of armour and warhorses. Until the Union of the Crowns in 1603 the Crown enforced the retention of the customary tenures but could never ensure that they were used for their proper purpose.

D. L. W. Tough wrote that 'decay is often used in Border papers with no exactly defined meaning; but the fact of decay in the second half of the sixteenth century is indisputable'. He summarised its causes as 'the hostility of the opposite nation and mismanagement'.[5] The chronic raiding and insecurity undoubtedly contributed to the further impoverishment of an already poor countryside. Labour and money were diverted to the construction of private strongholds but, significantly, not to the repair and maintenance of the major castles which had been an essential factor in the strategy of Border defence. In this respect at least 'the fact of decay' can be accepted in the literal sense. Yet it would seem that in general the 'hostility of the opposite nation' was a subsidiary cause, despite the abundant documentation of raiding. Raiding would have been at least checked had the old structure of leadership and military obligations remained intact, and the government would not have been faced with the constant appeals of its representatives for men or money, especially for money, to pay to fill the places of those who were bound by their tenures to give military service. Moreover, as a warden of the Middle Marches pointed out, the Northumbrians gave better service even than Yorkshiremen, if they could be induced to do so, 'knowing all the fords, passages and clans of Scotland'.[6]

By this argument, therefore, 'decay' was Northumberland's own response to the forces of the sixteenth century, themselves assisted by Tudor domestic policies. The exploits of Border reivers and chieftains are historic facts; the Border ballads in the main are true reflections of contemporary society. These aspects of Northumbrian history have however overshadowed other aspects of perhaps greater significance. In the sixteenth century the Northumbrian aristocracy and gentry began the transformation of the medieval landscape which was to end in the rural landscape of modern Northumberland. Throughout all the turmoil of Tudor Northumberland their position remained virtually unshaken. In this respect the aftermath of 1715 made more impression, through the sale of impoverished or forfeited Jacobite estates, than did Tudor monarchs. The roll of Northumbrian landowners of 1873[7] is a remarkable reflection of sixteenth-century Northumberland, both in regard to families and the relative size of their estates: the Duke of Northumberland with 186,616 acres; Charlton of Hesleyside with 19,730; Selby of Biddlestone with 25,327; Sir John Swinburn of Capheaton with 28,057; the Earl of Tankerville, of Chillingham, with 28,930; Sir John Haggerston of Ellingham with 14,285. These and a host of others with smaller estates perpetuate the position of sixteenth-century landowners, and to a great extent their geographical distribution.

To the Northumbrian historian C. J. Bates the county's history 'is essentially a drum and trumpet history from the time when the *buccina* of the Batavian cohort first rang out over the moors of Procolitia down to the proclamation of James III at Warkworth Cross . . . a history of the battles of kites and crows'. All Northumberland was a march, part of 'the Marches of England foranenst Scotland'.[8] More specifically the county comprised two marches, the East Marches and the Middle Marches. The West Marches included all Cumberland and Westmorland. In 1386 the marriage of Henry Percy, first Earl of Northumberland, to the widow of the Umfraville Earl of Angus, laid the foundations of the vast Percy territorial power in the North. By Tudor times this power had been recognised by the virtual monopoly within the house of Percy of the wardenships of the East and Middle Marches, and their holding of the offices of bailiff of Tynedale and constable of the royal castles of Bamburgh, Dunstanburgh and Newcastle. The Tudors made the wardens officers of the Crown to whom, in the absence of local support, they were constantly appealing for men and money. There was a brief but significant change of policy in 1527 when the sixth Earl (Henry Percy 1502–37) was restored to the position of his ancestors in order to reduce Northumberland to order.

Newcastle alone was exempt from any aspect of decay and was settled on the course which was to lead to the city's nineteenth-century eminence. Wills and inventories demonstrate that the wealth of its merchants could vie with the fortunes made in southern England and far surpassed the exiguous wealth of the country gentry.[9] The gentry for their part sent their younger sons into trade and the enrolments of apprentices show that many came from their ranks.[10]

Outside the walls of Newcastle few could deem themselves or their property safe. In 1524 English outlaws accompanied by Scots raided to within eight miles of the city. As late as 1596 Robert Carey had to report that the Scots had reached Alnwick, 'the strongest town in all Northumberland', whence they had carried off horses and oxen and left for dead a justice of the peace.[11]

Throughout Henry VIII's reign Northumberland was either disorderly or anarchic. For the Northumbrian countryman under Elizabeth I the kite and the crow over the line of a raiding party were not just the stage properties of Gothic imagination. Sir Walter Scott of Buccleuch, 'the bauld Buccleuch' of balladry, came into Tynedale plundering, burning and drowning, acting, as Sir William Bowes admitted, 'under the ancient immunity to kill whosoever they found under the red hand, possessing or driving stolen goods'.[12] Far down the North Tyne the trumpets of Robert Kerr of Cessford sounded defiance from the towers of Swinburn. Border habits of the period appear to have contributed the term blackmail to common use, the protection money often paid in meal or corn. 'Divers of her Majesty's loving subjects', ran the preamble to the statute Cap. xiii of 43 Eliz., 'are forced to pay a rate of money, corn, cattle or other consideration commonly called by the name of Black-Mail, unto divers and sundry upon or near the Borders, being men of name.' The preamble itself is a confession of failure in the North after one hundred years of Tudor rule.

The chronic insecurity was to a large extent caused by the failure of Tudor governments to find an effective substitute for local ties and loyalties, which were themselves based on ties of kinship and personal obligation, reciprocal bonds of protection and service. Loyalties such as these were not automatically transferred to a distant sovereign, still less to an official who was regarded as having usurped his position from its traditional holder and was in any case likely to be some 'inland' man from the South. The Northumbrian *surnames*, a term of late medieval origin, were analogous to the Scottish clans, though similarities were due to convergent evolution. The 'riding surnames' of North Tynedale and Redesdale – Halls, Charltons, Robsons, Milburns and others – presented an intractable problem to Tudor administrators. They formed kindred groups, holding land by virtue of membership of the kindred as well as by feudal tenure.[13] They were linked with the clans across the Border by language and customs, ties of marriage and alliance, mutual support and sanctuary against authority. Their dales provided an easy route for Scots raiders from the Border to the Durham boundary, and thence at need into Richmondshire in the North Riding. Their primary loyalty was to the kindred. Juries convicted under peril of 'the deadly feud . . . implacable without the blood and family destroyed'.[14] Even the combined influence of the formidable Earl of Surrey, victor of Flodden, and the judges of assize, failed to produce witnesses against eleven Borderers at Newcastle in 1523. Seventy years later a warden of the Middle Marches failed to coerce a Hexham jury to convict a member of the Heron family.

The administration sought to reduce the surnames to obedience by means of punitive expeditions. Hostages were taken to ensure the good behaviour of a kindred, but these were wont to escape or to be rescued by force. The chiefs or 'headmen' of the surnames for their part endeavoured to provide hostages who could be written off without serious loss if subsequent events brought them death by hanging or neglect in gaol.

In one important aspect of major policy the Tudors were successful. There was no serious invasion from Scotland after Flodden (1513). The reluctance of the Scottish nobility to cross the Border in force was confirmed at Solway Moss (1542). The Crown's always tenuous control of the North was at grave risk in 1536, and again in 1569–70; but despite Hunsdon's exasperated remark, that the North knew no prince but a Percy or a Neville, the military challenge of the old order ended, not ignobly, with the charge of the Dacre tenantry near Brampton in that bitter February of 1569–70. There was a brief rekindling of those ancient loyalties in the form of the devotion of the Earl of Derwentwater's tenants in 1715. After the flight of the Northern Earls the Crown's representatives were established in office more or less firmly; they displayed a marked uniformity in their failure to impose order and in their querulous condemnations of the Northumbrians.

From the bishop of Carlisle's reports of theft and extortion in the Northumberland of 1522 to Lord Eure's 'continual outcries on behalf of this wretched March', in 1596, officials wrung their hands over 'a miserable, distressed and wasted country'[15] and their own inability to effect more than fleeting improvements. The Middle Marches, *umbilicus morborum et malorum*, were in the worst plight; but Bowes had to inform the Queen personally in March 1597–98, that justice and authority were lacking everywhere 'so as upon the rings of all the Three Marches, as the tenth plough will scant be had, so not the twentieth armed man to furnish those places as they were wont'.[16]

Within the boundaries of the modern county Elizabethan Northumberland may have had a population of some 95,000 persons,[17] a density of 42·2 to the square mile. The difficulty of arriving at a firm estimate of sixteenth-century population is notorious and this is particularly true of the Border. It is reasonable to assume that Northumberland's harsh experience of war and brigandage in the fourteenth century, in addition to plague and famine, made the county even more thinly populated in relation to southern England. If so, the population had made a remarkable recovery in some two hundred years, from an estimated population of 25,210 and a density of 17·2 persons to the square mile in 1377.[18] Some indication of the relative position of sixteenth-century Northumberland may be obtained from comparison with Julian Cornwall's samples for the 1520s[19] with the densities added in brackets: Buckinghamshire 37,680 (50·8), Suffolk 90,500 (63·4), Sussex 35,590 (41·3), Berkshire 35,590 (49·4). It is true that there is a gap of a generation or more between the two sets of figures, but in other respects also Northumberland was at least a generation behind southern England.

Then, as now, Northumberland was dominated by Newcastle upon Tyne, the third city in the kingdom with a population of some 10,000. 'I have been forced to remain here longer than I meant to have done', Hunsdon wrote from Newcastle in 1587, 'first because there is no place within the Middle March, though Hexham, Morpeth and Alnwick all be set together, that is able to afford me and the gentlemen that are with me horse meat and man's meat for the night, the country is so bare.' The climate was harsh and may have been affected by the general climatic deterioration which set in during the century.[20] The Earl of Surrey, an experienced campaigner, complained in May 1523 of heavy rain and the coldest weather he had experienced at that time of year. In October 1542, when the harvest was good in England generally, the corn just across the Border was still in the fields and so wet with snow that it would not burn.

Northumberland was not self-supporting in corn. The routine maintenance of the Berwick garrison depended on supplies by sea from Yorkshire or East Anglia. In 1542 'few of the army found victuals, food or drink, between York and Newcastle'. Conditions were worse during the four-day march from Newcastle to Berwick. 'As for the oats', wrote the Earl of Hertford, 'as ye know they occupy them for food and drink'.[21] Nevertheless arable farming was more widespread and reached higher altitudes than in modern times. There are, for example, extensive areas of old ridge-and-furrow in the neighbourhood of Alwinton and Clennell, where evidence of the long-continued use of the plough on the steep slopes of the Cheviots is provided by the existence of lynchets, of which there are also impressive examples above the College Burn and on Humbledon Hill north of Wooler.

Relatively to its resources the country was overpopulated. In the wild country extending westwards from Rede and North Tyne towards the Bewcastle Fells and Liddesdale there were holdings which in the sixteenth century were required to support an armed and mounted man but which today are represented by a shepherd's cottage or tumbled stone in the grass and heather. In the 1580s there were two tenements in decay at Pundershaw in Wark Forest, and six on the moorlands above the Chirdon Burn, on Snabdaugh and Whitchester moors. East of North Tyne four tenements were in decay at Hawick, near Sweethope Lough, now, like Pundershaw, enveloped by the conifers of the Forestry Commission.

Tudor administrators recognised the connection between the pressure of population on land and the endemic raiding. In 1541 it was reported that both Tynedale and Redesdale were 'overcharged with an excessive number of inhabitants more by many than the profits of the same country may sustain'; and so 'the young and active people for lack of living be constrained to steal or spoil continually either in England or Scotland'.[22] A living of some sort was ensured by membership of the surname. Throughout the manor of Wark, all Tynedale from the Border at the Deadwater to the Alston fells, the tenants, it is recorded, 'reap and mow each their known ground separately, after the first crop they eat all in common, without stint or number; except in some places where the tenements lieth in several'.[23] Similarly with rights of pasture: they 'shield together by surnames, not keeping cattle according to the stint'. The economy was overwhelmingly pastoral. In Redesdale, the richer of the two dales, the 'known ground' of 168 tenants of Elsdon parish comprised 790 acres of arable (av. 4·7), 577 acres of meadow (av. 3·5) and 4960 acres of pasture (av. 30·1). The common grazing ground amounted to 13,550 acres, with a further 21,200 acres of 'certain high grounds' called summer shielings shared by all the inhabitants of the manor.[24]

Tynedale and Redesdale practised on a larger scale the predominantly pastoral economy of Northumberland as a whole, which was based on ample and often distant grazing grounds shared by groups of townships, such as the Shire Moor of Tynemouthshire. Shildon Common, east of Corbridge, was shared by eleven townships. Grindon Common was used by all the townships of the barony of Langley. Within townships such as Shilbottle and Hartley half the area was pasture. In a pastoral society the local landowner tended to assume many of the attributes of a tribal chieftain with an influence, derived from ties of blood and kindred, extending beyond the bounds of an estate. The gentry were rough, turbulent and clannish, differing in little more than degree from the headmen and chiefs of the 'riding surnames'. Under Elizabeth I they

Plate 2 Bamburgh Castle
Site of the original Anglian settlement of 547, later capital of Bernicia; the
keep was built by Henry II as one of the primary strategic fortresses of the
Border. In 1538 the castle was 'in great ruin and decay'. In 1575 it was 'in
utter ruin and decay'. Sir John Forster, Warden of the Middle Marches
1560–1595, was Captain of Bamburgh 1555–1602. Characteristically he added
to its dilapidation. Forster was in residence at Bamburgh when he barely
escaped assassination at the hands of Scots raiders who gained entry to the
castle in 1597. The photograph shows traces of old ridge-and-furrow which
abounds in Northumberland.

were still given to the pursuit of their quarrels in a series of murderous affrays recalling the England of the Paston Letters a century before.[25] Sir John Forster, for thirty-five years Warden of the Middle Marches,[26] had to fortify his official authority by local alliances and influence, but even he could not overcome the hostility of the gentry outside his circle. Insecurity put a premium on self-help, and on the support of the kindred and its allies. 'The gentlemen of Northumberland,' wrote Lord Eure, 'except a few are combined by tryst to save their goods to let outlaws pass, some favouring them for clan or marriage'.[27] Sir John Delaval found it convenient to make his own private treaty with the Halls of Redesdale, by which the Halls undertook to 'save and keep harmless the said Sir John, his heirs and successors'.[28] There was little support among the gentry for the Crown's religious policy – Cecil was informed in 1569 that there were not ten gentlemen in the country who favoured it.[29]

By the end of Elizabeth's reign gentlemen who had given good service on the Border found it preferable to withdraw and develop their estates. 'Divers gentlemen of good livelihood who had their habitations there, and kept good families of horse and foot, removed into the inland country whereby their houses have become farmholds upon great rents; or, what is worse, turned their grounds into pasture.'[30] The Earl of Northumberland at this time was kept in the South by government policy, and the lack of his local influence must have been a contributory cause of the markedly poor showing of his tenants at the musters.

Throughout the century the Northumbrian gentry were written off by Crown representatives as uncooperative and ungovernable. Early in 1543 John Dudley, Lord Lisle, reported to the Duke of Suffolk that

> as for order and watch to be kept upon the Borders, it is not possible to be holpen, without that the gentlemen of those parts would take some pains for their own surety; but such is their envy, hatred, disdain and malice among them, that one of them would see another's throat cut, rather than that they will rise to go to their doors to save their neighbour's goods; and if your Grace shall perceive such malice amongst themselves, as is not (I think) amongst no nation of the world, and that doeth these thieves and outlaws know, which maketh them so bold upon these quarters.[31]

Elizabethan officials reiterated these charges. Lord Hunsdon, warden of the East Marches and governor of Berwick from 1568 to 1596, echoed Lord Lisle. If the gentry would do their duty the

Queen would not be put to great charges; but 'such is their malice among them, and mistrust of one another, as though the fray came hard by their doors, they will not stir, unless it be some of their friends' goods of theirs that be taken away'.[32]

The distant government and most of its representatives were working against the grain of Northumbrian traditions and loyalties. Country gentlemen like Sir Henry Widdrington could on occasion be attended by one hundred horsemen, mostly of their own kin, but no similar effort was made to attend the musters.

In 1538 the muster of the East and Middle Marches produced a force of 2,766 equipped and mounted men excluding the 'Tynedale thieves', said to be 350 men with horses and harness, and the 'foot thieves' of Redesdale.[33] The musters of March 1579–80 produced only 323 men 'horsed and harnessed' from the East Marches, and 1145 from the larger Middle Marches. There was a further decline in 1584 when 267 equipped horsemen attended from the East Marches and 819 from the Middle. The musters of the Middle Marches on Stagshaw Bank and Abberwick Edge in 1595 produced a total of 136. On the last occasion only thirty-seven fully equipped horsemen appeared from the baronies of Langley, Bywell and Bulbeck, and from Hexhamshire, the Allendales and all Tynedale.

In 1580 the Privy Council enquired into the 'great decay of horses' on the Marches. The Earl of Huntingdon, President of the Council in the North, replied that decay was 'most plain'.[34] A further note[35] attributed the situation to leases by the Crown and lesser landlords who 'looked only to their profit, breeding cattle and not horses'; to 'the long peace'; the exactions of landlords in taking fines and gressoms from their tenants, thus causing tenants to keep cattle 'to manure their dear farms'; the absence of the keepers of castles and place of defence; the lease of Crown property to 'inland men'; and to the daily sale of horses to Scotland. It was also reported that land was being leased to Scots, who were immune from raiding, and that 'sundry towns where were many households' had been converted into sheep runs.

In the following year (1581) commissions were authorised, by Cap. iv. 23 Eliz. I 'to enquire what tenancies and houses of habitation since *anno* 27 Hen. VIII [1536] be decayed and not occupied by men able to serve as horsemen or footmen, according to the ancient duty of these tenancies, and to examine the probable cause of these ruins'. The Act elicited the report of 1584[36] with its detailed schedules covering 301 localities and townships throughout Northumberland, 178 in the Middle Marches, together with a handful of unspecified holdings in Haltwhistle parish, and 123 in the East Marches. By no means all townships in Northumberland are mentioned. Nor is it possible to reconcile the total of decayed tenements in the summary (407 in the Middle Marches and 947 in the East Marches) with the actual figures in the schedules. But the general impression is clear. It is a record of a traditional military society in dissolution.

In the Middle Marches no less than 158 townships failed to produce either horse or foot. Fifty-two were 'in decaie' or were described in similar terms; thus Sheepbanks, near Sharperton, was 'undone'. For Bolam the entry stated simply 'the towne was burnt'. Eighty-nine townships had been 'decaied' or 'spoiled' by the Scots, or, in respect of the earl of Northumberland's property in Tarsetdale, 'all slaine by Scotts'. Inevitably, damage by raiding was concentrated in North Tynedale, from Tepper Moor just north of the Roman Wall to Smalesmouth and Tarset, and in Redesdale. A belt of raiding damage also extended eastwards from Rothbury Forest to the Aln taking in Newton on the Moor, Glantlees, Shilbottle and Bilton. Harden House, a Selby property on the fells above Biddlestone, had been converted to pasture; this provides the only specific example of a change of use which might support the general reference in 1580 to the conversion to sheep pastures of 'sundry towns where were many households'. In Tynemouthshire six townships, Whitley, East Chirton, Preston, Murton, Earsdon and Backworth, were recorded as 'oppressed with encrease of rentes'.

In the schedule of the East Marches no reasons for decay are given. Of the total of 123 townships ninety-one could furnish neither horse nor foot, these included substantial villages belonging wholly or largely to the Earl of Northumberland, Long Houghton with twenty-seven tenements in decay, and Chatton with eighteen. Elsewhere Cornhill contained twenty-four decayed tenements, Doddington fourteen and Wooler twelve. Lowick was 'alle decaied'.

In Glendale, once the most prosperous area of Northumberland,[37] decline was equally marked. Homeldon township contained no less than twenty decayed tenements. There were another twenty in Hazelrigg, together with fourteen in Hetton and ten in Holburn. Lowick township, which had sent ten equipped men, and fifty-seven without equipment, to the muster of 1538, had lost no less than forty tenements. The little townships on the coast opposite Holy Island, Fenham, Goswick and Cheswick, had lost thirty-seven tenements between them.

The figures indicate that over wide areas of Northumberland the ground was being prepared by the elimination of holdings, and by

their increasing diversification in size, for the evolution of the large
farms and dependent rows of labourers' cottages which eventually
became characteristic of the Northumbrian landscape in the second
half of the eighteenth century. The process was particularly evident
in the East Marches which Pennant, in 1772, was to find 'miserably
depopulated, a few great farmhouses and hamlets . . . rarely scattered
over vast tracts'.[38] From the decay of the late sixteenth century
emerged the modern farm-hamlets of Glendale, such as those
between the Till and the Low, which together sent fifty-two equipped horsemen and 129 unequipped to the muster of 1538 and could
find none of either category in 1584; and the impressive farms and
wide fields of modern Bamburghshire, such as Shoreston, Fleetham
and Spindlestone, with twenty-eight decayed tenements between
them. Far in the western moorlands the decay of twenty tenements
'over Tarsettwater', of Roses Bower on the Warks Burn, and Wall
Shield remote under Thirlwall Common, presaged the great sheep
runs of the future.

The 'Abstract of the decaies and impoverishments of the East
Marches', in the report of 1584,[39] summarises the disorderly state of
Northumberland and also records economic factors as a potent
contributory cause of decay:

Causes of decaie	*Meanes to repaire*
Stelthe by the Scots their neighbours	For the inhabytants to followe hew and crye
Stollen goods seldom rescued by Justice without pryvate Revendge	A better waie of Justyce to be used at the daies of Truce
The disordered Cominge of the Scotts into Englande by daie lighte under subtile pretence	That no Scott come into Englande but first repayer to the Cunstable of ye nexte Englishe Towne, and show him the Cause of his Repayringe
Diverse waste Townes spoilede by the Scotts uninhabytede	For two fortress to be errectede upon the uttermoste partes of the borders
Want of Intertainment by the Prins in tyme of warrs too the Contrye gentlemen	A petycion for interteinement in tyme of warrs
Want of watchinge the waters	To fortiffie the bridges, and stope and watche the fords

Graunte of Leases in Revertion of Impropryate parsonages to Courtiers and suche other	That her Majestie woulde bestowe her impropryate parsonages and teithes on suche the Contrymen as have them in possessyon
Lettinge of tenements or fearme holdes to plowmen to halfe	That the farmer be an able man to serve on horsebacke, the horsse to be kepte by the owner and farmer
Occupieinge of farmeholds by the owners plowemen, and Catle be not Ressyant upon yt	The owner to find an able man in everye tenement
Tenements occupiede by plowemen by fearmers or Leasers	The fearmer or Leaser to finde a ploweman able to serve
Tenements taken from their tenants by the owner, and laide to inlarging of demaines	The owner to sett sufficient tenants to keepe horsse and Armour and weapon for service of the Contrey
Manye tenantes for feare dare not kepe horsse fit for service	To enforce the Scottes warden to Joyne in spearinge filinge and deliveringe all goods stollen whatsoever
The houldinge of lands by her Majestie duringe minoritie, and marriage of her subjectes the owners	That her Majestie woulde suffer those tenements and Lands to be in the hands of some one of the moste able frends that belongs to the said owner
Controversies amongste gentlemen and other of the marches	That the L.(ord) Governore of Barwycke and the L.(ord) Warden might for the moste parte be resyant upon the Charge to ende and determine all Controversies

The situation in the Middle Marches[40] was attributed to:

1. The Longe peace
2. Exactions of owners and possessours
3. Her Majesties possessions there leasede to Inlands men
4. Absence of Captens and Kepers of Castles fortes, and howses of diffence
5. Pryvate quarrels amongste the gentry
6. The dearthe and scarcetie of horses
7. The sale of horses into Scotlande

The report made plain the growing preoccupation with the most profitable use of land at the expense of military service. Landowners encouraged by the long peace with Scotland were now said to 'seeke their neereste comodytie converntinge their store of horses and furniture to store of cattle, and sheepe for the increase of their gaines . . . Regardinge more their proffites than their defence by the strength of their tenantes, and inhance their rentes, dryvinge the most parte of their inhabytantes first to sell their horses and furniture for payment thereof and nexte to provyde cattle for manurance.' Crown properties were 'more leasede since thende of the warrs, than they have bene usede at anie tyme before, to the greife and prejudice of sondrie fermours'.

The events of the sixteenth century did not lead to any permanent large-scale alienation of land outside the ranks of the Northumbrian gentry. Mary Tudor restored to the seventh Percy earl (Thomas Percy 1528–72) the estates which had been devised to the Crown in 1537. After the attainder and subsequent execution of the seventh earl in 1572 these estates passed to his brother. There were, however, frequent opportunities, both in the reigns of Henry VIII and Elizabeth, for the control of estates to pass temporarily into the hands of others who exploited them to the full. Inland men, 'sondrie persons not inhabytinge in the contrie', took their pickings. They had nothing to learn from Sir John Forster. 'I know not what authority is committed to Sir John Forster of the Earl of Northumberland's lands and leases', Hunsdon wrote to Burghley, 'nor what he has purchased thereof, but he takes the rule of all. It is a pity to see how Alnwick Castle and Warkworth are spoiled by him.' Hunsdon added: 'It was a happy rebellion for him . . . it was worth in spoils £3,000 or £7,000 to him'.[41]

The situation was unchanged in the last years of the Queen's reign. In 1592 Sir John Forster reported that little or nothing had been done to strengthen the Border since 1581. Since that year many of the gentry were said to have laid waste townships 'to make demesnes thereof for their own private commodity'.[42] Two years later it was reported that there were 1,157 decayed tenancies in the Middle Marches, including 338 in Hexhamshire, which had been scarcely included in the returns of 1584, and 284 in Tynemouth-shire.[43]

More enquiries followed. The instructions to Lord Eure, newly appointed warden of the Middle Marches, in October 1595, included a request for proposals to remedy the situation described by Lord Huntingdon as 'spoiling and burning in Redesdale and Tynedale, taking away lands from tenements; and lastly, too much subdivision of holdings'.[44] Sir William Bowes and Sir Thomas Fairfax, members of the Council in the North, were also instructed to report on the decay of tenancies caused by the Scots and by land-lords in the Middle Marches. In 1596 the situation in the East Marches was summarised in terms of horses:

By negligence and wilfulness of owners and farmers	152 horses
Converting tenements to demesnes or pasture, dividing and conjoining	48 horses
Excessive fines, improved rents, services and oppressions	188 horses
By Scots not denizens occupying lands in England	13 horses
By Scottish spoils and ransoms	139 horses
	540

There was also a loss of 1,245 horses in the Middle Marches 'by the like causes and murder of English subjects. The damage inflicted by Scots raids was estimated to amount to £15,876'.[45]

Spoils, ransoms and murder of English subjects were the normal occurrences of daily life, though the incidence varied according to the state of Anglo-Scots relations and of 'the tickle (*sic*) and un-certain government' of Scotland itself. Much depended on the will and ability of the Scots authorities to control their wardens and on the personal relations between the wardens of both kingdoms. 'The thieves' harvest', as Robert Carey termed it, officially lasted from Lammas to Candlemas, from August to February. After Candlemas 'all nights grow shorter, all cattle grow weaker, and oats growing dearer, the reivers feed their horses worst, and quickly turn them to grass'.[46] But in practice there was no close season. Many major raids involving 100 men or more took place in the summer, such as a destructive onslaught on the Ingram area by some 400 men in June 1587.

Despite the destruction and dislocation caused by raiding it is arguable that it was a contributory rather than the primary cause of the poverty of rural Northumberland. In the returns of 1584 raiding is one of several reasons cited to explain shortfalls in the musters though admittedly it accounts for over half the total of decayed townships. In 1596 the major reason given for the lack of horses, which implied the failure of a holding to support a mounted man, was economic. The long-term effects of ordinary raiding can be exaggerated. The destruction of dwellings which were no more than huts roofed with heather thatch could easily be repaired. Serious damage to the towers, peles and strong stone houses of the gentry and wealthier farmers required time, which was not usually available to a hard-pressed raiding party. Raids for revenge were more destructive; so too was damage by invading armies, though in this respect the English side of the Border in the sixteenth century never experienced the widespread and savage devastation which the Scots endured from the Earl of Hertford's army in 1545.

Raiding as a means of livelihood requires certain conventions if it is to be profitable. Bloodshed and unnecessary destruction were avoided if possible, in theory at least, by the Bedouin. On the sixteenth-century Border initial statements of damage were not necessarily expected to be believed but were the opening move in a long process of claim and counter-claim. Crops were not normally destroyed except in revenge. 'The Borderers will not willingly burn their neighbours', Hertford reported in 1545,[47] and accordingly Irish troops were used to destroy Scottish farms along the Bowmont and Kale Water. Human life was cheap, but prisoners were more profitable than dead men; farmers of Kirkaugh on the South Tyne, when following the fray in 1589, were captured with their horses and equipment and then ransomed for the substantial sum of £180.[48] Borderers on both sides were often cruel and ruthless. In their feuds they were remorseless, as Buccleuch demonstrated by a savage raid into Tynedale on Easter Sunday, 1597. But the ordinary reiver preferred to pick up his sheep or cattle quickly and quietly without running into too much trouble.

Flodden did not bring peace to the Border and for most of Henry VIII's reign the Marches were as disorderly as they were during the copiously documented reign of Elizabeth I. Yet the evidence of the report of Bowes and Ellerker in 1541[49] suggests that even in the earlier period, which included the more than usually disorderly years 1523–41, raiding was not responsible for the abandonment of villages on any significant scale even close to the Border line. Of the thirty-six townships in Glendale mentioned in this report, thirty-two containing 387 husbandlands, were described as 'plenished', 'well plenished', or 'now well plenished'. Moneylaws and Mindrum, both without tower or barmikin, and therefore exposed to 'great hurt in time of war', were in good order, despite the comment on Mindrum that 'in every appearance of a troublous world or war it is abandoned and left waste'.

Four small townships had been waste and unplenished 'since

before the memory of man'. Shotton had been waste for thirty years or more; Elterton for so long 'that it [could] not be remembered how many husbandlands it did contain'. These townships were situated particularly close to the Border line, in the hills between the College Burn and the Bowmont, and within easy raiding distance from Teviotdale. In a similarly exposed situation was the 10,000 acres of the lordship of Kidland, a tangle of narrow, steep-sided valleys whence the burns descend to the Upper Coquet from the Border ridge. Between the burns the fell tops provided a number of easy raiding tracks which gave access into the heart of Northumberland. It is not surprising that in 1541 Kidland had not been inhabited 'since Teviotdale was English'. The lordship was not to be repopulated until the eighteenth century.

Kidland however is the sole example of the abandonment of a substantial area on account of raiding. Elsewhere, as Professor Beresford has pointed out, 'the fact of destruction by an enemy meant that the marginality of a particular site became an immediate practical consideration'.[50] This could have occurred at Downham with its eight husbandlands 'waste by occasion of war'. The township was acquired by Cuthbert Ogle, the fighting parson, who built a tower but, in 1542, 'occupieth the said towne nowe with but two plowes of his owne. The resydue thereof he kepeth to medowe and pasture for his own cattall.'[51]

Damage and dislocation caused by raids clearly were a major factor in the impoverishment of Northumberland despite the problem of net loss or gain raised by the operations of the English Borderers. 'Scotland . . . seems to demand above £30,000 more than the English bills come to,' wrote the Earl of Huntingdon, adding 'not any such sum or near it has enriched the English by spoil or otherwise.'[52]

According to a report of 1594 damage in the Middle Marches since the twenty-sixth year of the Queen's reign amounted to £9,450. In the following year, however, Burghley was informed that the gentlemen of the Middle Marches claimed 'vehemently' that they had lost during the same period, since 1583, nearly £20,000. Bowes, well experienced in Border affairs, reported to Cecil in January, 1596–97 that, since 1587, raids on the East Marches had cost £10,458 and the Middle Marches had lost £29,098 during the same period. Eure reported losses amounting to £12,394 in the Middle Marches for the period 1567–93.[53] He found the details and dates imperfect and despaired of proof 'save by assize and the warden's honour'; that is by a picked Scots jury, since the complainants were English, at a day of truce, and by the Scots warden declaring according to his knowledge of the circumstances and on his honour whether claims of loss could be accepted. The figures suggest that since 1583 losses due to raiding had been running at a level of £1,000 to £3,000 a year.

Some indication of the constant erosion of the exiguous wealth of Northumberland towards the end of the sixteenth century can be obtained from the *Calendar of Border Papers*. Over 200 'attemptats' were reported between January 1587 and May 1590. These incidents differed widely in scale. They ranged between minor horse thefts, such as were by no means unknown elsewhere in England, to raids by 400 to 500 men. Losses were reported to have been of the order of 4,863 cattle, 3,550 sheep, 340 horses and 157 prisoners. In addition, losses of 'insight' or household goods were said to amount to some £2,582, and more than seventy houses were burnt. In 1557 Lord Wharton, then deputy warden for the three northern marches, had calculated losses on the basis of £4 for a horse, 20s a head for cattle and oxen, and 3s 4d for a sheep.[54] To compensate for inflation these values had been increased in 1563 and the tariff for the settlement of claims at wardens' meetings included 40s for an ox, 30s for a cow, and 6s for a full-grown sheep.[55] Even if allowance is made for the habitual exaggeration the contemporary reports indicate loss and damage on a scale unimaginable in southern England as, for example, in contemporary Essex.[56]

It is not possible to arrive at any firm estimate of the true cost of raiding to Northumberland's economy as a whole. Doubtless there were customary tenants enjoying the security of their tenure, and skilled in counter raiding and blackmail, who prospered. But the diversion of manpower, energy and resources entailed by chronic insecurity is demonstrated in stone in the Northumberland of today. Licences to crenellate manor houses were granted freely in the era of Bannockburn; and strongholds of various types multiplied through the centuries that followed. Not for the Northumbrian aristocracy and gentry of the sixteenth century were the palaces and country houses constructed for comfort and display in the South. An imposing private stronghold such as Doddington bastle was constructed as late as 1584. Bastle is derived from the French *bastide* or *bastille*. In Northumberland the term became used for strongholds of a substantial size, though smaller than a castle or a tower, and designed for defence. Peles, another form of defensive architecture associated with the Border, were originally the *palus* or 'pale', the structure of earth or wood surrounding an isolated house. This term in local usage became applied to private strongholds of stone smaller than bastles or towers but capable of defence against a raiding party. Both terms have tended to be used somewhat loosely. In writing on the 'Bastles of Cumberland and Northumberland' R. W. McDowall and Eric Mercer have applied

Plate 3 Longhorsley pele
Though popularly termed a pele this building is in fact a tower, a strong defensive building with relatively more comfortable accommodation. Probably constructed in the sixteenth century it is a good example of the type of building which a country gentleman active in Border life found necessary for his own protection in Tudor Northumberland. The Horsleys were a prominent Border family whose members had held offices such as the constableships of Bamburgh, Dunstanburgh and Warkworth.

the term bastle to defensive farmhouses built of stone and conform-
ing to a basic pattern.[57]

Whatever the strictly correct use of the terms 'bastle' and 'pele',
the fact is that Northumberland abounds in defensible stone houses
dating from the late sixteenth and early seventeenth centuries with
the *terminus ad quem* after the Restoration.[58] They are unique in
England, apart from Cumberland; that they were still being constructed in the seventeenth century is a reminder that James I did
not inaugurate a reign of peace on the Border. Relatively there was
an improvement; the Jacobean mansion added to the stark tower
of a previous era at Chipchase Castle in 1621 is in itself by implica-
tion a commentary on conditions in the sixteenth century.

Had the old military society and the pattern of local loyalties
remained intact it is unlikely that the dwindling of armed manpower
would have drawn the government's attention to the problem of
decay. The weakening of traditional obligations and authority,
the unpopularity of Crown policies among a substantial number of
the gentry and their followers, removed a barrier to the growing
conception of land as a source of wealth. After the collapse of the
rebellion of the northern earls few great landowners had the induce-
ment or the opportunity to support a body of tenantry ready and
able to follow them in battle. It is significant that the Ogle tenants
made a conspicuously good appearance at the musters, for Lord
Ogle was an active supporter of the regime. Catholic gentry such as
Sir Cuthbert Collingwood withdrew from the Border. Collingwood himself had been active against the Scots and had suffered
serious losses at the hands of raiding parties.

For a rural population that was increasing, despite war and
plague, there was a growing demand for land. Landlord and tenant
alike shared a common interest in the division of holdings to an
extent which rendered it impossible to provide 'horse and armour
for each tenement, to be held by an able man'.

The consequence of partible inheritance were explained in a note
explaining the decline of armed men from Tynedale and Redesdale
at the musters of 1580: 'Divers are unfurnished, for they have ever
had a custom, if a man have issue ten sons, 8, 6, 5, or 4, and sits on a
holding but of 6s rent, every son shall have a piece of his father's
holding'.[59] Moreover, 'the inhabitants of Northumberland . . . who
were formerly freed from subsidies etc. were bound to defend the
frontier at their own charges, as also were the inferior sort, who held
on low rents etc. . . . and by an ancient custom called tenant right'.[60]
Tenant right allowed the alienation of all or part of a holding. On

the extensive Crown manors of Wark on Tyne and Harbottle the tenants could sell the tenant right of their tenancies or any part thereof.[61]

Throughout Northumberland the division of tenements was creating uneconomic smallholdings which were less likely, in a later period, to afford a livelihood than would employment in prosperous Newcastle. Failure to fulfil the muster requirements for the Middle Marches in 1580[62] was attributed, in twenty-three out of over two hundred townships, lordships or other areas, to the small size and poverty of tenements in addition to the subdividing of gavelkind in Tynedale and Redesdale. The Earl of Northumberland's tenants of Barrasford 'say that they sit on holdings of 10s apiece and cannot keep horse or armour'. The twenty-one tenants of Headley and Headleywood and eleven tenants of Prudhoe claimed that they were not 'able because their holdings were only 8s or 10s rent'. Altogether ninety tenants in the earl's lordship of Prudhoe gave the same explanation. In Hexhamshire it was reported that 'six score' copyholders, who were tenants of the Crown and bound by their copies to provide horse and armour, were unable to do so because they did 'taverne' their land and dispose of it as if they were freeholders. In all 163 tenants in the Middle Marches claimed poverty due to the small size of their holdings, besides the copyholders of Hexhamshire, the men of Tynedale and Redesdale, and those who were described as 'tenants' without specification of number.

These muster rolls provide direct evidence of the economic forces which were weakening the old military society of Northumberland and endorse the reports of decay. The comments on the musters of 1580 disclose that in the East Marches arable land had been converted to pasture in the townships of Howtell, Hetton and Outchester; that in ten townships heavy fines and gressoms, or other exactions, were cited as the reasons for failure to provide horse and armour. Eleven townships of the Middle Marches gave similar reasons, while the tenants of Elswick and Benwell merely claimed that they could not serve 'as they did before the abbey of Tynemouth was suppressed'. Thomas Haggerston of Haggerston was actively raising revenue on his properties in both marches. Longframlington, for example, was recorded as 'in decay' in 1584. In 1580 it had been reported that nine tenants of this township were 'unable from their small holdings, and Mr Haggerston took great gressoms of them'.[63]

The disorders of 1569–70 made their own contribution to the

chronic disorder and ensuing damage to property. They also increased the opportunities for the exploitation of land. In 1580 twelve townships in the East Marches reported damage by the English rebels in conjunction with their Scottish allies. In the Middle Marches the barony of Langley had been 'spoiled by the Queen's garrisons'. The tenants of Amble and Hauxley complained of exactions by the Queen's officers. In the East Marches the townships of Budle, Beadnell, North Sunderland, Shoreston, Fleetham and Elford, all showing symptoms of decay in the report of 1584, were in the hands of the sheriffs who received the rents and profits 'but never answereth them or maketh any account, and the Queen gets nothing, yet unfurnished'.[64]

Rents were evidently being raised where possible though in this respect the Border tenures were an inhibiting factor. The only specific reference to increased rents in the comments on the muster of 1580 is at Sturton Grange, the property of Lord Eure, Warden of the Middle Marches. Charges made against Eure by his opponents in Northumberland included accusations that he was raising both fines and rents. He replied by claiming that while his own tenants paid willingly, the tenants of Lord Ogle, Sir Henry Widdrington and others 'would give double rent to be freed from their landlords' exactions', and that greater fines were being exacted by the lessees of Crown lands. He also suggested, apparently with some justification, that 'the gentlemen do not seem to trouble their heads with any other landlord but myself'.[65] Thomas Haggerston was certainly active in raising fines on his properties in both marches, including Old Etal and Doddington leased from the Crown. Swinhow, near Bamburgh, was another Crown property where the tenants complained of the fines levied by the lessee.

Specific examples of large-scale evictions for the conversion of arable to pasture are rare. Tawney, who made full use of Northumbrian material, warned that 'these isolated instances are obviously worthless as a basis for generalisation' though they did 'prove that writers who spoke of whole towns being depopulated were not romancing'.[66] The twelve husbandlands of Ross, north of Bamburgh, were converted to pasture about 1555.[67] Sir Thomas Grey expelled 'seventeen score' of the inhabitants of Newham, in Bamburghshire, towards the end of the century.[68] The pace and scale of conversion to pasture, evictions and the enlargement of demesnes were evidently increasing on the boulder clay of the coastal plain by the end of the century. At Seghill, for example, the tenants were expelled, their land converted into pasture and some 600 acres incorporated in the demesne.[69] By the 1590s the growth of coal mining in the Bebside-Cowpen area was demonstrating to the speculators the need for absolute control over land. Developments of this nature, however, were only emerging at the end of the sixteenth century.

Despite these examples, and the activities of Thomas Jackson of Berwick in using mortgages to expel tenants and to convert land to pasture at Outchester near Belford and Hetton in Glendale, large-scale evictions were not a major contributory cause of the decay of the Northumbrian Border. Instead there was a widespread process of piecemeal adjustments eating away at the structure of Border society, here a little and there a little, far-reaching in their cumulative effects. The reports of 1594 and 1596[70] describe this process. Tenements were being 'divided into several tenures, either by the landlords or the tenants themselves'. Landlords had 'taken demesnes into their own hands, and left the rest of the tenants to live as cottagers'. Tenants were 'overcharged by their landlords with continual carriage for the rebuilding of their houses, above the ancient rents and customs'. There was conversion of 'tenements to domains and pastures, dividing and conjoining, excessive fines, improved rents, services or oppressions'. Evidence of these activities extends across all Northumberland from the Tweed to the Pennines.

Surveys of Crown properties in the early seventeenth century demonstrated the effect of Border tenures in ensuring stability of rents, though not of course of fines and gressoms, during an inflationary period. It has been suggested that this stability may have been encouraged by the government as a defence measure and so financed the construction of the fortified farms and bastles so numerous on the Border.[71] The commissioners of 1604 found it possible to recommend enormous increases, from a total of £25 a year to £766 a year in the manor of Wark, and from £70 to £1,398 for the manor of Harbottle.[72] Similar increases were recommended for the manors of Bewick and Etal in Glendale. In Hexhamshire and the barony of Langley surveys of 1608 revealed that rents had been unchanged since the end of the fifteenth century.[73]

For some leaseholders and customary tenants this stability of rents throughout a century of disorder and inflation must have at least mitigated the general impoverishment of the countryside. It certainly failed to give a return to the Crown in the form of equipped horsemen, particularly in Hexhamshire and the wasted barony of Langley. If rents were stable fines were not. Old Etal and New Etal enjoyed the stability of rents common to the Crown manor of Etal, but neither township could provide horse or foot for the muster of March 1579–80. They explained that their inability was due to the payment of large fines to the Queen's lessees.

The government's necessary concern over 'decay' expressed in terms of diminishing armed manpower, the turbulence and drama of Northumberland's drum and trumpet history obscure the extent of the rural revolution which was gathering pace by the end of the sixteenth century. The 'wild and disorderly Border', as Lord Eure termed it, was already providing examples of changes in farming practices and management which were to take full effect in the eighteenth century.

The Percies, showing a remarkable capacity for survival, had retained through all vicissitudes the bulk of their estates, and the fifth and the sixth earls, like lesser landowners, had raised entry fines.[74] In the latter half of the century the earls and their local representatives were improving estate management and encouraging enclosure and the consolidation of holdings. In the earl's township of Long Houghton the system of scattered rigs, although it 'did give to every tenant like quantity for all sorts of land, yet it was so painful to them and their cattle, that for the most part the said tenants never did manure the ground properly, whereby they did fall into great poverty'.[75] Accordingly tenants and cottagers were to enclose their holdings 'with good dykes, set with quick wood and, where the same will not grow, with a stone wall'. At Ellingham, since already 'where any freeholder that hath a parcel of inheritance, where any spring of wood is, the same is enclosed to their best commodity', the earl was advised to do the same.[76] At Ovingham arable and pasture had been enclosed by 1585, with the result that in the following century the tenants acknowledged that their farms had been improved and accordingly petitioned the earl for the division of the remaining fields.[77] From another point of view these townships had been in decay since they failed to send equipped horsemen to the musters. They also present decay as a necessary preliminary of regrowth.

The Percy earls, themselves the embodiment of drum and trumpet history, were also the leaders in the field of agricultural improvement. The ninth earl (1584–1632) is a modern figure compared with the sixth earl (1502–37) who had representatives of the leading surnames of Tynedale and Redesdale hanged in the presence of the gentlemen of Northumberland. Called the 'Wizard Earl' on account of his interest in science and literature, he was sent to the Tower for alleged complicity in the Gunpowder Plot. Normally he lived at Petworth, in Sussex, where, as he informed the Privy Council, his principal occupations were building and gardening. In his time the gross income of his Northumbrian estates was substantially increased.[78] He is the appropriate precursor of Sir Hugh Smithson, married in 1766 to the Percy heiress and, as Hugh Percy, Duke of Northumberland, one of the great improving landlords of his age..

Eighteenth-century enclosure in Northumberland was to be primarily enclosure of the commons. By then the majority of the common fields had been divided. Tenant right fought hard for survival, but after 1603 James I lost no time in ordering its abolition on Crown estates and, by proclamation in 1620, its abolition elsewhere. Thus the tenants lost on an issue for which, in Cumberland and Westmorland at least, their forefathers had fought in the Pilgrimage of Grace.

In Northumberland, therefore, the 'decay of the Borders' was caused in the administrative and political fields by the Tudors' destruction of the traditional framework of local authority, loyalties and power, and by their failure to replace that framework by an efficient alternative. To this was added the alienation caused by religious policy. This situation removed a barrier of tradition which could have obstructed economic change. By Elizabeth's reign the evidence of economic change was rapidly accumulating: some wholesale evictions; some taking of tenements into demesne; some change of use from arable to pasture; the subdivision of holdings; the raising of rents where possible, otherwise an increase in fines and gressoms. The importance of land was seen to lie more in the cash it could provide, hence cattle for manure were more profitable than war-horses, and war-horses themselves could obtain cash by sale into Scotland. Farmers were paying more attention to improved farming practices, to the advantages of fences and the disadvantages of scattered rigs. These stirrings of economic change and growth existed side by side with the world of the Border reiver. They were more potent, less superficial, causes of 'decay' and regrowth.

After the Union of the Crowns and the abolition of the Border tenures a process already begun increased both in speed and scope. Thus, when Jacobitism no longer existed as a military threat, the landlords could carry to its conclusion what had begun in the sixteenth century. Then the peles and strong houses were collapsing into ruin above North Tyne and Rede. Kidland was being re-settled. The fells, empty save for black game and sheep, awaited the construction of the long stone walls of enclosure.[79]

NOTES AND REFERENCES

1. J. Brand, *The History and Antiquities of Newcastle upon Tyne* (1789), i, p. 121.
2. E. Hughes, *North Country Life in the eighteenth century: The North East 1700–1750* (Oxford University Press, 1952); C. M. L. Bouch and G. P. Jones, A *Short Economic and Social History of the Lake Counties 1500 1830* (Manchester University Press, 1961).
3. On this theme see Rachel Reed, 'The office of the Warden of the Marches', *English Historical Review* [EHR] xxxii (1917), and 'The political influence of the North Parts' in *Tudor Studies*, ed. R. W. Seton Watson (Longmans, 1924); also M. E. James, 'A Tudor Magnate and the Tudor State', *Borthwick Papers, No. 30* (1966).
4. *Calendar of Border Papers*, ed. J. Bain (Edinburgh, 1894–96) [CBP] i, no. 78.
5. D. L. W. Tough, *The Last Years of a Frontier* (Clarendon Press, 1928), p. 173.
6. Lord Eure in 1597, [CBP] ii, no. 854.
7. *Return of Owners of Land, 1873*, (1875), ii, Northumberland.
8. C. J. Bates, *History of Northumberland* (1895), p. iii. Procolitia is now Carrawburgh.
9. For example Surtees Society, *Wills and Inventories from the Registry of Durham*, Part I (1835), Part II (1860).
10. Surtees Society, *Newcastle Merchant Adventurers*, ii (1899), 'Enrollments of Apprentices and Admissions of Freemen'', pp. 185–381.
11. *CBP*, ii, no. 351.
12. *CBP*, ii, no. 616.
13. For the social organisation of the surnames see T. I. Rae, *The Administration of the Scottish Frontier 1513–1603* (Edinburgh University Press, 1966). Rae writes that 'The Border kinship groups of the 16th century known as surnames were not so much the survival of primitive tribal units as the result of processes in the 14th and 15th centuries when surnames (literally) emerged' (pp. 5–6).
14. *CBP*, ii, no. 323.
15. *Ibid.*, no. 268.
16. *Ibid.*, no. 758.
17. Tough, *op. cit.* p. 27, and also for the population of Newcastle.
18. J. C. Russell, *British Medieval Population* (University of New Mexico Press, 1948), p. 313.
19. Julian Cornwall, 'English Population in the Early 16th Century', *Economic History Review*, 2nd ser., xxiii (1970), 39.
20. H. H. Lamb, *The Changing Climate* (Methuen, 1966), p. 10.
21. *Letters and Papers, foreign and domestic, of the Reign of Henry VIII, 1509–1547* (London, 1862–1910; *Addenda*, London, 1929–32) [L&P], (11) ii (2) no. 4676.
22. J. Hodgson, *History of Northumberland,* Part III, vol. ii (Newcastle upon Tyne, 1828) pp. 233, 237, quoting the survey by Sir Robert Bowes and Sir Raufe Ellerker of 1541.
23. *Survey of The Debateable and Border Lands adjoining the Realm of Scotland and belonging to the Crown of England. Taken A.D. 1604*, ed. R. P. Sanderson (Alnwick, 1891), p. 52.

24. *Ibid.*, pp. 103–4.

25. Behaviour of this kind was not, of course, confined to Northumberland. See Lawrence Stone, *The Crisis of the Aristocracy* (Oxford University Press, 1965) pp. 223–54.

26. Sir John Forster was Warden 1560–95 with a short intermission when he was suspended on charges of misconduct. When he finally retired in 1595 he is said to have been 94 years old. On the authority of the *Dictionary of National Biography* (Supplement vol. ii) however he is believed to have been born about 1520. He died in 1603.

27. *CBP*, ii, no. 29.

28. *A History of Northumberland* [NCH], (Newcastle upon Tyne, 15 vols, 1893–1940), ix, pp. 154–5.

29. *Cal. State Papers, Dom., Eliz. I Addenda 1566–1579*, xv, p. 139.

30. *Cal. State Papers, Dom., Eliz. I Add. 1580–1635*, xxxiii, p. 359.

31. *Hamilton Papers* i, (Edinburgh, 1890–2), no. 296(1).

32. *CBP*, i, no. 563.

33. For the musters of 1538 the MS copy made by the Rev. J. Hodgson in the Library of the Society of Antiquaries, Newcastle upon Tyne, has been used. For the muster of 1579/80 see *CBP*, i, nos. 47, 50; 1584, *CBP*, i, nos. 253, 255, 259; 1595 *CBP*, ii, nos. 169, 170.

34. *CBP*, i, no. 74.

35. *Ibid.*, no. 75.

36. Public Record Office. An abstract of the Certificates of the Tenancies and the Fortes decaied upon the Borders since the 27th yere of Kinge Henry 8, *SP 15/28*.

37. For example in 1296: see *The Northumberland Lay Subsidy Roll of 1296*, ed. Constance Fraser, (Society of Antiquaries of Newcastle upon Tyne, 1968), p. xxii.

38. T. Pennant, *A Tour of Scotland* (Chester, 1776), ii, p. 279.

39. *SP 15/28*.

40. 'Causes of the decaie of servitors and weakenings of the borders cheifle in the Middle Marches', *SP 15/28*.

41. *Cal. State Papers, Dom. Eliz. I, Add. XXI*, pp. 393–4.

42. *CBP*, i, no. 786.

43. *CBP*, i, no. 277. In fact the totals in the summary add up to 915.

44. *CBP*, ii, no. 133.

45. *CBP*, ii, no. 323.

46. *CBP*, ii, no. 745.

47. *L&P*, xx (2), no. 400.

48. *CBP*, i, no. 668.

49. J. Hodgson, *History of Northumberland*, Pt iii, vol. ii, pp. 178–87.

50. M. Beresford, *The Lost Villages of England* (Lutterworth Press, 1963), p. 372.

51. Hodgson, *op. cit.* p. 183.

52. *CBP*,i, no. 893.

53. *CBP*, i, no. 998 for 1594 report; ii, no. 171 for 1595; ii, no. 485 for Bowes's report; ii, no. 410 for Eure's.

54. *Cal. State Papers, Dom. Eliz. I–James I, vi, 1601–1603; Addenda 1547–1565*, p. 451.

55. Rae, *op. cit.* p. 53.

56. E.g. F. G. Emmison, *Elizabethan Life; Disorder* (Essex Record Office, 1970), Appendix D.

57. See n. 58 below.

58. An attempt to achieve a tidy and consistent use of these terms is difficult. It was discussed by C. J. Bates, who had a wide knowledge of their medieval history and their colloquial use in the North. See *Archaeologia Aeliana*, 'Border Holds', 2nd ser. xiv (1891), 57–61 and 65. A modern work of great interest is Royal Commission on Historical Monuments (England), *Shielings and Bastles* (1970), especially Part ii, R. W. McDowall and Eric Mercer on 'Bastles of Cumberland and Northumberland.' This publication contains a fine range of photographs. The arguments for dating are at pp. 66–8.

59. *CBP*, i, no. 50.

60. *CBP*, ii, no. 462. Tough, *op.cit.* (p. 57) describes Border tenures as 'a special and very perplexing subject'.

61. *Survey of . . . Border Lands*, p. 51.

62. *CBP*, i, no. 50.

63. *CBP*, i, no. 47.

64. *CBP*, i, no. 78. 'Names of places in the East Marches where the Queen has any lands certified to be unfurnished of horse and armour.'

65. *CBP*, ii, nos. 652, 764.

66. R. H. Tawney, *The Agrarian Problem in the Sixteenth Century* (Harper & Row, 1967), p. 261.

67. J. Raine, *History of North Durham* (1852), p. 197.

68. *NCH*, i, 406.

69. *NCH*, ix, 69.

70. *Cal. State Papers Dom. Eliz. & James I Add. 1580–1625*, xxxiii, p. 359; *CBP*, ii, no. 323.

71. *Shielings and Bastles, op. cit.*, pp. 71–2.

72. *Survey of . . . Border Lands*, p. 135.

73. *NCH*, iii(1), 54; pp. 66–86 for the survey of 1547; pp. 86–104 for the survey of 1608. For Langley see L. C. Coombes, 'The survey of Langley barony, 1608', *Archaeologia Aeliana*, 4th ser., xliii (1965), 263, 268.

74. For studies of the Percy estates during this period see J. M. Bean, *The Estates of the Percy Family 1416–1537* (Oxford University Press, 1958). The fifth earl died in 1527, the sixth in 1537.

75. *NCH*, ii, 369.

76. *NCH*, ii, 246.

77. *NCH*, xii, 142.

78. A. Batho, 'The finances of an Elizabethan nobleman', *Eng. Hist. Review* ix (1957).

79. This essay is derived from a more detailed examination of factors to which necessarily brief reference was made in my *Northumberland Landscape* (Hodder and Stoughton, 1972).

The Squire of Conisholme

Conisholme is a tiny village, a straggle of farms and cottages grouped in ones and twos, set in the marshland of Lindsey, about midway between Grimsby and Mablethorpe. Even today it is scarcely larger than it was 400 years ago when the population numbered little more than a hundred souls: in 1524 there were twenty-five taxpayers, in 1563 twenty households.[1] Except that most of the buildings are of more recent date, and the little church of St Peter has been much reduced in size,[2] the scene cannot be very different from what it was on that bleak March day in 1528 when parson Thomas Laurence committed the mortal remains of John Langholme, esquire, to the earth, and later walked over to the manor house to write down the list of its contents while Edward Madyson and one or two other parishioners walked from room to room examining and appraising them.

So few are the ascertainable facts about this man the story might well end here with this commonplace event. His pedigree[3] is defective; his descendants have long since receded into the mists of history. What interest can his affairs hold for us in face of the already formidable literature on the gentry of Tudor England? Could it be that this short, unremarkable life of the unknown squire of a secluded village was more truly typical of his kind than the careers of the 'rising' gentry, founders of illustrious families whose rich archives have tended perhaps to inspire a onesided picture? For

numerically they formed at most a sizeable minority. We may
estimate that Lincolnshire contained upwards of 300 gentlemen in
the 1520s, most of them shadowy figures: in a small county like
Buckinghamshire it is possible to identify almost 100 (about seventy
families),[4] many of them solely because their names occur in tax
lists, certainly not from their achievements. Covering a wide range
of wealth, some clearly must have been of small account, jumped up
farmers and the like; but others, though equally elusive, were
unmistakably men of 'worship' in their own localities, esquires
proud of several generations of gentle blood, who quartered their
arms and lived on the rents of inherited broad acres.

To set the record straight we need answers to much the same
questions as have been asked about the more notable gentry families.
We must seek out Langholme's antecedents, ascertain his position
in the community, his income, way of life and aspirations; above all
why he is now all but forgotten. Through him we may feel our way
towards a more complete understanding of the provincial gentry in
the reign of Henry VIII. It is possible that he represented the average
esquire. The subsidy of 1524 assessed him at the median of £60 on
lands; an income exceeding £100 a year was rare in this class. But
this level of income was normally matched by personal property of
rather higher value, and yet the fact is that Langholme's was worth
very much less. Further, the evidence of feodary surveys is that the
median income of esquires was £80, and that his own was well
above average, in fact more than half as high again.[5] There is a conflict of evidence here which needs to be resolved, for more often
than not the only surviving records even of men of high standing
are their subsidy assessments and their wills. Thanks to two happy
accidents the sources for Langholme's biography are immeasurably
richer. His early death meant that his heir became a ward of the
Crown, and in consequence his lands were made the subject of a
feodary survey. Moreover, through some administrative muddle
his will was proved at Lincoln instead of the Prerogative Court of
Canterbury (which was the rule for estates extending into more than
one diocese) and thus for once the inventory of the goods and
chattels of a major landowner is available.

1

The facts of his life and antecedents are sparse. The family had first
appeared nearly two centuries earlier when Thomas Langholme

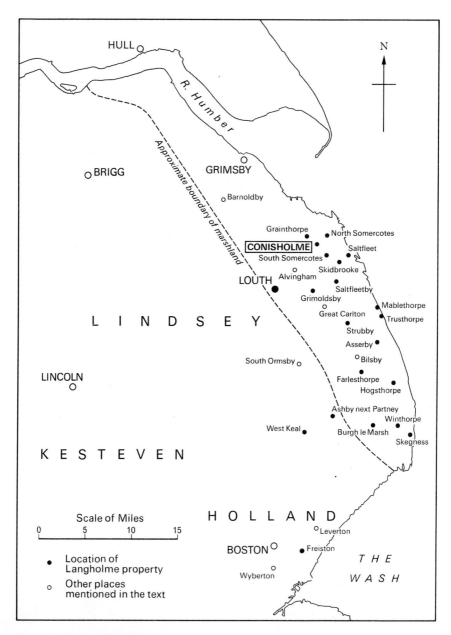

Fig. 2.1   Map of East Lincolnshire.

married the daughter of the last of the Conisholmes and acquired a moiety of the manor. His mother-in-law sold the other moiety with the advowson of the church to the influential Welles family in 1341. The early fifteenth century was the heyday of the Langholmes, spanning two, possibly three generations – it is impossible to be exact because the head of the family was nearly always called John. One of them was assessed at £40 for the income tax of 1436, his wife having £10 as well. Prominent in the business of landowning circles, as trustees, executors and mortgagees, they also filled the usual range of public offices: justice of the peace, escheator, feodary of the Duchy of Lancaster, deputy steward of the honour of Boling-broke, and burgess for Grimsby in several parliaments, 1426–53. One had campaigned in France, presumably in the retinue of Lord Clifford who granted him a life annuity in 1418. They were related to prominent families, and politically aligned with the Cromwell–Willoughby–Rochford group. Perhaps the association was too close, for the story terminates abruptly in 1461 with a pardon for their support of the Lancastrian cause. While great men usually managed to re-establish themselves after changes of regime, smaller fry could be, and no doubt were regarded as expendable, and with the deaths of the local Lancastrian magnates, Welles and Wil-loughby, at the battle of Towton, the Langholmes found them-selves in want of good lordship.[6]

Be the reason what it may, the family dropped out of sight for many years until, soon after the accession of Henry VII, another John married a lady named Anne whose maiden name is not recorded, but may very well have been Lyttylbury since their son referred in his will to his cousin John Lyttylbury. At any rate her jointure shows that she came of a considerable landed family. If the number of little figures on their memorial brass means anything, she bore her husband fourteen children, ten of whom died in infancy, leaving two boys and two girls.

Their eldest surviving child was John, who was born about 1493. His upbringing can only be conjectured. There might have been a school at Louth which he could have attended; he may have re-ceived some grounding in law at one of the Inns of Court, a practical form of higher education for members of the landowning class, and increasingly popular. At least by this date the rural gentry were by no means so unrelievedly boorish as Edmund Dudley pessimistically asserted. In 1515, at the age of twenty-two, he succeeded to his father's property, and probably shortly afterwards married Maud, daughter of Sir John Gilliott, sometime mayor of York, for Humphrey their eldest son was born in 1517–18. Five more sons followed: Christopher, George, Henry, Francis and Anthony. Towards the end of March 1528 he died aged scarcely thirty-five, having apparently achieved nothing. Like his immediate forebears, whom ambition seems to have deserted in obscurity, he held no public offices. Even the stewardship of the Wells manor, the other estate in Conisholme, was held by his cousin Lyttylbury. Although the considerations governing appointments to office in local administration are not known in any detail, it is clear that only a fraction of the gentry in any one shire served on the commission of the peace at a given time, and were normally much richer men than Langholme, though not invariably so.[7] He may simply have lacked the inclination since there is no sign of his having served even on the less important commissions, for sewers, subsidies, etc. Maybe he was a trifle on the youthful side, short of the fifth age of man.

> the justice,
> In fair round belly with good capon lined,
> With eyes severe and beard of formal cut
> Full of wise saws and modern instances.[8]

Whatever the reason the secluded life of a village squire effectively barred any prospect of augmenting the estate he had inherited, for which the fruits of office or the profits of commerce were essential.

II

As the standing of a gentleman was determined by his expenditure, 'the port, charge and countenance' he was able to support,[9] the first thing to establish about Langholme is his style of living. Let us, therefore, in imagination accompany Edward Madyson and his neighbours through the rooms of the manor house. Our first impression is something of a surprise, even shock, at the spartan simplicity of the furnishings. The accommodation was generous enough, but even though another half century would pass before William Harrison would be able to boast of 'the great amendment of lodging' he had witnessed in his lifetime, the paucity of contents almost taxes our credulity.[10]

[THE HALL]

In primis in the hall, j cownter	vj^s viij^d
The hangynges in the hall	vj^s viij^d
ij syd tabules	iij^s iiij^d
ij formes	viij^d
	Sum' xvij^s iiij^d

IN THE CHAMBER

j federbed with all thynges thereto perteyng — xvj^s

j old conter — xij^d

j chyst — ij^s

j lytell tabull — iiij^d

ij furmeres [forms?] — iiij^d

j hangynge — iij^s iiij^d

j old chyst — iiij^d

vij pare of lynynge shettes — xxiij^s iiij^d

vj pare of hardynge shettes — x^s

iiij towelles — xij^d

j tabull clowth — viij^d

iiij pylloberes — xvj^d

j federbed with a boster — vj^s viij^d

iiij pyllows — ij^s viij^d

[THE PARLOUR]

In the parler j federbed with j coverynge — vj^s viij^d

iij pyloberes — xij^d

[NETHER PARLOUR]

In the nether parler j federbed with a coveryng and a boster — x^s

ij chares & j furme — xij^d

ix cowshynges — ix^s

Sum' iiij^l xvj^s viij^d

IN THE LYTELL PARLER

In primis j bed with a materys and a coverlyd — iij^s iiij^d

[CHAMBER]

In on other chawmber j bed with ij materys and a coverlyd — ij^s

v jakes — xx^s

j pare of almmenreuyttes — x^s

viij pare of splynttes — x^s viij^d

ij salyttes — iiij^s iiij^d

j hangyng — ij^s

Sum' lj^s iiij^d

IN THE BUTTERY

In primis ij peses of syluer — v^l

ij salttes of [silver] — xl^s

xij syluer spones — xxx^s

j holl garnyshe of old putcr — xx^s

j chawynge dyshe — xvj^d

v candylstykes — iiij^s iiij^d

xij napkynges — ij^s

iiij tabull clothes — v^s

lytell cowbord ij^s

Sum' x^l iij^s viij^d

IN THE KHETCHYNGE

In primis v brasse pottes xv^s

iij pannes of brasse xiij^s iiij^d

ij spyttes and j pare of cowberdes ij^s

brokyn brasynge morter ij^s

j fryynge pane viij^d

brolyngyern vj^d

j pare of mosterd querns xvj^d

ij dresynge bordes viij^d

Sum' xxxv^s vj^d

IN THE BRUHEWS

In primis j bord iiij^s iiij^d

j pare of malt quernes ij^s

iij tobbes iij^s

ij saltynge trowghtes & j bord ij^s

Sum' x^s iiij^d

The total value of the contents of this home amounted to £20 12s 2d, rather less than half a personal estate of £43 3s 2d. For convenience it may be roughly summarised thus:

	£	s	d
Furniture		17	8
Bedding, linen, hangings	5	10	0
Implements and utensils	2	10	6
Pewterware	1	0	0
Silverware	8	10	0
Armour	2	4	0

Some estimate of how Langholme stood in relation to other Lincolnshire gentlemen can be made by comparing him with a few contemporaries whose total personalty or, as in one case, domestic effects, were similar to his.[11]

Name	Household			Farm			Total			Debts		
	£	s	d	£	s	d	£	s	d	£	s	d
Langholme	20	12	2	22	11	0	43	3	2	—	—	—
Ormesby	12	12	10	21	0	0	33	12	10	−10	3	4
Friskeney	26	17	0	17	4	8	44	1	8	—	—	—
Morys	16	16	8	33	1	8	49	18	4	+15	9	0
Leyke	22	0	0	35	0	0	57	0	0	−46	0	0
Clement	26	7	0	146	4	8	172	11	8	—	—	—

Ignoring debts, of which he had none, and concentrating on movables, Langholme ranked fifth in total wealth and fourth in household effects. Then as now individual notions as to what made a home must have varied, but considered as a whole there is not a great deal to choose between any of these; Conisholme manor was, however, decidedly less inviting than some houses since the trappings of war hardly contributed to home comforts.

It is evident that Langholme's standard of living was no better than that of men who were his social inferiors, for that is what they were, 'mere gentlemen' who almost certainly owned comparatively little land[12]; 'gentleman farmer' seems to be the aptest description, especially for Clement. At the same time he ranked well above Richard Delfe of Barnoldby who was worth only £21 altogether and lived in a small house the contents of which came to just £8 2s. Little better off than many a husbandman, Delfe's farm was wretchedly stocked; he seems to personify the type of status seeker at whom Sir Thomas Smith aimed his tart observation: 'no man hath hurt of it but he himself, who hereby will bear a bigger sail than he is able to maintain'.[13]

To place Langholme among his peers we may refer to the inventory of John Asserby, esq. of Bilsby[14] who had died the previous September. Unfortunately the values were omitted (as most provokingly were those for the sumptuous Sussex home of the courtier Sir John Gage a generation later),[15] and attempts at reconstruction by reference to other inventories prove unsatisfactory: wildly differing values used to be assigned to apparently similar articles, probably because the appraisers had little to go on, whereas for livestock, etc. they could quote current market prices. None the less, it is obvious at a glance that Asserby's home was much the more comfortable, although his income, assessed at £40, was much smaller.[16] His house was similar, but it was furnished altogether more comprehensively and comfortably. An estimate in the region of £40 might not be exaggerated since there were several pieces of silver gilt, in addition to plain silver, and a handsome girdle encrusted with a ruby and six pearls. Langholme possessed few pieces of silver 'which', he wrote sadly in his will, 'is all my plate'. Asserby shows that a gentleman could live very reasonably on £40 a year without needing even to farm – he may be assumed to have been employed as steward in the service of his brother-in-law Sir Andrew Billesby.

In common with many others belonging to this period Langholme's inventory ignores clothing. The wardrobes of the other five gentlemen were priced at from 31*s* 8*d* to £4. Few are itemised, but Antony Morys's included two doublets, two coats, jacket, bonnet, and two pairs of hose, worth 33*s*. This obviously is not a complete outfit, but presumably other things were not considered worth pricing; perhaps none of Langholme's were. It is worth pausing here to observe how few garments most people seem to have possessed in those days; only in the rare case of the inventory of a very rich man (such as Gage) do we notice fine garments in any quantity. Langholme is sure to have dressed plainly, if the meagre contents of his house are any guide. Nor is there any mention of his purse, though it would be hard to imagine a well lined one. Most Conisholme men seem to have managed on little or no ready cash, and so did many gentlemen. Roger Clement of Wyberton had £2 in hand, while John Fryskeney's money was totalled with his plate.

Take away the silver and the armour, and what remained in the manor house was not significantly more than might be found in any yeoman's house, like, for example, Thomas Kecher of Leverton who also died in 1527. None the less, there was no one in any way comparable at Conisholme, where all the farmers were small men whose household effects, rarely itemised, were mostly valued at between one and two pounds.[17]

III

The state of the home farm complemented Langholme's household in many respects.

IN THE STABULL

In primis j hors	xiij^s iiij^d
iiij yonge mares	xx^s
j cowpull of oxen	liij^s iiij^d
vj kye	iij^s
j cowpull of sters	xxiiij^s
sters	x^s
v yonge bestes	xxiij^s iiij^d

IN THE YARD

In primis j wayne with all thynges pertenyng therto	v^s
ij plowghes	ij^s

IN THE WOLL HOWS

lx stons of woll	xij^l
Sum' xxij^l	xj^s

This was not a comprehensive stock. Salt marsh farmers specialised in sheep and in fattening the cattle bred on the middle marsh.[18] Few arable crops were grown, perhaps even fewer in Conisholme than in most other parishes. Although the majority of surviving inventories were drawn up before the spring sowing, the omission of standing wheat from most of them testifies to the subordinate role of crop husbandry here. In one dated just after the harvest in 1549 'all the hay' was priced at 53s 4d compared with 13s 4d for 'all the corn'. The glebe terrier of 1577 described 71¾ acres, of which three only were arable.[19] There was nothing unusual, therefore, in Langholme's failure to sow any wheat in the autumn before he died, or in the absence of any store of grain in the barn. He concentrated on the cattle for which the marsh was famous. None the less, his stock was barely what was to be seen in any average peasant's farm-yard. Pigs were not much kept in the marsh, while no Conisholme inventory mentions poultry. The horse, which he probably rode himself, and the mares represented a common number of such animals in this village. With few implements itemised the demesne farm somehow fails to convey an air of bustle and activity. It compares unfavourably with those of other gentlemen, even of many peasants.

The most puzzling feature is the wool which was worth more than the rest of the farm stuff put together. Where did it come from? Most other gentlemen farmers kept three or four score sheep; Roger Clement had no fewer than 680, and flocks of 100 or more were not uncommon on the saltmarsh. The median size of peasants' flocks was forty. Since Clement had eighty stones of wool in his barn, Langholme's sixty must have represented the clip of at least 500 beasts, if not more.[20] The absence of sheep takes some explaining. They could of course have been sold off; as we shall shortly see there are reasons for thinking that Langholme's financial state was precarious. Alternatively he may have been a dealer in wool in a small way, although as a businessman he is unconvincing. A further possibility is that he pastured his flock on the coastal marsh in North Somercotes where he had a large holding, and that it was overlooked by the valuers. Unlikely though this may seem, things did get left out of inventories, including a valuable piece of jewellery in Asserby's case. Some form of share cropping is a possibility, but in that case one would expect a large landowner to own the sheep. Speculation apart, Clement's flock were worth over £48, so that 500 head would have added some £36 to the value of Langholme's estate.

The character of his farming must remain something of a mystery.

This glimpse implies that he attempted little more than keeping his family supplied with necessaries, and hence the question must be asked, was his land under-used? The size of the home farm may be indicated by the 155 acres specified in his inquisition post mortem. A survey taken in 1634, however, implies a demesne of 658 acres – more than half the parish area of 1270 – although since Langholme's day his moiety of the original manor had been reunited with the other.[21] Wool was clearly the only product of commercial signi-ficance, and since there were so few cattle most of the land must have been occupied by sheep. Their absence lends colour to the notion that they had been assigned to his creditors, for both his earlier circumstances and present poor household combine to give the impression that money was tight. Here was a man who, whether from choice or necessity, did not identify himself with the go-ahead, profit conscious brand of gentry, but remained content to live the life of a rentier. But since a mild flutter in wool involved no risk of losing caste we are at liberty to speculate that, like many another man in need of cash, he had ventured to play the market and suc-ceeded only in burning his fingers by choosing to do so in a time of war and economic dislocation.

IV

If there was no hint of opulence in the manor house, the owner was still a rich man compared with the villagers. His personal wealth must have roughly equalled everybody else's put together with the exception of Thomas Laurence, rector 1509–32, who, although his personality is not recorded, enjoyed a comfortable £9 13s 5½d a year, according to the *Valor Ecclesiasticus*. The twenty-five tax-payers of 1524 included two middling farmers assessed on goods at £10 and £7, respectively, seven lesser men at £2 to £3, and fifteen others taxed on wages at £1, each of whom would have owned a few trifling possessions. A few poor households may have escaped taxation. This structure corresponds broadly with the survey of 1634, allowing for the possibility that there had been intakes from the waste and amalgamations in the interim, and that in 1524 part of the parish might have been farmed by someone living in an adjacent village.[22] There were two large farms, 135 and 168 acres, six (possibly seven) medium and small ones, 12 to 50 acres, and six cottage holdings of seven acres and less.

The distinctive feature of the 1524 return is that precisely three-

fifths of the taxpayers were wage earners, a very much higher
proportion than the average of 42 per cent for the wapentake of
Louthesk as a whole. Some were day labourers, cottagers with an
acre or two of land; a few might have been farm servants. Although
this list is restricted to bare names, the rolls for parts of Sussex show
that farmers assessed at £10 not infrequently kept a servant, even
two, and there are examples of £2 taxpayers who did so.[23] But it
should not be too readily assumed that many Conisholme peasants
could afford full-time labour. The only obvious employer was the
squire, and the inference is that he kept seven or eight servants at
least.

Society demanded that gentlemen keep households commensurate
with their status and incomes, and signs of retrenchment were apt
to bring sharp protest.[24] If Langholme's establishment was as large
as we suspect the annual cost would have been considerable. In the
earliest extant assessments 20s was in fact the annual wage for a
common servant in husbandry, and was probably the rate most
widely paid. Living in a remote district, Langholme might have
paid somewhat less, but it was usual to add 6s 8d for a livery, and he
probably employed some women and boys for a pittance; all had
also to be fed, over and above a large family.[25] Housekeeping on
this scale could have left little margin for luxuries.[26]

Besides owning as much as the rest of the parish put together,
Langholme was the richest man for miles around, apart from
Christopher Yers over at Great Carlton whose assessment was
identical; and since old Mrs Anne Langholme, now living at
Alvingham (probably in retirement at the Priory), had £50 a year,
they were the richest family in all the wapentakes of Louthesk and
Ludburgh. William Skipwith of South Ormsby (who was shortly
to acquire the wardship of young Humphrey) had 200 marks a
year, but he lived miles away. The Lincolnshire gentry were not a
wealthy lot. A fragment of the anticipation of the subsidy listing
fifty men, mostly in Kesteven, rated only twelve at more than £60,
seven of them being Stamford merchants; not a great many more
can be traced in Lindsey. Nor was the district especially prosperous.
Although marshland people as a whole enjoyed a relatively high
average standard, 97 per cent of the inhabitants of the wapentake
were assessed at under £20, indeed nearly nine out of every ten had
less than half this amount. Even Louth, the centre for north-east
Lindsey, was no more than an average market town, its richest
inhabitant having £60 in goods, while a couple more had £50
apiece. Further, the medieval prosperity of Lincolnshire now lay in

the past. The parts of Lindsey paid no more tax than in 1334, while the national yield had doubled, and its population fell by nearly 4 per cent between 1377 and 1563, with the dramatic decline of the city of Lincoln by more than half adding the final significant touch.[27]

Langholme's income had been assessed at £60 a year. But, as the consequence of his premature death, his estates passed into Crown wardship, and the resulting survey revealed a net income of no less than £129 11s 0¾d. Against this, however, was charged his mother's dower of £37 8s 6d while her subsidy assessment shows that she had got him to raise her allowance to £50. Moreover, his father's will made twelve years earlier had saddled him with heavy commitments: his sister Anne was allotted eighty marks (£53 6s 8d) on her marriage, and young Elizabeth £40. It is not improbable that there were substantial pious bequests similar to those John himself was to make, as well as the memorial brass to be placed in the parish church. A total equal to a year's income can readily be envisaged, while at the same time the area of the estate was reduced by a bequest to his brother Thomas of lands in Saltfleetby. Their father had executed a feoffment to the uses of his will, a normal practice by which an estate was vested in a group of feoffees appointed to carry out the deceased's final dispositions; the object was to get round the rigid common law rule which excluded younger sons from inheriting any share of real property. To meet such heavy charges borrowing was inevitable if the final resort of selling off a part of the estate was to be avoided, and it is all but certain that the debt had not been cleared by 1524. The missing flock of sheep, not to say the frugal housekeeping, could have been directly linked with the final satisfaction of his creditors. The irony is that after ten years or so of hard slogging he was cut off in his prime at the very moment when he could begin to look forward to better times.[28]

This glimpse into the finances of a single family demonstrates how its tax assessment could legitimately be reduced to less than half its gross income. It thus furnishes a vital clue to understanding the mechanism of the entire subsidy of 1524–25, which in turn promotes confidence in the subsidy as a measure of comparative wealth. Assessments were made on net values, whether income or capital, after sundry charges, both recurrent and occasional, had been allowed. Among the former would feature such items as rent; even Langholme had to pay out at least £8 4s 4d to various lords, his revenue of £130 being over and above these liabilities. Again, since 20s was the regular wage paid to boarded servants it is clear that day labourers must in effect have been allowed subsistence costs, for their earnings should have been substantially higher. Assessments of goods are matched by inventories (which rarely represent the poorest people) which prove that there was nothing abnormal in a peasant farmer owning a personal estate of less than £10 or even £5. And most revealingly, glosses on a few subsidy returns illustrate graphically how a man's circumstances could be drastically altered by a single event. When the instalment for 1525 came to be collected in the Aylesbury hundreds of Buckinghamshire one-fifth of the taxpayers secured reductions on their previous assessments, most by 20–40 per cent, but a few by much more: in one extreme instance £63 was cut to £13. As in the case of a man at Cold Higham, Northants, 'by his oath and oath of his neighbours', the commonest grounds were crop failure and loss of cattle, but there were other incidents of business including entry fines, lawsuits, and losses due to 'evil debtors'. Family occasions also supervened. Weddings, funerals and prolonged sickness were all expensive. The goods made over to two of his sons when they married cut the assessment of Thomas Smythe of Gayton from £27 to £16, while the ordination of a Great Missenden youth cost his father £9 out of an original £20.[29] Allowing that taxpayers would have made the most of their liabilities and hardships, such details of the process of assessment furnish good evidence that most cases were examined with considerable care. They lend support to the theory that Langholme was a man who had to contend with many financial difficulties, and if corroboration is needed the debts of some of those gentlemen whose inventories have been summarised above indicate how greatly they could reduce a person's net assets at any given time.

There is a corollary that is frequently overlooked. Given that tax assessments refer to the situation on the day they were made and that a person's financial state could alter substantially virtually overnight, it follows that statements of wealth made at different dates, and also for different purposes, cannot on their own invalidate the evidence of the subsidy. On the surviving evidence Langholme's basic £130 was reduced by the £50 assigned to his mother. This implies that he should really have been assessed at £80 in 1524, but does not preclude the possibility that he was able to claim further allowances. Inevitably an exaggeration of liabilities, a general tendency to round down must be understood, but the final outcome need never be treated as necessarily misleading. Here, indeed, it is the seeming discrepancy which, combined with some shreds of circumstantial evidence, enables us to sketch a few additional details into what would otherwise have to remain a very bare outline.

Most of John Langholme's estates were in Lincolnshire, strung out over twenty-five miles from Grainthorpe to Skegness, and comprising twenty-four separate holdings ranging from large ones such as the 300 acres in Mablethorpe right down to the tiny parcel in Grainthorpe which produced only 1s 2d a year. The only two manors were Conisholme and Freiston, and both were mesne tenancies. All that was held in chief of the Crown was ten acres in West Keal, with a further twelve in Ashby next Partney being held of the Duchy of Lancaster as the fortieth part of a knight's fee. Conisholme itself was but a moiety of the original manor, and the inferior one. Although the partition had been effected (some two hundred years earlier) to endow the heiress of the former owners on her marriage to the first Langholme, it was held of the other manor which, along with the advowson of the church, now belonged to the heirs of the last Viscount Wells. In point of size they were probably about equal, the Wells manor yielding £19 6s 8d annually, Langholme's £19 17s 11d, with each perhaps controlling up to 600 acres.[30] The estate looks anything but a planned, efficient whole, rather a miscellany of parcels added as and when the opportunity presented itself. The sole unifying feature was the fact of its situation in the rich marshland, except for the tiny portions in Ashby and West Keal. Also marshland was Maud Langholme's jointure in Norfolk, consisting chiefly of Pannell's manor in Walpole, and accounting for a good sixth of the gross value.[31]

The stages of formation can only be conjectured. Marriages had clearly added more than half of what there was by 1528. But although John and his father had acquired the two largest blocks in this fashion, there are grounds for supposing that the real expansion had taken place in the heyday of the family's fortunes, a hundred years earlier, and had long ceased. Recent gains were no doubt balanced by losses. There was the land in Saltfleetby which had been allotted to Thomas Langholme, and since the family seems to have been prolific similar provisions for younger sons and daughters must have been made more than once. An earlier alienation is implied by the quitclaim which William, kinsman of some previous John Langholme, executed in 1478 in favour of a certain John Newton in respect of a sizable property in Tetney and Howton. And since the former MP for Grimsby had served on the commission of the peace for Kesteven in 1439–42, he must then have held land there which had since passed out of the family.

V

Prominent among Langholme's scanty effects was the small collection of armour including jacks (protective coats), sallets (helmets), splints (worn on the arms), and a pair of almain rivets (probably thigh pieces), worth, at £2 4s 8d, more than double the value of the furnishings of the hall. It was indeed only the gear worn by common archers and billmen of the shire levy, although it might also have been preferred to the costly knight's harness by a gentleman of limited means, especially since the English fought on foot. In keeping with everything else here it was rather a job lot. No weapons are listed, though it is hard to believe that he did not wear a sword when he rode abroad.

To the extent that it could instantly fit out two men with adequate harness,[32] and three or four more if promptly supplemented from other sources, this gear assumes a significance far greater than its estimated cash value. Although the ancient Statute of Winchester enjoined every man to arm himself for home defence and every township to maintain a common stock of harness, it was honoured mostly in the breach. Musters taken in 27 southern counties in 1524 recorded harness for only 27·6 per cent of the able-bodied population, and since several shires were obviously undermustered the true proportion must have been much lower. As things stood less than a tenth of the men of several Midland counties could be armed from local resources. In Rutland, adjoining Lincolnshire, there was enough harness for only 14 per cent of its 732 able men. The military survey of 1522, compiled in painstaking detail, furnishes a very exact picture of the actual situation. There were eighty-seven complete harnesses, no fewer than fifty-nine of which were owned by gentlemen and nine more by their retainers, leaving the commonalty almost entirely dependent on the gentry for equipment. Things were rather better in Lincolnshire by 1539, the result, perhaps, of the increased preparedness pursued by the government in response to a deteriorating international situation. Most townships now provided a communal harness, although one still observes the foremost members of the gentry each furnishing ten or twelve armed men from their households, and lesser men doing so in proportion.[33] Among the gentlemen farmers examined John Friskeney alone possessed a complete harness; Morys had a sword.

Just as the administration of the countryside depended wholly on the good will of the gentry,[34] so did their contribution of men and arms form the essence of Henry VIII's military system. For want of a professional army he encouraged great landowners to take responsibility for supplying soldiers, tacitly ignoring the Acts against livery and maintenance, and in 1518 appointed gentlemen of known loyalty as captains, licensing them 'to retain a good and competent number of our subjects' ready horsed and harnessed whenever required for service. Unlikely though Langholme was to have belonged to this organisation, the mere fact of his possessing a good deal of equipment underlines the vital role of even the most retiring of gentlemen in underpinning the Tudor state, the crude reality of armed might on which it was more than once seen clearly to rest when a breakdown of order threatened.

No more than eight years were to pass before the Lincolnshire peasants actually rose in rebellion (in 1536); indeed the first demonstrations broke out in Louth, and the rector of Conisholme itself was later indicted for treason.[35] This Lincolnshire rising was part of a more widespread rebellion known as the Pilgrimage of Grace which engulfed the whole of the north of England. The causes were a complex mixture of religious, political and economic grievances of which the most prominent were opposition to Protestantism and the dissolution of the monasteries coupled with resentment by the magnates at their replacement in the Royal councils by 'upstarts' like Cardinal Wolsey and Thomas Cromwell; by the gentry at higher taxation; and by the peasants at rising rents and enclosures.[36] The general story is well known; all too little attention has been paid to the practical aspects which made such rebellions a mortal threat to the body politic, yet caused most of them to peter out tamely.

Here, as in every other peasant rising, one of the first moves was to oblige the gentry to turn out, for the muster of able-bodied men could not be truly effective without captains to lead them (and probably bear the brunt of any fighting), and access to the little local armouries which is what many manor houses were. The thousands of peasants who eventually assembled outside Lincoln must have appeared more angry than warlike. While some hundreds would have carried the regulation bows and bills, and many more would have improvised ugly weapons out of scythes, the dearth of side arms and protective gear would have been acute and thoroughly inimical to good morale when face to face with the fully armed retinues of the magnates backed by the resources of the royal arsenals.

The gentry found themselves initially in a dilemma. Men like Langholme were individually too weak to defy mobs of enraged farmers and labourers, however ill armed. Thanks to the supineness of Lord Hussey, skulking in his castle at Sleaford instead of vigorously organising them as a peace-keeping force, the only course open to them was to play along – some of course were sympathetic – and wait on events while trying to keep control of most of the arms. When, within days, the Duke of Suffolk began concentrating forces at Stamford, the gentlemen slipped away to rally around the standard of law and order. Leaderless and defenceless, the rebel host melted away too and the rising collapsed ignominiously. That it had momentarily appeared dangerous was due largely to Hussey's ambiguous attitude gravely imperilling the basis of public order, and by the standards of the time his execution a few months later was amply justified.

In a similar situation in Devonshire and Norfolk in 1549 the gentry panicked and lost control of the situation. Where they actually supported the people, in Yorkshire in 1536, the king's lieutenant dared not risk a fight and was obliged to fall back on negotiation: the Pilgrimage of Grace collapsed when they pulled out. The only popular revolts that were self-sufficient were those in Cornwall in 1497 and 1549, and for the same reason they culminated in severe pitched battles, a description that hardly fits the grisly farce at Dussindale which terminated Kett's rebellion. In that county the gentry were mainly men of limited resources, while an exceptionally high proportion of the populace owned 'whole harnesses'[37]; in fact in 1524 it could field at least 1,700 fully armed men besides many more partially equipped. And in 1549 the Cornishmen only went down before the assault of a powerful force of veteran mercenaries.

But almost everywhere else the Crown could count on the landowning class – perhaps one per cent of the population – with their handful of retainers to ward off the dangers of civil strife by prompt and effective action. Like Langholme, many of them were usually absorbed in their private affairs, but in times of crisis the balance was apt to rest in their hands simply because they were armed and the majority of country folk were not.

VI

The final act of John Langholme's short life was the making of his will on 27 February 1528, a fortnight before he died. He had already conveyed all his lands to his cousin John Lytylbury and other

feoffees to hold to the uses to be stipulated in his will, the only way
of providing for younger children before the enactment of the
Statute of Wills in 1540. To each of his five younger sons he assigned
five marks a year for life, plus a couple of breeding swans on attain-
ing the age of twenty. The feodary survey offers a garbled summary,
mentioning only four boys, but crediting Maud, their mother, with
an annuity of ten marks, whereas all she was intended to have (apart
from her dower) was the conventional secondbest bed with its
appointments. As the heir Humphrey naturally got the residue of
the estate, and was to have all the silver, and the residue of the swans
on coming of age. These swans add a pleasant gentlemanly touch.
Keeping them was quite widespread, and limited by law to men
who had a minimum income of five marks from land. They were
bred for the table, and could be a source of some profit, though not
to Langholme, one imagines.[38] There were few small legacies
outside the family: 12*d* apiece to Robert Bagot, and to Thomas
Toynton his godson who was probably the son of the man of the
same name who witnessed the will, and may have been Langholme's
servant since he had been assessed on wages for the subsidy. Again
the feodary interpolates an annuity of 13*s* 4*d* to a certain Richard
Clerke who was possibly an elderly servant.

Considering his limited estate the provision for religious purposes was generous, not to say extravagant. He charged the income
of the estate with £2 13*s* 4*d* to purchase a cope and other vestments
for the parish church, and £20 to pay an honest priest to say masses
for the repose of his soul for the next four years. If this turned out
to be parson Laurence it is possible to make the spiteful comment
that he resigned the living almost exactly four years afterwards when
the young squire was still only fourteen and the prospect of a similar
windfall looked hopelessly remote. John also directed that the
residue of his goods should be disposed of for the health of his soul.
There is no hint of provision for the poor, but then the marsh was
relatively free of destitution. Many contemporary testaments,
especially of peasants, include a small gift to the mother church of
Lincoln, and something for the parson for tithes 'forgotten'. The
absence of these, coupled with the ample provision for his obsequies,
strongly implies that he was a man of deep piety who scrupulously
observed his duties to the Church.

So closed an uneventful life, and yet one that in all essentials
must have closely resembled those of many hundreds of rural
gentlemen who were neither rich nor poor, and rarely aspired to do
more than live quietly on their rents and enjoy the esteem of their

bucolic neighbours. Raising his family, overseeing his estate, and the pleasures of the chase constituted a full life for the squire of Conisholme, for aught we know to the contrary. In view of his early death it may well have been that his constitution was not robust. Indeed the whole strain may have been below average physically. So far as can be judged longevity was not a marked feature: Humphrey was to follow him to the grave in 1538 without having attained his majority, and Christopher the second son only just reached fifty. Perhaps after all it was some want of vitality that held the family back. They did not, so far as is known, profit from the secularisation of the lands of the Church; in 1550 Christopher's income was reported to be 200 marks, virtually the same as his father's, before deductions.[39] In the end it was not unfitting that no special monument was raised to John's memory, and that Gervase Holles, the seventeenth-century antiquary should find only his parents' brass[40]; any simpler inscription was almost certainly erased in the course of subsequent drastic alterations to the fabric of the church.

When Christopher died in 1571 his son Henry sold out, and the estate shortly came into the hands of Sir Christopher Wray, a lawyer and politician of a fundamentally different stamp from the retiring Langholmes. Whether Henry had inherited little more than his father's debts, or simply took the decision to pull up his roots and seek fortune elsewhere, the family faded quietly into the mists of history, and the death of old Anthony, the last of John's children, in 1592 finally terminated a connection which had endured for 250 years.

A brief glimpse into the twilight years of a single family is too narrow a foundation for any theory of the role and aspirations of the 'silent majority' of the mere country gentry. Few, if any, left any records; perhaps they kept none except for their essential 'evidences' or title deeds. It may be that they were fundamentally unbusiness-like and so failed to change with the times. In this they were not alone: the collected works of William Shakespeare are the only substantial record of the life of the most renowned self-made gentleman of the age, and no one could possibly accuse him of lack of enterprise. In passing one cannot help remarking the wry comment on fashionable educational dogma implied by the contrasting fortunes of the man privileged by birth and inherited wealth on the one hand, and the 'disadvantaged' youth who left school with 'small Latin and less Greek' on the other. In the effacement of the Langholmes we can detect failure to surmount the challenge of an increasingly fluid social structure in which the emergence of new families could not but be offset by the decline of old and respected ones. Having prospered in the age of so-called bastard feudalism, they were perhaps unable to adapt successfully to a situation in which they could no longer look to some magnate to advance their interests.

NOTES AND REFERENCES

1. Public Record Office [PRO], E.179/138/478; BM, Harl. 618, f. 11.
2. T. Longley, 'Some work of our forefathers in a quiet marsh parish', *Louth Antiquarian and Naturalists' Society* (1900), 3–10.
3. A. R. Maddison, ed. *Lincolnshire Pedigrees,* ii, Harleian Society (1903), 580.
4. See J. Cornwall, 'The early Tudor gentry', *Economic History Review*, 2nd ser. xvii (1965), 473–5.
5. *Ibid.*, pp. 462–5.
6. R. C. Dudding, 'Conisholme', *Reports and Papers of the Architectural and Archaeological Society of the County of Lincoln*, xli, pt 2 (1933), 134–6; *Calendar of Close Rolls, passim*; H. L. Gray, 'Incomes from land in England in 1436', *English Historical Review*, xlix (1934), 636; A. Rogers, 'Parliamentary Electors in Lincoln-shire in the Fifteenth Century', *Lincolnshire History and Archaeology*, 3 (1968), p. 76; J. C. Wedgwood, *History of Parliament, 1439–1509: Biographies* (1936), p. 525, *Register* (HMSO 1938), p. 202.
7. Cornwall, *loc. cit.*, 466–9.
8. Shakespeare, *As You Like It*, ii, vii, 153–6.
9. Sir Thomas Smith, *De Republica Anglorum*, ed. L. Alston (Cambridge University Press, 1906), p. 34.
10. Lincoln Archives Office, inventory 2/54; printed by C. W. Foster, ed. *Lincoln Wills,* ii, Lincoln Record Society, x, (1918) 64–6.
11. Lincoln Archives Office, inventories, 10/130, 10/140, 10/179, 11/26, 11/161.
12. Cornwall, *loc cit.*, 462–3: feodary surveys indicate a maximum estate of £30; owners of larger incomes mentioned in subsidies may really have been gentlemen, in any case the median is roughly the same in each source, approximately £16.
13. Sir Thomas Smith, *op. cit.* p. 41. The inventories (Worcester diocesan probate registry) of John Praty and Daniel Bentwich of Yardley, 1554, depict gentlemen living in wretched conditions.
14. *Lincoln Wills*, Lincoln Record Society, x, 50–2.
15. R. G. Rice, 'The household goods of Sir John Gage . . .', *Sussex Archaeo-logical Collections*, xlv (1902), 114–27.
16. *PRO* E.179/136/310.
17. Lincoln Archives Office inventories, 2/25, 10/60, 12/117, 13/50, 15/79, 17/38, 18/96, 19/51, 21/48, 31/857, 34/229, 39/2. *Lincoln Wills*, Lincoln R.S., x, 85–6: Kecher's total was £23, household contents £8; the list of items is very similar to Langholme's.

18. See Joan Thirsk, *English Peasant Farming* (Routledge, 1957), ch. 2.

19. Lincoln Archives Office, Conisholme parish documents; inventory 17/38.

20. That is, an average of 1·65 per fleece, a reasonable weight; excluding lambs, just over 2 lb. apiece. In 1595 an upland flock averaging 1,800 head produced 157 stone: Thirsk, *op. cit.*, pp. 90–1.

21. *PRO*, E.150/562/16; Lincoln Archives Office, Longley 1/15.

22. The survey of 1634 is available only in a (summarised?) transcript which is not altogether clear. In 1524 Alvingham Priory owned 168 acres, cf. a similar farm in the survey; Dudding, *loc. cit.*

23. *Lay Subsidy Rolls, 1524–25,* ed. J. Cornwall, Sussex Record Society, lvi (Lewes, 1956), *passim.*

24. *Discourse of the Common Weal,* ed. E. Lamond, (Cambridge University Press, 1929), pp. 81–2.

25. Tawney and Power, *Tudor Economic Documents,* i, 335 (Longmans, 1924); C. H. Williams, *English Historical Documents, 1485–1558,* v (1967), 995–6; *Records of Buckinghamshire,* xiii (1934–40), 282; *HMC, Hastings Report,* i, 354.

26. Cf. Sir Walter Scott's assertion (*Waverley,* ch. xxi) that Highland chiefs lived plainly in order to be able to meet the demands of hospitality, attaching great importance to the number of their dependants and clients.

27. PRO, E.179/136/310, 306, 138/478; E.314/14, 41; B.M. Harl. 618; J. C. Russell, *British Medieval Population* (University of New Mexico Press, 1948), p. 135; Thirsk, *op. cit.* p. 55; Lincoln Archives Office, Longley, 1/16.

28. PRO, Wards 9/129; Dudding, *art. cit.*, p. 135.

29. PRO, E.179/155/131; *Subsidy for the County of Buckingham, 1524,* ed. A. C. Chibnall and A. V. Woodman, Bucks Record Society, viii (Aylesbury, 1950), 8–10.

30. Lincoln Archives Office, Anc. 7D/6.

31. C. Parkin, *Topographical History of the County of Norfolk* (1808), ix, p. 112.

32. Details of military organisation from J. J. Goring, 'The military obligations of the English people, 1511–58' unpublished Ph.D. thesis, London, 1955. The 'whole harness for a man' included sallet, gorget (for the throat), jack and splints. 'Almain rivets' was also used as a collective term for harness other than sallet and gorget. Contemporary illustrations show that splints were not always worn, especially by archers.

33. *Letters and Papers, Henry VIII,* iv, 972; PRO, E. 36/36, SP 1/145, fo. 34 ff.

34. K. Pickthorn, *Early Tudor Government: Henry VII* (Cambridge University Press 1934), p. 72.

35. Lincoln Archives Office, Longley, 1/16.

36. See J. D. Mackie, *The Earlier Tudors, 1485–1558* (Oxford University Press, 1952), pp. 385–93.

37. PRO, E.315/77, 78.

38. N. F. Ticehurst, 'The Swan marks of Lincolnshire', *Reports and Papers . . . of Lincolnshire,* xiii, part 1 (1936), 59–141. No Langholme mark is extant.

39. Dudding, *loc. cit.*

40. Gervase Holles, *Lincolnshire Church Notes,* ed. R. E. G. Cole, Lincoln Record Society, i (1911), 247.

Dearth and Disease
in Staffordshire, 1540–1670[1]

The Cambridge Group for the History of Population and Social
Structure are stimulating a deeper understanding of English demographic history, and the local historian who aspires to be more than
an antiquarian now has to add their *Introduction to English Historical
Demography* to his shelf of essential reference works. The exploitation
of a wide range of sources previously neglected except by the
genealogist has become general, and no one could now dispute
E. A. Wrigley's claim that 'the dark ages of population history ended
in 1538, not in 1837'.[2] Furthermore, our knowledge of other related
subjects is being advanced at the same time, notably the history of
climate and the history of disease; while the chronology of harvests
and famines in the early modern period has been pioneered by
Professor Hoskins.[3] In consequence, it is becoming possible to
build up a series of local studies, like Professor Hoskins's own
monograph on Devon,[4] which will eventually enable us to observe
the chronology and geographical distribution of demographic
crises, whether caused by malnutrition or by disease.

   The present study attempts to contribute to this growing body of
information by taking the county of Stafford from the beginning of
parish registration until about 1670, a convenient date which
coincides roughly with the end of bubonic plague in England. The
intention is to establish a chronology of crisis, based largely on
surviving registers, and to see how far the crises coincide with those

recorded for other regions. It does not claim to be a comprehensive study of all the possible aspects of crisis, nor to have exhausted all the available sources. One particularly regrettable omission is that no systematic price data for grain crops have yet been discovered for the area. In the absence of such data, the national price series printed by Professor Hoskins, Dr Bowden and Mr Harrison (see note 3) have been utilised, but it must be remembered that their grain series are almost all drawn from southern sources. In especially bad years like 1587–88 and 1596–98, a dearth could be nationwide, but normally harvest failures were more limited, and the application to Staffordshire mortality rates of explanations based on southern harvests can be made only with severe qualifications.[5]

The county of Stafford (Fig. 3.1) is one of those transitional between the highland and lowland zones of Britain. Its northern and southern parts are mainly uplands with poor soils, dispersed settlements, and a largely pastoral economy until industrialisation. But the Trent and its tributaries, flowing across the central plain, have created there a richer lowland region which was much nearer the classic Midland pattern of nucleated villages and a good deal of arable farming. Population, now at its densest in the northern and southern conurbations (the Potteries and the Black Country), was then concentrated rather more in the lowland vale and its outliers. The largest centres of population in 1563 were Lichfield, Wolverhampton, Stafford, Eccleshall, Walsall and Uttoxeter, all of them with populations of between one and two thousand. Altogether, the county was thinly peopled in comparison with many other regions; its total population was perhaps 40 or 50,000 in the midsixteenth century and 90 or 100,000 a century later.[6]

The demographic history of the county is very obscure before 1538, and is likely to remain so in the absence of adequate sources. Clearly, like the rest of England, it suffered terribly from the Great Pestilence, a devastating epidemic probably compounded of both bubonic and pneumonic plague. It took hold in Staffordshire by May 1349, and on at least one manor it killed every free tenant.[7] Even in such a terrible year, the county may have escaped a little more lightly than other regions because of its small and scattered population. In both Cheshire and Staffordshire one-third of the beneficed clergy seem to have died, an appallingly high rate but even so (with Huntingdonshire and Oxfordshire) the lowest rate in the country.[8] No other late medieval epidemic is well recorded in Staffordshire, though research on such sources as court rolls may identify lesser peaks of mortality. The county is unlikely to have

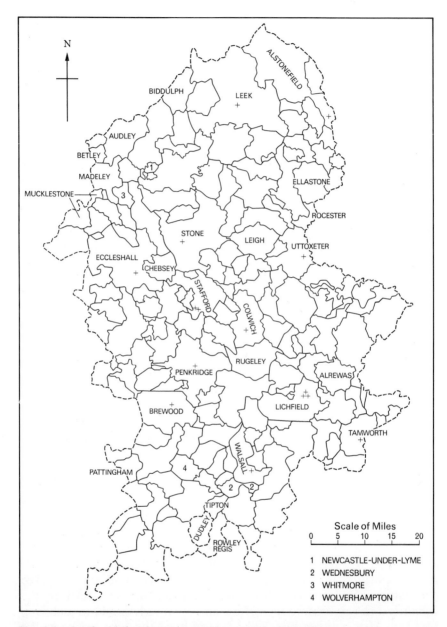

Fig. 3.1   Staffordshire, showing parishes mentioned in the text. In the case of large parishes, the location of the church is indicated thus: +

escaped the nationwide pestilences of 1361, 1368–69, 1371, 1375, 1390 and 1405; and if the climate was already worsening during the fourteenth and fifteenth centuries,[9] then one would expect more frequent bad harvests, with famines and with lowered resistance to disease, as well as the declining total population and contraction of cultivation which are already well established. Staffordshire certainly shared in the widespread contraction of settlement in the later Middle Ages, and at least eighteen villages and hamlets – possibly many more – disappeared between the 1320s and the 1530s.[10]

A number of Staffordshire parish registers begin in 1538 or the years immediately following, enabling a reasonable chronology of demographic crises to be constructed from that time onwards, despite the obvious underregistration, and even complete cessation of entries, that frequently occur in those early years. The first epidemic clearly evident from the registers occurred in the summer of 1551. At Betley nine parishioners were buried in June – as many as in a normal year – while in the adjacent parish of Audley there were twenty burials between 15 June and 6 July. In the Moorlands the epidemic was at its worst in July, when fourteen were buried at Ellastone and twenty-eight at Alstonefield; in both cases a single month saw the equivalent of a normal year. The Ellastone register explicitly ascribes the deaths to 'a generall sweate', and that of Audley to 'the greate sweate'. The sweating sickness, perhaps a form of influenza, had first struck England in 1485, and 1551 was the year of its fifth and last appearance. It broke out at Shrewsbury in March and spread rapidly as far as Yorkshire and Devon, so much so that one witness called it 'the Posting sweat, that posted from town to town thorow England'.[11] This nationwide epidemic, though presumably microbial, was probably assisted by the weakness caused by malnutrition, for a deficient harvest in 1549 had been succeeded by a very bad one in 1550, with grain prices a third above their usual level.[12]

After only a six-year respite, 1557–59 saw an even worse nationwide epidemic, which has been tentatively identified by Professor F. J. Fisher as a virulent form of influenza.[13] Again, malnutrition may have been an important contributory factor, for although the harvests of 1557 onwards were normal, 1555 and 1556 had been the only two successive dearths (that is, with prices over 50 per cent above the average) during the whole period 1465 to 1636.[14] There is considerable, if sporadic, evidence for the mortality in Staffordshire. Thirty-seven parishioners of Leigh were buried in 1557, the highest figure for any year before 1670, with a peak of nine in March.

Betley had a high total in 1557 (fifteen) and a higher still in 1558 (eighteen), though neither was large enough for the monthly distribution to be meaningful. The adjacent parish of Audley escaped in 1557 but was badly struck in the following year with twenty-six burials. The register of Tamworth begins on 4 March 1557; it records the enormous total of ninety-five burials between then and the end of the year, and a further thirty-one in the first three months of 1558. (By contrast, average burials were only forty a year during the healthy period 1566–75.) Unfortunately the register breaks off in April 1558 and is not resumed for sixteen months; and the registers of other, widely scattered, parishes have similar lengthy gaps at just this time: Alstonefield, Mucklestone and Rowley Regis.

These lapses in registration, all occurring at the same period, suggest that the epidemic may have been so severe that the registers were simply abandoned. Confidence in this suggestion is strengthened by a comparison with a group of Yorkshire parishes, where all but one of the registers ceased to be kept during 1558, and where other sources show clearly that the epidemic was exceptionally severe.[15] There is also the fact that, in Staffordshire as elsewhere, the commissioners of musters recorded the epidemic in making their returns to the privy council, a most unusual step. The Staffordshire commissioners reported on 27 February 1559 that they had been able to muster a good number of footmen 'notwithstandinge the greate mortalitie of late within the same [county] & as yet not seasid'.[16] Similar references were made that month by the commissioners for Cheshire, Nottinghamshire and Salisbury, Cheshire's return being particularly welcome as an explicit statement from a county adjoining Staffordshire.[17] The Cheshire commissioners returned a low quota, attributing this to 'extreame sicknes aswell the plage as Quarterne and other extreame diseases wherwithe this Shire hath bene this ij yeres past and yet is sore vysyted'; and a later reference to the Cheshire epidemic called it 'the newe sicknes'.[18] It should be stressed that 'plague' was a blanket term employed by contemporaries for epidemics, and was not restricted to bubonic, pneumonic and septicaemic plagues. Indeed bubonic plague, a summer killer, could not have been the cause of a lethal winter epidemic. It is most likely that Cheshire and Staffordshire, like other parts of the country, were suffering mainly from a new virus infection – hence the retrospective label of 'the newe sicknes' to distinguish it from previous epidemics.

This epidemic died away at the end of the decade, and there

followed a lengthy period free from really general epidemics. If the
county was in line with the areas of surviving grain price series, one
reason will probably have been better nutrition. After the terrible
harvests of 1555 and 1556, there followed sixteen harvests in a row
of average quality or better.[19] During such a relatively healthy
period, one can observe the way in which epidemic diseases like
bubonic plague were becoming more and more an urban scourge,
and were ceasing to devastate the country as a whole. The towns of
Elizabethan England, after all, were unhealthier than the countryside: many urban parishes had a normal surplus of burials over
baptisms, so that for towns to maintain their size, let alone to grow,
a constant flow of immigrants from the country was needed.

The years 1563–64 saw the first case of a serious epidemic recorded
only in urban registers. There was a very severe plague in London
between July and December, 1563, accompanied or followed by
outbreaks at Derby, Leicester, Stratford and Canterbury in that or
the following year,[20] and the towns of south-east Staffordshire
were also struck. Tamworth's register, after a gap of several years,
resumed on 20 December 1563 with the entry 'The names of them
that were buried of the Plague', and significantly this was followed
by forty-three burials listed for the first half of 1564, without a
single baptism or marriage until June. From July 1564 to November
1565 there was a complete gap, probably an indication that the
epidemic continued to rage. It could not have been solely bubonic
plague, but a possibility would be bubonic plague in the summer
alternating with a winter disease.[21] It is not clear how far other
Staffordshire towns were affected. The Stafford and Newcastle
registers do not record exceptional mortality, but Lichfield is known
to have suffered severely in 1564, and on 10 November 1564 the
Bishop of Lichfield said that many of the corporate towns in his
diocese were then suffering from the plague.[22]

Between 1565 and 1578 no widespread and exceptional mortality
seems to have been recorded. There are one or two local exceptions,
as for instance at Stafford in the first quarter of 1570 and the second
quarter of 1571, but the rates in such cases are not high enough to
establish an epidemic beyond doubt. But in 1579 there is again clear
evidence for a widespread urban epidemic, if by urban we include
the growing semi-industrial parishes of the Black Country as well
as the older towns. Wednesbury in April 1579 reached its highest
Elizabethan monthly burial figure, and at Wolverhampton 'plague'
is recorded to have begun on 28 July, though the register for the
period is now missing and the total of burials is not known.[23] At

Tamworth plague burials were recorded from 12 July, and though only a few burials that year are specifically attributed to 'plague', all of them in Wilnecote, the epidemic was plainly active in the town itself. There were 105 burials during 1579 (as against an average fifty during the rest of the decade), with a peak of nineteen during the month of August.

High mortality recurred in 1587–88, perhaps owing to malnutrition, since no 'plague' is mentioned, and the deficient harvest of 1585 had been followed by a bad harvest in 1586.[24] The rural parish of Audley had thirty burials in 1588, its highest total of the century, but most other known cases of heavy mortality are again urban. Newcastle-under-Lyme had increasing mortality during the period 1585–88, reaching a peak of forty-six burials in the harvest year 1587–88, and falling back to sixteen in 1588–89. The pattern was similar at Stafford St Mary's, culminating in eighty-nine burials in 1587–88, and at Tamworth, with peaks of seventy-four in 1587–88 and seventy-one in the following year.

Only five years later, the towns were struck again. The neighbouring county town of Derby endured 'plague' for a whole year, from October 1592 to October 1593,[25] and by the summer the Staffordshire towns were also affected. As the Mucklestone register put it, there was 'a great plage in Staffordshire', and Lichfield and Newcastle 'were gretly vesyteth'. According to Newcastle's own register, 'magna pestis graseatur' on 18 August 1593, and the number of burials climbed steeply – eight in September, seven in October, eleven in November and twelve in December – before falling off in the New Year. Altogether there were fifty-seven burials in 1593, three and a half times the average for the rest of the decade. Stafford was struck slightly later, the first plague burial being entered on 13 December, and mortality not being exceptionally heavy that winter. Hardest struck of all was Lichfield; its registers do not survive so early, but its mortality was explicitly recorded in the register of nearby Alrewas: 'This yeare in the summer time, 1593, their was a great plague in England ... and in Lichfeeld their died to the number of xj hundred and odde and as at this time of wryting not cleane ceassed being the 28 of November.' This figure may imply that Lichfield was already copying London in keeping weekly bills of mortality, as it certainly did in 1645–46. If the population of the combined Lichfield parishes was really 6,000, as it was stated to be in 1604,[26] then a mortality of over 1,100 is perfectly credible; but a population of 6,000 seems a wild overestimate. Perhaps more reliable is the artless testimony of the vicar of Alrewas, like his colleague at Mucklestone, to the exclusively urban nature of the plague. Both placed the entries on town plagues in their registers simply as major items of local news; and it is significant that the burial rates in their own parishes were normal that year.

The Lichfield epidemic continued into 1594 before dying away.[27] A little later, in the winter of 1596–97, four prisoners in Stafford gaol died within six weeks 'by the visitation of God', perhaps an indication of an outbreak of 'gaol fever' or typhus, which was a dreaded killer in county towns with crowded prisons.[28] But these limited epidemics quickly paled before another general crisis in 1596–98, the first to scourge country as well as town since the late 1550s, and likewise connected with harvest failures. There was a nationwide dearth, well known from literary sources, and corroborated by the price indices which show deficient harvests in 1594 and 1595, followed by a dearth in 1596 and a bad harvest in 1597 – the largest run of consecutive harvests of below average quality during the whole sixteenth century.[29] And on this occasion there is sufficient corroborative evidence that the north-west Midlands shared in the general crisis. Mucklestone parish register, for instance, records exceptional grain prices between Michaelmas 1594 and Michaelmas 1597, and cites the current prices at nearby Market Drayton. They reveal that oats reached a maximum (18s the strike) at Michaelmas 1595, and wheat, rye, barley and French wheat a year later (19s 6d, 15s, 13s 4d and 12s respectively). Likewise at Nantwich, just across the county boundary, the parish register, a private diary and business accounts all confirm a huge rise in grain prices during 'the greatt Darthe', and it is recorded 'that greate syckness by ffamyne ensued & many poore dyed thereoff'.[30]

Mortality was heavy in many Staffordshire parishes, though not in all. Newcastle, for instance, suffered much less than in the previous harvest crisis ten years before; but the neighbouring market-village of Betley did not. It had seventeen burials in 1596–97, sixteen in 1597–98, and fourteen in 1598–99, as against an average of eight in the previous ten years. In the south, the harvest year 1596–97 saw forty burials at Wednesbury and forty at Brewood, in each case about double the usual death rate, while in 1597–98 Wednesbury's total rose further to forty-three. In most cases January proved to be the worst month, as one might expect if harvest failure was a major cause; and at Tamworth the register was quite specific about the mortality. 116 were buried there in the harvest year 1597–98, double the usual number, and the climax was reached with twenty-three burials in March, as many as usually died in the whole winter quarter. A terse note after the March entries states that 'Dyvers died of the blouddie flixe, at which tyme the darth of corne somwhat abated by reason of Deathe & Danske [Danzig] Rye'. In other words, the scarcity was reduced by imports of Baltic grain, and because dysentery (the bloody flux) had carried off many hungry mouths.

Mortality generally returned to normal during 1598, and there was no further sharp increase after the bad harvest of 1600, perhaps an indication that it did not seriously affect the county. Instead, in 1603–5, there was a return to the pattern of urban plague. This one began with bubonic plague in the London suburbs in March 1603, probably brought over from the Low Countries, and it killed over 30,000 in the capital that year, or about 15 per cent of the population.[31] From there it spread during that summer and the following year to most English towns and many rural areas; but in Staffordshire it seems to have been largely confined to the towns, and the growing industrial villages of the Black Country. At Walsall an epidemic was heralded by a plague-burial on 30 October 1603, and altogether at least seventeen parishioners died of 'plague' between then and the following March, but this cannot have been bubonic plague because of the seasonal incidence. At Tipton there was clearly an epidemic in 1604, forty-two burials occurring that year as against twenty-two during the whole previous decade; and here the monthly distribution was consistent with bubonic plague, thirty-nine of the forty-two burials taking place during the three months August to October. The first seven burials in late August were all of members of the Nightingale family, and four other Nightingales died during the first half of September; this concentration of mortality among certain families is again what would be expected of bubonic plague. On 8 September two justices of peace levied an assessment on nineteen southern parishes 'for the relief of the poor in Typton township infected with the plague'.[32]

If Tipton can be regarded as an urbanising rural community, the same cannot be said of Colwich, where the register suggests an epidemic in July of 1604, or of Oulton township near Stone, which was 'infected with the sicknes' during the following winter, six houses being affected and twenty-six people isolated.[33] But in general it was the towns which fell victim. Once again the clerk of Mucklestone, a rural parish which escaped, is the most explicit witness:

> this yere [1604] was an Universall plage, u.z.
> Srowesberry, Wichchurch, Lichefeld, Eccleshall, Chebsey, Panckriche, Staffard, Stone, Olton, Addersly, Chester Cyty, Nanntwich,

Weddensbury, Northwiche, Alldringgain, Anlym, Hodnet,
Usxenton pochshe, The cyty of Coventrey, Warwicke, Bristol, York,
London, Glocester cityes.

It seems, however, that the plague may have been shortlived in the Staffordshire towns, or else less virulent than in other years. In some of the urban registers, such as Stafford and Penkridge, the burial rates were little above normal, although Newcastle's has a gap for most of the year which may be ominous. One danger with the county's urban registers, however, is that they often cover large parishes taking in rural townships as well as the urban nucleus, so that a purely urban epidemic may escape notice unless the burial entries identify the victims' addresses as well as their names. At Eccleshall, a small market town with an enormous parish, the total burials for 1604 (forty-two) were about average, but an analysis of addresses by townships shows that the totals are concealing the epidemic in Eccleshall town. Thirty of the forty-two burials in 1604 were of townspeople, whereas usually they accounted for only about a quarter of parish burials. Of the thirty, twenty-two were buried in the three months June to August, a monthly distribution consistent with bubonic plague.

This seems to have been the last widespread series of epidemics before the Civil War. It was followed by nearly forty years in which serious epidemics were few, isolated, and almost entirely urban. Tamworth provides good examples of isolated outbreaks: it suffered severely in 1602 (with a peak of fourteen burials in September), escaped in 1603–5, but had at least eight 'plague' burials in the last quarter of 1606 in a minor local epidemic. Wednesbury experienced high mortality in 1607 and 1608, mainly in the winter months; and Wolverhampton in March and April 1613, and again in March 1614. Dudley, a Worcestershire enclave in Staffordshire, suffered a devastating plague in 1616–17; and in April 1617, when it was still raging, the townspeople petitioned Quarter Sessions for relief, asserting that many were left destitute and that nearly 150 children had been orphaned.[34] A notable absence of plague occured in 1625, for in that year London was heavily struck, and the previous major epidemics in the capital – in 1563, 1593 and 1603 – had all been reflected in the county. In October 1626, however, plague did flare up again in Tamworth.[35]

Nevertheless, the 1620s were a period of distress, for if epidemics were less common, dearth was present instead. The grain price indices do not note any bad harvests between 1601 and 1629,[36] but they are drawn from other areas and may not always reflect the position in Staffordshire. Certainly, many of the county's registers suggest that dearth was abroad in the second and third decades of the century. Deaths of wanderers and of the destitute are scattered throughout the registers, but they become much more common just at this period. In 1613–14, for instance, two wanderers died at Pattingham, one a woman travelling from Surrey to Shropshire, and the other a boy 'coming from or near Madeley': they may well have been the weakest members of families on the road, looking for food and work. In 1618–19 'a suckerlesse pore woman destitute of Maintenance' was buried at Rocester, followed by 'Hewgo Hall, cotager, gravatus paupertate'. Most striking of all is a series of grim entries from the Brewood register:

5 Mar. 1618	A certaine poor man dying in the crosse
30 Sep. 1618	Yevan, a poore wandering boy
23 Mar. 1619	Margaret, a poore wandering wench, dying in the crosse
1 Aug. 1621	Edward Smith, a poore childe dying in the church porch
22 May 1623	A certaine poore childe dying in the church porch
19 Oct. 1623	A poore man dying in Thomas Johnsonne his barne, whose name we knowe not
27 Sep. 1624	A poore wandring boy, whose name is unknowne, dying at Sommerford
26 June 1625	Thomas Pooler, a poor wandring boy
26 Sep. 1625	A poore wandring man
23 Oct. 1625	A poore wandering woman
30 Nov. 1625	A poore wandring man, unknowne

It is unlikely that Brewood had an exceptional number of starving travellers passing through, and more likely that the clerk was simply keeping a more detailed register. If so, such deaths may have been common all over the county, and this would fit with the evidence from other areas. There was heavy mortality all over the North in 1623, perhaps a combination of famine and bubonic plague, and, uniquely, a parish register in Cumberland attributed at least eleven deaths to starvation.[37] The evidence needs comparisons with other areas, but it raises the question whether the highland half of England did not suffer from a general crisis of subsistence in the early 1620s, which has not been reflected in the lowland-based grain price series. On the whole, crises of subsistence, familiar in seventeenth-century France, have not been established for England, but this may prove to have been an exception.

The 1630s seem to have been a relatively healthy decade in Staffordshire: entries of deaths of wanderers become rare, and mentions of 'plagues' are few. There was a widespread plague in

1631 in London, Yorkshire, Lancashire, and parts of Wales and the Marches, but it seems to have spared Staffordshire. Later in the decade, however, limited urban epidemics did occur. The register of Wolverhampton, after a gap in the summer of 1635, shows high mortality from September to January. In 1637 Birmingham and Kidderminster, just over the county boundary, both seem to have suffered a 'great contagion',[38] though it is not apparently reflected in Staffordshire. And during Lent 1638 there was a 'time of sicknesse' in Stafford, though not severe enough to cause exceptional mortality.[39]

The 1640s, by contrast, saw the worst epidemics in the county since the series of 1603–5. As in other areas, the first Civil War of 1642–46 coincided with, and no doubt helped to cause, widespread sickness, chiefly in the towns; 1642 was generally an unhealthy year, and parishes as widely spread as Newcastle, Stoke, Eccleshall, Stafford and Wolverhampton suffered increased mortality, though not of the order of a major epidemic. Stafford suffered particularly throughout the war, perhaps because of its military and garrison functions. A series of special street cleansing orders, beginning in December 1643, probably indicates anxiety about disease, and by 2 January many prisoners in the town were sick of some contagious disease. Furthermore 'the feaver', probably typhus, took hold in the common prison by June 1644. In July 1646 the Committee of Accounts in the town said there had been a 'late breaking forth of the sickness in Stafford and other places in this county', but in August the town was described as having suffered from plague 'for a long tyme', so perhaps it was only a recrudescence of diseases which had become endemic. The 'plague' was still present, at all events, in February 1647.[40] The monthly distribution of deaths cannot be plotted, since the town's two registers are incomplete for the period; but it is clear that bubonic plague cannot have been the only killer disease, as it is active only in summer.

During 1645–47 plagues became widespread, Lichfield suffering especially heavily. There is no adequate coverage from parish registers, but fortunately a note survives written by Elias Ashmole (a native of the city) listing total deaths, by streets, for 1645–46. Altogether 821 died during the year, probably at least a third of the population, which numbered some 2,500 twenty years later.[41] The 'plague' was still present in July 1646, when Ashmole's mother fell victim to it, and possibly throughout the following winter. In February 1647 Isaac Smith, 'sicknes then cruelly handlinge him', dictated his will through the bedroom window, a clear indication of contagious illness.[42]

Tradition credits Leek with a serious plague in 1646–47,[43] and though the registers are too badly kept to confirm this, they do suggest high mortality throughout the Civil War. Uttoxeter, in contrast, seems to have escaped entirely in 1646, and to have been able to send relief to other places which were less fortunate.[44] In the Moorlands, the large rural parish of Alstonefield had at least one recorded plague burial (31 July 1646), although its total of burials for the year was low; and it was not the only case of rural plague. A letter from a justice of the peace written some time in 1647 concerned 'divers persons suspected to be infected with the plague' at Rushton Grange.[45]

The twenty years after these epidemics were relatively healthy, though as usual there are scattered suggestions of isolated epidemics. Rugeley, for instance, suffered high mortality in 1649 and 1650, and Newcastle during the years 1651–55. The most notorious outbreak of the period was of course the Great Plague of London in 1665, the last major bout of the bubonic pandemic which had begun in England in 1348. A few small provincial outbreaks are also recorded for 1665, notably the well-known Derbyshire example at Eyam.[46] Staffordshire yields at least one hint of an epidemic at this period, when a yeoman of Lichfield died in the autumn of 1665. The appraisers did not venture to enter his town house to make an inventory because of 'those deingorous times', though they were able to catalogue his farming gear.[47]

After 1666 bubonic plague died away in England, and the last outbreak accepted by Professor Shrewsbury as bubonic was a small Cornish one in 1671.[48] Admittedly, the terms 'plague' and 'pestilence' remained in use for some time: in Staffordshire, Edward Mainwaring of Whitmore bought 'plague water' in 1676 and 1687, and paid 'pest fines' for Biddulph in 1678 and 1687.[49] But it is most unlikely that bubonic plague can be intended. After all, it was only during the seventeenth century that plague acquired its present connotation of a specific bacterial disease, and it was not until the nineteenth century that it was clinically distinguished from epidemic typhus.[50] The seventeenth century, indeed, marks a great divide in English pathological history, and not only because medical knowledge was advancing rapidly. Bubonic and pneumonic plague disappeared, and other killer diseases became prominent (or were more clearly diagnosed) instead. Smallpox and measles, for instance, were first noticed under the Tudors, but did not become major epidemic diseases until the seventeenth century. Both are occasionally recorded in Staffordshire and Cheshire after the middle of the century,[51] though the registers before the eighteenth century name causes of death too rarely for an analysis of these and other diseases to be possible.

The most striking feature of the bouts of high mortality in the period under review is the contrast between 'plague' and other causes. 'Plague' was evidently an omnibus term for several killers, including one or more winter diseases, and possibly summer diseases other than bubonic plague. But the epidemics so described by contemporaries fall into a pattern: they rarely lasted more than a year at a time, and were almost exclusively urban. Whereas the Great Pestilence of 1348–50 had scourged town and country alike, its successors in the sixteenth and seventeenth centuries were urban killers – most frequent and heavy in London and the large cities, and rather less common in the smaller towns. In the countryside, 'plague' deaths were very few indeed, and the notoriety of the lethal outbreak at Eyam in 1665 has masked its untypicality. As to why certain diseases should have become urban in character, the pro-verbially insanitary state of Tudor and Stuart towns is probably sufficient explanation.

Mortality affecting town and country alike fell into two categories. One was the periodic dearths resulting from harvest failures; these were less lethal than epidemics, and they rarely caused a death rate as high as did 'plague', but they could drag on for several years given a run of poor harvests, and were especially dangerous if they coincided with the arrival of disease, since they weakened resistance. The other category consisted of the epidemics distinguished from 'plague' at the time, notably the virus diseases of 1551 and 1557–59. These caused death rates at least as high as 'plagues', in rural as well as urban parishes. The former was an outbreak of a disease, the sweating sickness, which had been introduced as recently as 1485, and the latter, significantly dubbed 'the new sickness', was ap-parently without precedent. This must have made them more deadly than diseases longer established, against which partial im-munity could be built up; but their virulence probably owed as much to synchronisation with malnutrition as to the nature of the diseases themselves. Even a really serious harvest crisis, like 1596–98, unaccompanied by an epidemic, only doubled the usual death rate, but the virus diseases of the 1550s, both coming on the heels of bad harvests, were much more lethal.

It cannot be stressed too often that the medical identification of epidemics before the eighteenth century is difficult. Nevertheless, there seems little reason to doubt that those urban 'plagues' of the seventeenth century which struck in the summer months were normally bubonic. There is confirmation that this was so from the more copious London records; and for Staffordshire it is often a reasonable assumption when the epidemic has the right seasonal distribution and occurs simultaneously with a London 'plague'. Now bubonic plague died out in England around 1670; and the reasons for this are far from clear. One reason often put forward, which may be a partial explanation, is the replacement of the black rat by the brown; but perhaps at least as important was the Great Rebuilding of rural England to which Professor Hoskins has directed our attention,[52] and which can be documented for Staffordshire as well as for most other English counties. The construction of better built and more sanitary housing must have been a great deterrent to rat infestation and therefore to bubonic plague; and the consequent improvement in health must have considerably offset the results of overcrowding as the seventeenth-century population increased.

Long-term trends, however, do not provide an appropriate note on which to conclude a discussion of epidemics. To contemporaries facing a crisis of mortality, the short term – immediate survival or not – was what mattered. What happened to the population during such crises, and how long-lasting were its effects? Many parish registers are not suitable for answering such questions, either because of underregistration during a crisis, or because the absolute numbers of entries are too low to provide statistically significant results. However, three examples from registers not subject to these objections are presented here in graph form (Fig. 3.2 to 3.4). Baptisms, marriages and burials are plotted on a quarterly basis, each New Style year commencing with the winter quarter (January to March inclusive). Somewhat arbitrarily, all baptismal totals have been advanced by nine months and called 'conceptions', a method which does allow mortality to be synchronised with fertility. (The resulting figures do not of course represent all conceptions, but only those resulting in live births.)

Figures 3.2 and 3.4 monitor the effects of 'plagues', a probably bubonic outbreak at Tamworth in 1579 with a summer peak, and the Newcastle epidemic of 1593 with maximum mortality in November and December. This seasonal difference apart, both cases reveal a similar pattern of burials. First, the normal seasonal oscillation was broken by a steady rise over four or five quarters, suggesting an already unhealthy situation. Then came a rapid

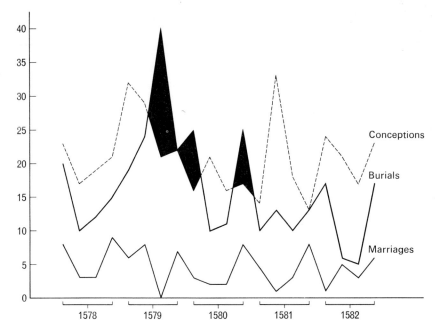

Fig. 3.2   Tamworth: epidemic of plague, 1579.

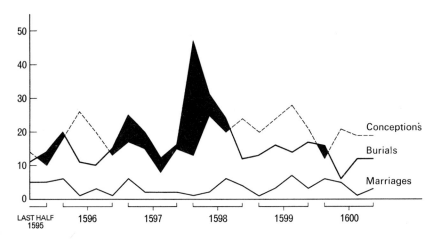

Fig. 3.3   Tamworth crises of 1596–8.

increase to the first and greatest mortality peak, followed by an equally rapid fall. The next phase saw a continuing decline – punctuated by lesser peaks of burials – to an abnormally low level, presumably because the epidemic had already carried off many of those who would otherwise have died over the next year or two. And finally the burial rate returned to its normal level, in so far as the word normal has any meaning when applied to an age of highly unstable death rates.

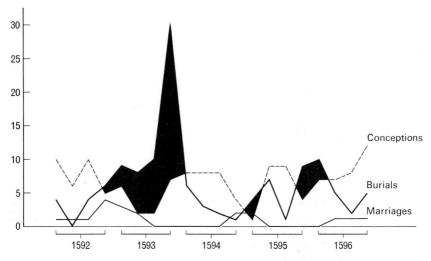

Fig. 3.4   Newcastle-under-Lyme: epidemic of plague, 1593.

The Tamworth mortality of 1596–98, on the other hand, supports the identification of famine, rather than disease, as the primary cause. The register, as has been seen, is quite explicit about a climax of dearth and accompanying dysentery in March 1598. Figure 3.3 shows a pattern of mortality in reverse order to that of 1579–80, as well as one spread out over a longer period. A first burial peak in the winter of 1596 was succeeded by a lull and then by a second and more severe mortality in the following winter. Again burials declined in the summer, though not as low as previously, and then came the third and highest peak in the winter of 1598, after which the death rate declined sharply. This is the thumbprint of dearth, mortality reaching a climax three to six months after a bad harvest, and a succession of winter peaks each more severe than the one before, until the harvests improve. It is the pattern identified by Professor Hoskins as typical of pre-industrial England:

. . . 'meagre yield-ratios of 1:3·0 or 4·0 . . . were the rule in the middle ages and even in many countries till the eighteenth century.' This meant that a large part of the arable had to be kept for growing the next year's seed. It also meant that a bad harvest, by reducing the yield ratio to a dangerously low level, almost automatically ensured another bad harvest from a sheer deficiency of seed. In very bad years the rural population must have staved off the worst of their hunger by consuming part of next year's seed-corn. . . . So one bad harvest tended to generate others, possibly cumulatively, and the sequence could only be broken by a year in which the weather came to the rescue and doubled the yield, so restoring the 'normal' balance between bread-corn and seed-corn.[53]

Such a crisis was naturally more acute in a semi-urban parish like Tamworth than in purely rural areas, since the countrymen lacked the usual rural surplus of grain to exchange for the goods and services of the townsmen.

The graphs also confirm the patterns discovered in many regions for the other vital statistics. While burials climbed to a peak, marriages and conceptions fell to a minimum, and when the crisis passed, the three movements were reversed, though less violently. Finally, some two years after the onset of the crisis, the three rates resumed a state of approximate equilibrium, rising and falling at the same time. Weddings were naturally more disrupted during a short, severe epidemic than during a long-drawn-out subsistence crisis. During both sample epidemics weddings ceased altogether at the height of the crisis, and at Newcastle in 1593–94 none were celebrated during five successive quarters. Similarly, conceptions, which normally moved in tandem with the death rate, fell sharply at the onset of a demographic crisis. Each of the two epidemics is marked by a two- or three-year 'scissor movement', the first and worst mortality being followed by a sharp fall in the death rate and a corresponding increase in conceptions, to produce a surplus of conceptions over burials, and then by a repetition of the same sequence once or twice more on a lower scale. The fluctuations in conceptions are not as self-explanatory as those in weddings, but they can plausibly be explained by changes in two variables: the deaths of a considerable proportion of fertile marriage partners, and that lowered fertility of the survivors which is a common feature of famines and epidemics.

It seems, therefore, that much of the loss of life was swiftly repaired by a rise in births. This rise was not as pronounced as the mortality it succeeded, but that was not necessary, for the available evidence suggests that the norm was an excess of baptisms over burials. That being so, the ravages of an epidemic could be quickly made good in terms of numbers, though of course the age structure would be distorted, and for some time afterwards the proportion of the population who were economically self-supporting would be lowered. It may occasion some surprise to assert a Staffordshire baptismal surplus as normal throughout the period, since in some other areas a rapid rise in population under Elizabeth was followed by a much slower rise, or even stagnation, in the early and mid-seventeenth century. However, almost all the parish registers of the county which have been analysed in full reveal a baptismal surplus during most decades of the seventeenth century no less than the sixteenth.[54] It is therefore no surprise that the county's population more than doubled in the period under review, from 9,000 house-holds in 1563 to nearly 21,000 in 1665.[55] By contrast, the national population did not quite double over a period half as long again, if we accept Cornwall's 2·8 million for England in 1545, and Glass's 5·2 million for England and Wales in 1695.[56] It would be too crude to contrast these two pairs of figures as absolute totals in an absence of really reliable data, but there do seem reasonable grounds for postulating a population growth more rapid and sustained in Staffordshire than in England as a whole. To pursue the possible causes of the growth would be to go beyond the limits of this essay, but it may well be linked with the growth of rural and semi-urban industry in the county. That is not to argue, however, that in-dustrialisation precipitated the increase in population. On the contrary, it could well be that the causal link, if there was one, was the other way round. Joan Thirsk has demonstrated that in most of Staffordshire pastoral farming was combined with other occu-pations, especially small-scale industry,[57] and no doubt a large growth in population provided a considerable incentive to practise such dual careers, or even to move over to full-time industry if the land became unable to support the extra mouths.

NOTES AND REFERENCES

1. This essay is based mainly on printed parish registers, and on unprinted registers (both originals and transcripts) at the County Record Office, Stafford, to the staff of which I am indebted for much help and kindness. References are not given for data taken from the registers, but parish and date are instead cited in the text. Two classifications employed in the text require explanation. (i) The terms 'calendar year' and 'harvest year' are employed for years beginning

respectively on 1 January and 1 August, and the year starting on 25 March (used in most of the registers) is not employed here. (ii) Descriptions of the quality of harvests ('bad', 'deficient', etc.) are in accordance with the definitions employed in Professor Hoskins's articles (see n. 3).

2. E. A. Wrigley, ed., *An Introduction to English Historical Demography* (Weidenfeld & Nicolson, 1966), p. xi. 1538 was the date at which Thomas Cromwell ordered parish registers to be kept, and only a handful begin before then. It is often asserted that Tipton (Staffs.) has the earliest register in England, starting in 1513, but Mr. Mander convincingly showed that '1513' is a simple error for 1573: Staffordshire Parish Registers Society (1923), *Tipton Parish Register*, ed. G. P. Mander, pp. iii, iv.

3. 'Harvest fluctuations and English economic history, 1480–1619', *Agricultural History Review* xii (1964), 28–46; and 'Harvest fluctuations and English economic history, 1620–1759', *ibid.* xvi (1968) 15–31. These, in the absence of other data, were based solely on wheat prices. Later, P. Bowden, in his 'Statistical Appendix', *The Agrarian History of England and Wales,* iv (Cambridge University Press, 1967), pp. 814–70, published data for other grains, and from this a revised chronology was calculated using all grain prices: C. J. Harrison, 'Grain price and analysis and harvest qualities, 1465–1634', *Agric. Hist. Rev.* xix (1971), 135–55. References here to harvests before 1634 are based on Mr Harrison's data, but Professor Hoskins' categories are retained. Average prices 10 to 25 per cent above the 31-year moving average are taken to indicate a 'deficient harvest'; those 25 to 50 per cent, a 'bad harvest'; and those 50 per cent or more above, a 'dearth'.

4. W. G. Hoskins, 'Epidemics in Tudor Devon', repr. in his *Old Devon* (David and Charles, 1966), pp. 132–48.

5. Another missing source, but one which could be supplied by patient research, is a collection of climatic data for the county. There is a little evidence that the English climate was deteriorating in the Tudor and Stuart periods (H. H. Lamb, *The Changing Climate*, Methuen, 1966, pp. 10–12, 174–5), and Mr Chalklin has suggested that bad weather, coupled in towns with overcrowding and insanitation, was a much more important cause of disease than malnutrition (C. W. Chalklin, *Seventeenth-Century Kent: a Social and Economic History*, Longmans, 1965, pp. 40–1).

6. Population figures for 1563 and 1665 in *Staffordshire Historical Collections* [*SHC*] (1915), lxix–lxxii. A multiplier of 4·5 to 5 persons per household has been employed.

7. *SHC* (1913), 130–1.

8. J. F. D. Shrewsbury, *A History of Bubonic Plague in the British Isles* (Cambridge University Press, 1970), p. 56.

9. Lamb, *op. cit.*, pp. 8–10, 174–5.

10. P. V. Bate and D. M. Palliser, 'Suspected lost village sites in Staffordshire', *Transactions of the South Staffordshire Archaeological and Historical Society*, xii (1970–71), 31–6.

11. C. Creighton, *A History of Epidemics in Britain from A.D. 664 to the Extinction of Plague* (Cambridge, 1891) [Creighton, vol. i], pp. 237–81. For the sweat in Yorkshire, not known to Creighton, see D. M. Palliser, 'Epidemics in Tudor

York', *Northern History,* viii (1973) 50.

12. Harrison, *loc. cit.,* 153.

13. F. J. Fisher, 'Influenza and inflation in Tudor England', *Econ. Hist. Rev.,* 2nd ser., xviii (1965), 120–9.

14. Harrison, *loc. cit.*

15. Palliser, 'Epidemics in Tudor York', p.51.

16. Public Record Office, SP 12/2, No. 42.

17. *Ibid.,* nos. 26, 38, 45.

18. *Ibid.,* no. 38; *Child Marriages, Ratifications, Divorces, &c.,* ed. F. J. Furnivall (Early English Text Society, original series, 1897), cviii, 139.

19. Harrison, *loc. cit.*

20. Creighton, i, pp. 304–9.

21. Recent writers have disagreed over the nature of winter epidemics which often alternated with summer diseases. Shrewsbury, *op. cit.,* pp. 125, 161–3 etc., prefers typhus and famine-fever, and dismisses the possibility of pneumonic plague. C. Morris, 'The plague in Britain', *Historical Journal,* xiv (1971), 205–15, prefers pneumonic plague and insists that it can operate in winter.

22. T. Harwood, *The History and Antiquities of the Church and City of Lichfield* (Gloucester, 1806), pp. 304, 526; *SHC* (1915), 369.

23. S. Shaw, *The History and Antiquities of Staffordshire* (1801), ii, pt. 1, p. 163; Staffordshire Parish Registers Society, 1932: *Wolverhampton Parish Register,* Part I, ed. G. P. Mander, p. 2.

24. Harrison, *loc. cit.*

25. R. Simpson, *A Collection of Fragments illustrative of the History and Antiquities of Derby* . . . (Derby, 1826), i, pp. 87, 368–9; Creighton, i, p. 357.

26. *SHC* (1915), lxxiv.

27. Harwood, *op. cit.,* pp. 268, 304, 527.

28. Creighton, i. pp. 374–86, 395; Shrewsbury, *op cit.,* p. 110.

29. Harrison, *loc. cit.,* p. 154 (figures for all grains). For wheat alone, the position was worse, with dearth in two successive years.

30. J. Hall, *A History of the Town and Parish of Nantwich* . . . (Nantwich, 1883), pp. 112–13. Burials in Nantwich numbered 40 in Dec. 1596 and 49 in Jan. 1597, each about a normal *year's* total.

31. Creighton, i, pp. 474–92; Shrewsbury, *op cit.,* pp. 266–9; F. P. Wilson, *The Plague in Shakespeare's London* (Oxford University Press, 1927), pp. 85–113. E. A. Wrigley, 'A simple model of London's importance . . . 1650–1750', *Past and Present,* no. 37 (1967), 44, estimates its population *c.* 1600 as 200,000.

32. *SHC* (1940), 176.

33. *Ibid.,* 213.

34. J. Roper, *Dudley: the Seventeenth Century Town* (Dudley Public Library, 1968 reprint), pp. 4, 5.

35. Staffs. Parish Register Society, *Tamworth Parish Register,* part I (1917), p. 1. The 1626 entries have not been printed, and the original has not been examined.

36. Harrison, 'Grain price analysis', p. 154.

37. W. G. Howson, 'Plague, poverty and population in parts of north-west England, 1580–1720', *Transactions of the Historic Society of Lancashire and Cheshire,*

cxii (1961), 33, 34, 39, 40; P. Laslett, *The World We Have Lost* (Methuen, 1965), pp. 114–17.

38. C. Gill, *History of Birmingham*, Volume I: *Manor and Borough to 1865* (Oxford University Press, 1952), p. 50; Roper, *op. cit.*, p. 7.

39. K. R. Adey, 'Aspects of the history of the town of Stafford, 1590–1710' (unpublished M.A. thesis, University of Keele, 1971), p. 32. I am grateful to Mr Adey for permission to use and quote from his thesis.

40. D. H. Pennington and I. A. Roots, *The Committee at Stafford 1643–1645: the Order Book of the Staffordshire County Committee* (*SHC* 4th series, i, (1957)), 4, 26, 51, 124, 138–9; Adey, *loc. cit.*, pp. 32–34.

41. Harwood, *op. cit.*, p. 306; H. Thorpe, 'Lichfield: a study of its growth and function', *SHC* (1950–51), 183.

42. *Probate Inventories of Lichfield and District 1568–1680*, ed. D. G. Vaisey, *SHC*, 4th series, v (1969), 73.

43. J. Sleigh, *A History of the Ancient Parish of Leek* (1st edn, 1862), p. 28.

44. F. Redfern, *History of the Town of Uttoxeter* (London etc., 1865), pp. 242–3.

45. Edward Mainwaring's book of expenses 1674–92 (unfoliated), in the possession of Mr Rafe Cavenagh-Mainwaring of Whitmore Hall (the letter is stitched in between the pages of expenses for Dec. 1685 and Jan. 1686). I am grateful to Mr Cavenagh-Mainwaring for permission to consult and cite this manuscript.

46. Creighton, i, pp. 680–7; Shrewsbury, *op. cit.*, pp. 510–29.

47. *Lichfield Inventories*, ed. Vaisey, p. 151.

48. Shrewsbury, *op. cit.*, p. 537.

49. Edward Mainwaring's book of expenses (unfoliated), *SHC*, (1933), pt II, 72, 76, 77.

50. Shrewsbury, *op. cit.*, pp. 1, 125, 141. See however Morris, 'The plague in Britain', pp. 211–15, for a contrary view.

51. Rocester register, 30 April 1649; Edward Mainwaring's expenses, April 1676.

52. W. G. Hoskins, 'The rebuilding of Rural England, 1570–1640', *Past and Present* iv (1953), 44–59, repr. in his *Provincial England* (Macmillan 1963), pp. 131–48.

53. Hoskins, 'Harvest fluctuations 1480–1619', pp. 32, 33.

54. For the exceptional case of Walsall, where the Mollesley Dole accounts furnish precise figures from 1619 onwards, see E. J. Homeshaw, *The Corporation of the Borough and Foreign of Walsall* (Geof. J. Clark Ltd., Walsall, 1960), pp. 4–6. Walsall's population increased by 123 per cent from 1619 to 1699, with a cumulative rise of over 10 per cent per decade for much of that period.

55. *SHC* (1915), lxix–lxxii.

56. J. Cornwall, 'English population in the early sixteenth century', *Economic History Review*, 2nd ser., xxiii (1970), 32–44; D. V. Glass and D. E. C. Eversley, eds, *Population in History* (Edward Arnold, 1965), p. 204.

57. J. Thirsk, 'Horn and thorn in Staffordshire: the economy of a pastoral county', *North Staffs. Journal of Field Studies* ix (1969), 1–16.

New Crops and their Diffusion:
Tobacco-growing in
Seventeenth-century England

Substantial changes in the structure of agriculture and in the quantities of food produced have been brought about at different times in man's history by the introduction of new crops. Englishmen could cite as examples the introduction of clover and turnips; Irish, German and Polish historians the potato; French, Spanish and Italians maize. Sometimes the innovation is attributed to one man, as Sir Walter Raleigh is credited with the introduction of the potato to Ireland.[1] Sometimes it is attributed to its first publicist, as the introduction of clover as a field crop is attributed to Sir Richard Weston, or turnips to Lord Townshend. But while these attributions make colourful biographical history, they do not go to the heart of the matter. Explorers who bring back plants from their voyages, and the writers of persuasive books are only individuals singled out for obvious reasons from a large company of players. In reality the success of a new crop depends on its cultivators. It is they who experiment with it, measure its contribution to their food resources, decide if it will find a ready sale at the market, and judge how its cultivation can be fitted into their pattern of agricultural work. They are the supreme arbiters; it is they who determine whether the crop shall spread rapidly, slowly, or not at all.

But who are 'they', and what governs their decisions? 'They' are cultivators, but they are not always one homogeneous class. Their enthusiasm for an innovation must survive the test of the crop's economic attractiveness, *and* the demands it makes on their technical skills, their capital, and their labour resources. If enthusiasm does survive, it will vary in degree among different classes of farmers according to the social framework in which their lives are set. If the new crop takes hold among the peasantry, it may be counted a minor miracle, so notoriously slow are they in adopting novelties. In short, a successful new crop has a complex economic and social history involving several layers of explanation. The deeper layers are rarely explored for our sources of information are too meagre. We have to be content usually with a superficial account of its progress, studded with the names of one or two astute plant importers or eloquent writers. The phases of the story that involve the cultivators are shrouded in mystery.

Tobacco-growing in England, however, is a different case. It began to take hold early in the seventeenth century, and was almost immediately banned by the government. Yet the crop proved to be remarkably tenacious and popular, being taken up with alacrity by large numbers of peasant cultivators. In fifty years it spread into twenty-two counties in England and Wales, and to the islands of Jersey and Guernsey. Since the government had to fight a long-drawn-out battle, lasting over seventy years, before tobacco-growing was eradicated, its history is unusually well documented. An exceptional opportunity occurs of observing how a novel crop was first introduced, and, more remarkably, how it became firmly established among poor husbandmen, the group normally most reluctant to risk its fortunes on new-fangled ventures.

II

Ralph Lane, the first governor of Virginia, and Francis Drake are usually given credit for bringing tobacco to England in 1586. They introduced Sir Walter Raleigh to tobacco-smoking, and he became its first publicist. Seed was brought from America in the sixteenth century for the interest of English botanists, to be grown in their physic gardens and nurseries. But it does not necessarily follow that cultivation on a large scale began under their impetus. It is possible that field cultivation was encouraged by observations and experience of growing tobacco picked up by someone in another country in Europe. The plant (*nicotiana tabacum*) had been brought from Brazil to Portugal probably before 1530. In 1560 the French ambassador in Lisbon, Jean Nicot, was given some seeds by the distinguished Portuguese archivist and historiographer, Damião de Goes, and despatched them to France. It is not thought the plant had been brought much earlier to Spain: the Spanish physician Francisco Fernandes, sent by Philip II of Spain to Mexico to investigate the country's commercial potential, brought back seed in 1558 with the practical possibilities of cultivation in Europe in mind. It is thought that commercial tobacco cultivation did not start in France, despite Nicot's action, until 1626, seven years after it had begun in England.[2] If any country in Europe is to have credit for teaching English growers, it is more likely to have been Holland, where the crop was growing in 1610, and where by 1615 it was firmly established around Amersfoort, later to become a principal centre.[3]

Nevertheless, the influence of European experience on English tobacco-growers still remains in doubt, since the first book of instruction on the subject, *An Advice how to plant Tobacco in England . . . with the Danger of the Spanish Tobacco* by C.T., published in London in 1615, is clearly written by someone with an accurate knowledge of the methods used to grow and cure it in the West Indies.[4] In the next four years much experience was to be had from Virginia too. The Virginia plantation had been in existence since 1607, and tobacco was the staple crop from 1616 onwards.[5] By 1619 when the Tracy family of Toddington, Gloucestershire, was engaged in tobacco-growing around Winchcombe, one younger member, William Tracy of Hailes, near Winchcombe, was actively associated with the Virginia Company, recruiting men for the Virginia plantation. He sailed to Virginia in the first half of 1620 and was appointed a member of the Council of Estate there in June. His correspondence in 1620 included at least one letter from his 'cousin' Timothy Gates, parson of Winchcombe, whose wife allowed some of her land to be used to grow tobacco. He also wrote many letters to John Smyth of Nibley, who was ordering good tobacco seed from Virginia in 1619, and who sold English tobacco to Virginia in 1621.[6]

The impetus to grow tobacco commercially in England, therefore, could have come from one of a number of different sources or from the combined influence of several. By 1619 tobacco was finding its way into an increasing number of yards and gardens in Westminster and London, where the apothecaries were willing purchasers, and it was no longer certain that their purposes were only medicinal.[7] The first commercial grower of tobacco on a large scale had trading connections with Holland. But the strongest evidence is that which links Gloucestershire gentry with the Virginia Company. The full significance of this association is elaborated below.

III

The first firm evidence of tobacco cultivation on a field scale in England dates from 1619, with some slight hints that a trial crop had been grown in the previous year.[8] The land used for tobacco lay in the neighbourhood of Winchcombe, Gloucestershire, and the promoters of the enterprise were two Londoners, John Stratford, Salter, and his partner Henry Somerscales, gentleman, of Gray's Inn. The identity of these two gentlemen repays closer investigation.

When Henry Somerscales entered Gray's Inn in 1605 he was described as the son of Robert Somerscales, esquire, of Gainsborough, Lincolnshire.[9] In a subsequent lawsuit two London salters who sold English tobacco wholesale claimed their first acquaintance with Henry in 1618. This is a slender but corroborating clue that the tobacco venture with John Stratford was first planned in that year and not earlier.[10] Henry Somerscales had doubtless acquired his skill with tobacco through the similar interests of his father. In May 1619 Robert Somerscales was seeking a patent 'about tobacco' from the Crown, much to the alarm of the Virginia Company. When the Company's officers investigated the scheme, they decided that it was 'very prejudicial' to them, and must be stopped. They seem to have succeeded, for, after a meeting was arranged in May 1619 with the Attorney General and Mr Somerscales, no more was heard of it. A year later, in May 1620, Robert Somerscales concocted another project which he put before the Virginia Company. It required a capital sum of £15,000 which was to be raised from among adventurers in the Virginia Company, and was concerned with 'the curing and ordering of tobacco'. Somerscales was introduced to the Company as 'a very fit man . . . who is very skilful in curing that plant, whereby it may be made more profitable than it is'. The scheme was approved by the Company in July 1620, but it is not referred to again in the Company's records and Robert Somerscales thereafter disappears from sight.[11] Meanwhile his brother, Henry, was engaged in tobacco growing in Gloucestershire. From January until December 1619 it was a legal activity; thereafter it was banned.

In 1625 Henry Somerscales petitioned the Privy Council from Coates in Nottinghamshire, a small hamlet a few miles from

Gainsborough, claiming to be a poor man who had spent his whole estate in 'finding out and perfecting the mystery of planting and curing tobacco'. His 'impoverishment' was that of a gentleman rather than a labourer, however, for he admitted having just spent £30 travelling twice to London to reclaim confiscated tobacco. He had been hard hit by the government's ban on tobacco-growing, and he now sought a new but associated occupation. He wanted a warrant to seize all English and Spanish tobacco and suppress all tobacco plantations throughout England, his reward being half the tobacco so seized which he could then sell for the support of himself and his family.[12] Three months later, in September 1626, the Privy Council gave Henry Somerscales, 'gentleman of the county of Nottingham', the job he desired: he was ordered to search and seize all tobacco found growing in Buckinghamshire, Lincolnshire, Yorkshire, and elsewhere.[13] No more is heard of him after this and he may have died at Lincoln in 1634.[14]

Such meagre biographical information does nothing to explain how the Somerscales family learned the mystery of tobacco-growing. They could have talked to the gardeners of London, read C.T.'s book, lived in Virginia, the West Indies, or Holland, or even, perhaps, learned from Dutch settlers in England or from Dutch traders. They lived near Gainsborough, which was a modest but developing trading port on the Trent, which had regular contact via Hull with the Netherlands.[15] Speculation on this point is unprofitable, but some additional facts concerning Henry Somerscales's circumstances should be noted here, for though in the mid 1620s he stood at the centre of a fragile web of tobacco-growing connections in Lincolnshire, he had been more firmly established in this business in Gloucestershire in 1619, and some of the social and geographical features of his Gloucestershire partnership are repeated here.

Somerscales's home was in Coates, possibly Coates Hall, an address which seems to make modest claim to being a manor house.[16] But Coates was only a hamlet in Habblesthorpe parish, and even Habblesthorpe itself was not a fully fledged village, never having had a church though it once possessed a chapel. These two townships comprised a small parish of just over a thousand acres consisting of low-lying land along the banks of the river Trent. The manor of Habblesthorpe and Coates was already divided between two lords in the early fourteenth century, and subsequently the land became further subdivided.[17] In 1612 one landowner was Michael Bland, gentleman,[18] and it seems reasonable to suppose that there is a connection between him and the Michael Bland who was also sought out in August 1626 by an emissary of the Privy Council because he was suspected of growing tobacco at Utterby in the Lincolnshire marshland. Bland was not at home when his august visitor called, for he was being pursued by his creditors and dared not show his face in his own house. The royal messenger judged him 'very poor', and so fearful that he had to live away from home, leaving his wife and children alone at Utterby. His crop of tobacco, intended for medicinal purposes, occupied only a tenth of an acre.[19]

In tracing Henry Somerscales's associates, we have been led into a byway. But the fragments of his story seem to associate tobacco-growing with parish gentry, even poor gentry, making their way not in the congenial environment of deferential village society, where the gentry were acknowledged leaders, but in a less propitious countryside, on the damp, ill-drained lands of river floodplains and in marshland, where they lived alongside tough peasant communities endeavouring to get a living from their pastures and meadows. Only the shadowy outline of the story emerges here, but it gains in clarity when set beside the story from Gloucestershire, where a few years earlier Somerscales had grown tobacco on a grander scale in partnership with John Stratford.

John Stratford was a member of the London Salters' Company. Several other members of his family were also making their way in the same company in the first two decades of the seventeenth century when, by all accounts, the company was at the height of its prosperity.[20] John Stratford's business interests were multifarious: as an acquaintance put it later, when Stratford fell on evil days, he had 'too many trades and occupations'. In partnership with his brother Ralph and two others he was engaged in soap-boiling and soap-trading. At the same time he was buying land with borrowed money and paying out substantial sums each year in interest.[21] He also traded in broadcloth, which he sold to the Eastland merchants, taking in exchange wheat, rye, linen yarn, and rough flax. In his own account of his career, he described flax as the chief commodity of his trade, which he put out to be dressed by the poor in London and the country. The Netherlands merchants ruined his business when they started to bring in flax ready dressed, and so he turned to tobacco-growing.[22]

John Stratford was first and foremost a merchant of London, and in his partnership with Somerscales it was he who was responsible for the despatch of tobacco from Gloucestershire to London for subsequent resale. But John Stratford's native county was Gloucestershire, for he was a younger son of an old gentry family living at

Farmcote, two miles east of Winchcombe. His forebears had been gentlemen in Leicestershire and Nottinghamshire, but he came of a prolific junior branch which had struck roots in Gloucestershire some two or three generations earlier.[23] His tobacco-growing enterprise, therefore, brought him to Winchcombe, in part, at least, because he could there enlist the cooperation of a great number of kindred and neighbours.

The division of function between Somerscales and Stratford as 'co-partners and parting fellows' was nowhere made explicit, but everything points to a working arrangement whereby Somerscales attended to the planting and curing while Stratford was the more experienced salesman. Partnerships to grow tobacco, however, did not depend on merchants alone, but involved others in a larger co-operative enterprise: the merchants owned little or none of the land which they selected for planting.

The crop was best grown on land that had lain under grass for many years, and since leases of old pasture and meadow contained clauses forbidding ploughing under penalties, landowners had to be consulted and their permission given to grow the crop. The cultivator of the land might be an employee of the merchant if the merchant chose to lease the land direct from the landlord, but just as often he was a tenant farmer who agreed to cultivate the land for tobacco on contract with the merchant. His role was a responsible one, for planting, transplanting, watering, weeding, and pruning were laborious tasks, and required care if the plants were to be nursed into full production. In the early autumn the leaves had to be picked individually as and when they ripened; the harvest could last a month or more from the beginning of September until early October. The cultivator, therefore, had to be in constant attendance and employ extra labour at busy times.

The curing of the tobacco was another skilled operation which the grower was not necessarily competent to undertake alone. The leaves were left to dry in the sun, and then heaped together until they began to ferment. They were then hung up to dry for three or four weeks, taken down and heaped again until fermentation started a second time, and then again spread out to dry. Curing occupied about six weeks altogether until the beginning or middle of November, when the crop was ready for despatch to the salesman in London. The merchant knew most about curing, and curing was critical in determining the final value of the crop. He kept a close eye on the last stage in the process to see that nothing went wrong; he or his representatives were at hand in the autumn, if not all through the summer as well. Tobacco cultivation in these pioneering days, therefore, usually (though not invariably) established a partnership between three groups of people, landlords, cultivators and merchants, and they shared the expenses and profits equally between them. Since Stratford and Somerscales were already partners with their own division of function, their contracts divided the profits equally between four persons.[24]

The merchant initiated the planting of tobacco by seeking out suitable land and negotiating with landlord and tenant. John Stratford's first contacts were made in February 1619 with Gloucestershire gentry, whom he already knew and who knew each other. The plan to grow tobacco evidently caused something of a stir in the district: high rents were being offered for tobacco land, and the gentry kept each other up to date with the gossip about the new crop's lucrative possibilities. The gossip and the bargaining came to light in a lawsuit in 1621 when local people were called to give evidence at an enquiry at Winchcombe. Such a congerie of distinguished gentry assembled on one day in 1621 in Winchcombe that the rest of the townsfolk could well have mistaken the gathering for the opening of Quarter Sessions.

The dispute about tobacco contracts set John Stratford and Henry Somerscales at loggerheads with Thomas Lorenge, gentleman of Cleeve. Lorenge had an interest in eight acres of land in Bishops Cleeve which had been leased for tobacco. Two of these acres he occupied himself, six he let to John Lorenge, yeoman.[25] Both had been parties to the negotiations with Stratford and Somerscales,[26] and they produced many knowledgeable witnesses.

Evidence was given by Giles Broadway, esquire, of Postlip, owner of Bishop Cleeve manor[27] where several pieces of land had been taken for tobacco growing. His daughter was married to another younger John Stratford of the same family.[28] Broadway had made a tobacco-growing agreement with Stratford and Somerscales, and had also persuaded Alice, wife of the parson of Winchcombe, Timothy Gates, to do likewise. Bartholomew Smyth, gentleman of Tewkesbury, gave evidence because he had surveyed and measured land designated for tobacco. Christopher Merret, mercer and gentleman of Winchcombe and landowner at Cleeve, was called because he was well informed, through conversation with neighbours, on the tobacco contracts. He was, incidentally, the father of Christopher Merret, who later became a prominent member of the Royal Society and joined its Georgical Committee in 1662.[29] Henry Izod, gentleman of Toddington, Gloucestershire, gave evidence because he was present (whether as witness, party or scrivener, is not made clear) when bonds were drawn up binding tobacco merchants, growers and landlords.[30] John Parsons of Overbury, Worcestershire,[31] was present to explain how he had contemplated letting some of his land for tobacco but had fallen out with John Stratford on the terms of the agreement, and had settled with someone else instead. Francis Thorne, gentleman of Sudeley in Winchcombe parish, disclosed that he was in partnership with others who had made offers to take up land for tobacco in competition with Stratford.[32] Other witnesses included yeomen growers of tobacco, and a husbandman and labourer who had helped with the planting and weeding.

Since tobacco-growing depended upon partnerships, much bargaining and bond-taking accompanied them. John Stratford, planning well ahead to ensure that he had enough land in successive years to grow a worthwhile crop, negotiated some leases for four years. He soon learned the error of pledging to pay such high rents into the uncertain future. His first crop in 1619 occupied one hundred acres altogether,[33] but in December 1619 the government banned tobacco-growing, and Stratford was saddled with obligations entered into by bond to pay for another three years rents which were only justified if the land bore this one uniquely profitable crop.

In a second lawsuit, in which John Stratford tried to wriggle out of another obligation to pay a high rent for four years, we see the other side of the coin, the calculated risks taken by landlords who allowed their land to be used for a novel crop. John Ligon, gentleman, was persuaded after much cajoling by Ralph Wood, his tenant, to permit ten acres of his land at Arle Court, Cheltenham, to be used for tobacco. The land was good pasture, situated near the farmhouse, and the owner hesitated before he allowed it to be ploughed up, since little other grazing ground was available so near at hand. The ploughing involved the destruction of a good orchard and the felling of forty or fifty trees. But the high rent offered – £80 in place of the £13 per annum paid by the sitting tenant – swayed him. When Stratford had taken one crop of tobacco and could plant no more, he grew a crop of barley. After that the land was abandoned, and Ligon was left with a weed-ridden plot, tumbling down to grass, for which his tenant would now only offer half the previous rent of £13.[34]

Ligon's information on the comparative rents paid for 'deep, good' grassland and for tobacco – £13 compared with £80 – sheds our first glimmer of light on the economics of the new crop. It was a subject on which witnesses were prepared to be expansive, and on which they offered remarkably consistent evidence. The contracts evidently did not all take the same form. Sometimes the merchant offered a larger rent and took all the responsibility for cultivation, planting, harvesting, and curing.[35] In at least one case the occupier of land appears to have cultivated the tobacco and then sold the growing crop to the merchant. But more often than not the merchant offered landlord and tenant a partnership before the ground was planted. On this footing the tenant took responsibility for cultivation, paid all labour costs as they occurred, and the partners settled up at the end, sharing expenses and profits equally.

Land chosen for tobacco was old pasture or meadow whose average value was reckoned at £2 an acre, though sometimes it fetched only 25–30s, and sometimes was worth as much as £4. Tobacco merchants, offering a partnership with landlords and growers, rented it for £5, £6 13s 4d and even £8 an acre. Such rents included payment for buildings too, for barns and storehouses nearby were essential for drying the tobacco leaves after picking.[36]

John Lorenge's two acres of land yielded 819 lb of tobacco or almost 410 lb an acre.[37] It was taken to London by carrier in February 1620 and received by Thomas Drinkwater, salter of Friday Street, on Stratford's behalf.[38] He valued it as 2s per pound or £81 18s altogether. Rent and the costs of cultivation had amounted to £29 leaving a clear profit of £52 18s. Since there had been four parties to this enterprise, John and Thomas Lorenge, and John Stratford and Henry Somerscales each received £13 4s 6d.

In this example, rent and cultivation per acre had cost £14 10s; the net profit amounted to £26 9s per acre. In another example, Edward Stratford, Somerscales's local representative, who supervised the cultivation and curing of 15–16 acres in a parish next to Cleeve,[39] claimed that rent and charges amounted to £16 an acre, while the crop sold for only £10 an acre. Thus a loss of £6 an acre had been incurred. In a third example, Somerscales wanted to dissolve a partnership at the eleventh hour and carry on on his own because a crop growing on eight acres of Sir John Tracy's land promised a bumper harvest. He offered Tracy £450 plus 50 lb of tobacco plus £25 as a gratuity to Sir John's daughter, Anne. If we value 50 lb of tobacco at 2s per lb, making £5 in all, Somerscales was offering £480 for eight acres or £60 an acre. Tracy had pledged himself to bear the costs of cultivation, which by the end of the harvest would have amounted (at an average of £15 an acre) to £120, of which he had expected to recoup half from Somerscales.

On the most unfavourable reckoning, namely, that Tracy was now expected to bear the full cost of cultivation, harvesting and rent, he would have finished with a profit of £45 an acre. Somerscales still had to make his profit; and we may well ask on what basis he arrived at his offer. He could expect a crop of at least 410 lb per acre, or 3,280 lb altogether, for which, at 2s a lb, he would have received only £328, a good deal less than the price he had offered Sir John Tracy. However, there are many speculative calculations in this example. Tobacco valued at 2s a lb was a very moderate, even low, wholesale price; prices varied widely between good, medium, and poor quality. Another grower of tobacco, John Ligon, alleged that in the same year that Lorenge's crop was sold, some English tobacco was selling for 10s, 12s, 16s, and 18s per lb. Presumably these were retail prices. It is difficult to be exact about the price range since wholesale and retail prices cannot always be disentangled,[40] but there is such a large gap between a moderate wholesale price of 2s and a high retail price of 18s that the merchant grower evidently had the possibility of getting substantially more than 2s a lb for a good crop. This is doubtless why Somerscales tried to buy Sir John Tracy's crop outright. He had only to sell it for 4s a lb (£656 altogether) to be handsomely in pocket.

The possibility of high prices for good quality tobacco makes sense of another contemporary statement by John Ligon that on his crop of ten acres of tobacco at Arle Court, John Stratford made a profit above all charges of servants, labour, and rent of £600–700. Ten acres could have produced 4,100 lb of tobacco, which, at 2s a lb, would have earned only £410. But at 4s it would have earned £820, thus covering all charges and leaving, as Ligon claimed, just under £600 clear profit.[41] In short, a reasonable net profit on an acre of tobacco in 1619 was £26 9s, but on a very good crop it could easily be four times as much, reaching nearly £100 an acre.

Tobacco-growing was thus a highly speculative venture which, at its most successful, could bring in superlative profits, even by the standards of London merchants. The hazards, of course, were many. The English weather was unreliable – 1619 was a good year, but the years 1620–22 were wet and cold and wholly unkind to the ripening crop.[42] Moreover, although the domestic demand for tobacco was rising rapidly, supplies from Spanish America, the West Indies and Virginia fluctuated sharply, and so affected unpredictably the price of English tobacco. One of John Stratford's opponents in law claimed that in 1620 an excessive supply caused prices to fall. But when the Virginia Company secured the ban on the growing of English tobacco, a shortage was anticipated, and instead of drawing in his horns, John Stratford hastened to buy large stocks from all and sundry, to bide his time until the price rose.[43]

In the event the hazards involved in tobacco-growing turned out to be greater than any of the merchants and growers anticipated, because of the inordinate influence exerted by the Virginia Company on the government. In no other European country did merchants and planters manage to secure a total prohibition on domestic cultivation for the sake of the colonial trade, and it is not perhaps surprising that English merchant-growers were caught unawares. But it is also clear that tobacco-growing had developed within one or two years of the first experiments all the attributes of a wild speculation, which was of the merchants' own making. The trials were not cautiously entered into; the merchants dreamed of making a quick fortune before too many others caught on to the same idea. They burst upon farmers and landlords in Gloucestershire with the same excitement with which they might have entered Ali Baba's cave, couching their proposals not in cautious terms, but offering high rents and the promise of high profits. They imported into the farming community a mentality and a commercial ethos which was the very air they breathed in London, but was surely alien to agricultural society. London merchants were not, of course, entirely guileless when they offered to share their profits equally with their neighbours in Gloucestershire – in fact, they were sharing the risks as well. They were also using their farming partners to supply liquid capital they did not wish to find for themselves. And they had ways of changing their contracts midstream when they saw in a growing crop the promise of a superabundant harvest. But what the London merchants offered was profit far in excess of any that farmers normally received in agriculture, whether from dairying, cattle-raising, or corn-growing. The profit from a thirty-acre farm in the early seventeenth century has been estimated at £14 10s. The average annual earnings of a farm labourer was £9.[44] Compared with these sums, £26 9s clear profit from one acre of tobacco land was riches indeed.

For a short while the merchants held the whip hand while they alone knew the full mystery of cultivation, and they strove to keep it a mystery as long as possible. In the lease with Thomas Lorenge, Stratford and Somerscales insisted on a promise that he would not grow tobacco anywhere else within ten miles of Cleeve.[45] They had other yet more devious ways of guarding their secrets. When Somerscales decided to buy out Sir John Tracy's interest in eight acres of tobacco, it was, he later maintained, because he wished to take full charge of the drying process and prevent Sir John and his servants from learning anything about it. In renting Lorenge's land, moreover, he believed that he and Stratford had forestalled two other gentlemen of Winchcombe parish who were trying to rent it because it adjoined another of their plantations, and their rivals wished to spy on them.[46]

It is not essential to know whether the suspicions of Somerscales and Stratford were justified or baseless; the fact that they nursed them reveals the atmosphere in which London merchants pursued their schemes and enlisted others. They imported into the countryside of the West Midlands a commercial and speculative boldness, with which they infected gentlemen and other well-to-do farmers. But while the latter played their due part as compliant agents of London adventurers, they did not abandon their country caution. They insisted on bonds, four-year contracts, and the like before they agreed to surrender their land for tobacco, and these were upheld in the courts when tobacco growing was no longer permitted. Stratford had to fulfil his promises, even though it bankrupted him, while the local gentry emerged unscathed. When Stratford and his associates gave up tobacco and embarked on yet another scheme – flax-growing this time – they left in the hands of the local population a store of knowledge which did not go to waste.

IV

At this point a closer look at the economy and structure of society in this part of Gloucestershire makes a necessary prelude to the later history of tobacco-growing there. Winchcombe lies in the Vale of Tewkesbury, a broad vale watered by the rivers Severn and Avon and numerous smaller streams. Tobacco-growing proved successful throughout this vale and the contiguous Vale of Evesham.

Most of the land consists of liassic clays that are heavy and difficult to work under the plough. Large areas consisted of ancient pastures and meadows, and those which lay along river banks that were liable to flooding were bound to remain so.[47] Whenever enclosure took place in the sixteenth and seventeenth centuries it usually resulted in the land being converted from arable to pasture.[48] At the same time a generally easy-going attitude towards small piecemeal enclosures prevailed in pastoral country like this, and people expected their neighbours to assent to small adjustments.[49] Thus the chief characteristic of the vale parishes was their extensive grasslands, which often included extensive commons, shared between town-ships.[50] These were the mainstay of their economy despite the presence of islands of sand and gravel on which the settlements and some of the arable lay, and despite the persistence of common fields, many of which were not enclosed until the eighteenth or nineteenth century.[51] The farming specialities of the region were dairying, cattle-raising, and -feeding, while those villages on the Cotswold slopes which had extensive sheep pastures kept many sheep. As in all pastoral regions other sidelines were welcome: the vale lands boasted fruit orchards, some hops, flax, and a linen industry, as well as other handicraft occupations like glove and clothmaking and stocking knitting.[52]

The agricultural conditions for tobacco were, therefore, entirely suitable. Contemporaries believed that it grew best on a moist loam, and that it needed animal dung in great quantity.[53] The Vale of Tewkesbury could provide both, though it was one of the (probably justified) complaints of those who opposed tobacco-growing that so much dung was put on the land that the corn fields suffered.[54] The necessary agricultural work also interlocked neatly with that of other arable crops. The seeds were sown in prepared seedbeds in February and were ready for planting out in the middle of April or even May, when other arable crops were safely in the ground and did not demand much attention, and before the hay harvest was ready. Picking began when the corn harvest was finished, in the second half of August, and continued until the end of September when drying began. This lasted until the beginning of November.[55] Tobacco could not have been a more convenient crop for employing casual labour without interfering with the cultivation of essential food crops.

The labour demands of tobacco-growing were readily met in a community having plenty of unused or underused casual labour. And while this was a common characteristic of pastoral com-munities generally, few possessed the almost unlimited supply of the Vale of Tewkesbury. The explanation for this situation lies in the past history of the Vale, which contains some unusual, perhaps even unique, features. A first look at the structure of its society shows none of the clear cut hierarchical features associated with the classic villages of Midland England. The pattern of settlement was that associated with scattered hamlets. Winchcombe parish accom-modated eleven hamlets; Bishops Cleeve had seven; most other parishes had at least three. Nor did the villages invariably hold the commanding position one expects to find at a parish centre.

Sometimes the villages themselves seem to have started as two hamlets that coalesced, rather than as a single community.[56] Such resident gentry as there were in the parish often lived in the hamlets and not in the village.[57] Some hamlets grew in size in the sixteenth and seventeenth centuries at a faster rate than their parent villages. Authority, such as it was, did not reside uncompromisingly and permanently in one place, but was liable to waver as people moved around from one township to another in the parish.

This impermanence of power reflected other impermanences in the structure of landed society in the region. Much land had belonged to the religious houses of Westminster Abbey, Deerhurst Priory, and Evesham Abbey until the Dissolution. These estates passed to new owners in the mid-sixteenth century. But so also did many manors belonging to the bishops of Worcester and Hereford, whose consolidated properties were compulsorily exchanged by Queen Elizabeth in 1560–61 for a collection of rents from impropriate rectories. A remarkable number of estates in this area thus came on to the market in the second half of the sixteenth century, and were sold by the Crown to absentee owners who forged no permanent attachment to their new acquisitions. In James's reign many of them changed hands yet again, sometimes twice over.[58] Some were dismembered in the process, and the freeholders became firmly entrenched as the ruling class in the community.[59]

The strength of the freeholders could, however, be traced back to a longer chain of causes. Their ranks had not been thinned in the fourteenth and fifteenth centuries by land consolidations that occurred elsewhere. Rather the reverse had happened: demesnes had been leased out, lands in villeinage enfranchised, and many holdings fragmented.[60] One ecclesiastical landlord, at least – Westminster Abbey – was remarkably lenient in its demands for rent and permissive in its attitude to the subdivision of land.[61] Thus the freeholders remained an influential and numerous group; customary tenants on some estates claimed unusual liberties; and no concerted effort by the gentry in the sixteenth century, thrusting or patiently striving , undermined this state of affairs.

Without the constraining influences of watchful and status-minded landlords, the peasantry sought their livelihood in pursuits which exploited their principal asset, their labour resources. Labour intensive crops (not only tobacco, but fruit and vegetables as well) enabled them to hold their own in the sixteenth and seventeenth centuries, and to survive into the nineteenth and twentieth – to the astonishment of modern observers, so accustomed to recording another turn of events.[62] As the writer of the Land Utilisation Survey of Worcestershire remarked of the adjoining Vale of Evesham:

> The development of the vigorous peasant communities of the [Avon] valley, though one of the most fascinating chapters in the rural history of the last hundred years has attracted little attention from the outside world, and detailed information on the course of events is meagre in the extreme. It is nevertheless an aspect of Worcestershire life that cannot be passed over.[63]

The towns of the region matched the rural areas: authority spoke in muted tones, as tradesmen with an independent turn of mind ran their own affairs. Tewkesbury became a self-governing community in 1610; the two large estates of Tewkesbury Abbey and the Honour of Gloucester were both divided and sold in the sixteenth century, and the latter handed over to Tewkesbury Corporation by the Crown in that year. Thereafter its inhabitants governed themselves and developed their economy in a way that suited poor rather than rich men. The river traffic on the Severn maintained a volatile population of bargemasters, trowmen, and fishermen. A cloth industry persisted, and although by the early eighteenth century it was said to be in decline, stocking knitting took up the slack when cloth manufacture lost impetus. Wild mustard seed was gathered in the surrounding countryside to make the famous mustard balls which attracted notice from every traveller. Further employment was found in market gardening – the excellence of Tewkesbury carrots was widely proclaimed – and the growing of other labour intensive crops, among which was tobacco. All these were activities which required small cash resources but many pairs of hands.[64]

Winchcombe was a smaller market town in the Vale that was losing its trade in the seventeenth century, probably in favour of Tewkesbury. Tobacco was introduced at a time when the manorial lord showed little interest in the place. Winchcombe Abbey had owned the manor till the Dissolution when it passed to the Crown. In 1610–11 James I sold it to Sir George Whitmore, a London merchant and later lord mayor, and his brother Thomas, absentee owners who did nothing to assert their authority. Courts were not regularly kept, and when tobacco-growing started, labourers flocked into the town without let or hindrance. When another Whitmore took over the estate and showed an unwonted interest in the rents in 1636, he found a few docile tenants who were prepared to pay more for their houses. But effective power over the tenantry lay with less accommodating tradesmen who could rally the towns-

folk to put on a fine display of enraged resentment. It started with a
chorus from the fiery tongues of scolds, raising their voices to 'God
save the King and the laws, and they and their ancestors had lived
there, and they would live there', and moved on to more spirited
action with hot spits and scalding water. A court case in 1638 revealed
that many single family houses had been turned into tenements in
the previous twenty years to house two, three, and even four
families. The lord's agent also accused the recalcitrant tenants of
spoiling orchards, and converting orchards and gardens into arable
land – a form of words that seems to contain a veiled reference
to tobacco cultivation.[65]

Sir William Whitmore's idea of lordship did not coincide with
that of Winchcombe's inhabitants. But it also seems to have been at
odds with the accepted conventions of the local gentry, who were
modest, unpretentious men, who felt strong bonds of sympathy and
fellowship with their neighbours of all classes. William Higford, a
gentleman of Alderton, another tobacco-growing parish, who
before his death in 1657 wrote some advice for his grandson, seemed
to speak for them all when he urged his heir 'to make yourself
rather less than you are', to keep his first place in his affections for his
friends, and then for his neighbours (by which he meant the gentry).
But then he added:

> The next companions will be your tenants who are your neighbours
> . . . . they hold of you by fealty (that is fidelity) to be faithful unto you
> for the lands they hold. You must in relation [= return?] give them
> protection whereby they may follow their excessive labours. Your
> ancestors have been moderate in their fines, and I trust God will bless
> you the better for it. Let these men of bread enjoy and eat the bread,
> which they dearly labour for and earn.[66]

Society in the Vale of Tewkesbury was not a rigid hierarchy with
clearly defined, even widening, gaps separating the classes. It had its
share of gentry, but they were modest, parish gentry without class
pride, or the desire or means for ostentation, and entirely without
ambition 'to rule over their neighbours as vassals'.[67] They identified
themselves with the interests of their neighbours and tenants, who
were independent-minded peasants, smallholders and tradesmen of
no more than middling wealth. And in this egalitarian society
labourers moved around freely without interference, indeed with
the connivance, of lords.

It is difficult to capture in words the spirit of a local community
which mirrors the truth and is not an illusion of the biased beholder.

But this account is similar to that of a contemporary, John Corbet, chaplain to the Gloucester garrison, who described the civil war struggles in Gloucestershire and portrayed the same people.

> There was no excessive number of powerful gentry. . . . But the inhabitants consisted chiefly of yeomen, farmers, petty freeholders, and such as use manufactures that enrich the country, and pass through the hands of a multitude; a generation of men truly laborious, jealous of their properties, whose principal aim is liberty and plenty; and whilst in an equal rank with their neighbours, they desire only not to be oppressed, and account themselves extremely bound to the world if they may keep their own. Such, therefore, continually thwart the intentions of tyranny. . . . The countryman had of his own, and did not live by the breath of his great landlord; neither were the poor and needy at the will of the gentry, but observed those men by whom those manufactures were maintained that kept them alive.[68]

Social egalitarianism in the Vale of Tewkesbury goes a long way to explain the unusual phenomenon which so hampered the Cromwellian Council of State, and later the Privy Council, in their fierce efforts at stamping out tobacco-growing between the 1650s and 1690. The gentry were in firm alliance with the peasantry, and none of them cared a fig for government orders. Rarely has a government acted so directly at variance with the opinion of *all* classes in the local community as in its determination to stamp out tobacco-growing.

V

Lawsuits show that gossip about tobacco and the economics of growing it circulated freely among neighbours in the Winchcombe area of Gloucestershire. To believe that the mystery of cultivating and curing it could long remain a secret was a vain hope. Since one acre of tobacco land properly planted requires 10,000 plants,[69] a veritable army of helping hands is needed in the planting season. Moreover, much of the work could be done by women and children, and who are more observant and adept at prying out and remembering the secrets of any skilled task than children? But the factors which ensured the survival of tobacco in the Vale of Tewkesbury when the government banned it and the capitalist entrepreneurs had departed, were economic and social: first, the continuing financial rewards – not any longer on a scale that was sufficiently enticing to fortune-hunting London merchants, perhaps, but still eminently satisfactory to West Midland family farmers; secondly, its use of the one factor of production which they had in abundance, hand labour; thirdly, the persistence of a ready market for English tobacco which survived alongside the demand for Virginian tobacco for another seventy years. Tastes were not yet highly developed for any one leaf, and since tobacco smoking had quickly become a habit among all classes, a wide range of prices was paid for it. Different markets were known to take different qualities: it was sold locally, and in London, exported to Ireland, and the Low Countries, or it was mixed with Virginian or Bermuda tobacco, and found its way into tobacconists' shops under the guise of pure West Indian or American tobacco.[70]

The Privy Council's ban on tobacco, first announced in December 1619, was only fitfully enforced for the next few years. In 1626–27 the Council became aware that the crop had spread from the Winchcombe area and was being grown in thirty-nine places in Gloucestershire, seventeen in Worcestershire, and one in Wiltshire.[71] In 1628 it was growing 'in very great quantity' in Jersey and Guernsey.[72] From then until 1639 Gloucestershire along with Worcestershire (that is, the Avon valley and Vale of Evesham) were deemed the principal centres, but in the latter year it was newly reported growing in Monmouthshire.[73] After 1640 official attention was diverted to other matters, and the tobacco growers enjoyed twelve tranquil years of tobacco cultivation.

In April 1652 the Council of State in the course of a new and thoroughgoing survey of its commercial policy passed a fresh Act forbidding tobacco-growing. When the growers raised an outcry, a conciliatory Act in September 1653 allowed them to continue to grow the crop on payment of excise. Such a compromise was not to the taste of the Virginia merchants, who promptly intervened to procure a fresh ordinance in April 1654 ordering the act to be fully enforced.[74] A year later they seem to have feared some weakening of the Council's resolve, and this time pressed their attack on to the enemy's ground by describing the harmful effects of tobacco-growing on local agriculture.[75] The Council of State, swayed by the trading arguments, but more by its fiscal interest in the import duties on tobacco, decided in March 1655 not to grant any further suspensions of its orders.[76] Meanwhile tobacco-growing had spread still farther afield. In 1655 it was reported in fourteen English and Welsh counties: Oxfordshire, Sussex, Gloucestershire, Worcestershire, Herefordshire, Warwickshire, Wiltshire, Shropshire, Staffordshire, Somerset, Monmouthshire, Radnorshire, Montgomeryshire and Denbighshire.[77] All official efforts to stamp it out met with tough local resistance, especially in Gloucestershire.

At the Restoration the Virginia merchants again weighed in quickly with a fresh petition against tobacco-growing.[78] Again they won the ear of the Privy Council, and an Act prohibiting the crop was duly issued late in 1660.[79] Its enforcement engaged the personal attention of the Privy Council for the next twenty-eight years, as tobacco spread into still more counties: Brecknockshire was mentioned for the first time in 1666, Yorkshire and Essex in 1667, and Flintshire in 1668. 'A much greater quantity than in former years' was growing in 1666; 'many large plantations' were described in seven counties in 1667; ten counties received reminders of the law in 1668.[80] But it was always the customs officers at Bristol who were the recipients of more letters than anyone else, and the counties of Gloucestershire, Worcestershire, Herefordshire, Warwickshire and Monmouthshire, which were singled out for the most assiduous attention. The last order from the Privy Council against tobacco-growing was given in 1688–89.

Is it fanciful to think that when William of Orange came to preside at the Council Table, it was he who brought the campaign quietly to an end? Throughout the 1660s and 1670s troops of horse had been used every summer against poor men and women who were scraping a livelihood from small plots.[81] William III came from a country where tobacco supported many small peasants, and where, far from being an illegal crop, it was the basis of a modest but flourishing industry. To an outsider, the draconian measures of the Privy Council must have seemed out of all proportion to the offence. At the same time, it must be admitted that by 1688 the ferocity with which the policy had been pursued throughout the 1660s to 1680s, had brought it close to success – it had already intimidated growers in areas where it was less firmly established than in Gloucestershire.[82] Furthermore, the price of Virginia tobacco was falling and the public taste for this rather than any other leaf was growing. When the government dropped its more ferocious expedients against tobacco growers, it was on the verge of victory after a prolonged and bitter war.

One final question remains to be answered. Who were the assiduous growers of tobacco in the years between 1620 and 1690, and how did the alliance of landlords and cultivators survive the withdrawal of the London merchant entrepreneurs? It is difficult to discover much about the growers in counties other than Gloucestershire. The lists of their names which the Privy Council regularly demanded, and sometimes actually received, do not seem to have survived. But in the Vale of Tewkesbury, tobacco growers can sometimes be identified personally. By 1634 tobacco was avowedly a poor man's crop: poor men claimed to be excused by their poverty from observing the prohibition on its cultivation.[83] The sympathy if not active participation of landlords, however, continued to be reflected in the reluctance of JPs to heed the Privy Council's orders. In 1634 and 1636, these orders were addressed to men such as Sir John Tracy, lord of Toddington, and Timothy Gates, parson of Winchcombe, both of whom had been involved with John Stratford in the tobacco-growing contracts of 1619.[84] They clearly had no heart for the task, and yearly reminders from the Privy Council did not change their attitude. 'All the justices do refuse to give warrant for the peace and is rather a hindrance than always helpful', wrote a melancholy soldier in 1658. He was saddled with the responsibility of destroying tobacco around Cheltenham, assisted by a cornet who would not act, and without a major to turn to for advice. His horsemen from the county had to be hand picked since so many were themselves 'dealers and planters'.[85] In the 1630s the appointed destroyers of tobacco had been labouring men from the neighbourhood, hired by the constables at a daily rate.[86] Doubtless, some of these also had had a hand in planting the very crops they were asked to destroy. No wonder that no one could be found to enforce the law with enthusiasm. As late as 1667 John Vaughan, high sheriff of the county of Herefordshire, was handed an order from the Privy Council, but 'seemed by his action to slight it and refused to receive it'.[87]

When the Council of State issued its ordinance against tobacco in April 1654, 110 Winchcombe tobacco growers signed a petition in protest. They were of all classes. One was John Harvey, reputed to have £60–80 per annum of free land, and a ringleader in the battle against higher rents demanded by the manorial lord in 1638.[88] He and nine other growers had contributed to the subsidy of 1641–42, which did not fall on poor men.[89] In 1671 it is possible to identify among hearth tax payers twenty-five people of the same names as the petitioners of 1654: one had a four-hearth house, five had three hearths, eight had two hearths, three had one, and eight were too poor to pay.[90] The wills of other signatories to the 1654 petition similarly suggest that growers were a socially mixed group, some belonging to the middling ranks of the peasantry with sufficient cash to employ labour in busy seasons, while others were men who could plant only a rod or two of tobacco, and found the necessary labour within the family circle. Some were styled yeomen, some were craftsmen who thus had more than one source of income. No one openly referred in official documents to tobacco land, but bequests such as those made by Christopher Merret, mercer, of properties possessing 'courts, orchards, and gardens', and 'one barn adjoining the same orchards and gardens' seem to be euphemisms for tobacco plantations.[91]

No one in the later seventeenth century was so treacherous as to suggest that the Justices of the Peace were themselves growing tobacco, but it was certainly growing on their land. And the risks of the crop were still shared – indirectly by landlords, who collected high rents and faced the possibility of non-payment by unsuccessful growers, but directly now by tenants and poor labourer-planters, the latter taking the ground from tenants in return for half the crop. Thus cooperative agreements were still the order of the day, but they had spread down the social scale and involved an even poorer class of labourers working tiny plots. Such men did not hedge their risks with bonds and covenants, and so have left no records behind, but an informer in 1667 makes the position clear. He found tobacco growing

> upon the High Sheriff's land, the bishop's land, and scarce one of the justices but on their land tobacco is planted, possibly without their privity. The tenants set their ground to planters that are poor people who plant and give half the crop for the use of the ground. So, if destroyed, the planter loseth, the tenant loseth his half of the crop, and thereby is disabled to pay his rent.[92]

Directly or indirectly, all classes in the community, landlords, tenant farmers, and labourers had an interest in tobacco. It was still a crop that passed 'through the hands of a multitude'.

VI

Three conclusions of wider significance emerge from this study of tobacco growing. While it seems an almost invariable rule that innovations in agriculture in the early modern period were first adopted by well-to-do gentry or merchant-entrepreneurs who could afford to take risks, the peasantry evidently were not slow to take them up when they suited their economic and social circumstances. This conclusion obliges us to look more carefully at innovations which did not spread quickly, for it is likely that the explanation for their poor success lay in the economic and social constraints of cultivation and marketing rather than in the ignorance and stubbornness of peasants.[93]

Secondly, well authenticated figures on the profits to be had from tobacco oblige us to pause before we reject what otherwise would seem to be extravagant claims by contemporary writers of the profits to be drawn from other special crops. Walter Blith, writing in 1653, gave examples which historians have tended to dismiss as wild exaggerations. Saffron, he said, might cost £4 an acre to cultivate, yield anything from 7 or 8 to 14 or 15 lb per acre, and bring in an average return of £36 an acre, or, for a very good crop, over £70. One acre of indifferent liquorice might sell for £50–60, excellent liquorice for £80–100. At the best price of £14 per cwt one acre of hops could sell for £168 and yield a clear gain of £100. A gardener could make £100 an acre out of vegetable growing. In the light of the evidence on tobacco, these rates of profit are not incredible.[94]

Thirdly, the wide range of prices for different qualities of product is of vital importance for understanding the market in horticultural, industrial, and other special crops. Saffron sold at anything between 24s and £14. Tobacco prices varied just as widely according to the quality, and according to what Blith called 'the ebbings and flowings of the market'.[95] In short, anyone who strikes an average price for these crops is ironing out most of the evidence so carefully garnered for us by contemporaries to show why horticulture, market gardening, and other specialised crops secured such a following among the farming population of seventeenth-century England.

NOTES AND REFERENCES

1. G. B. Masefield, 'Crops and livestock', in E. E. Rich and C. H. Wilson, eds, *The Cambridge Economic History of Europe*, iv (Cambridge University Press, 1967), pp. 277–8

2. Sarah A. Dickson, 'Panacea or Precious Bane. Tobacco in Sixteenth Century Literature', *Bulletin of the New York Public Library*, vol. 57 (1953), 549–66.

3. V. R. I. Croesen, 'Tabakscultuur in Nederland', *Agronomisch-Historisch Jaarboek* (1940), 3–4.

4. The author also speaks of the results already achieved by growers in England and France, but since he names Gerarde's *Herbal* and the French writers, Olivier de Serres and Car. Stephanus (Charles Estienne), his remarks could have been derived from a reading of French and English herbals and horticultural textbooks.

5. A. Rive, 'The consumption of tobacco since 1600', *Economic History* (1926–9), p. 59.

6. S. M. Kingsbury, *Records of the Virginia Company* (1906), i, pp. 296, 303, 139,

141, 143, 379, 144; H. Willcox, *Gloucestershire: a study in local government* (Yale University Press, 1940), p. 159. For Timothy Gates, see p. 83.

7. C. M. MacInnes, *The Early English Tobacco Trade*, (Kegan, Paul, Trench, Trubner, 1926), p. 79.

8. One witness, John Ligon, in a lawsuit discussed more fully below, made ambiguous reference to a crop before that of 1619, Public Record Office [PRO] C2, Jas. I, S28/18.

9. J. Foster, *Register of Admissions to Gray's Inn, 1521–1889* (1889), p. 110. Three branches of the Somerscales family, of gentle birth, lived in the Grimsby area of Lincolnshire (A. R. Maddison, *Lincolnshire Pedigrees*, 1902–6, iii, pp. 906–9).

10. PRO Req. 2/308/44.

11. Kingsbury, *op. cit.*, i, pp. 218, 219, 370, 364–5, 398, 403.

12. PRO SP 16/2, no. 117.

13. *Acts of the Privy Council, Colonial, vol. i, 1613–80*, p. 109.

14. *Calendar of Administrations in the Consistory Court of Lincoln, 1540–1659*, Index Library (1921), p. 338.

15. I. S. Beckwith, 'The river trade of Gainsborough, 1500–1850', *Lincolnshire History and Archaeology*, no. 2 (1967), 3–4.

16. Information reaching the Privy Council in 1626 named Henry Somerscales of Goatshall as a persistent tobacco-grower (*Acts of the Privy Council, June–Dec. 1626*, p. 194).

17. W. White *History, Directory, and Gazetteer of Nottinghamshire* (1844), under Habblesthorpe.

18. Thoroton's *History of Nottinghamshire*, republished by John Thoresby, vol. iii (1796), p. 302. Richard Bland of Habblesthorpe was a Treasurer of the county in 1627, an office usually filled by gentlemen and esquires (H. Hampton Copnall, compiler, *Nottinghamshire County Records. Notes and Extracts from County Records of the Seventeenth Century* (1915), p. 13).

19. PRO SP 16/34, no. 40.

20. J. Steven Watson, *A History of the Salters Company* (Oxford University Press, 1963), p. 54.

21. PRO Req. 2, Bdle 308/45.

22. PRO SP 14/180, no. 79.

23. The Stratford family was so prolific that it is difficult to establish from the Stratford pedigree of 1623 which John Stratford was the salter of London. In lawsuits his brother Ralph is mentioned, also the fact that he married one of the daughters of Peter Robinson of London. The most likely candidate in the pedigree is John Stratford, the seventh son of John Stratford, but he is shown to have married Margaret, daughter of William (or Robert) Tracy, and his family tree omits two brothers of John, Giles and Ralph (H. Chitty and John Phillipot, *The Visitation of the County of Gloucester, 1623,* Harleian Soc. xxi (1885), 157). For additional information on John's family, see PRO Stac 8, Bdle 266, no. 24; Req. Bdle 308/45; C2 Jas. I, S3/11.

24. This and the following paragraph are based on information in two lawsuits, PRO Req. 2, 308/44 and Req. 2, 399/68.

25. That John and Thomas Lorenge were kinsmen is made clear in John's will,

though the exact relationship is not specified (Gloucester Public Library, Will dated 8 Dec., 1626).

26. PRO Req. 2, 308/44.

27. *Victoria County History, Gloucestershire* [*VCH Glos.*], viii, (1968) 8.

28. Probably grandson of John Stratford, who was the cousin of our John Stratford.

29. The express purpose of this committee was to promote agricultural improvement, and spread a knowledge of new crops. Christopher Merret undertook to compile a list of plants grown in England, and this is doubtless the origin of his *Pinax Rerum Naturalium Britannicarum* (1666), a list of plants and animals found in Britain. Under tobacco he simply says 'cultivated in several places, especially in Winchcombe, Glos'.

30. Christopher Merret's will shows that Henry Izod was his uncle (Gloucester Public Library, Will dated 31 Dec., 1624).

31. This John Parsons is almost certainly the one whose family had been buying up land in Kemerton parish since the end of the sixteenth century, and became resident and influential landowners there until the present century (though the name was changed to Hopton). Kemerton was a tobacco-growing village, lying next door to Overbury, Worcs. In Overbury parish, Conderton was named as a tobacco-growing township in 1627 (*VCH Glos.,* viii, 212; *Acts of the Privy Council, Jan–August, 1627,* p. 409).

32. This is one of two or three hints that other contractors besides Stratford were looking for tobacco land at the same time. On this, see note 46 below.

33. PRO SP 16/57, no. 14. That John Stratford planted 100 acres is also implied in his statement of the costs he anticipated, when he planned his first year. He reckoned on a labour cost of £1400. Another £1800 for rent and land was itemised separately (PRO C2 Jas. I, S3/11).

34. PRO C2 Jas. I, S 28/18.

35. *Ibid.*

36. PRO Req. 2, 308/44; Req. 2, 399/68; C2, Jas. I, S28/18.

37. The yield of an average crop of tobacco in Ireland in the early nineteenth century was 1200 lbs, three times the yield quoted here (BPP 1830 (565) x, 12).

38. A Thomas Drinkwater was Master of the Salters Company in 1663 (Watson, *op. cit.*, p. 145).

39. Edward Stratford, gentleman of Winchcombe, was almost certainly one of John Stratford's many kinsmen.

40. For other evidence from 1621 of poor quality tobacco, worth 2s and 2s 6d per lb, and of good quality at 6s 8d, see PRO Req. 2, 397/122. Thorold Rogers gives some illustrations of widely varying prices for different qualities at later dates in the seventeenth century (*A History of Agriculture and Prices in England,* (7 vols, 1866–1902), vol v; *1583–1702,* (Oxford), pp. 467–8).

41. PRO C2, Jas. I, S3/11.

42. PRO C2, Jas. I, S28/18.

43. *Ibid.*

44. Peter Bowden in Joan Thirsk, ed., *Agrarian History of England and Wales, vol. iv., 1500–1640* (Cambridge University Press, 1967), pp. 653, 657.

45. It may be that in imposing this condition Somerscales was anticipating that his brother would receive a patent of monopoly for growing tobacco. See above, p. 79.

46. There are some slight references in PRO Req. 2, 308/44 to tobacco-growing ventures that did not involve Stratford. A Mr Harris had been in partnership with Francis Thorne of Sudeley 'in a former year', and they had made £70 an acre on tobacco. John Harvey had also been in partnership with Thorne at some stage. But Thorne was described as a servant of Giles Broadway who co-operated with Stratford in growing tobacco, so that it is impossible to distinguish with any certainty an independent venture.

47. *VCH Glos.*, contains numerous illustrations. See vi, 195; viii, 114.

48. See, for example, *VCH Glos.*, vi, 189, (1965).

49. PRO Req. 2, 308/44; C3, 227/58.

50. *VCH Glos. passim.* Deerhurst common, shared between Deerhurst and Leigh was four miles in length even in 1779 (*VCH Glos.*, viii, 42). Cleeve Hill, consisting of 1002a. of common land, was shared between four townships in the late nineteenth century. It was still common in 1964 (*VCH Glos.*, viii, 2).

51. Doubtless because of the many freeholders.

52. *VCH Glos., passim*; Thirsk, *Agrarian History*, pp. 67–8.

53. A sandy loam is nowadays considered most suitable for tobacco.

54. PRO SP 18/98, no. 16.

55. BPP 1830 (565) x, 9, 113, 114, 136.

56. See, for example, Alderton (*VCH Glos.*, vi, 189); Elmstone Hardwicke (*VCH Glos.*, viii, 50); Kemerton (*ibid.*, p. 209); Apperley (*ibid.*, p. 34).

57. See, for example, *VCH Glos.*, vi, 190.

58. As at Broadwell (*VCH Glos.*, vi, 52), and Bishops Cleeve, Southam, Stoke Orchard, Prestbury, Uckington, and Elmstone (*VCH Glos.*, viii, 8, 10, 72, 52, 53).

59. As at Broadwell (*VCH Glos.*, vi, 52–3), Beckford, Ashton under Hill, and Woolstone (*VCH Glos.*, viii, 254, 246, 247, 107). Woolstone is my identification of the tobacco-growing township named 'Worston' in the Privy Council's list of 1627 (*Acts of the Privy Council, Jan.–Aug., 1627*, p. 409).

60. See, for example, Bishops Cleeve, Southam, Stoke Orchard, Gotherington, Prestbury, and Woolstone (*VCH Glos.*, vii, 14, 74, 106).

61. Barbara Harvey, 'The leasing of the Abbot of Westminster's demesnes in the later middle ages', *Econ. Hist. Rev.*, xxii, pt 1 (1969), 22, 26.

62. For the survival of market gardening, see *VCH Glos.*, viii, *passim*. The nineteenth-century gazetteers commonly describe property in these villages as 'much subdivided'. Enclosure and tithe awards give more precise information: for example, at Prestbury in 1732, 77 people received allotments of land, of whom 61 received less than 20 acres apiece (*VCH Glos.*, viii, 76); Elmstone Hardwicke in 1839 had 80 holdings of less than 50 acres out of a total of 93 (*VCH Glos.*, viii, 55).

63. K. M. Buchanan, *The Land of Britain, Part 68, Worcestershire* (Geographical Publications, 1944), pp. 649–50.

64. *VCH Glos.*, viii, 110 ff.

65. PRO E 134, 14 Chas. I, Mich. 31. The date of this dispute is 1638, not 1662 as I wrongly stated in 'Seventeenth-century agriculture and social change', *Agricultural History Review* xviii (1970), Supplement, 165.

66. W. Higford, 'Institutions or advice to his grandson', *Harleian Misc.*, ix, (1810), 585, 588–90. William Higford was a signatory to a petition in 1626 on John Stratford's behalf, when Stratford sought protection from his creditors (PRO SP 16/57, no. 14, ii).

67. *A True and Impartial History of the Military Government of the City of Gloucester . . ., 1647, Somers Tracts*, v (1811), 303.

68. *Ibid.*

69. BPP 1830 (565) x, 111–12.

70. PRO C2, Jas. I, S3/11; *CSPD 1631–3,* p. 224; *Harry Hangman's Honour . . .*, (1655), Thomason Tract, E 842 (13), p. 3.

71. *Acts of the Privy Council, Jan.–Aug., 1627*, p. 409.

72. *CSPD 1628–9*, p. 329.

73. PRO PC2/50, p. 564. Between 1636 and 1640 the Privy Council gave more attention to the licensing of tobacco retailers than to the iniquities of growers.

74. PRO SP 18/72, no. 65; SP 25/75, p. 712; SP 25/76a, pp. 43–4.

75. PRO SP 18/98, no. 16. It is suggested that Cromwell favoured a gentler policy towards the tobacco growers because Royalist agents were active in Gloucestershire and the neighbouring counties (MacInnes, *op. cit.*, p. 103).

76. SP 25/76a, pp. 43–4.

77. PRO SP 25/76a, pp. 44, 130; SP 25/76, pp. 123–4.

78. PRO PC 2/55, pp. 140, 171.

79. *Statutes of the Realm*, v, 297 (12 Car. II, c. 34).

80. PRO PC 2/59, pp. 62, 507; PC2/60, p. 36; PC 2/58, p. 396; SP 29/212, no. 108; PC 2/60, p. 36.

81. PRO PC 2/57, pp. 57, 117; PC 2/58, p. 165; PC 2/59, p. 529; PC 2/69, pp. 32, 312. The last order about destroying tobacco from the Customs Commissioners is dated 27 June 1689 – *Acts of the Privy Council, Colonial II, 1680–1720*, p. 135.

82. Those who defied the law were brought personally to the Privy Council Table (PRO PC 2/59, pp. 530, 539, 561, 562; PC 2/60, p. 58).

83. PRO PC 2/44, p. 109.

84. PRO PC 2/44, p. 109; PC 2/46, p. 266.

85. PRO SP 18/182, no. 50. For other examples, see HMC 12th Report, Appendix VII, 52; *Cal. Treas. Books, 1676–9*, v, pt 1, 330.

86. PRO PC 2/45, pp. 27–8.

87. PRO PC2/59, p. 532.

88. PRO SP 18/72, no. 65. A John Harvey was bailiff of Winchcombe in 1632 (Gloucester Record Office, Winchcombe Bailiffs' Accounts, P 368 M I 1/2).

89. PRO E 179/116/528.

90. PRO E 179/247/14.

91. Gloucester Public Library. Will dated 31 Dec. 1624.

92. PRO SP 29/212, no. 108.

93. A conclusion to which Professor Mendras was led in a recent investigation

into the resistance of French peasants to hybrid maize (H. Mendras, *La Fin des Paysans,* Colin, 1970 edn., pp. 121 ff., esp. pp. 125–8).

94. Walter Blith, *The English Improver Improved* (1653), pp. 249, 225, 247, 273.

95. *Ibid.*, p. 225.

5

MICHAEL HAVINDEN

Lime as a Means
of Agricultural Improvement:
The Devon Example

> He that found out the way of fertilizing of land with Lime or Marle
> (though by accident) did a more charitable deed in publishing thereof
> than if he had built all the capital Hospitalls in England.
> GABRIEL PLATTES (1639).[1]

Despite this enthusiastic advocacy agricultural historians have not in
general devoted very much attention to the role of lime as a source of
higher cereal yields. Although it is well known that lime, like ground
chalk, marl and calcareous seasand, neutralises excessive soil acidity,
it is not so generally realised that soil acidity not only reduces the
yields of crops on unmanured land but also prevents manures from
exercising any effect. This point was underlined by an agricultural
journalist, writing in 1818, who said that the use of lime on the
Mendip hills in Somerset had restored the value of dung 'which
previous to liming had no sensible effect' – and by this means the
value of the land had been raised from four shillings to forty shillings
an acre.[2] Thus even if the chronic shortage of animal manure which
afflicted British agriculture before the invention of artificial fertilisers
in the mid-nineteenth century had been completely overcome, an
increase in cereal yields would still have depended on a concurrent
neutralisation of soil acidity in the many parts of Britain where the
soil is naturally acid. These areas are very extensive, especially in the
west and north of the country. Since lime and chalk dissolve in
water and are washed out of the soil by heavy rainfall, continual

replacement is needed in such areas. An estimate of the extent of lime deficient soil in Britain made in the late 1930s produced the following results.[3]

TABLE 5.1   *Acres of crops, grass and rough-grazing* (millions)

	Total	Lime-deficient
England	26	10
Wales	4·5	2·5
Scotland	15	4
Total	45·5	16·5 = 34%

Thus slightly over one-third of the land in Britain was lime-deficient at a time when the use of lime was at least 400 years old. It seems highly likely therefore that the proportion of lime–deficient soil in the sixteenth century was considerably higher.

The national survey also conceals major regional variations and it is probable that in natural conditions practically the whole of western counties like Devon suffer from lime deficiency. A survey of Shropshire in 1930 based on ten years' work revealed that about one-third of the county was acid (some parts very acid) and that only about 5 per cent of the soils did not need any lime. Similarly in eastern parts of England, where rainfall is much lower, soil acidity can still be a serious problem. A survey of 27,000 acres in east Suffolk in 1939 showed that 9,517 acres (about 35 per cent) were in immediate need of liming. Nor is the fact that soils lie on a chalk or limestone subsoil any guarantee that they will not be acid, especially if they have been left as pasture for a long time. This was manifest in H. W. Gardner's experiments in Hertfordshire in 1932–35 where old grass land in the St Albans area growing on soils consisting of light chalk, medium loam with flints and glacial gravel produced the following results.[4]

Category	%
Not acid	10
Slightly acid	6
Moderately acid	22
Very acid	47
Extremely acid	14

Thus 90 per cent of these soils required liming despite their chalky subsoil.

It is however not surprising that historians have not always fully grasped the significance of the problem of soil acidity, since contemporaries were themselves in the dark about it. The belief that lime, chalk and marl (a term which comprises a variety of mixtures of chalk and clay) were in themselves plant foods persisted well into the nineteenth century, and with it the belief that lime was to some extent a substitute for manure, and not a necessary partner to it. This view was held by the early improvers. Thus the true significance of lime was not emphasised by the great publicists of agricultural improvements like Arthur Young, William Marshall and their contemporaries (even though they recognised that lime was important) and has thus not found a prominent part in the historical literature.

Nevertheless it comes as something of a surprise to discover that Lord Ernle in his classic history of English farming has only four references to lime (all quite cursory) in a work of 472 pages, especially as having been a prominent land agent and a former Minister of Agriculture he can hardly have been ignorant of technical matters. Nor have his editors added more than a few references in the 1961 reissue of Ernle's work. [5]

Other recent books have given the subject more prominence, especially as there has been a growing realisation of the importance of the sixteenth and seventeenth centuries in the history of agricultural improvement, springing in part from Professor Hoskins' pioneering studies. [6] This was the period when the use of burnt lime, as opposed to chalk or marl, seems to have begun. Eric Kerridge was the first historian to give major emphasis to the spread of liming from the sixteenth century as a key development in raising agricultural production (see below) and the subject has not been neglected by other scholars (especially Joan Thirsk), yet it remains true that it occupies a relatively minor position in the total picture. [7]

The amount of work which has already been done indicates that burnt lime was being widely used all over Britain by the mid-eighteenth century and that a national study of the origin and spread of the practice would be a large task. However some of the more important factors may be isolated and clarified if the field of study is narrowed to one county. For this purpose Devon has some advantages. In the first place it was known for its advanced farming practices in the mid-seventeenth century, Oliver Cromwell having said that it exceeded all other counties in this respect. [8] Thus the question of the extent to which liming was responsible for this relative pre-eminence is relevant; for although Devon was not the first county to use lime on a large scale, it was one of the improvements of the sixteenth century to which Professor Hoskins has drawn attention.[9]

All along the north and south coasts of the county the mouldering remains of disused lime kilns stand, sometimes peeping out of dense undergrowth like ruined medieval castles, for which they are occasionally mistaken. Many estuarine, river and inland sites have also been discovered, but it is only recently that industrial archaeologists have begun to carry out the search in a systematic way and doubtless many more sites will be discovered as this work proceeds. The pioneer was the late Dr A. H. Shorter whose work forms the basis for Fig. 5.1. This map shows 374 lime kilns in Devon of which 57 per cent (215 kilns) were located on the south coast and its estuaries, 27 per cent (100 kilns) on the shorter north coast and the remaining 16 per cent (59 kilns) in mid-Devon. The map also relates the kilns to the calcareous rock formations and shows that no farm in Devon was very far from a lime supply.[10] The map does not relate to any particular period of time, and all these kilns were not in operation simultaneously, although the majority were probably in existence by the late eighteenth century.

Literary references to the use of lime in Devon agriculture are also fairly abundant and it is clear from the works of the late eighteenth century surveyors like Robert Fraser, William Marshall, and Charles Vancouver that lime was being used almost universally by Devon farmers buttressed by covenants in leases specifying the quantities to be applied when pasture was being ploughed up for cereal growing.[11] Many of these leases survive in the Devon Record Office and elsewhere, and may be combined with deeds, lime-kiln accounts, estate correspondence and old maps, to provide yet another rich source of information.

Although this study can make no claim to be a complete survey it seeks to provide a framework for establishing some of the main trends; especially the chronology of lime's diffusion in Devon farming and, in conjunction with this, the causal and limiting factors involved. These fall roughly into three separate but interrelated categories: technical, economic and legal.

Technical aspects include the knowledge of the process of lime burning (which in fact is very ancient, lime having been burnt for mortar in Roman times and possibly much earlier) and the knowledge of its use to raise crop yields, which may also be ancient, though was not widely diffused until the sixteenth century. Developments in kiln building and transportation would also come under this category to some extent.

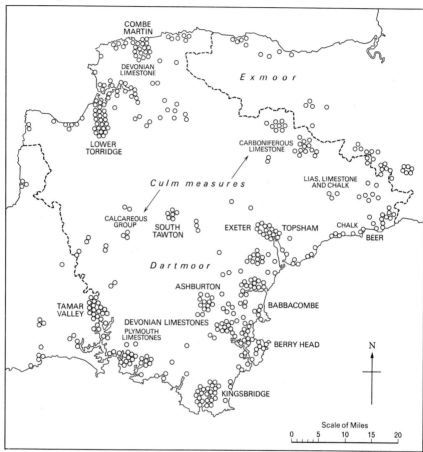

Fig. 5.1   Old lime kilns in Devon. (Reproduced by kind permission of Thomas Nelson & Sons Ltd. This map is based on one in *Southwest England* by A. H. Shorter, W. D. Ravenhill and K. J. Gregory, 1969, p. 137. A considerable number of recently discovered lime kilns have been added to it.)

The economic category is obviously very comprehensive and closely related to the technical since the adoption of new techniques often depends much more on their profitability than on their mere availability. It includes not only the general movements of prices and costs in the national economy, but also economic factors more specific to Devon, especially the relationship between the cost of applying lime and the price received for the extra yield obtained. In this situation the cost of transporting the lime from the kiln to the farm was often more important than the cost of the burnt lime itself. Thus the state of the roads, waterways (and by the early nineteenth century, canals) was always an important factor in the situation, and was frequently the most crucial.

The other vital element was the amount of extra cereal yield which was obtained by the use of lime. Yields are always very important in the economics of cereal-growing, because the costs of cultivation (ploughing, harrowing, sowing, harvesting, etc.) are relatively fixed and do not rise anything like proportionately to increases in yield, so that an improvement which increases the yield per acre is likely to react very noticeably on the farmers' profits.

Finally there is the legal category to which Vancouver attached the major importance. He believed that the insertion of covenants into leases forced farmers to undertake regular liming, and thus keep their land in good heart, whether it was to their particular economic advantage or not. Fortunately this is a matter which can be tested to some extent by an examination of surviving leases to see how important covenants were at different periods of time. (What is unfortunately not so easy to assess is the extent to which covenants were enforced – but this is not a serious problem as will appear later.)

Before describing the development of liming in Devon in more detail it may be helpful to summarise briefly the role and uses of lime in agriculture.

The primary function of lime is to neutralise soil acidity which inhibits the growth of most agricultural plants. The action of micro-organisms in the soil is constantly creating nitric acid. This nitric acid can be neutralised by combining it with a calcium compound, such as chalk or lime, to form the neutral salt, calcium nitrate. This is the usual form in which plants take up their nitrogen. Thus to a limited extent chalk or lime does act as a plant food, but it should be emphasised that the quantities of nitrogen thus absorbed by plants are very limited and do not affect yields to any significant extent.

The simplest way of applying a calcium compound to the soil is to find one which exists naturally in a form which is sufficiently soft to break up for spreading, and sufficiently soluble to act reasonably quickly. Chalk and marl have been historically by far the most common calcium compounds used in agriculture. Their use is extremely ancient and was described by Pliny the elder (*c.* AD 23–70) in his *Natural History*. He explained how marl enriched the soils of the Gallic lands in France and Britain, and distinguished six different types of marl. In Britain a white marl (probably chalk) was taken from a considerable depth in the ground and its beneficial effects on the soil were said to last for eighty years.[12]

Chalk and marl were spread on the ground in small lumps and gradually disintegrated by the action of frost, thaws, rainfall and drying winds causing them to crumble and dissolve. They were however relatively slow to act, and of course were not available in many parts of the country. The alternative was limestone, but this is hard and difficult to break up and is relatively insoluble unless reduced to a very fine powder. This was difficult to achieve by mechanical means (though modern machinery enables finely ground limestone powder to be used today) but could be easily done by burning. When limestone (calcium carbonate) is heated to a dull redness it begins to decompose (at *c.* 550°C) and to give off its carbon dioxide. The result is quicklime (calcium oxide) a compound not found in nature. It takes about two tons of limestone to produce one ton of quick lime.

Quicklime is an unpleasant substance to handle because it absorbs moisture and gives off a fierce heat in the process. However, once spread on the land it rapidly combines with soil moisture or rain to form slaked lime (calcium hydroxide) – a fine powder which will gradually dissolve in water. It is over a hundred times as soluble as limestone, and also considerably more soluble than chalk, as well as containing much more calcium oxide than either. Hence the great significance of burnt lime for agricultural improvement.

Although the primary function of liming is to neutralise soil acidity there are also some important secondary benefits. Lime improves soil structure. On light land it reduces the formation of a caked or loosely cemented surface layer of soil which delays the emergence of newly germinated seeds. On heavy soils it increases the friability, opening up the soil and allowing water and air to penetrate more easily. This makes the soil easier to work, reducing the power needed for tillage and increasing the number of days when the soil can be cultivated. Other benefits are the prevention of finger and toe disease in turnips and the elimination of certain weeds such as sheep's sorrel, spurrey and knawel which flourish in acid soils; they may however be replaced by other weeds which prefer a neutral soil.

The quantities of lime which are necessary at different levels of acidity and on different types of soil are now known and are given in Table 5.2 for reference. Acidity is measured on the pH scale with

7 as the neutral point. Readings above 7 indicate alkalinity and readings below 7 indicate acidity. It is surprising how accurate Devon farmers had become by the eighteenth century in assessing

TABLE 5.2   *A guide to the lime-requirements of arable mineral soils of average humus content*

		Estimate of lime-requirement calcium carbonate, tons/acre		
Acidity class	pH as measured	Light soils	Medium soils	Heavy soils
A. Not acid	6·6 or above	A rotational dressing may be advisable		
B. Slightly acid	6·5 to 6·1	$\frac{1}{2}$	1	$1\frac{1}{2}$
C. Moderately acid	6·0 to 5·6	$1\frac{1}{4}$	$1\frac{3}{4}$	$2\frac{1}{4}$
D. Very acid	5·5 to 5·1	2	$2\frac{1}{2}$	3
E. Extremely acid	5·0 to 4·6	3	$3\frac{3}{4}$	$4\frac{1}{2}$
F. Exceptionally acid	below 4·6	4	not usually encountered	

Source H. W. Gardner and H. V. Garner (see note 1) p. 64

lime requirements considering that they knew nothing of the scientific basis of what they were doing. Rule of thumb and observation had produced a more-or-less correct customary dressing of 40 Winchester bushels per acre in North Devon and 75 in South Devon.[13] These would weigh about 1·5 and 2·75 tons respectively – quite close to the range of dressings of between 1·25 tons (for light land) and 2·25 tons (for heavy land) recommended by Gardner and Garner for soils of moderate acidity (pH 6·0 to 5·6) – though not perhaps quite enough for really acid land.

THE RISE OF LIMING IN DEVON

The earliest literary references to the use of lime in British agriculture date from the sixteenth century, but the fact that burnt lime was used to prepare mortar for building in Roman times and in the Middle Ages means that it is not impossible that it was spread on the land as well.[14] Its use may even have originated from the observation that plants grew particularly well near kilns, where lime had been spilt.

In fact Fitzherbert was quite familiar with burnt lime in 1523.[15]

Referring to land improvement he wrote 'Another maner of mendyng of errable lande is to mucke it, marle it, lyme it, or dong it.'[16]

He also has a passage describing how old arable land which had reverted to bush or moss could be improved by the process of paring off the turf and burning it (called Devonshiring or Denshiring) and then applying marl. He praised farmers in Cheshire and Lancashire for using this method but did not mention any other locality specifically, although he lamented that the use of marl had fallen into disuse since former times. He thought that fear of increased rents may have discouraged tenants from improving their lands in this way, but wondered why freeholders were not more active, since all the profit was theirs.[17]

However on the use of burnt lime he was quite specific, 'And in many countreis (i.e. counties) where plentie of lyme stonne is the husbandes do bren the lyme stonne with wode and secole and make lyme thereof: and do set it upon their landes as they do their dong and do sprede it in lyke maner the whiche they call moche better than dong for lyme is hote of hymselfe.'[18] This passage is interesting for several reasons. It indicates that coal (secole) was replacing wood as the kiln fuel and that lime was being used in many counties, as well as the quaint idea that it was the heat in dung and lime which contributed to soil fertility. Another passage also indicates that a trade in agricultural lime existed: 'he that hath lymestone maye bren it with coole and wode and make lyme wherwith he may lyme his grounde and that wyll bring good corne or he maye sell his lyme at his pleasure.'[19] Kerridge has commented that it is not surprising that lime

> became the farmers' standby almost everywhere, especially as coal fuel now reduced the cost of producing many of its forms. . . . after 1560, and still more after 1590, liming, or chalking, though not in itself an entirely new practice, grew so greatly in extent, frequency and volume, that it became effectually revolutionary.[20]

References to liming indeed come from a great number of counties, though they are more common in the north, west and east of England than in the great arable area stretching from Dorset in the south to Yorkshire in the north, where a wide range of chalk and limestone-based soils made acidity less of a problem. Lime was particularly useful where old pastures and rough grazings were being converted to corn-growing as was happening all over the north and west. Northumberland, the Lake counties, Lancashire and Cheshire were prominent users, as were the Border counties and much of Wales, especially South Wales and Anglesey. Many old forests were being cut down and the land converted to farming and again liming was specially necessary on their acid soils. Areas affected were the wealden vales of Kent and Sussex, the Chilterns, the forests of Wiltshire, Dorset and Somerset in the south, and the midland forests like Sherwood farther north.[21] John Norden noted in 1607 that in 'Shropshire, Denbighshire, Flintshire and now lately in some parts of Sussex they fetch limestone, erect kilns, and burn it on their own farms'.[22] Prominent also were the south-western counties of Devon and Cornwall.

Contemporaries were well aware of the importance of lime. In 1578 R. Merrick wrote of Glamorgan that 'now of late years, since the knowledge or use of lyminge was found, there groweth more plenty of grayne'.[23] In the House of Commons, in 1621 John Smyth of Nibley in Gloucestershire stated that the fear of dearth was gone because 'Our husbandry, by marlinge, chawkinge, sea-sand, lyminge, more earth, oadynge old pastures, plowing up warrens, parks and wood growndes, with god's ordynary blessinge, freeth us from that feare'.[24]

By the mid-seventeenth century Walter Blith could declare in the *The English Improver Improved* (1652) that whole counties which were formerly barren were now growing corn because of lime.[25] Some allowance for exaggeration has to be made, for bad harvests could still cause serious shortages of wheat in the eighteenth century, the years 1740 and 1756 being very bad and 1709 nearly disastrous.[26] All were however war years when imports were restricted.

One of the earliest references to the use of lime in Devon farming was made by John Hooker, alias Vowell (1526–1601) a well-informed antiquarian who had been Chamberlain of the city of Exeter. He noted the use of lime in 1599, but did not indicate for how long it had been used.[27] An account of Devon written in 1630 by Tristram Risdon (c. 1580–1640) suggested that the practice was fairly recent. Risdon who lived in north Devon at Winscott Barton near Torrington wrote that

> of late, a new invention hath sprung up, and been practised amongst us, by burning of lime, and incorporating it for a season with earth, and then spread upon the arable land, hath produced a plentiful increase of all sorts of grain where formerly such never grew in any living man's memory.[28]

Risdon's opinion was confirmed by his fellow antiquarian Thomas

Westcote (1567–*c*. 1640), who lived at West Raddon near Crediton in mid-Devon.[29]

This suggests that the last quarter of the sixteenth century was the time when liming began in Devon agriculture, but there are earlier references to lime kilns. These probably existed to supply the building trade, but it is possible that there may have been a localised agricultural use as well.[30]

The Exeter Customs Rolls also begin to record imports of limestone in the late sixteenth century. Three 'stone boats' were recorded in 1589–90 and twenty-eight in 1601–2 when there were also another twenty-seven carrying fish as well as limestone. Some of this limestone was no doubt used for building, but a reference to an old man dying on the lime kiln at Topsham in 1613 indicates that lime burning had already been established.[31] The rapid increase in limestone imports also suggests that agricultural demand had been added to that of building.

It is not easy to discover the sites of the early kilns but scattered references show that they were quite widely distributed by 1650. An early reference relates to Axmouth on the south-east coast, where a lease of 1606 stated that John Mallack, the occupier of enclosed grounds called Blacklease and a parcel of waste ground lying between his barn and the churchyard 'may dig marl, chalk and stones, and burn lime upon the premises for their betterment'.[32] A slightly later reference comes from an inventory of 1630, which shows that John Stangcombe, a husbandman of Ilsington, a village on the eastern fringe of Dartmoor below Haytor, had 'Marrell stones in a lyme kill' worth 40 shillings. Marrell is a corruption for marble, the name which is attached to many limestones in Devon. He also had 'certen yeeres to come in a chattell lease concernynge libertye for fetchinge and carryenge of Marrell stones' worth 6s 8d.[33] A lime kiln was built at Exeter quay in 1634, possibly replacing an earlier one.[34] In 1646 a lime kiln was included in the lease of a fourth part of five closes of land in the manor of Pridhamsleigh, two of which were called Great and Little Twinewood.[35] Pridhamsleigh is in Staverton parish and is situated about two miles south of Ashburton. Extensive limestone quarries are still being worked nearby. These references all come from south Devon but an inventory of 1644 from Swimbridge near Barnstaple shows that north Devon was also involved. Robert Rosyer, a clothier at Swimbridge, was also a lime burner, being owed £5 for lime and having tools for his kiln and quarry worth 13s 4d.[36]

In fact it would not be surprising if further research uncovered more references to early kilns in north Devon than in the south, because there is reason to believe that the practice of using burnt lime on the land may have spread to Devon across the Bristol Channel from South Wales, where the industry had developed at an earlier date. South Wales possessed ample supplies of cheap coal and limestone, and although Devon had plenty of limestone it was always dependent on the import of Welsh coal, known as culm. This was true for kilns on the south coast as well as the north.

The origins of the use of lime on farms in south Wales have not been fully established but F. V. Emery refers to a rent roll at Horton in West Glamorgan dating from the reign of Henry VIII which refers to a 'kill-place' for lime-burning; and at Landimore in 1639 there were 'Quarries of Limestones where Tenants time out of mind have used to burn their lime for the composting of their lands'. Emery believes that the trade to Devon was also of long standing and states that

> despite a general belief that the convertible farmers of Devonshire and elsewhere began liming about 1600, it can be shown that in North Devon at least kilns were burning Glamorgan limestone in the mid-sixteenth century. It was exported from places like Porteynon in Gower with a story of cross-Channel trade in stone right through to the 1870s.[37]

The next major reference to the spread of liming in Devon dates from 1667 when Samuel Colepresse supplied answers to a number of queries made by the newly founded Royal Society as to the state of agriculture. In answer to the question, 'what peculiar preparations are made use of to these soils for each kind of grain: with what kind of manure they are prepared: when and how and in what quantity the manure is laid on?' he replied, with seasand, seaweed, dung and

> with Lyme (in our westerne parts the best, of marble: but easterne with chaulke, or freestone) which is most proportionate for cold, drie, clayie grounds: and is the only dressing of all sandy moulds. Tis carried from the kilne in to the fields from Rudemas till Lammas about 16 hogsheds in an acre, and cast into furriers plow'd on purpose, 4 foote broad, $\frac{1}{2}$ deep, round the field, and some athwart amongst the loose earth: and by that time the limestones are slatcht, or reduc'd to a flower, in the beginning of August, (the best), some September, that, and the earth, well mixt, are carried out, and equallie cast abroad over the whole field: the effects of which dressing, (say some,) may be perceived 20 years after: and serves indifferentlie for all graine. This is not us'd in Cornewall, or westerne parts of Devonshire till of late, and that, by but a few, who being

sencible, that their ground is glutted, and surcharg'd with sand, begin
to furrow, and lyme their ground, thereby not only dressing it for
their present tillage, but raise and strengthen it for the future.[38]

Unfortunately this passage is not very precise about the extent
to which lime was being used in the 1660s, but its reference to the
practice being new in the western part of the county implies that it
may have been fairly common elsewhere. The reason why lime was
beginning to replace seasand may also have been partly economic.
Even though coal had to be imported it may have been cheaper to
burn the local limestones (especially in south-west Devon) than to
cart expensive seasand overland from the north coast like the monks
of Tavistock Abbey did in the Middle Ages.[39]

It is also probable that by 1750 burnt lime was being used throughout Devonshire. As noted earlier when Dean Milles circulated the
Devon clergy asking for information about the history of their
parishes and included questions about agriculture, he received
answers to his query on manures from 220 parishes all over Devon
(see Fig. 5.2). Of these 186 applied lime (84·5 per cent), 30 used
seasand or marl as a substitute, and only 4 (1·8 per cent) used no
calcareous manures. From the distribution of the parishes which
used lime it seems highly likely that most of the parishes which did
not bother to reply were also using lime.[40]

It may be suggested tentatively that the use of lime was adopted
by the better farmers between about 1550 and 1650 and spread to
the remainder in the following century. This supposition is supported by Marshall's statement of the 1790s that in west Devonshire 'lime, . . . I understand, has been more or less used, here, for
about sixty years', that is since the 1730s.[41] As lime was particularly
associated with the conversion of old pastures to wheat-growing by
means of peat-burning it may also be suggested that the spread of
lime was associated with the rise in wheat prices shown in Fig. 5.3.
However there is evidence from north-western England that lime
was frequently used to improve pastures, so that meat and dairy
prices may also have been important. Such evidence also exists for
Devon but to a lesser extent.[42] It seems likely that periods when the
curve was rising particularly sharply would be periods when the
use of lime spread most rapidly. If this was the case the periods 1530
to 1600, 1625 to 1650, 1685 to 1700 and 1750 to 1815 would be
particularly important, although it may be necessary to allow some
time lag between a high price stimulating investment in kiln
building and the actual production of lime. Bearing this in mind, it
looks as though the generally high level of wheat prices in the war

years, 1689–97 and 1702–13, may have been specially important for lime diffusion.

Ideally it would be desirable to correlate the price data with evidence of kiln building, but since the latter is fragmentary the

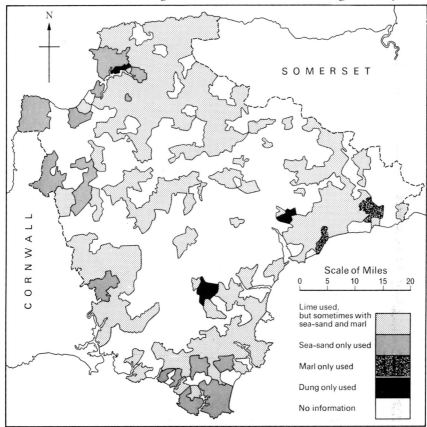

Fig. 5.2. Recorded use of lime, sea sand and marl in Devon *c.* 1750. Blank areas = no information. (Information kindly provided by Mr Robin Stanes from Dean Milles' parochial enquiries, 1747–56. The original MS is in the Bodleian Library, Oxford.)

most that can be done is to present a few surviving examples which at least indicate that this was a period when lime-burning was spreading. For instance in north Devon in 1700 the Barnstaple Corporation granted a licence to one Hierson for boats and barges to pass to the lime kiln with lime and culm.[43] Also in north Devon in 1708 a yeoman of South Molton called John Scott made a covenant with Elizabeth Squire the owner of a tenement called Bridge

(now included in the grounds of Lord Fortescue's estate at Castle
Hill in Filleigh) which enabled Scott to 'dig and burn limestone in
the tenement called Bridge for the next twenty years'. He was also
to deliver to Elizabeth Squire, or her assigns or servants, or the
'workmen at the kilns where such limestone should be burnt' 300

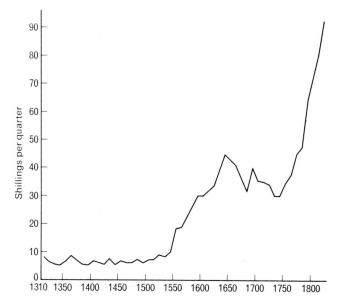

Fig. 5.3   Exeter wheat prices – decennial means. (Shillings per quarter
adjusted to Winchester bushels by W. H. Beveridge.)

Source Adapted from graph in William H. Beveridge, 'A statistical crime of the seventeenth
century', *Journal of Economic and Business History*, i (1929) p. 524. The 'crime'
discovered by Beveridge was that prior to 1670 the Exeter market was using a
bushel containing 10 gallons instead of the 8 gallons in the Winchester, or national,
bushel.

bushels of lime which was to be given free to a certain John Pasmore
for use on his land.[44] Pasmore was presumably a tenant farmer.

The lime trade of the Exe estuary was also in a flourishing condition. In 1711 at least eight lime kilns were operating on one small
stretch of the estuary alone – the three miles of east bank between
Countess Wear and Exmouth. Thomas Pidgeon and Abraham
Gibbs had kilns at Countess Wear, Robert Spiring had one at Topsham 'a little below the key towards Exmouth', and John Chappell
had no fewer than five in the Glass House area.[45] There were
doubtless other kilns elsewhere on the estuary at this time.

DEVELOPMENT AND DECLINE

The steep and continuous rise in grain prices after about 1750 shown in Fig. 5.3 ensured that the use of lime continued to spread. References to kilns in the major producing areas shown in Fig. 5.1 become relatively abundant, and by the early nineteenth century, observers like the Reverend Thomas Moore were beginning to sound like precursors of modern conservationists in their fear that the lime burners were squandering irreplaceable natural resources. Moore wrote in 1829 that the owners of the beautiful cliffs around Berry head and Babbacombe in Torbay were 'literally retailing the picturesque and beautiful by weight and measure'.

The use of lime and the construction of kilns had also spread into new areas like the Kingsbridge and Tamar estuaries to supply lime to farmers who had previously relied on seasand from the south coast which was low in calcareous content. Abraham Hawkins, writing about the Kingsbridge area in 1819, noted that the use of seasand had much declined in the previous forty years or so, and that whereas there had once been thirty-two barges dredging sand from the bar by the mouth of the estuary only three or four remained. Instead limestone was brought from Cattedown near Plymouth and burnt in recently constructed kilns.[46] Construction of kilns must have proceeded rapidly in the area between 1750, when Hawkins said that the two kilns at Salt-mill quay just south of Kingsbridge had been 'the only buildings of this kind in the neighbourhood',[47] and 1808–14 when the annual production of lime was between 50,000 and 60,000 hogsheads – about 15–18,000 tons.[48] Such a production would have required at least 18 kilns on the assumption that each kiln could produce 1,000 tons a year, which the large kilns at Halton on the Tamar estuary were capable of doing when pressed.[49] Their more normal production was 500 to 600 tons though, and at this rate some thirty kilns would have been needed to achieve the Kingsbridge area production. The ruins of twenty-three kilns survive on the Kingsbridge estuary and at least three more are known to have existed.[50] Some however had even lower production figures. Yalton kiln on the southern coast of Southpool Creek near East Portlemouth produced only 1,300 hogsheads (about 394 tons) in the burning season 1792–93.[51]

Lime seems to have replaced sand at a slightly later date on the farms in the Tamar valley. Frank Booker states that most of the Tamar valley kilns were built between 1770 and 1830 and that some twenty survive on the lower part of the river below Gunnislake (some of course being on the Cornish bank). The lime trade on the

Tamar reached its peak between 1810 and 1850 and then gradually declined owing to the competition from artificial manures, which were readily available from the growing chemical industry in Plymouth.[52]

The advantages of using lime were widely recognised by the agricultural writers of the eighteenth century, but it is difficult to move beyond their general statements to specific examples of the extent to which the use of lime raised the production of cereals and grass. Indications sometimes emerge from farm or bailiffs' accounts such as those made by Lord Fortescue's agent Mr Hole for the years 1762 to 1769. He managed the Barton of Castle Hill, the seat of the Fortescue family near South Molton in north Devon. According to Mr Hole he had raised the annual value of the Barton fields from £373 8s in 1762 to £517 in 1769 – a rise of £143 12s or 38 per cent. This had been achieved by various improvements in management and manuring of which the use of lime had been prominent. This emerges from Hole's comments on the rises in annual value for particular fields. For instance he says of a field called Church Broomeham, containing about 15·5 acres, that its annual value had risen from £12 7s 6d to £17 10s. It had been first dressed 'for turnips with 80 bushels of lime in an acre, and only one crop of barley taken after it. It was afterwards dressed over upon the green side with dung.' A field called Quarry Close containing 29 acres had been increased in annual value from £16 to £31 10s. It was 'broke up and tilled in the year 1766 and let out with a dressing of 80 bushels of lime an acre'. Similar comments were made for several other fields.[53] Of course not all the improvement in value can be credited to liming, but it looks as though lime could increase the annual value of land by some 25 to 30 per cent at least.

More generally Robert Fraser in his report on Devon farming (1794) provides some figures for the costs of liming and expected wheat yields which can be combined with price data to illustrate the relationship between income and yields. This information is plotted in Fig. 5.4 which reveals the dramatic way in which profits rise with increased yields when basic costs are fixed. Fraser points out that the price of lime depended on the price of Welsh culm and the distance of the kiln from the place of import. At Totnes, at the head of the navigable Dart, when culm was 10s 6d per quarter, lime cost £3 10s per acre. Tillage and harvesting etc. cost about £1 10s, so that the total cost of producing an acre of wheat was £5. However since the benefit of lime was felt for at least three crops (and often for more) it is not necessary to charge the whole cost of the lime to the first crop. It may reasonably bear one-third – or £1 3s 4d, which reduces the total cost to £2 13s 4d per acre. Fraser said that farmers expected yields of 26 to 30 bushels, which at the 1793 price

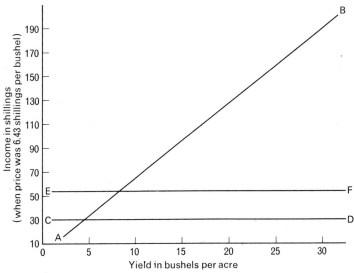

AB = Income obtained from one acre of wheat
CD = Cost of tillage for one acre (without lime)
EF = Cost of tillage per acre (with lime at one-third of its total cost which is spread over
3 crops)

Fig. 5.4 Relationship between yields of wheat and costs of production in 1793, when the wheat price was 6·43 shillings per bushel.

of 6.43 shillings per bushel would have produced the following satisfactory results[54]:

	£	s	d
30 bushels of wheat	9	12	11
less costs of tillage and lime	2	13	4
Profit per acre	6	19	7
26 bushels of wheat	8	7	2
less costs of tillage and lime	2	13	4
Profit per acre	5	13	10

Fraser thought however that these yields were probably above the average for south Devon which was nearer to 20 bushels per acre. Even at this reduced yield a profit of £3 15s 3d would have resulted.

The interesting question then arises: what would the profit have been if no lime had been applied? Naturally the answer depends on how much the absence of lime would have reduced the yield. If it be assumed that the yield would have fallen by 25 per cent – that is to 15 bushels – then allowing for the saving in lime costs the resultant profit would have been £3 6s 8d. The reduction in profit of 8s 7d per acre might not seem very significant (though it would come to nearly £9 if 100 acres of wheat were grown). But it is probable that the absence of lime would have reduced the yield even more than 25 per cent, perhaps to 10 or 12 bushels. At 12 bushels the profit per acre would have been only £2 7s 2d.

Whatever the precise extent of the profitability of lime Fraser had no doubt about its general usefulness in South Devon agriculture. He concluded this section of his report with the following words

> However much it may be the custom to think, that in a country so distant from the metropolis, the people know little of the theory of agriculture; yet I am fully convinced, that in point of practice of cultivation, the labour and care of manuring their lands, there are no people in any district of England of equal extent, where there is so much good husbandry as in the south of Devon.[55]

William Marshall, whose book on south-western farming was published two years after Fraser's, also praised Devon farmers for their use of lime. He indicates how lime production had become a specialised business and notes that

> 'The LIME KILNS of Devonshire are large, and of an expensive construction; some of them costing not less than thirty or forty pounds each. But their duration is in proportion: one that has been built thirty years is still firm and sound on the outside. The walls are of extraordinary thickness; wide enough, on the top, for horses to pass round the kiln, and deliver stones. . . .
> The stones are brought up from the water side, on horseback or upon asses; and, being distributed round the top of the kiln, are there broken, and thrown into the kiln with shovels; without the extra trouble of carrying them in baskets; a saving, probably which counterbalances the apparently extra expense of carrying up the unbroken stones, on horseback, instead of in carts: so that we have here, as in many other instances, in Rural Management two roads, of similar length and expediency, leading to the same ends.'[56]

Plate 4 Lime burning at Clovelly on the north Devon coast, 1833.

Marshall also noted that lime was sometimes used to improve grassland as well as cereals and came across an instance near Torrington in north Devon.[57]

Charles Vancouver's report on Devon farming in 1808 described lime as 'the prevailing article of manure in most parts of the county' and gave copious details of varying rates of application in different regions.[58] Vancouver includes a striking example of how recently reclaimed land could be made fertile when well manured with lime. He tells how Mr King of Fowlescombe (a farm about eight miles north of Kingsbridge in Loddiswell parish) obtained a yield of 28 bushels of wheat per acre from 70 acres of reclaimed moorland near Blackdown hill fort. The land had been cleared of rocks by blasting, and had been pared and burned and well dressed with lime at the rate of 60 double Winchester bushels to the acre before the wheat was sown.[59] Nevertheless this was a remarkably high yield from reclaimed moor.

Farmers were also prepared to travel long distances for lime. The accounts left by an unnamed farmer who apparently occupied Nymet Barton farm in Nymet Rowland parish in mid-Devon, show that between 27 July and 1 September 1824 his carts made twelve trips to South Tawton for lime, a distance of about ten miles. But much more remarkable were the six trips made all the way to Topsham between 18 September and the 16 October 1824.[60] This was a distance of over twenty miles. Since there were many kilns closer than Topsham it would appear that the Topsham lime burners were the only ones who could supply lime at that period. Possibly other burners had ceased work during harvest time, when general demand would have been slack.

Other evidence shows that lime kilns could supply farmers over a large area. The accounts of William Ford, who produced lime at Branscombe on the south-east coast about five miles east of Sidmouth, showed that he supplied lime to farmers in no fewer than twenty-seven different parishes in the years 1786–88. These ranged in a semicircle around Branscombe from Seaton on the coast to the east, round to the parishes north of Honiton, like Awliscombe and Buckerell, back to coastal parishes like Otterton to the west of Sidmouth. The distances were about eight miles along the coast in either direction and about twelve miles inland to parishes like Talaton and Payhembury.[61]

Some surviving lime kiln accounts suggest that lime production could be very profitable in certain circumstances, though such accounts need to be treated with some caution since they are not drawn up in a form which would be acceptable to a modern accountant, and they contain certain important omissions. However it is possible to provide reasonable estimates for these. An example of such a profitable lime kiln was at Budleigh Salterton which belonged to Lord Rolle of Bicton, near Sidmouth in East Devon.[62] A particularly good year was 1806, when the cost of producing lime (limestone, coal, transport, labour, etc.) amounted to £675 19s 11d and the proceeds of sales (2,731 hogsheads – about 683 tons[63] – of lime at 6s each and 263 hogsheads of lime ashes at 3s each) to eighty-four customers amounted to £858 13s 6d. This left a credit margin of £182 13s 7d. However, this was not all profit because certain items like depreciation, rent and interest on capital are not included. The problem is to know how much to allow for such items. It depends mainly on the size of the initial capital investment in the lime kiln. Marshall said that a kiln cost £30 to £40 in 1796, and so an estimated £50 for 1806 (when prices were higher) would seem reasonable and may even be too high, especially as we do not know when the kiln was built and it may have been considerably earlier. If it be assumed that the kiln lasts for 10 years (they often lasted twenty to thirty years in fact) a depreciation allowance of 10 per cent (i.e. £5) should also be added to the costs. There is also the question of working capital. Lord Rolle seems to have worked his kiln in partnership with an Exeter banker and shipping merchant, Matthew Lee Yeates, to whom he made advances to cover expenses. This was especially necessary since most of the farmers to whom Lord Rolle sold lime bought it on credit. Indeed many were his own tenants and paid for their lime when they paid their quarterly rents. However by the end of the year Lord Rolle had received all his working capital back again so it would only seem necessary to charge to kiln expenses the interest which Lord Rolle would have had to pay if he had borrowed this money – 5 per cent of £676, or £33 15s. Even this is something of an overestimate because Lord Rolle received at least half of his working capital back during the year.

It is also necessary to charge interest on the investment in the kiln, say 5 per cent on £50, or £2 10s, and to make some allowance for the rent of the land on which the kiln stood, for which £5 would probably be over generous.

On these assumptions the accounts can be amended in the way shown overleaf to yield a profit of £136 8s 7d.

If this profit be expressed as a rate on the assumed initial investment of £84 (£50 for the kiln and £34 for interest on working capital) it works out at 162·5 per cent. Such a high rate can hardly

			£	s	d
Income from sale of lime and ashes			858	13	6

Less costs:	£	s	d			
Limestone, coal, labour, etc	675	19	11			
Rent of land for kiln, say	5	0	0			
Depreciation of kiln, say 10% of £50	5	0	0			
Interest of fixed capital, say 5% of £50	2	10	0			
Interest on working capital at 5% of £676	33	15	0			
				722	4	11
Profit				136	8	7

have been typical and calls for some comment. Firstly the accounts may be defective and some items of expense may have been omitted. Secondly Lord Rolle was in a special position. As we have seen nearly all his eighty-four customers were his own tenants who were obliged by the covenants in their leases to spread lime on all land which they brought into cereal cultivation from pasture at the rate of 10 hogsheads per acre. At 6s a hogshead this cost them £3 an acre. Their leases did not actually specify that they should buy this lime from Lord Rolle's kiln, but it was probably generally understood that they were expected to do so. It should however be pointed out that £3 an acre was not an above-average price. In fact it was less than the £3 10s which Fraser quoted for Totnes lime in 1794, previously referred to.

It thus appears that although Lord Rolle enjoyed some of the advantages of a monopoly seller he did not exploit these unduly (and he had competitors along the coast such as the Branscombe kiln). It seems rather that during the Napoleonic wars when grain prices were abnormally high (see Fig. 5.6) farmers were prepared to spend a lot of money on lime, and as labour costs were generally low, a productive kiln was highly profitable – even though limestone had to be brought from Torbay and culm from South Wales.

The question of covenants in leases leads on to the consideration of whether legal pressure was an important cause of the use of lime. We have seen that Charles Vancouver (1808) attached great importance to this, noting that leases usually specified that land being brought back into cultivation for cereals from pasture by means of paring and burning should be dressed with 80 Winchester bushels of lime per acre and adding that 'the expensive article of lime would frequently be omitted, did not the leases expressly provide for the tenants laying on that quantity of lime per acre'.[64]

From this it would seem that the insertion of such covenants in leases must have been an important element in persuading farmers to use lime in the first place. Yet when we examine a random sample of fifty-three leases made between 1650 and 1829 a rather different picture emerges (Table 5.3). We know from the evidence of the Milles enquiries, *c.* 1750 that the use of lime was more or less general by the mid-eighteenth century, so we should expect to see that the insertion of lime covenants into leases was also fairly general. In fact of the thirty-one leases made before 1770 only eleven contained lime covenants, and only four of these date from before 1750. In contrast nearly all the leases made after 1770 contained covenants (fifteen out of eighteen).

It is true that this sample covers too long a period of time for the leases for any single decade to have statistical significance and the fact that there are no covenants in the ten leases before 1730 is probably accidental. Nevertheless the general picture presented by Table 5.3 – of landlords following a trend already set by farmers,

TABLE 5.3   *Devon leases and lime covenants, 1650–1829*

Period	No. of Leases	No. with lime covenants	Period	No. of Leases	No. with lime covenants
1650–59	1	—	1740–49	4	2
1660–69	—	—	1750–59	6	1
1670–79	1	—	1760–69	9	6
1680–89	—	—	1770–79	9	8
1690–99	1	—	1780–89	2	1
1700–09	2	—	1790–99	2	1
1710–19	3	—	1800–09	2	2
1720–29	2	—	1810–19	2	2
1730–39	6	2	1820–29	1	1
			TOTALS	53	26

and not initiating it, can be reinforced if a larger sample from the years 1730–49 be examined. Those were the crucial years for the theory. Unless it can be shown that covenants had come to predominate in this period, it cannot seriously be argued that pressure from landlords was an important cause of the use of lime. In fact a sample of thirty leases taken from this period shows that only five contained lime covenants – a mere 16·6 per cent. This sample may be treated as random because the leases were randomly drawn from Devon as available, and not according to any plan. On the assumption that there were about 20,000 farmers in Devon in the mid eighteenth century – which seems reasonable[65] – there is a 95 per cent probability that the proportion of landlords who inserted lime covenants into leases was not greater than 30 per cent and not fewer than 4 per cent.[66] It seems fair to conclude that covenants were not a major cause of the spread of liming before 1750.

This conclusion can be reinforced by evidence from individual farms. Only a few of many examples can be given here. For instance in north Devon leases for three farms in the Fortescue's manor of Mortehoe show that covenants were introduced in the 1760s. At Ousborough farm the lease for 1765 contained a covenant while its predecessor of 1755 did not. At Overwoollacombe Barton the lease of the 1767 specified that '40 bushels of good hot well burnt lime, or 100 seams or horseloads of good salt seasand or 250 seams of good rotten dung' should be spread per acre of pasture broken for corn crops. Its predecessor of 1751 contained no covenant. At Broadmead the lease for 1764 had a lime specification of 50 bushels, and again its predecessor of 1754 had no covenant.[67]

There could also be considerable variation within regions. For instance a lease of 1748 for land in east Devon at Dalditch in East Budleigh parish specified that lime should be applied at the rate of 8 hogsheads per acre (48 to 64 bushels depending on whether the 6 or 8 bushel hogshead was being used). In contrast a lease in nearby Harpford parish had no covenant as late as 1777 and it was not introduced till 1800 (at 10 hogsheads to the acre). Neither of these farms had entered the Rolle estate when these leases were granted.[68]

It may be said in defence of landlords that the long Devon leases granted for ninety-nine years or the lives of three named persons (whichever was the shorter) restricted their opportunities to influence their tenants, but this was not as serious as it appears at first sight because the tenants frequently renegotiated the leases by buying in new lives for a down payment, or surrendering the leases to move elsewhere, etc. As the examples quoted indicate, leases did not usually run for much longer than ten years before such an opportunity presented itself. This tendency for landlords to follow in the wake of tenants' improvements, rather than to initiate them is also in line with the wider national evidence discussed by Habakkuk and Mingay. Neither found that landlords did much to improve agriculture by progressive leases in the first half of the eighteenth century, and Mingay quotes William Marshall's opinion in 1796 that 'it is from the superior class of yeomanry and from some few principal tenants that we must expect to learn the best practice of the country'.[69] As Hoskins has pointed out Devon was a county where the yeomanry were well established.[70]

It seems likely that the role of landlords in Devon was to drive the laggards into the fold by forcing all tenants to comply with the standards of farming set by the best. However there may have been a considerable time lag before landlords were generally persuaded to perform this function.

The use of lime began a steady decline from the 1840s as farmers increasingly substituted the new chemical fertilisers for it. It is curious that the old illusions about lime being a fertiliser should have continued so long after the publication of Liebig's work on agricultural chemistry in 1842 had clearly elucidated the principles of plant nutrition for the first time. But the decline was long and continuous and was encouraged by the agricultural depressions of the periods 1879–96 and 1921–35, until it reached crisis proportions. The discovery of the serious nature of lime deficiency in the mid-1930s, as the result of the experimental work of people like Gardner, referred to at the beginning of this chapter, led to the government's decision in 1938 to promote a crash programme of liming, encouraged by subsidy as part of its war preparations. Subsidy payment has continued ever since, though is soon to cease.

However, the old kilns mostly survived into the early twentieth century, and one hardy veteran at Topsham was still burning in the early 1930s. In 1850 White's *History, Gazeteer and Directory of the County of Devon* recorded some forty-three limeburners in twenty-seven different locations, and it is known that this directory is far from complete.

Even when quenched forever lime kilns could still be put to artistic use and perhaps a fitting epitaph to their long reign may be provided by the history of an early casualty. In 1769 when the grounds at Castle Hill were being extended a problem arose about what to do with the old lime kiln. The agent, H. Hilliard wrote to Lord Fortescue in London on 26 November,

> Some preparations are making for the little Improvement of the old lime kiln – clearing the Rubbish, and picking up some stone for it. It may have the appearance of a Fort given to it, and will fall into several principal Points of View, when a few Bushes in a Hedge Row are cut down, which at present obstruct the View from the Platform. I shall do myself the Honour to send your Lordship a Sketch before I make the alteration.

Having received Lord Fortescue's approval, Hilliard reported on 5 January 1770 that the conversion was finished and added: 'I have taken the liberty to hang a Port-Cullis in the arch fronting the Meadow Park Wood which gives it a good deal of Spirit.'[71]

The chief conclusions of this chapter must remain tentative until more extensive work has been done on the documentary sources for the use of lime on farms, such as accounts and leases; and on the construction of lime kilns including a field survey of existing remains. Generally it seems that the role and function of lime as a factor in raising agricultural productivity by neutralising soil acidity has been underemphasised by most agricultural historians both nationally and locally. It seems to have been very rare before the fifteenth century (though further research amongst medieval records may modify this date) and to have spread in Devon in the late sixteenth century possibly stimulated by the example of South Wales via the coal and limestone trade. Liming was probably adopted by the better Devon farmers between 1550 and 1650 and was very widespread by 1750. Economic factors especially high grain prices in war years, such as the periods 1640–60 and 1689–1713 seem to have been more important than legal pressure from land-lords via covenants in leases. These were not at all general before 1770. However after that date, the continued rise of grain prices coupled with the widespread use of covenants probably caused every Devon farmer to take up liming. The practice reached its peak during the Napoleonic wars but remained important until the mid-nineteenth century, after which it slowly faded away, until revived by government stimulus in the late 1930s.

NOTES AND REFERENCES

1. Gabriel Plattes, *A Discovery of Infinite Treasure* (1639) quoted by H. W. Gardner and H. V. Garner, *The Use of Lime in British Agriculture* (Spon, 1953), p. 14.
2. *The Alfred* (a local paper published in Exeter, 14 April 1818).
3. Gardner and Garner, *op. cit.,* p. 4.
4. *Ibid.,* pp. 2 and 3.
5. Lord Ernle (R. E. Prothero), *English Farming, Past and Present* (6th edn, Heinemann, 1961) with introduction by G. E. Fussell and O. R. McGregor (first published 1912).
6. Especially 'The Leicestershire farmer in the sixteenth century' in *Essays in Leicestershire History* (Liverpool University Press, 1950) and 'The Leicestershire

farmer in the seventeenth century', reprinted in *Provincial England* (Macmillan, (1963).

7. Eric Kerridge, *The Agricultural Revolution* (Allen & Unwin, 1967), pp. 247–8; Joan Thirsk, ed. *The Agrarian History of England and Wales* vol. iv (Cambridge University Press, 1967) and J. D. Chambers and G. E. Mingay, *The Agricultural Revolution, 1750–1880* (Batsford, 1966).

8. Anthony Powell, *John Aubrey and his Friends* (1948), p. 91, cited by H. P. R. Finberg in *Tavistock Abbey* (2nd edn, David & Charles, 1969), p. 115.

9. W. G. Hoskins, *Devon* (Collins, 1954), pp. 95–6.

10. A. H. Shorter, W. D. Ravenhill, and K. J. Gregory, *Southwest England* (Nelson, 1969), pp. 136–8. I am grateful to Mrs Shorter and Professor Ravenhill for permission to reprint this map, to which some additional lime kilns have been added. See also Frank Booker, *The Industrial Archaeology of the Tamar Valley* (David & Charles, 1967), pp. 69–81 for a description of lime kilns in the Tamar Valley.

11. Robert Fraser, *General View of the County of Devon* (1794); William Marshall, *The Rural Economy of the West of England* (1796), and Charles Vancouver, *General View of the Agriculture of the County of Devon* (1808; repr. David & Charles, 1969).

12. Cited by Gardner and Garner, *op. cit.*, p. 12. This section is largely based on their work which should be consulted for further technical details if required. See especially pp. 25–6, 33–6, 95–7.

13. Robin Stanes, 'Devon agriculture in the mid-eighteenth century: the evidence of the Milles enquiries' in M. A. Havinden and Celia M. King, eds., *The Southwest and the Land* (Exeter University, 1969), p. 51. The Winchester bushel was the standard bushel from the reign of Henry VII until 1826. It was a round vessel with a plain and even bottom which was $18\frac{1}{2}$ inches in diameter. The sides were 8 inches high and the capacity was 2,150·42 cubic inches. There were 8 Winchester bushels in a Winchester quarter which was 97 per cent of the subsequent Imperial quarter.

14. For references to Roman lime kilns in the works of Marcus Cato and the use of lime on the roots of vines, olives and cherries in the works of Pliny, see Rev. John M. Wilson, ed., *The Rural Cyclopedia* (Edinburgh, 1849) p. 176. For medieval references to lime kilns for building mortar see L. F. Salzman, *Building in England down to 1540* (Oxford University Press, 2nd ed, 1967), pp. 149–50. For the early use of marl and lime in agriculture see Dorothea Oschinsky, ed., *Walter of Henley and other treatises on estate management and accounting* (Clarendon Press, 1971) pp. 144, 179 and 329 and R. A. L. Smith, *Canterbury Cathedral Priory* (Cambridge University Press, 1943), p. 137.

15. Sir Anthony or John Fitzherbert, *The Boke of Surveyeng and Improvements* (1523). In *Old English Farming Books* (Crosby Lockwood, 1947) p. 5, G. E. Fussell reverses a previous preference for John as the author and prefers his brother, Sir Anthony a prominent lawyer, on the grounds that John was an obscure squire not mentioned in *Fuller's Worthies*.

16. Fitzherbert, *The Boke of Surveyeng and Improvements* (1523), f. 42 (back).

17. *Ibid.*, f. 45.

18. *Ibid.*, f. 48.

19. *Ibid.*, f. 50.

20. Kerridge, *op. cit.*, p. 248.

21. Thirsk, ed., *op. cit.*, pp. 67, 75, 117–18, 133–4, 159–60, 167, 180. Kerridge, *op. cit.*, pp. 106, 121, 132, 162–72, 203, 207, 219–21, 244–50.

22. John Norden, *The Surveyor's Dialogue* (1607), p. 227.

23. Kerridge, *op. cit.*, p. 249.

24. Cited by Kerridge, p. 345.

25. Cited by Kerridge, p. 250.

26. W. G. Hoskins, 'Harvest fluctuations and English economic history, 1620–1759', *Agricultural History Review*, xvi (1968), 16.

27. William J. Blake, 'Hooker's synopsis chorographical of Devonshire' *Transactions of the Devonshire Association,* xlvii (1915), 343–4. Blake transcribed the first eleven pages of Hooker's manuscript which is in the British Museum (Harleian MS 5827).

28. Tristram Risdon, *The Chorographical Description or Survey of the County of Devon* (1811) p. 11. The passage quoted was not added by the later editors who indeed praised Risdon for his remarks about lime.

29. Thomas Westcote, *A View of Devonshire in 1630* (ed. Rev. George Oliver and Pitman Jones, Exeter, 1845) p. 56. Again the reference is in the original manuscript.

30. For instance references to kilns occur in Cambridge University Library, Additional MSS 3298m.1, lime burner's accounts, Widworthy, 1446–7; PRO, E.315/385 survey of Woodford in Plympton (c.1525); PRO SC 11/174, Rental of Yealmpton, 1548, and SC 11/168, Rental of Stokenham 1548–9. (I am grateful to Dr. Harold Fox for these references). For the kiln at Chudleigh in 1549 see W. G. Hoskins, *Devon* (1954), p. 263 and Exeter City Record Office 48/14/78/1; and for the kiln at Bellamarsh between Chudleigh and Newton Abbot see E. A. G. Clarke, 'The estuarine ports of the Exe and Teign with special reference to the period 1660–1860. A study in historical geography', unpublished Ph.D. thesis, University of London (University College of the South West – now Exeter University – 1956) p. 419.

31. Clarke, *op. cit.*, p. 419 and p. 425.

32. Devon Record Office, Petre papers, 123 M/L 767.

33. Margaret Cash, ed., 'Devon inventories of the sixteenth and seventeenth centuries', *Devon and Cornwall Record Society* xi (1966), 43.

34. Clarke, *op. cit.*, p. 423.

35. Exeter City Record Office, 48/14/120/5ab.

36. Cash, *op. cit.*, p. 75.

37. F. V. Emery, 'West Glamorgan Farming, c. 1580–1620', *The National Library of Wales Journal*, 9 (1955), 399–400. Devon sailors paid a fee called 'Mainboard' or 'Cliffidge' for the right to load limestone. A reference to this occurred in a survey of the demesnes of Oxwith Manor, Gower, made *c.* 1545–55. By 1708 Oxwith was exporting 1,698 tons to north Devon (112 shipments). I am grateful to Mr. Emery for this information. Interestingly, limestone did not appear in north Devon port books of this period because it was unloaded on the seashore opposite the kilns, but Welsh coal and culm were copiously recorded.

See G. J. D. Dunstan, 'The sea-borne trade of Barnstaple, Bideford and Ilfra-combe, 1680–1700' (unpublished B.A. dissertation, Cambridge, 1972). I am grateful to Mr. Dunstan and Dr. Harold Fox for this information. For a good account of early Welsh liming, see Henry Owen, ed., 'The description of Pembrokeshire by George Owen of Henllys, Lord of Kemes' (1603) *Cymmrodorion Record Series* no. i, Part 1 (1892) 70–1; and B. E. Howells 'Pembrokeshire farming, c. 1580–1620', *National Library of Wales Journal*, ix (1955), 239–50, 313–33 and 413–39.

38. R. G. F. Stanes, ed., 'A georgical account of Devonshire and Cornwalle, Samuel Colepresse (1667)' *Transactions of the Devonshire Association*, xcvi (1964) 279–81.

39. H. P. R. Finberg, *Tavistock Abbey: a study in the social and economic history of Devon* (David & Charles, 1965) pp. 89–94.

40. I am grateful to Robin Stanes for this information, derived from his study of the original Milles MSS in the Bodleian Library, Oxford.

41. William Marshall, *The Rural Economy of the West of England* (1796), i, p. 156.

42. I am grateful to Dr. Joan Thirsk for this point.

43. Devon RO, MS list of Barnstaple records (in custody of North Devon Athenaeum, Barnstaple) lease no. 332.

44. Devon RO 1262M Fortescue leases, South Molton 1. The reference to the covenant of 1708 occurs in a sale of 1725.

45. Clarke, *op. cit.,* pp. 423–31.

46. Abraham Hawkins, *Kingsbridge and Salcombe with the intermediate estuary historically and topographically depicted* (1819), pp. 82–3.

47. *Ibid.,* p. 62.

48. Gordon Mingay, ed., *The Agricultural State of the Kingdom, 1816,* Documents of Social History, ed. Anthony Adams (Bath, Adams & Dart, 1970), p. 64.

49. Frank Booker, *The Industrial Archaeology of the Tamar Valley* (David & Charles, 1971), p. 76.

50. I am grateful to Mr Robert Pim and Mr A. M. Chitty for information about lime kilns on the Kingsbridge estuary.

51. Devon RO, 1399M/7/16.

52. Booker, *op. cit.,* pp. 73–7.

53. Devon RO Fortescue MSS 1262/M/E 1/27.

54. Fraser, *op. cit.,* p. 21. The wheat price is from W. H. Beveridge, 'A statistical crime of the seventeenth century', *Journal of Economic and Business History*, i (1929). The year 1793 was chosen as being the year prior to Fraser's date of publication and therefore the probable one to which his lime costs refer.

55. Fraser, *op. cit.,* p. 23.

56. Marshall, *op cit.,* i, pp. 56–7.

57. Marshall, *op. cit.* ii, p. 52.

58. Vancouver, *op. cit.,* p. 113.

59. Vancouver, *op. cit.,* p. 307

60. Devon RO, Nymet Rowland farm accounts, 1107M/E1.

61. Exeter City RO, Diary and accounts of William Ford, 1786–91, transcribed by Elijah Chick, MS/26.

62. Devon RO, Clinton (Rolle) MSS, 96M/Box 2/12. I am grateful to the Devon RO for the loan of some notes on these records made by Miss J. Synar, a former member of the staff.

63. This assumes that the Budleigh hogshead, like the Branscombe one referred to previously (see note 61) contained only 6 bushels and not the customary 8, and that therefore 4 hogsheads weighed 1 ton.

64. Vancouver, *op. cit.,* pp. 140–1.

65. This calculation was made by taking the estimate for Devonshire population in 1750 of 306,524 (see Phylis Deane and W. A. Cole, *British Economic Growth, 1688–1959* (Cambridge University Press, 1962) p. 103) and assuming that there were five persons per family to arrive at an estimate of 61,305 families. If it be assumed that about two-thirds of these were rural (i.e. *c.*40,000) and one-half of the rural families were farmers, the estimated 20,000 farmers results. The estimate is probably too high because Deane and Cole believe the 1750 population figure is too high (possibly by as much as 30 per cent) and my estimates for the proportion of rural families and farmers may also be too high. However the validity of the sample would be altered only marginally if the number of farmers was considerably larger or smaller.

66. The sample has been submitted to a confidence interval test on the assumption that only 1 in 10 of the farmers had leases which fell due in this period (i.e. 2,000 leases). I am grateful to Dr Rolf Ohlsson of Lund University, Sweden (a visiting colleague) for advice and assistance with this section.

67. Devon RO, Fortescue leases, 1262M.

68. Devon RO, Clinton-Rolle MSS, 96M/Box 36/12 and Box 55/6.

69. From Marshall's *Rural Economy of the Midland Counties* (1796) cited in G. E. Mingay, *English Landed Society in the Eighteenth century* (Routledge, 1963) p. 166. See also H. J. Habakkuk, 'Economic functions of landowners in the seventeenth and eighteenth centuries', *Explorations in Entrepreneurial History,* vi (1953) 92–4.

70. W. G. Hoskins, *Devon* (1954) pp. 78–92.

71. Devon RO Fortescue MSS, 1262/M, E/29/17.

6

Vernacular Building in the Oxford Region in the Sixteenth and Seventeenth Centuries

The study of vernacular building can be approached in two ways: by the investigation of the surviving physical structures and by the examination of relevant documentary evidence. Ideally the two should be combined, but there are difficulties in doing this. At the detailed level it is often not possible to relate the most informative documents to particular buildings, certainly where houses in the country are concerned. At the general level the sheer mass of material, both physical and documentary, makes it impossible for all but a team of full-time researchers to undertake a comprehensive assessment of developments in a large area over a substantial period of time.

The present study is limited to a consideration of documentary evidence, but it is concerned with the changes that took place in a whole region over almost two centuries. Its purpose is twofold – to determine the pattern of building development in the area around Oxford between 1500 and 1700, and to throw light on the economic and social conditions which made such developments possible. Basically information has been derived from a single type of document – the probate inventory – and over a thousand of these have been analysed.[1]

The inventory, the study of which was pioneered by Professor Hoskins, is a list, with valuations, of a deceased person's goods and chattels, and was required for the proving of the will. Of course, like all historical documents it is not without some shortcomings. The appraisers, usually friends and neighbours, were sometimes inaccurate and careless, not indicating the occupation of the deceased or omitting the names of the rooms. Furthermore the document represents only a minority of the people.[2] Nevertheless, it is of immense importance in showing how ordinary folk lived, what furniture they used, the different and often changing functions that their rooms fulfilled and the way in which their houses developed over a long period.

Plate 5 A house erected in the latter part of the fifteenth century and now used as a tractor shed at Church Farm, Long Wittenham, Berkshire. It is of cruck construction, having pairs of curving wooden 'blades' (revealed here in the gable end) springing from ground level to support the roof. (Photo, 1960)

The study of vernacular building in this country, carried out on a regional or subregional scale and using documentary evidence, is not new. Professor Barley has established many of the characteristics of smaller dwellings in the Trent Valley, depending largely on evidence obtained from probate inventories.[3] He followed this with two important general surveys of farmhouses and cottages but, excellent though these are,[4] they clearly need to be supported by more detailed investigation of particular areas. The present study is an attempt to remedy that deficiency so far as the Oxford region is concerned.

Plate 6a The interior of Cruckfield Cottage, Long Wittenham, showing a portion of the original medieval house, possibly dating from the early fifteenth century and still in part open to the roof. The chimney-stack on the left is a later insertion. (P. S. Spokes, 1958)

Economic and social conditions are particularly relevant during the period under review for it embraced what has come to be known as the Great Rebuilding, the outlines of which were first traced twenty years ago by Hoskins.[5] Briefly, the sixteenth century was a period of great inflation which saw prices rise more than fourfold. During the next fifty years there was a further rise, but of only 30 per cent, and it was restricted to only 9 per cent in the second half of the seventeenth century.[6] Farmers reaped exceptional benefits, freeholders especially but many leaseholders and copyholders as well,[7] for while their costs remained relatively low, their selling prices rose rapidly if irregularly. Moreover, as they were able to provide many necessities for themselves, they were largely protected from the fluctuations of the open market.

The farmers' growing affluence was shrewdly employed. Their first reaction was to extend and consolidate their holdings and increase their stock. This continued throughout the middle and later decades of the sixteenth century, and during this period the majority in many parts of the country were content to go on living in houses of medieval or submedieval type which were quite out of keeping with their new prosperity. Small, dirty and sparsely furnished, these dwellings at their simplest usually contained only a main living room open to the rafters, with perhaps another room on the ground floor or a rough loft contrived in the roof space by laying boards across the beams (Plates 5 and 6a). Functions were ill-defined in such restricted quarters, and the same room would be used for sleeping and storage. The century was nearing its end before the farmers began to relax and enjoy their wealth. Now, desiring greater comfort and privacy and possibly looking for an opportunity to impress their neighbours, they either extended their medieval dwellings or built entirely new ones (Plate 6b). A complete first floor was incorporated to accommodate an increased number of rooms, and this increase, together with the vastly improved furnishings, gradually led to a greater discrimination between room functions.

Most of the earlier structures had been of timber and wattle-and-daub, and if no alternative materials were available these persisted. But if building stone was easily obtainable this handsome and more durable substitute was used for the new farmhouses, barns and other outbuildings. This remarkable movement – the Great Rebuilding – extended over the whole of southern and midland England and much of the north. It apparently began around 1570, though in certain areas it did not start until some decades later, and it was generally brought to a close by the Civil War. In other parts of the country the commencement was delayed still further. It seems that rebuilding in the east Midlands did not begin until after the Restoration, and then it was normally carried out in brick.[8] Some of the northern counties had to wait until the eighteenth century.

Plate 6b Though it was probably extended in the first half of the sixteenth century, Cruckfield Cottage, Long Wittenham, admirably illustrates what became more commonplace later on. A two-storeyed wing of post-and-truss construction, containing six rooms, has been added to the earlier cruck-framed dwelling of only one storey. The external chimney-stack is later. (Photo, 1960)

How did the farmers of the essentially agricultural Oxford region respond to the favourable economic conditions of the sixteenth century? When did they decide to extend or rebuild their houses and when did the movement cease? Before answering these questions it is necessary to define the region itself which consists, for the purpose of this survey, of that area of Oxfordshire and Berkshire which is bounded on the north by the line of the Cotswold Hills and on the south by the Chilterns and Berkshire Downs (see Fig. 6.1). It extends marginally into the upland masses to embrace the fringe parishes, but in those directions its limits are natural; elsewhere they follow the artificial lines of the county boundaries as in 1972, that of Buckinghamshire to the east and those of Gloucestershire and Wiltshire to the west. The area thus defined is of a considerable size, measuring more than 800 square miles.

Geologically it is, in broad terms, simply compounded, being divided into five distinct parallel belts lying on a south-west to north-east axis. These comprise three ranges of high land with two intervening valleys. To the north is the dipslope of Oolitic Limestones which form the Cotswolds and their eastward extension. South of

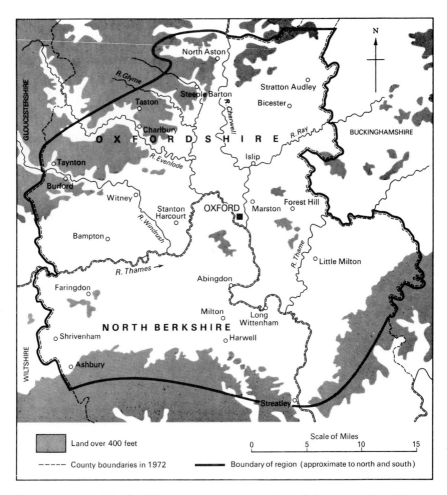

Fig. 6.1   Map of Oxfordshire, showing the location of places mentioned in the text.

that is the Oxford Clay vale, followed by the comparatively low, irregular ridge of the Oxford Heights, which contain the rubbly Corallian and Portlandian Limestones. Then comes the vale of Kimmeridge and Gault Clays, more loamy and therefore more fertile than the Oxford Clay, and finally the Chalk scarpland of the Downs and Chilterns.

The area as a whole was easily accessible, with good communications. By the sixteenth century it was traversed by a number of main roads, some of national importance, and stretches of the Thames carried considerable local traffic. Being fertile, well watered and not over-wooded, the region had never demanded the cultivation by scattered and isolated farmsteads which the bleaker northern and western highlands had enforced on those who colonised them. Its economy and way of life were overwhelmingly agricultural, based on a pattern of settlement that was almost completely established by the eleventh century,[9] and which has persisted substantially unchanged into the twentieth. The unit of settlement was the village, or the hamlet at the least. The most densely populated areas were the belt of Gault Clay and Greensand lying at the foot of the southern scarp, and the wide gravel terraces of the upper Thames. Settlements were also established along the valleys of such upland rivers as the Glyme, Evenlode and Windrush, but the dank clay vale stretching north-east from Oxford attracted fewer people.

There was only one city in the region, Oxford itself, but many thriving market towns with Witney, Bampton, Burford, Bicester, Abingdon and Faringdon among the most notable, and it was in some of these that industries for processing agricultural products – fulling, blanket-making and tanning, for example – were centred. As early as the fourteenth century there were few places that were more than five or six miles from a weekly market,[10] and still, towards the end of the seventeenth century, Robert Plot could claim that looking north-east from a hill near Taynton on a clear day he could see ten market towns.[11]

The one major industry not related to agriculture was that of quarrying and working stone. Before 1500 there was already a concentrated exploitation of the vast and varied limestone deposits – in the Great Oolite and the Corallian measures – which were used for buildings of quality within and well outside the region. By the seventeenth century the area embraced two contrasting vernacular building styles. Broadly speaking, limestone and stone slates were employed in the north and west, with fields bounded by dry-stone walling. In the south and east the timber and thatch tradition was firmly rooted (see Plates 5 and 6b), with comparatively few enclosures surrounded by hedgerows.[12] The villages along the narrow ridge of the Oxford Heights, lying on the border between the two forms, partook to a certain extent of both. These settlements had their own quarries, but their stone houses were often roofed with thatch and their fields were usually hedged. It seems, however, that the stone houses in the intermediate belt (see Plates 7 and 8a and Figs. 6.2 and 6.3) replaced earlier, less substantial dwellings of timber-framed construction,[13] and even in those areas where there was apparently no departure from tradition the visual evidence indicates

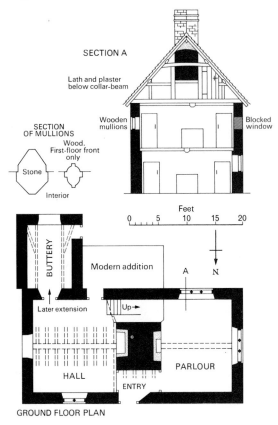

Fig. 6.2   Plan of Fletcher Farm House, Little Milton, Oxfordshire.

that many fine vernacular buildings were erected within a relatively short period, measurable only in decades, as completely new structures or as extensions to older ones. They can be associated, in fact, with the Great Rebuilding.

The social status of the people being studied is shown in Table 6.1.[14] Virtually all included there were dependent on the land in some degree or other; even the craftsmen and tradesmen usually had at least an acre or two and a few head of livestock. Two criteria were observed in selecting the inventories and in defining further the limits of the survey. These were, firstly, that the deceased house-holder should be of yeoman status or below and, secondly, that he should occupy a house of nine rooms or less, nine rooms being adjudged a reasonable upper limit to the size of a yeoman's dwelling.

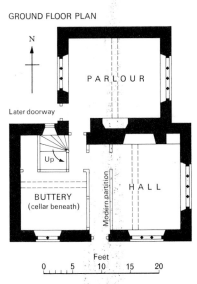

GROUND FLOOR PLAN

Fig. 6.3   Plan of The Garage, Little Milton, Oxfordshire.

However, while these criteria do complement each other, they also conflict to a certain extent. A minority of yeomen lived in houses containing over nine rooms and a small proportion of gentry lived in houses with less, so these, too, have been incorporated.

How did the different social groups fare during the long period from the latter part of the sixteenth century down to 1700? In the majority of cases the statistical evidence is too inadequate for any valid deduc-tions to be made; there are simply not enough samples. The craftsmen and tradesmen are an exception to this, but there are so many different occupations represented here that it would be misleading to generalise about them. There is, in fact, sufficient evidence relat-ing to only two groups, the yeomen and husbandmen, but they are by far the most important.

Despite their importance, however, it is impossible to give a complete definition of either. Even Bacon could only describe the yeomen as 'middle people of a condition between gentlemen and cottagers or peasants'. The yeoman ranked above the husbandman in the social scale (the latter in turn stood above the cottager with little or no land), but this superiority did not rest on a clear-cut

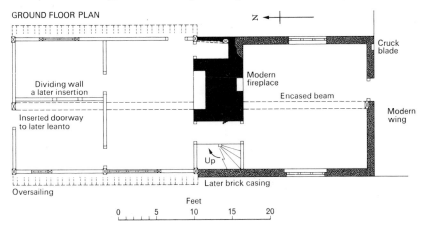

Fig. 6.4   Plan of Church Farm House, Long Wittenham, Oxfordshire.

distinction between freeholder and lease- or copyholder. Though to a large extent the yeoman could be associated with freehold and the husbandman with copyhold tenure, this was not inevitable and both competed for leasehold property. In fact, the term 'freeholder' was loosely used at that time and often included farmers who held long leases extending over several generations. Nor was wealth always a sound indication of status. The yeoman was generally richer than the husbandman, but there were many exceptions to this rule, for there was no clear line of demarcation. In 1640, for example, there were yeomen with a personal estate of less than £50, yet in the same year a husbandman worth £554, though occupying only a three-roomed house, died in the parish of Steeple Barton.

Some of his contemporaries in the reign of James I maintained that the yeoman, a prey to unscrupulous landlords and exorbitant entry fines, belonged to a disappearing class. But if some sank into poverty more had profited by inflation, and it could be more truly claimed that the yeoman stood a better chance of becoming a gentleman than a pauper. Judging from the evidence in Table 6.1, however, it can be seen that in the Oxford region, at any rate, far from moving up or down the social scale, he was most likely to remain where he was. After all, his position was an enviable one; it was dignified, responsible and respected, and free of certain irksome duties and impositions, financial or otherwise, that the gentry were

TABLE 6.1 *Social status of persons making wills (percentages in brackets)*

	(N. Berks. only) 1539–50	1578–1600	1616–20	1636–40	1666–70	1696–1700
Gentry	1 (2)	2 (1)	2 (1)	6 (3)	2 (1)	3 (1·5)
Clergy	1 (2)	1 (0·5)	2 (1)	5 (2·5)	3 (1·5)	1 (0·5)
Yeomen	— —	16 (8)	33 (16·5)	35 (17·5)	58 (29)	72 (36)
Husbandmen	9 (18)	74 (37)	50 (25)	56 (28)	25 (12·5)	19 (9·5)
Craftsmen/ tradesmen	3 (6)	14 (7)	30 (15)	27 (13·5)	50 (25)	44 (22)
Labourers	— —	2 (1)	9 (4·5)	8 (4)	5 (2·5)	8 (4)
Widows/spinsters	4 (8)	16 (8)	39 (19·5)	41 (20·5)	36 (18)	36 (18)
Not stated	31 (62)	74 (37)	35 (17·5)	22 (11)	21 (10·5)	17 (8·5)
total sample	49★ (98)	199★ (99·5)	200 (100)	200 (100)	200 (100)	200 (100)

★ one person had two separate properties

called on to bear. Small wonder, then, that one of the minor social phenomena of the seventeenth century, in this area at least, was that the yeomen more than quadrupled in number and almost entirely, it is clear, at the expense of the husbandmen. There was no specific economic basis for this, for the term 'yeoman' had no clear economic meaning, but the change must be attributable in part to a stimulus given to social aspirations by the increase in wealth.

Throughout the century a steady growth in prosperity, though mild compared with the vast profits made in Elizabeth's reign, helped an increasing number of husbandmen to cross the indefinable barrier between them and yeoman status. The process can be observed time and again when an inventory refers to a husbandman's personal estate whereas his will describes him as the yeoman he aspired to be. Clearly the metamorphosis took time while the neighbours adjusted themselves to it, but it was achieved, and the transition is outlined in Table 6.1. In the latter part of the sixteenth century the husbandmen constituted by far the largest group and outnumbered the yeomen by over four to one. By 1620 the gap had narrowed and there was now a discrepancy of only 50 per cent. This position was maintained for the next twenty years. A generation later it was the yeomen who predominated, enjoying more than double the numerical strength of the husbandmen. This trend continued, and in 1700 there were four yeomen for every husbandman in the area. Of course the husbandmen in their turn gained new members from those lower in the social scale. For example, in 1636 a man recorded as a day labourer in his inventory was described as a husbandman in his will. But this influx was limited and can have compensated little for the drain from above. In little more than a century the relative size of the two groups was completely reversed.

The rise in the level of wealth in the region is illustrated in Table 6.2. As real estate is not valued in the inventories the table in fact understates the true position, but one advantage is that the figures are therefore weighted less heavily against those who were too poor to make a will. In the early North Berkshire sample covering the 1540s 60 per cent of the people had a personal estate of less than £20. By the end of the century in the region as a whole this proportion had been reduced to 32 per cent, though only 8 per cent were worth more than £100. The most marked development came between 1600 and 1640 when the number of people worth less than £20 fell by a third whilst the group of those worth over £100 multiplied fourfold. After 1640, it seems, much of the impetus was lost. The national economy was now less inflationary and conditions were not

TABLE 6.2   *Personal wealth as shown in the inventories*
(percentages in brackets)

	(N. Berks. only) 1539–50	1578–1600	1616–20	1636–40	1666–70	1696–1700
less than £10	16 (32)	34 (17)	19 (9·5)	17 (8·5)	14 (7)	14 (7)
£10–20	14 (28)	30 (15)	36 (18)	27 (13·5)	29 (14·5)	36 (18)
£20–30	2 (4)	25 (12·5)	18 (9)	21 (10·5)	21 (10·5)	22 (11)
£30–40	2 (4)	21 (10·5)	25 (12·5)	23 (11·5)	24 (12)	14 (7)
£40–50	6 (12)	21 (10·5)	16 (8)	9 (4·5)	14 (7)	11 (5·5)
£50–60	4 (8)	12 (6)	14 (7)	11 (5·5)	7 (3·5)	8 (4)
£60–80	2 (4)	17 (8·5)	12 (6)	11 (5·5)	19 (9·5)	17 (8·5)
£80–100	3 (6)	19 (9·5)	15 (7·5)	17 (8·5)	14 (7)	14 (7)
£100–200	1 (2)	11 (5·5)	30 (15)	38 (19)	33 (16·5)	29 (14·5)
£200–300	— —	4 (2)	11 (5·5)	15 (7·5)	9 (4·5)	18 (9)
over £300	— —	2 (1)	4 (2)	9 (4·5)	15 (7·5)	17 (8·5)
total sample	49★ (98)	196★†‡ (98)	200 (100)	198†‡ (99)	199‡ (99·5)	200 (100)

★ one man had two properties
† no valuations given in one inventory
‡ one person insolvent

so favourable to the farmer as they had formerly been. The political situation was also unstable. Whatever the cause, from that date to the end of the seventeenth century the proportion of those worth less than £20 was more or less constant at or just below 25 per cent, and those with a personal estate of over £100 remained at around 30 per cent. There was some variation in the intermediate levels without a significant pattern emerging, though the percentage of those worth over £300 increased gradually and consistently.

Any specific indication of the relative wealth and standing of the yeoman and husbandman is difficult to obtain from the inventories for two reasons. First, the omission from the documents of information about real estate makes the gap between the two groups seem narrower than it actually was, for the yeoman was normally a much bigger landholder; second, the evidence of the personal estate itself can be suspect, so comparisons are sometimes uncertain, as are changes in a single group's fortunes. The main reason for this is that the inventories frequently refer to an apparently poor yeoman or husbandman who has in fact retired from full-scale farming, just keeping back a few animals and a patch of land and perhaps living more or less independently in a part of the house now relinquished to his son. Such documents are misleading about both house size and personal estate, but they are often easy to detect and were omitted from the survey. Some, though, are heavily disguised and a few have probably been missed. For these reasons the findings below relating to wealth must be regarded as rather tentative, though the deductions of average house sizes are valid.

Table 6.3 shows that in the last decade of the sixteenth century the median value of the yeoman's personal estate stood at about £90, about twice as much as the husbandman's median estate at that time. From 1600 down to the outbreak of the Civil War, the period when most of the rebuilding was taking place, the yeoman's median estate rose by 67 per cent to just over £150, but the husbandman's rose by only 27 per cent. The average yeoman was now two and a half times richer than the average husbandman.[15] In those four decades or so the gap between the two had widened, but this could probably be largely explained by the elevation of the more prosperous husbandmen to the ranks of the yeomen, a factor which would prevent the husbandman's median estate from rising in proportion. After 1640 the continued loss of the richer members of the group led to a fall of 25 per cent in the husbandman's median estate during a period of modest inflation. The yeoman was more fortunate, but the median value of his estate did no more than

TABLE 6.3 *Median values of personal estate* and average house sizes*

Period	YEOMEN			HUSBANDMEN		
	No. of Samples	Median Estate	Average No. of Rooms	No. of Samples	Median Estate	Average No. of Rooms
1590–1600	13	£90 10s } rise of 67%	4–5	38	£46 10s } rise of 27%	3–4
1636–40	29	£153 10s	c. 7	47	£59 } fall of 25%	4–5
1696–1700	51	£154 10s	6–7	13	£44	4–5

* to the nearest 10s.

remain constant, and in real terms it probably declined a little. By 1700, however, it was three times as great as that of the husbandman.

How does the pattern of wealth relate to the construction and improvement of houses in the region during the sixteenth and seventeenth centuries? One major drawback to establishing this is the lack of detailed information on the costs of erecting the wide range of buildings (varying in size, materials and quality) at different periods. One can only gain a rough idea from occasional pieces of evidence. For example, a building contract of 1516, earlier than the Berkshire sample of inventories, describes in some detail a farm-house to be built at Holywell, Oxford, for the Warden and Fellows of Merton College.[16] It was of two storeys, with the stone walls 18 ft in height, 3 ft thick on the ground floor and 2 ft 6 in thick on the upper floor. It had a ground floor hall with a fireplace 8 ft wide and a parlour containing a fireplace 4 ft wide. In the rooms above these there were two further fireplaces and two stone 'widdrawts' or privies. There were numerous windows throughout. This building was uncommonly substantial, it was unusual in having two indoor privies, and it cost £29 to erect. This must be an indication of the upper limit to the cost of vernacular building in the area at that time. A hundred years later, in 1618, Robert Loder of Prince's Manor Farm, Harwell, in North Berkshire, apparently laid out £6 10s 'aboute my Chimney . . . making my staires, my window & selling [ceiling] & plastering'.[17] This work, which must have represented the substantial modernisation of an older house, was no doubt Loder's contribution to the rebuilding movement and it gives some idea of the scale of costs incurred then.

It is far more profitable to look at the general picture and to concentrate on house sizes as expressed in the numbers of rooms prevailing throughout the period. A major problem was deciding which rooms should qualify for inclusion in the tables, particularly in view of the haphazard arrangement of some of the inventories. Only those clearly belonging to the main structure have been admitted, principally the hall, kitchen, parlour, chambers, buttery, cellar and lofts. The shop and outhouses have been excluded unless there is some indication (for example, a chamber overhead) that they are part of the main building.

Detailed information about the number of rooms listed in the inventories at different periods is shown in Table 6.4.[18] In the sample of fifty Berkshire inventories for 1539–50 only half contain valid evidence. It would be unwise to deduce too much from such a small selection, but it is significant that there is no house recorded

TABLE 6.4   *Number of rooms mentioned in the inventories (percentages in brackets)*

	(N. Berks. only) 1539–50	1578–1600	1616–20	1636–40	1666–70	1696–1700
none	23 (46)	81 (40·5)	64 (32)	51 (25·5)	48 (24)	43 (21·5)
1	3 (6)	9 (4·5)	4 (2)	3 (1·5)	4 (2)	—
2	9 (18)	31 (15·5)	34 (17)	16 (8)	4 (2)	5 (2·5)
3	8 (16)	29 (14·5)	22 (11)	19 (9·5)	26 (13)	19 (9·5)
4	2 (4)	20 (10)	20 (10)	25 (12·5)	29 (14·5)	35 (17·5)
5	3 (6)	10 (5)	18 (9)	25 (12·5)	30 (15)	24 (12)
6	—	9 (4·5)	13 (6·5)	14 (7)	13 (6·5)	24 (12)
7	—	1 (0·5)	10 (5)	16 (8)	12 (6)	16 (8)
8	—	5 (2·5)	6 (3)	7 (3·5)	11 (5·5)	13 (6·5)
9 or more	—	3 (1·5)	6 (3)	17 (8·5)	16 (8)	14 (7)
doubtful	2 (4)	2 (1)	3 (1·5)	7 (3·5)	7 (3·5)	7 (3·5)
total sample	50 (100)	200 (100)	200 (100)	200 (100)	200 (100)	200 (100)

as having more than five rooms. The dwelling with few rooms clearly preponderates, and twenty out of the twenty-five relevant inventories relate to a medieval or submedieval type having three rooms or less. With regard to the later period for which more documentary information is available, there is evidence in the table of a definite pattern, even allowing for a fair margin of error in sampling. The medieval type of house, that of three rooms or less, was still predominant in the region in 1600. Those inventories which mention individual rooms show that at that date over half of the houses were of this limited size, about a third were of middle size (four to six rooms), and less than a tenth had seven rooms or more. In fact the proportion of small houses must have been much higher: in the early part of the period at least, the majority of inventories in which no rooms are recorded appear to relate to dwellings of three rooms or less; moreover, many people who occupied houses like these would be too poor to make a will and therefore cannot be included in these calculations. The table, then, is weighted throughout against the small house, though to what extent it is impossible to say.

It seems clear that the Great Rebuilding in the Oxford region, if it had been begun before 1600, was not very far advanced by then. But afterwards it progressed very rapidly and was substantially completed by the outbreak of the Civil War. From approximately 1600 onwards the number of houses having over three rooms rose steadily until by 1640 it had more than doubled; the following sixty years saw an increase of less than 20 per cent. As one would expect, the pattern of development followed reasonably closely the growth in personal wealth described earlier. In wider terms the period of highest activity was unexceptional and much the same as that in many other parts of southern England.

With regard to the different types of house recorded in the inventories, the medium-sized dwelling of four to six rooms had established its predominance by 1640, and its numbers continued to grow over the remainder of the period. It was the large house, however, that was most dramatically affected by the rebuilding. Between 1600 and 1640 the number of dwellings with seven rooms or more increased fourfold, though afterwards it remained fairly constant. In the same period the number of small houses fell by almost a half. This, too, remained constant for a few decades, then declined again towards the end of the century. There was no resurgence of the small house such as Hoskins found at Wigston Magna in Leicestershire.[19] On the other hand the house of one to three rooms was in no danger of extinction in the Oxford region. Taking into account the labouring poor not represented in the inventories it is probable that at least a quarter – possibly approaching a half – of the houses in 1700 were of three rooms or less.

The pattern of house sizes does not correspond exactly with the distribution of wealth between the two major social groups. The husbandman's dwelling did not diminish in proportion to his personal estate in the second half of the seventeenth century, which indicates that a reasonable minimum standard of domestic comfort, represented by the four-roomed house, had come to be accepted by the majority. But throughout the whole period there was a difference in size between the average houses of yeomen and husbandmen. As shown in Table 6.3, before 1600 this discrepancy was not so marked and the dwelling of four rooms was common to both, but it became far more noticeable as a result of the rebuilding. By 1640 the characteristic sizes were established for both groups, a house of six or seven rooms for a yeoman and of four or five rooms for the husbandman, and these remained unchanged throughout the century. Of course these houses, especially the larger ones, would contain different combinations of rooms but, judging from the inventories, a three-roomed dwelling would commonly consist of a hall, a lower chamber and an upper chamber or loft. A house of four rooms usually included a hall, a kitchen and two chambers, and a frequent combination in the six-roomed house consisted of a hall, a parlour, a buttery and three chambers.

However, if we are to obtain some understanding of what it was like to live in those times, we must get away from averages and percentages and look more closely at the inventories themselves. Richard Churchhouse of Taston died in 1592. Described as a labourer in his will he is one of the class of very poor who rarely appear in documents as individuals. His inventory is brief,[20] for it required only a few words to indicate the starkness of his existence in his one-roomed hut. His possessions consisted of a covering for the bed, three pairs of sheets and a bolster; a table cloth; two pots, two kettles, a frying-pan, two candlesticks, two platters, one porringer and a saucer; a cover (for the fire, probably); a load of wood; a brandiron (fire-iron supporting logs?); and all the other implements belonging to the house. These, his worldly goods, were valued at 18s 8d.

Compared with Churchhouse, his contemporary, Nicholas Hore, a yeoman of Marston who died in 1593, lived in splendid fashion as can be seen from his inventory, which is worth quoting in full.[21]

In the hall two tables, one cupboard, four joined
stools with glass and wainscot and other furniture
in the same hall   40s

In the parlour one joined bedstead, a featherbed
and curtains, a flock bed, a round table with forms,
'seelings' (wainscot) and glass windows and
also other implements   £6

In the little chamber two chests with hemp and
other implements   30s

In the next chamber a bedstead, two coffers with
wool, two coverlets, three blankets with other
implements   50s

In the chamber over the hall a joined bedstead, a
featherbed, a coverlet, three blankets, a bolster,
a pillow, a chest with other implements   £3 13s 4d

In the chamber over the entry a bedstead, a
featherbed, a coverlet, a quilt, two chests with
other implements   £4

In the maids' chamber one bed, a cupboard, two
blankets, a coverlet with other implements   40s

In the loft over the maids' chamber two beds,
three coverlets, two blankets with other
implements   40s

In the first room without one chest, a rack with
wheat and other implements   34s 4d

A rack, eight sacks, two sheets with corn and
other implements   £3

In the kitchen and brewhouse tables, forms,
cheese press with other implements   10s

Brass pans, pots of brass and other implements   £6

A furnace, a settle, a mill and other implements   £4

In the malthouse one vat with barley in the same   40s

A cheese press, a stone and other implements   5s

Forty quarters of malt appraised at   £20

For lumber over the kitchen   10s

Plough timber over the malthouse with other
implements   26s

In the little stable plough timber and cart timber   20s

In the oxhouse one scaffold with plough timber   20s

In the rickyard two hovels with beans and other
things   £3

Two loads of hay		20s
Three ladders		6s
One hovel with straw and other implements		40s
Three carts with furniture thereunto, ploughs, gear, harrows, chains and yokes	£5	
One sheep house with racks and hovels	£3	
All the wood about the yard	£12	
Two ricks of wheat with hovel posts, standers and barley in the barn	£45	
Sheets, towels, tablecloths, napkins and other napery ware	£13	
Sheep racks and hurdles		7s
Pewter dishes and other vessels		30s
Four hundred sheep	£150	
Eight oxen, seventeen kine	£50	
Five horses	£10	
Bacon		40s
Fourteen hogs	£4	
Hens, geese and ducks		10s
Seventeen acres of wheat on the ground	£9	
Barley and beans sown in the ground	£10	
Sum total	£386 10s 8d	

In his large house containing about nine rooms, Hore lived in considerable comfort. He had wainscot in the hall and parlour, and glass in the windows there. The fact that the glass is recorded at all is an indication that it was a prized possession – and a movable one, too. The other window spaces were probably filled in with lattice 'made either of wicker or fine rifts [strips] of oak in checkerwise',[22] with shutters to keep out draughts and marauders. Glass is mentioned in only eight of the inventories dating from before 1600. References to it in the seventeenth century are also rare, but this is because after 1600 it became a more common feature of domestic comfort and soon ceased to be valued as a movable fixture belonging to the tenant or occupier (see Plate 8b).

There are one or two incongruous details in Hore's inventory – sleeping in the parlour, for example. Room functions in the sixteenth century were not always similar to those with which we are familiar today. Indeed they were sometimes markedly different and often underwent considerable change in the period under review. The main developments in the Oxford region are best examined not by further study of individual inventories but by looking separately and in detail at the most important rooms of the house, relating local features where necessary to a wider context.

Plate 7 The Garage, Little Milton, Oxfordshire, a substantial yeoman's house · dating from 1600 or soon after. It has a cellar, a hall, parlour and buttery on the ground floor, three chambers on the first floor and above these a loft extending over the whole. The improved living standards are indicated particularly by the massive chimney-stack and the large windows. The roof was probably thatched originally. (Photo, 1960)

The principal room was the hall: in fact the medieval small house at its simplest consisted of this one room, open to the roof. Here the occupants cooked, ate, relaxed and slept, and often stored their goods. When additional rooms were contrived in medieval and submedieval times, and even when a whole complex was introduced during the Great Rebuilding, the hall remained as the nucleus of the scheme, the eating and living room of the family, and it continued to be so down to 1700 and beyond. When there was no separate kitchen cooking was still carried on in the hall. In one or two of the documents a bed is recorded there as well, but these are isolated cases. Occasionally in an inventory, even though the other rooms are mentioned by their individual names, the hall is referred to as the 'house' or the 'dwelling house', which further emphasises that it was regarded as the most important part of the structure.[23]

In the southern half of the region, including the whole of North

Plate 8a Fletcher Farm House, Little Milton, might well have been occupied by a well-to-do husbandman and was no doubt erected at the same time as the barn in the background, dated 1638. Originally it contained a hall and parlour on the ground floor, two or three chambers on the first floor and two rooms in the loft above. The roof was once thatched. (Photo, 1960)

Berkshire, the main living room is always described as the hall, but in the north it is referred to on a number of occasions as the 'hall-house'.[24] This term also stresses the room's importance and it is applied to dwellings of six and seven rooms as well as to some having only three. It is unlikely that it was a failing medieval survival for it is first recorded in 1619 – though it was obviously in use well before that date – but instead of dying out as the century progresses the term becomes more and more popular, and the greatest number of references is found in the sample of 1696–1700. Its use seems to be restricted to a definite area and it is because of this that the examples, just over ten in all, are significant. It is recorded at

Bicester and Stratton Audley in the north-east of the region, and at places roughly within the same latitude either just within or on the fringe of the Cotswolds. These appear to form a southern boundary line and the term was probably more widespread to the north. In fact it can be substantially associated with the upland area.

Plate 8b Fletcher Farm House. Window in the chamber over the hall. (Photo, 1960)

The chamber ranked second in importance after the hall. In the Oxford region it was usually the first room to be added to it in sub-medieval times. A chamber, sometimes more than one, is recorded in two-thirds of the inventories listing individual rooms in the earliest Berkshire sample of 1539–50. In the seventeenth century chambers comprised between a quarter and a half of the total number of rooms under the main roof.

In the sixteenth century the chamber was always primarily a sleeping room, though complete specialisation of function was slow and it often contained tables at which meals were presumably served. After that it was sometimes used solely for storage. It began in the rural dwellings as a ground floor addition to, or subdivision of, the hall, and down to about 1600 the majority were of this type.[25] But it is clear from the inventories that even before 1550 a small proportion of chambers were being placed on the first floor. When at the end of the century and in the following decades new houses were built with complete first floors, this type quickly became predominant. However, the ground floor chamber did not disappear; in many of the new buildings it persisted beneath those introduced above it. In 1620 about a half of the houses recorded in the inventories still had a ground floor sleeping chamber. Their numbers decreased in the course of the century, but even in 1700 the arrangement still continued, though in North Berkshire no more than an eighth of the 'middle-class' houses adhered to it and in Oxfordshire the proportion was probably smaller than this.

After the chamber the earliest room to develop a separate function was the kitchen. It is actually listed in over a quarter of the Berkshire samples of 1539–50, and may be implied in a small proportion of the other inventories of that period in which no rooms are mentioned by name. In almost every case it was used for cooking. As the century progressed the kitchen became more common, and in the seventeenth century, it is to be found in the great majority of the houses recorded in the inventories.

Again in most cases the kitchen was primarily the cooking room, but it would often combine a secondary function. According to Barley the Trent Valley kitchen in the seventeenth century differed little in use from the dairy or milkhouse.[26] In the Oxford region it did not lose its identity to this extent, but in a small proportion of inventories it is clear from the furnishings and implements listed there that the hall was being used for cooking and the kitchen was employed in its secondary capacity. There are examples of it serving as a milkhouse, a brewhouse, a buttery, a storage place for general lumber and even, on rare occasions, as a sleeping room for the servants. However, in a very small number of inventories the process is reversed. In these the main living and cooking room is described as the kitchen, and the hall is omitted altogether. These examples are late, two being recorded in 1700 when the inventory of a Witney butcher refers to 'the dwelling Roome or kitchen'.

The kitchen was usually an integral part of the house, though it could be completely detached from the main structure. The reasons for this arrangement and for its survival are obscure, but fear of fire was probably the most important. The detached kitchen derived from medieval times and earlier, but though it was generally dying out in the seventeenth century it was far from dead. Barley and

Hoskins could find no indication of detached kitchens in Trent Valley and Leicestershire inventories,[27] but Fox and Raglan discovered a few surviving examples of seventeenth century date in Monmouthshire,[28]. and the set of surveys made in 1631–32 of the Wiltshire estates of the first Earl of Pembroke and Montgomery shows that of the 355 houses for which there is unequivocal information about 5 per cent had them.[29]

Evidence of similar survivals in the Oxford region is contained in a maximum of twenty or so inventories and glebe terriers,[30] about 2 per cent of the total number of samples. They extend in date from the late sixteenth to the end of the seventeenth century, the greatest number lying in the first forty years of the period. On the whole the evidence is not explicit but it nevertheless seems to be valid. In two inventories, for example, relating to a yeoman of Marston (1636) and to a yeoman of Stanton Harcourt (1670), both a kitchen and an old kitchen are recorded. In each case the former room is the cooking place and an integral part of a good-sized house. The old kitchen is apparently detached, a survival of the medieval dwelling that was replaced during the Great Rebuilding.[31] A terrier of 1634 for the parsonage of Milton records a dwelling house 'and an old Kitchen neere vnto it' (i.e. not adjoining).

In most cases a detached kitchen is suggested when the room is listed among the outbuildings after the appraisal of the main structure has been completed, and this interpretation is supported when the cooking implements are kept in the hall. Occasionally there is a specific reference, particularly in glebe terriers, to an 'out kitchen' or an 'outer kitchen', and as late as 1698 a widow of Forest Hill was keeping general lumber in her 'kitchen or outhouse'.[32] In fact in the Oxford region in the seventeenth century it appears that the detached kitchen was rarely, if ever, used as a cooking place. It was more likely to be used for brewing than for anything else.

The parlour was never really common in the region in the sixteenth and seventeenth centuries. In the Berkshire sample of 1539–50 only two inventories out of fifty record it, and the proportion does not increase appreciably before about 1620. As a result of the rebuilding the parlour appears more frequently from the second quarter of the century onwards, but in 1700 it is still listed in no more than a fourth of the inventories. It seems to have been more popular in Oxfordshire than in North Berkshire.

The parlour was always on the ground floor. It began in the sixteenth century as a sleeping room, and it often continued as such down to 1700 and beyond. But before 1620 the bed was being taken out and the parlour was being used as a withdrawing room, better furnished and more comfortable than the hall. It usually had a fireplace but no cooking was done there, though the parlour was sometimes used for dining and was referred to as the dining-room in the house of an Abingdon linendraper in 1668. The new use as a withdrawing room quickly became fashionable and from the 1630s onwards the parlour ceased to serve as a bedroom in the majority of cases.

The buttery, occasionally referred to as the spence or drinkhouse (the latter term was rarely used), was essentially a ground floor room where the barrels of beer were stored.[33] The pewter and other tableware was frequently kept there; it also served as a general lumber room and was sometimes used for cooking. It commonly opened off the hall or kitchen, though in some cases it adjoined the parlour. The buttery is recorded in one or two inventories before 1550, and at the end of the century is still found in only a small proportion of the houses. After 1600 the number rises. In the first half of the seventeenth century probably about a quarter of the middle-sized dwellings in the region had a buttery; by the end of it roughly half of them had one.

The cellar can hardly be regarded as an important room, but it is worth consideration. It does not appear in the inventories until after 1600, and therefore in the countryside it can be related directly to the rebuilding. It might be incorporated at that time in the extension to a medieval dwelling, but it seems more likely that it was part of a completely new building. A blacksmith of Streatley in 1618 had a cellar in a house that in all probability had only two other rooms, and there are a few examples throughout the century of cellars in houses that consisted of only four or five rooms. On the whole, however, it is to be associated with dwellings containing at least six rooms, and more particularly, nine rooms or more.

Judging from the inventories cellars were not common in the seventeenth century, though there was a very marked increase in their numbers at the end of the period. The cellar was a useful extra room for storing odd equipment and lumber, but its prime function was to take the barrels of home-brewed beer. Even in those few houses that had two cellars both fulfilled much the same purpose.

Limitations of space make it impossible to deal adequately with furnishings and fittings, which increased in quantity, quality and variety from the late sixteenth century onwards.[34] However, certain features are worth examining in some detail for the light which they throw on the domestic standards of the time. Through-

out the sixteenth century the common means of access to the upper
floor of the house was the ladder. It persisted throughout the seventeenth century and, if one includes those poor dwellings not represented in the documents, it was probably still used in the majority
of houses in the region. Certainly the ladder continues to be listed
in the inventories, often located in the house as distinct from the
farmyard. Its particular functions are rarely recorded, but there is an
unequivocal reference of 1669 to the 'Ladder to goe into the chamber' in a dwelling of submedieval type which contained only two
other rooms, the 'Hall house' and a 'Little Drinckhouse'.

A feature of the Great Rebuilding, however, was the introduction
of the fixed staircase, which could be more easily accommodated in
a new and larger dwelling. This is indicated generally by archaeological evidence (see Figs. 6.2, 6.3 and 6.4), but documentary support
is not always forthcoming. For example, the first stairs recorded in
the village of Wigston Magna, Leicestershire, were in a yeoman's
inventory of 1642.[35] In Emmison's study of Bedfordshire inventories for 1617–19 no stairs are recorded at all.[36] The first of the sampled
inventories from the Oxford region to refer to stairs is consequently
quite early. Dated 1595, it relates to a yeoman of Stratton Audley
living in a five-roomed house and mentions the spinning wheel and
press at the top of the 'steeres', which were clearly of quite roomy
construction. Nor was this innovation confined to those of yeoman
status. In 1618 a husbandman in the parish of Shrivenham lived in a
house consisting of only a hall, a buttery and a chamber with a loft
over it. But he was a fairly prosperous man with a personal estate
amounting to over £52 and though he had not enlarged or rebuilt
his dwelling he had installed stairs. There are numerous other
references in later inventories, but undoubtedly stairs were to be
found in a higher proportion of houses than is suggested by the
number of examples quoted above. Being fixed they would only
be mentioned incidentally in the inventories, which were concerned with recording movable goods.

One discovers little from the inventories about sanitary arrange-
ments, but the lack of information is in itself significant. The garde-
robe (a fixed internal privy) is never mentioned, though this is not
surprising for it would generally be associated with a higher class
of housing and was, in any case, part of the structure. It seems that
the chamber pot was not very common. Close stools (commodes)
are listed, but in only five out of over a thousand documents and then,
as one would expect, only in the homes of well-to-do yeomen and
tradesmen. The earliest reference (1588) in the inventory of a Witney

baker is to 'a Square borde with a close stoole in the same' in the chamber over the hall, and the latest in 1698 is to a Charlbury yeoman who had a close stool in his parlour. On the whole it was kept in the upper part of the house. Having made all possible allowances the fact remains that well under 10 per cent of the households in the region had any form of indoor sanitation, including chamber pots, in the sixteenth and seventeenth centuries. The overwhelming majority of the people were dependent on a crude latrine in the garden. Despite the revolution in housing standards life for even the well-to-do in the seventeenth century was in some of its aspects still primitive.

Briefly in conclusion this study has established that there was a consistent pattern of development in vernacular building in the Oxford region during the sixteenth and seventeenth centuries. Housing standards rose dramatically during the period, the most intense activity, the Great Rebuilding, being concentrated roughly between 1600 and 1640, associated with a marked rise in personal wealth during the same decades. Attention has been drawn to the startling increase in the number of yeomen during the seventeenth century, achieved largely at the expense of the husbandmen, and an attempt has been made to draw more precise lines of demarcation between the two social groups in terms of personal wealth and size of house. So far as room functions are concerned the trend was one of increasing specialisation over the period, and there is evidence that in some places the old detached kitchen survived until at least the latter part of the seventeenth century. As regards terminology the use of 'house' and 'hallhouse' for the principal living room suggests that, in some respects, is a case for bringing the dividing line between northern and southern cultures much farther south than has hitherto been permitted.

In general, the picture that has emerged is an unexceptional one. The Oxford region takes its place in the mainstream of the Great Rebuilding movement and its pattern of domestic life during the sixteenth and seventeenth centuries can be firmly associated with southern England. Much more remains to be discovered. Despite the many surviving structures in the area the physical evidence outside Oxford is largely unstudied.[37] Time is short, for the increased affluence and mobility of today have brought the rural parts of the region under great pressure from commuters who live in the countryside but look to the town. We are now in the age of the Great Improving and much may be destroyed through ignorance or indifference. The widespread archaeological exploration of these smaller dwellings is a vital necessity. At least the first steps have now been taken in providing a documentary basis for this.

NOTES AND REFERENCES

1. Professor Hoskins was among the first to appreciate and exploit the potential of this particular type of document, and he has used it widely and sensitively, especially to illustrate early farming practices in 'The Leicestershire farmer in the Sixteenth Century', in *Essays in Leicestershire History* (Liverpool University Press 1950), pp. 123–83. F. W. Steer, *Farm and Cottage Inventories of Mid-Essex, 1635-1749*, (Essex Record Office 1950), is a good introduction to the probate inventory, and there is a useful collection, too, in F. G. Emmison, 'Jacobean household inventories', *Beds. Hist. Rec. Soc.,* xx (1938) drawn mainly from the years 1617–19. An interesting selection of more direct relevance to the Oxford region is to be found in M. A. Havinden, ed., *Household and Farm Inventories in Oxfordshire, 1550–1590*, HMSO HIST. MSS Comm., JP 10 and Oxfordshire Rec. Soc., 44 (1965). The difficulties inherent in analysing probate inventories are discussed in M. W. Barley, 'Farmhouses and cottages, 1550–1725', *Economic History Review,* second series, vii, no. 3 (1955), 291–306.

The wills and inventories for Oxfordshire and Berkshire are deposited in the Bodleian Library, Oxford, in the collections MSS Wills Oxon and MSS Wills Berks. The former contains documents filed in the Oxford Consistory and Archdeaconry Courts; the latter incorporates the probate records of the Court of the Archdeacon of Berkshire. Records relating to peculiars (parishes exempted from the normal jurisdiction of the diocese) are not included in the two collections. However, the peculiars, being relatively small, are of little consequence in a general survey such as this.

The sampling method adopted was dictated by the nature of the documents themselves and by the time available. The object was to obtain samples of valid inventories that were large enough for worthwhile conclusions to be drawn. A total of 150 Oxfordshire and 50 Berkshire inventories was decided upon for each sampling period, and these were selected in random fashion but spread as evenly as possible over the years. The standard periods were set at five years each, a length of time that would reflect conditions with a fair degree of uniformity. But suitable inventories are only thinly scattered in the sixteenth century, so the early sampling periods had to be extended if sufficient documents were to be obtained. Consequently the period 1578 (the date of the first Oxfordshire inventory) to 1600 was taken as being equivalent to the later ones of five years each, and as the Berkshire inventories begin in 1539, a further period 1539–50, relating to Berkshire alone, was introduced to give some idea of the conditions prevailing in the first half of the sixteenth century.

The samples had to be taken at suitable intervals to illustrate the trends in housing development. An interval of twenty years was selected as being reasonable, and ideally this should have been maintained throughout the series. However, in the sixteenth century the documents were too limited in number for this to be possible, and the seventeenth century, to which most of the inventories relate, was a troubled period, so the sampling had to be planned in such a way that it would avoid the upheaval of the Civil War and the Commonwealth. The final sequence is as follows: 1539–50 for Berkshire, then for Berkshire and Oxfordshire together 1578–1600, 1616–20, 1636–40, 1666–70 and 1696–1700. The sampling was not taken beyond 1700 because the practice of making inventories generally declined in the eighteenth century and because, in the Oxford region, the visual evidence indicates that the great period of building activity was over by then.

The vast majority of the inventories inevitably refer to houses in the countryside, because that was where most of the people lived. A small percentage of the documents relates to town houses, but it was felt that this would not invalidate any conclusions which might be drawn about rural conditions.

2. Barley, *loc. cit.*, 292. After comparing the number of wills proved with the number of adult burials recorded in a parish in the peculiar of Southwell and setting this against certain Trent Valley villages, he came to the conclusion that 'it is clear that inventories in general relate to less than half the population, and within these limits the decline in their numbers after 1700 is such as to render comparisons dangerous'. However, in his assessment of wills as a proportion of adult burials during the period 1570–1725, his lowest *calculated* figure is 21 per cent and his most generous *estimate* only 40 per cent. Furthermore, a will is not always accompanied by an inventory. Certainly in the collections for Oxfordshire and Berkshire a high proportion of wills do not have inventories with them. Thus one might well claim that inventories in general relate to no more than a third of the people.

Nevertheless it appears that the samples in the present survey are of respectable size. (I am indebted to M. A. Havinden for bringing the following sources of information to my notice.) P. Deane and W. A. Cole, *British Economic Growth, 1688–1959*, (Cambridge University Press, 2nd edn, 1967), p. 103, gives estimates for the Oxfordshire population in 1701 as 84,005 and for Berkshire as 76,790, making a total of 160, 795. The Oxford region, as defined for this study, might have contained half this, i.e. 80,000 people – perhaps 15–20,000 families. Thus 200 inventories represent a 1 per cent sample, or larger, of all *families*.

The figures relating to mortality confirm this. Deane and Cole (p. 131) give an average death rate in 1701 of 30 per 1,000 people in Oxfordshire and 32·1 per 1,000 in Berkshire. If this is applied as a further average of 31 per 1,000 to the 80,000 people in the Oxford region at that time, it works out as 2,480 deaths a year (*c.*1700) or 12,400 deaths over the period 1696–1700. The 200 inventories thus represent 1·6 per cent of all deaths, *including children*. All of these calculations relate to the end of the survey period. Two hundred inventories would represent a larger sample at earlier points in the seventeenth century when the population of the area was smaller and the death rate higher.

3. Statistical analysis of the Oxfordshire and Berkshire inventories largely follows the methods adopted in Barley's pioneer study. These seemed to work satisfactorily in practice and this approach should make it easier to compare results.

4. M. W. Barley, *The English Farmhouse and Cottage* (Routledge, 1961), and 'Rural housing in England', in J. Thirsk, ed., *The Agrarian History of England and Wales*, vol. iv: *1500–1640* (Cambridge University Press, 1967), pp. 696–766.

5. W. G. Hoskins, 'The rebuilding of rural England, 1570–1640', *Past and Present*, no. 4 (1953), 44–59, reprinted in Hoskins, *Provincial England*, (1965), pp. 131–48.

6. Based on median indices calculated for the first and last decades of the sixteenth century, the 1640s and the last decade of the seventeenth century from statistical tables in E. H. Phelps-Brown and S. V. Hopkins, 'Seven centuries of the prices of consumables, compared with builders' wage-rates', *Economica*, new series, xxxiii (1956), 312–13. The pattern accords closely with the rise in median values for the average prices of all agricultural products in the same decades during the period 1500–1649 (see Statistical Appendix in Thirsk, *op. cit.*, pp. 847–50).

7. Copyholders were tenant farmers with prescribed obligations to their landlords. Their rents and entry fines were often low and landlords had some difficulty in raising them owing to the constraints of earlier manorial custom, on which they were based.

8. Barley, 'Farmhouses and cottages, 1550–1725', 293–4.

9. A. F. Martin and R. W. Steel, eds., *The Oxford Region* (Oxford University Press, 1954), p. 103.

10. *Ibid.*, p. 108.

11. R. Plot, *The Natural History of Oxfordshire* (2nd edn, rev., 1705), p. 69. The market towns were not particularly large settlements by modern standards. For example, it seems from R. H. Gretton, *The Burford Records*, (1920), 189–91, 207–9, that Burford had some 700 inhabitants in the 1540s, about 1,000 in the 1590s and approximately 900 in the 1680s.

12. Also, in the south-west, 'clunch' or chalkstone from the Berkshire Downs was used locally. For example, it was employed in the construction of Ashbury church in the fourteenth and fifteenth centuries and of the old manor house, parts of which date back to before 1500. There is evidence in the same village of its use in vernacular building as late as the seventeenth century.

13. D. Portman, 'Little Milton – the rebuilding of an Oxfordshire village', *Oxoniensia*, xxv (1960), 50.

14. Table 6.1 shows that people of all degrees of social status were represented throughout the whole of the study period (there were doubtless yeomen and labourers among those in the 1539–50 sample whose inventories did not state their occupation). The proportions of gentry and clergy remain small, as one would expect. At the other end of the social scale the proportion of labourers is fairly constant throughout the seventeenth century. That of craftsmen and tradesmen rises irregularly but progressively. These features seem part of a consistent pattern, strongly supporting the view that any changes reflected in the inventories over the study period were real ones and not statistical illusions brought about by substantial variations in the practice of making wills and inventories.

15. Compare these findings with those of Hoskins in 'The Leicestershire farmer in the seventeenth century', *Agricultural History*, xxv, (1951), 12, subsequently reprinted in Hoskins, *Provincial England*. In that county the median value of

husbandmen's personal estates rose by about 60 per cent between 1588 and 1640. At the outbreak of the Civil War the average yeoman was well over twice as prosperous as the average husbandman.

16. L. F. Salzman, *Building in England down to 1540* (Clarendon Press, 1952), pp. 570–1. This farmhouse seems to be the original part of the surviving Holywell Manor (see Royal Commission on Historical Monuments, *An Inventory of the Historical Monuments in the City of Oxford,* 1939, pp. 182–3).

17. G. E. Fussell, ed., *Robert Loder's Farm Accounts, 1610–20*, Camden Soc., third series, liii, (1936), 157.

18. No assumptions have been made, for purposes of analysis, about the number of rooms that might be referred to in inventories where none have been listed by name or where the evidence is confused. They have simply been recorded in the Table under 'none' and 'doubtful'. Of course, though there is a high proportion of inventories that do not give the names of the rooms, these have not been excluded as being invalid, for the other information contained in the document is relevant. Furthermore, to discard them might well result in serious distortion.

19. W. G. Hoskins, *The Midland Peasant,* (Macmillan, 1957), p. 301.

20. MSS Wills Oxon, 10/3/34.

21. MSS Wills Oxon. 29/2/27.

22. William Harrison, *The Description of England,* ed. G. Edelen, (Cornell University Press, New York, 1968), p. 197. Harrison's portrait of Elizabethan society first appeared in 1577. A second, revised edition was published in 1587.

23. 'In 1700 the frontier between those who still called the living-room the *house,* in the northern fashion, and those who used the southern word *hall,* ran through south Lincolnshire, Leicestershire and Staffordshire' (Barley, *The English Farmhouse and Cottage,* 260–1). The evidence in the Oxford region suggests that this dividing line may require revision.

24. The term was also used in Yorkshire, for example (see S.O. Addy, *The Evolution of the English House,* revised J. Summerson, (Allen and Unwin, 1933), p. 80.

25. Barley (*The English Farmhouse and Cottage,* 44) points out that the use of 'chamber' for ground floor rooms, including sleeping rooms, distinguishes the south-eastern counties, as far north as Bedfordshire and Oxfordshire, from the rest of England where functional names such as parlour and buttery were in general use in Elizabethan times.

26. 'Farmhouses and cottages, 1550–1725', 297.

27. Barley, *ibid.,* 298; Hoskins, *Midland Peasant,* p. 287. Barley, however, found that they were sometimes suggested in glebe terriers, an ecclesiastical record of the buildings, land, tithes and other emoluments associated with a particular living.

28. Sir Cyril Fox and Lord Raglan, *Monmouthshire Houses,* iii, Welsh Folk Museum, (1954), 115–19.

29. E. Kerridge, ed., *Surveys of the Manors of Philip, first earl of Pembroke and Montgomery, 1631–2,* Records Branch of Wilts. Arch., and Nat. Hist. Soc. (1953). Information on the evidence for detached kitchens in the surveys from Hoskins, *Midland Peasant,* p. 287.

30. The glebe terriers for Oxfordshire and Berkshire are also deposited in the Bodleian Library in the collections MSS Oxf. Archd. papers, Oxon b. 40–41 and MSS Oxf. Archd. papers, Berks c. 185–6. They are scattered at intervals throughout the seventeenth century, but most of them date from the period 1634–85. Many, however, are invalidated by their cursory reference to the main building.

31. It may well be, as Hoskins tentatively suggests (*Midland Peasant*, pp. 287–8), that the detached kitchen in some cases occupies the old medieval dwelling house, which was allowed to remain when a new one was erected·nearby in the late sixteenth or early seventeenth century. Occasionally in the Oxford region a detached kitchen implied in the inventories is closely associated with another outbuilding – a millhouse or brewhouse, for example – which could indicate a former two-roomed house. But there is no definite evidence for or against the theory, which can really be tested only by archaeological investigation.

32. It seems that the outer kitchen was often attached to other outbuildings which might in turn be attached to the main structure, but the kitchen would be detached in a sense in that it would be removed from the living quarters and there would be no internal communication between them.

33. In the 1570s the wife of William Harrison, a contemporary chronicler, would make 200 gallons each month at a cost of 20*s*. (Harrison, *Description of England*, ed. Edelen, pp. 137–8).

34. Further information on these is to be found in D. Portman, 'The Development of Smaller Domestic Architecture in the Oxford Region from the late fifteenth to the early eighteenth century,' 1960, chap. 4 (unpublished B. Litt. thesis presented at Oxford University and deposited in the Bodleian Library).

35. Hoskins, *Midland Peasant*, p. 290.

36. *Ibid.*, p. 291.

37. Some limited investigations have been carried out, e.g., D. Portman, 'Cruck houses in Long Wittenham', *Berks. Arch. Journ.*, lvi (1958), 35–45; 'Little Milton – the rebuilding of an Oxfordshire village', *Oxoniensia*, xxv (1960), 49–63, by the same author; and J. M. Fletcher, 'Three medieval farmhouses in Harwell,' *Berks. Arch. Journ.*, lxii (1965–66), 45–69. J. Fletcher has also made a wider study of a particular feature in 'Crucks in the West Berkshire and Oxford region', *Oxoniensia*, xxxiii (1968), 71–88. However, as yet there is no comprehensive assessment to match that made by Wood-Jones of the area immediately to the north of the region, covering the period 1300–1800 (see R. B. Wood-Jones, *Traditional Domestic Architecture of the Banbury Region*, Manchester University Press, 1963).

Kentish Family Portrait

To a student of sixteenth- or seventeenth-century England, one of the most remarkable features of Victorian society is the enormous size of the leisured and professional classes. In the reign of Queen Elizabeth I or James I the social order still consisted predominantly of peers, knights and squires; merchants, tradesmen and craftsmen; yeomen, husbandmen and labourers. There had always been some professional people, of course – clerics, notaries, lawyers, doctors, schoolmasters – and there is plenty of evidence for the expansion of their numbers during the seventeenth century, or in a city like York in the sixteenth. Yet before the Civil War there was very little that was truly comparable with the thousands of 'private residents' recorded in the 'Court Lists' of mid-Victorian directories. These 'Court Lists' or 'Court Directories' consisted largely of the leisured classes and the upper echelons of the professions. In the county of Kent alone the 'Court Directory' in Kelly's *Post Office Directory* of 1870 lists more than 16,000 'private residents'.[1] Of these about 7,000 lived in the Greater London area, in such parishes as Greenwich, Woolwich, Lewisham, and Plumstead, and these must more properly be regarded as belonging to the metropolis. Yet in the county proper, in the towns and villages of the genuine countryside, there were at least 9,000 families who were carefully distinguished in the directory of 1870 from the manufacturing, commercial, and farming classes of the shire.

Of these 9,000, about 500 or 600 were titled magnates or landed gentry living on the rents from their estates. The remainder, or more than 8,000, consisted predominantly of professional people and families evidently living in the style of gentry, supported by their own private means, although not possessing any considerable landed property. Few of these 8,000 appear in the *Return of Owners of Land, 1873*, which lists all the 7,800 proprietors in Kent possessing more than an acre of land, and none of them appears with any property to speak of. Of course the compiler of the directory of 1870 drew his net as widely as possible so as to avoid giving offence. We need not believe that everyone in his Court List was, in any recognisable sense, a 'gentleman'. Yet, when all allowance is made, it is clear that there was a very large class of families of independent means in the county; and this class of 'pseudo-gentry', as the present writer has ventured to call them, was very largely a creation of the two centuries or so before Queen Victoria. The 9,000 families must have represented about 50,000 people in the county as a whole out of a total population (outside Greater London) of 550,000 inhabitants.[2] It is true that this class of persons was exceptionally numerous in Kent. Quite apart from the strictly 'leisured' class, the professional classes in the county were more numerous than in any other part of England – to wit 30,000 in 1861 – though the figures for Lancashire, Hampshire, Yorkshire, and Devon (with 24,000 – 29,000 each) came close to those for Kent.[3] Yet the rise of the pseudo-gentry was by no means a peculiarity of Kent or of southern England. It was also very striking in counties such as Devon and Northamptonshire, for example, and it was to be found in greater or less degree in every part of the kingdom.

There is no space in these pages to pursue the history of this class as a whole; but it is arguable that their social rise between Charles I's reign and Queen Victoria's formed as important a development in English history as the more frequently discussed rise of the landed gentry in the generations before the Civil War. It was during their period of emergence, in the eighteenth century, that the word *class* itself came to acquire its modern connotation of a division of society according to status. It was not used in this sense in the seventeenth or early eighteenth century, and according to the *Oxford Dictionary* its current meaning did not come into literary use till about 1770. In the present writer's opinion this semantic development was intimately connected with the emergence of the pseudo-gentry in this period as a distinct and self-conscious social order.

Broadly speaking the origins of the pseudo-gentry may be

grouped under two headings. A large number derived from entirely new families who had risen from the ranks of local husband-men, yeomen and tradesmen, often during the later seventeenth and eighteenth centuries. Such families rarely at any time in their history possessed much landed property: they often rose into the lower echelons of the armigerous class, but they were not closely allied, in Kent at least, with the major historic gentry of the county like the Derings, Twysdens and Knatchbulls. By no means all the pseudo-gentry stemmed from yeomen and tradesmen, however. A very large number, possibly the majority, were landless descen-dants of the old county families of Kent. During the seventeenth and eighteenth centuries many of these ancient dynasties – Boyses, Denne and Filmers, for example – had proved remarkably prolific. As their numbers increased, their comparatively modest estates proved incapable of supporting their younger sons as well as the eldest in the style of gentry. These landless scions of the old stock were thus driven to augment their fortunes by some other source of wealth – trade, church, law, navy, army, or the like – in order to maintain their port as gentlemen.

This essay traces the history of a single example of a pseudo-gentry family, that of the Kentish historian Edward Hasted (1732–1812). Owing to the historian's own passion for recording facts and to the magpie habits of his descendants, it is possible to reconstruct a more intimate and telling picture of the Hasteds than is normally possible with families of this standing. They were not, it is true, in all respects typical of their class, since for a short period in the eighteenth century, unlike most of the pseudo-gentry, they held con-siderable landed property. Yet in their changing social attitudes and their varying economic fortunes between the sixteenth century and the nineteenth they reflected many characteristic developments of their period and their class.

The Hasteds were not an ancient family in the sense of deriving from one of the great county dynasties of Kent. They were typical, rather, of those newly leisured families who stemmed from the ranks of yeomen and tradesmen. Neither were they an ancient family in the sense of remaining rooted for centuries in a single spot, like the Cholwiches and Sokespitches of Devon, whose history has been recounted by Professor Hoskins with such insight and illumination.[4] They were, however, a profoundly local family in the sense that they originated in the county at a very remote period and remained throughout their history rooted in the same area. The surname itself is still found in Kent and the adjoining parts of Sussex, beyond which even today it is rarely met with. In its varying forms it occurs twenty-four times in the current telephone directories for the Canterbury and Tunbridge Wells areas, which between them cover Kent and East Sussex.[5] There are grounds for believing that all those who now bear the surname in Kent, and possibly some scores of others bearing another local surname, that of Isted, may be descended from a single common ancestor in the early medieval period. None of those who bear the surname of Hasted today, however, can be closely related to the branch of the family described in these pages. Though the historian had a large family, his descendants died out in both the male and the female line in the 1850s. With their extinction the historian's branch of the family itself came to an end.

Despite the fact that Edward Hasted and his great *History and Topographical Survey of the County of Kent*, with its 7,000 pages and three million words, have been household words in Kent for nearly two centuries, there is no biography of the author and no history of the family in print. Until recently the only serious account of the historian was the brief and not entirely accurate notice in the *Dictionary of National Biography*. So far as the *History* and its author are concerned, the present writer attempted to compile a more complete account for the Introduction to the new edition of the *History and Topographical Survey*, published in 1972.[6] The present essay attempts to bring together the available evidence for the history of the family as a whole.

Although there is no history of the Hasteds, the surviving evidence, if scattered and amorphous, is in fact considerable. Neither of the two collections of Hasted family papers is particularly extensive, but almost every document they contain is of some significance. The Hasted manuscripts in the Eastgate House Museum at Rochester consist principally of rentals, estate documents, and legal papers; correspondence relating to the historian and his descendants; and a diary and account book of his son, the Rev. Edward Hasted of Hollingbourne.[7] This collection is particularly interesting for the light it sheds on the economic vicissitudes of the family between 1750 and 1850: the vast expenditure on the *History*, the eventual loss of the family estates, the imprisonment of the historian for debt, and the ruses his children were driven to adopt in order to maintain their standing as gentlemen.

The Hasted papers in the Maidstone Museum are more extensive than those at Rochester and contain two items of particular interest.[8] The first is a collection of letters of Edward Hasted to Thomas Astle of the British Museum between 1763 and 1801. These provide a remarkable picture of the English antiquarian world of the time, with its delightful *camaraderie* of learning and pleasure. Many contemporary scholars appear in the letters, including Bryan Faussett, Sir Joseph Ayloffe and Andrew Ducarel.[9] The second item at Maidstone is the 'Anecdotes of the Hasted Family', compiled by the historian himself in 1800, whilst imprisoned for debt in the King's Bench. Of all the family papers the 'Anecdotes' are certainly the most interesting. Indeed, although they are incomplete, breaking off after the first few pages of 'Book the Second', about the year 1770, they form an extraordinarily revealing record of a family of minor gentry during the late seventeenth and eighteenth centuries. They run to about 12,000 words, and their artless yet graphic phrasing sheds a vivid light not only on the personalities of the Hasteds but on the subtle nuances of contemporary class distinctions and the niceties of domestic manners. They record in remarkable detail the changing social habits of a family that hovered uneasily, during these generations, between wealth and poverty, between gentility and trade.[10]

FAMILY FOREBEARS

In the family's own account of its history, the Hasteds of Kent derived from a family of Hampshire gentry named Hausted. According to this version the Rev. John Hausted of Hampshire, an Elizabethan divine who died in 1596, married a sister of Sir Coniers Clifford by whom he had a son John, whose son Laurence, of Sonning in Berkshire, was the historian's great-great-grandfather.[11] These family claims to a genteel ancestry of some antiquity were accepted by Edward Hasted the historian, but they were dismissed with scorn by the editor of the 'Anecdotes' in 1904.

> It has generally been assumed . . . that Edward Hasted was a man of position in the county. . . . This can hardly be accepted as a correct account. Joseph Hasted, the historian's grandfather, was born in the city of Canterbury in the year 1662, of a respectable yeoman stock which had been settled in or near Canterbury for at least a hundred years previously, and there seems no ground whatever for assuming any connexion with the Hausteds of Hampshire or elsewhere.[12]

These strictures are too positive. Hasted was certainly a man of some position in Kent, both as a landowner and as an unusually active JP: and the inaccuracy of many of the editor's statements and references does not inspire confidence in his version of the story generally. The truth, as we might expect, is both more complex and more interesting.

The historian can probably be acquitted of conscious dishonesty in accepting the family tradition, but it is practically certain that his paternal ancestry was entirely Kentish in origin. One cannot be absolutely sure on this point because it is just possible that he himself was in possession of evidence proving his descent from Laurence Ha(u)sted of Sonning which has since disappeared.[13]

The historian's ancestry is definitely traceable only as far back as his great-grandfather, Moses Hasted of St Peter's parish in Canterbury, who married Mary Goslin, of the same parish, in St Alphege's church in 1657.[14] Thus far there is no dispute, and Hasted himself gives the facts quite correctly. Unfortunately it is impossible to say positively who was the father of Moses Hasted. According to the family tradition repeated by the historian, as already remarked, he was Laurence Ha(u)sted of Sonning. The editor of the 'Anecdotes' talks vaguely of 'respectable yeoman stock', but he cites no precise evidence for this assertion and so far as Moses Hasted's immediate forebears are concerned it is probably wrong. Moses Hasted himself was certainly not a yeoman; he was a tailor in Canterbury and most likely a native of the city, though he may possibly have come from outside it since he acquired his freedom in 1671 by purchase, not by apprenticeship or inheritance.[15] The fact that he was a tailor (not usually at all a wealthy occupation at this date) makes it unlikely, though not absolutely impossible, that he came of an armigerous family of some standing in Hampshire and Berkshire. The fact that it was only with his son Joseph that the family assumed the coat of arms that Hasted himself bore reinforces these doubts, although Joseph was permitted by the Heralds to adopt the coat of the Hampshire Hausteds. The most interesting piece of evidence in favour of a local origin, however, is the fact that the family surname of Hasted is found in Canterbury at least as early as 1544, when George Haysted, son of John Haysted, was baptised in the church of St George.[16] It is possible that these Haysteds were not ancestors of the historian; the connection cannot at present be absolutely proved; but with so unusual and localised a surname it is difficult not to think that there was a definite link with Moses Hasted.

What in fact is the origin of the historian's surname? There can be very little doubt that the Canterbury family was in fact simply one branch of a fairly numerous clan of Kentish husbandmen and small yeomen in the fifteenth to nineteenth centuries, whose surname was spelt in a bewildering variety of ways: Hasted, Haisted, Heighsted, Heysted, Haysted, Hoysted, Hysted, Hyested, Histed, Highsted.[17] Despite this variation in spelling, it is virtually certain that all these forms represent the same patronymic and ultimately the same family. Rural dialects could still be highly localised in this period, and it is of some significance in this connection that the historian's own family evidently pronounced their name as Hay-sted, a form that in Kentish speech might well be assimilated with that of Hoysted and Hysted. The common modern pronunciation of the name as Hassted is simply a vulgarism with no historical validity.[18] Certainly the Hasteds, Heysteds, Heighsteds, and Hysteds were related: occasionally, indeed, these different spellings occur in the same will. It is just possible that the Hoysteds were of a different family, but it does not seem at all probable. As has already been remarked, another characteristically Kentish surname, that of Isted, may well stem from the same root.

Although the family of Hasted and its variants was fairly widespread in Kent, it was particularly associated, outside Canterbury, with a small group of eight or nine parishes in the centre of the county, lying between Faversham, Sittingbourne, Hollingbourne, and Lenham. This suggests that it most probably originated at a farm settlement in this area, a mile or so south of Sittingbourne, called Highsted or Highsted Forstal.[19] The suggestion is confirmed by the appearance of Highsted in medieval records in such forms as *Heystede* and *Heghstede*. The historian of Kent, one suspects, might not have been entirely gratified to find that he had so many lowly relations; but it would undoubtedly have appealed to his sense of local patriotism to learn that he was far more completely Kentish than he thought.

Today Highsted Forstal is a pleasant but unpretentious red brick farmhouse, probably dating from about the end of the eighteenth century, and lying in a hollow of the downs. The name itself is an ancient one, however, originating soon after the Conquest if not earlier and recorded in feet of fines in the late twelfth century. Originally Highsted (the 'high place') must have referred to the settlement on the hilltop above the present farm, whilst the 'forstal' in the valley beneath it, like most places bearing this local suffix (= 'fore-stall', or enclosure in front [of a house]) was doubtless a subsequent settlement formed from it. Though it cannot be proved conclusively, there is presumptive evidence that all those bearing the surname of Highsted and its many variant forms may have derived from a single common ancestor of this name who held Highsted in the late twelfth century. There are many hundreds of Kentish families with precisely this kind of origin. Like their counterparts in Devonshire, as Professor Hoskins has described them, they frequently assumed their surnames from the farm settlements they carved out of the uncolonised woodland during the two centuries or so following the Conquest. This was the ultimate origin not only of families of pseudo-gentry like the Hasteds, but of great county dynasties like the Twysdens of Twysden, of families who throughout their history remained obscure village gentry like the Blaxlands of Blaxland, and of many more who never rose above the rank of yeoman or husbandman, like the Wickendens of Wickenden. The Highsteds, Heighsteds, and Hasteds could thus have hardly had a more characteristically and completely Kentish origin.

So far as the present writer knows, the family surname has remained thoughout its history an entirely local one. The name of Hasted does occur, it is true, in Suffolk, particularly in the neighbourhood of Bury St Edmunds; but the Suffolk Hasteds had a different origin, probably deriving from the village of Hawstead near Bury.[20] It is curious to note that one of the earliest instances of the name Hasted or Hysted in a Kentish will refers to the parish of Hollingbourne, where the last representative of the historian's family in England, his eldest son Edward, died as vicar 330 years later in 1855. Equally curious is the fact that in 1851 this vicar was employing as a gardener or odd-job man a villager of the name of Hysted, who must have been his own very distant kinsman and who was probably a descendant of the original Hysteds or Heysteds of Hollingbourne in Henry VIII's reign.[21]

From Moses Hasted onwards the pedigree of the historian's branch of the family is minutely and correctly recorded in the 'Anecdotes'. Of Moses himself little is known except his remarkable marital persistence in wedding three successive wives bearing the name of Mary, by all of whom he had children.[22] The portrait supposedly of him in the Maidstone Museum, in which he is represented as a splendidly bewigged Cavalier of the Restoration period, must be incorrectly attributed, though it came from the Hasted family collection. Despite what the family later came to believe about its origins, and what the Heralds were induced to believe about them, there is no reason to think that Moses was ever anything more than a moderately well-to-do tailor in Canterbury, though his second wife was the daughter of a minor armigerous family at Faversham. The Hasteds thus represented the kind of pseudo-gentry who thrust upwards from below rather than those – like the historian's own antiquarian friends William Boys and William Boteler – who were landless descendants of medieval knights and Tudor squires.

It was Moses's son Joseph, by his first wife Mary Goslin of Canterbury, who was the real founder of the family fortunes. Joseph was clearly a man of remarkable character, though whence he derived his surprising gifts it is impossible to say. He was born in 1662 and died in 1732. He was apprenticed first to his father in Canterbury and then to a painter stainer, probably in the dockyard at Chatham. The painter stainer eventually became Chief Painter to the Royal Navy at Chatham, and Joseph Hasted not only succeeded him in this employment but married his kinswoman Katherine, daughter of Richard Yardley of Abchurch Lane, London, whose wife, a Miss Walker, was the sister of Joseph's master. Although Richard Yardley and his wife's family were themselves London tradesmen, they both came of minor armigerous families who had many kinsmen in the Chatham and Rochester area of Kent, who were of the same social standing as themselves. The marriage marked, therefore, a definite social advance for the Canterbury tailor's son, who as already remarked signalled his progress by assuming a coat of arms of his own, derived from that of the Hausteds of Hampshire.[23]

His advance was more than social. By some means which is not altogether obvious he also managed to acquire very considerable wealth. According to the historian it was acquired by means of his office as Chief Painter to the navy.

> The great emoluments of this employment arose from the vast cost which the gilding of the sterns and other carved work of the Men of Wars [*sic*] occasioned, the expense of which, as the navy increased, was so enormous that it was wholly left off at the end of that or at the beginning of the next reign of King George I, and common paint was instituted in the room of it. On this change Mr Joseph H[asted] resigned his place as not worth the keeping, and at first he was partner with his [wife's] uncle, and on his death succeeded solely to it.[24]

However his wealth was acquired, and whether honestly or not, Joseph Hasted was certainly a very shrewd man of business. After leaving the royal service he began gradually to amass the landed property in Kent which formed the basis of his son's and his grandson's inheritance. This consisted chiefly of scattered farms and small parcels of land in a dozen different parishes, mostly near Rochester, whose value by the time of his death amounted to nearly £1,000 per annum. He also speculated to some extent in the financial world of the time, though he lost heavily in the South Sea Bubble. In acquiring landed property in this way Joseph Hasted was in a sense not entirely

typical of the new pseudo-gentry class of his time. But his farm-
lands in fact constituted a form of investment rather than the basis of
a manorial estate. About half the land was rented, principally on long
leases from All Souls College, and it consisted of no solid block of
freehold property to root the family in the countryside, but a number
of widely separated farms.[25] Joseph himself continued to live in
Rochester till his death and neither his son nor his grandson seems to
have lived on their rural properties. Though very conscious of their
armigerous status, they were never genuine country squires in the
traditional sense of the word. Neither did they ever intermarry with
the greater landed families of the county such as the Oxindens,
Derings, Twysdens, and Honywoods. Their world always remained
that of the urban gentry, the professional classes, and the small
parochial squires of the county.

Joseph's character comes out vividly in his grandson's account in
the 'Anecdotes'.

> After his coming into possession of the above estates, he retained a
> parlour in each of his principal farms, both at Newington and
> Halstow, to which he used frequently to ride and pass a day . . . to
> see after his workmen and repairs, and see after the management of
> his estates. It is remarkable that he generally chewed rhubarb whilst he
> was on these excursions, which he found an excellent preventive
> medicine against agues and bad airs and fogs. [Several of his farms
> were in marshland parishes.] Being looked on at Chatham as very
> kind, [he and his wife] were looked on accordingly with much respect.
> Their housekeeping was exceeding plentiful, but their visitors who
> partook of it were in general their relations.[26]

By his wife Katherine Yardley, who was clearly as great a character
as her husband – she was furious when she found, at the age of nearly
seventy, that her life-interest in his estates was dependent on her not
remarrying – Joseph Hasted was brought into touch with a whole
circle of little gentry and pseudo-gentry families around Rochester
and Chatham. It was a purely local and highly inbred connection.
Amongst them, besides the Yardleys, were the Chicheleys, Austens,
Ayersts, and Bryants, 'who were all called cousins and kept up an
intimacy as such and were nearly related'.
picture of the housekeeping of his grandparents, who might have
stepped out of the pages of *The Mill on the Floss*.

> According to the fashion of the times their hours were early; they rose
> in the morning at 5 o'clock and played together at backgammon till
> breakfast at 8 o'clock; they had at morning [?] some thick cake and

mead; they dined at 12, drank tea at 4, and supped at 8. He brewed his own beer, which he prided himself much in, especially his strong beer, which he kept to the age of several years. Their beverage after dinner was elder wine, which as well as several other sorts [Mrs Hasted] made herself, being an excellent housewife.[27]

Their only child, Edward, was born in 1702 and was the father of the historian. Both his father and his mother were nearly forty when he was born. With him we leave behind the homely gentility of his mother and her country cousins around Rochester, and the newly made wealth of his strong-minded father, riding about to his Kentish farms chewing rhubarb. With the new generation a certain metropolitan sophistication seems to characterise the family. Edward was bred up to the law in London and became a barrister. He went into partnership with the comptroller of the City, of which he became a freeman, and his wife, too, was a thorough Londoner. She was Anne, daughter and coheir of Joseph Tyler, a London goldsmith, by his wife Elizabeth, daughter and heir of John Dingley, another gold-smith in the city. Through the Dingleys, who came of an ancient Hampshire family, the Hasteds were connected with one of the wealthiest families in England, the Hoares of Stourhead in Wiltshire; for Richard Hoare, the banker, had married a daughter of Robert Dingley of Lamorbey Park in Kent, who was Anne Hasted's first cousin.[28] Anne was in fact the only character in the Hasted family history who was not of Kentish origin.

Despite their rise in the social scale and their London habits, Edward and Anne Hasted by no means cut themselves off from their kinsmen in Kent. Every summer during his father's lifetime they went down to Chatham to spend a few weeks with Edward's parents.

[But] the early hours of the old folks no more than the method of passing their time by no means agreed with the young ones used to the modern fashions of London; and my grandfather used frequently to say, in joke, That there was no knowing what to do with these young Londoners, their late hours and their new-fangled fashions.[29]

Soon after his father's death in 1732, Edward Hasted retired from his practice of the law and left London. He rented a house at Hawley, in the parish of Sutton-at-Hone,

where he lived as a country gentleman, respected and beloved by all for his good nature, affability, and constant readiness to oblige and render himself serviceable to all his neighbours. . . . By his knowledge in the law he became exceedingly useful at all meetings of the gentry of the county on the business of the county.

He was a jovial, generous-hearted man and the pleasures of his life consisted in entertaining his neighbours, in cultivating his garden, and in music.

> He promoted cheerfulness and good neighbourhood on every occasion, for which purpose he established a monthly concert, of which he was steward and treasurer, in the adjoining market-town of Dartford, which flourished with much celebrity till his death, when, losing its chief director, it soon declined. At the same time his wife set forward a Public Breakfast weekly on a Saturday, being the market day, for the Ladies of that town and its neighbourhood, of which she was patroness.[30]

Quite clearly there was a pronounced contrast between the social habits and ideals of this generation of the family and those of Edward's prudent and provincial parents. 'My father's little establishment,' the historian wrote of his youthful days at Hawley, in the countryside of the Darent valley,

> consisted of a coachman and footman, livery servants, 3 maidservants, and a housekeeper, a person they had long known in friendship in a better state of life, but who by misfortunes had come to decay. To these I may add an upper and under-gardener. He had a coach and chariot, 3 coach horses, a riding horse for himself and one for his servant, and 3 cows. His table was plentiful without ostentation, accompanied with a cheerful welcome to all his friends, of whom he had generally one or perhaps two, being his old cronies and schoolfellows, in the house as visitors to him. . . . The livery he gave his servants, however preposterous they would be looked on now [in 1800], were quite congenial to that time: a light blue suit with small gilt buttons down to the bottom of the skirt, a pair of scarlet stockings, a blue and gold shoulder knot with gilt tassels, and a very broad gold lace on a square cocked hat.[31]

By his wife Anne, Edward Hasted had six sons, of whom the historian was the youngest, and one daughter. He died suddenly from apoplexy at the age of thirty-eight in 1740. His wife survived him for more than fifty years, dying at the age of ninety in 1791.[32] Anne Hasted figures prominently in the 'Anecdotes', and she strikes one in a sense as rather a lonely and tragic character. 'My mother, poor woman,' says the historian, 'had an excessive pride, which predominated on every occasion and made most people rather disgusted with her acquaintance, which they of course in future rather avoided than otherwise.'[33] Her pride consisted in an inordinate regard (to some extent shared by her son) for her connection with the

Dingleys. The ancestral Dingley knighthood of which she made so much was in fact a long way back in her pedigree, and it is not hard to understand the disgust of her Kentish neighbours, who tended to be rather free and easy, and had probably never heard of the Hampshire Dingleys.

This lofty and not very sensible woman had many sorrows and humiliations to bear in her lengthy life. When her husband died she was still in her thirties, and her youth and total inexperience in business left her an easy prey to unscrupulous lawyers and misguided acquaintances, who between them succeeded in dissipating much of her substance. She soon had to part with her country house at Hawley, and for a few years she lived at Rome House, on the outskirts of Chatham, which her husband had inherited from his grandmother's family, the Walkers. Nevertheless, she still maintained a considerable establishment, consisting of 'a coachman, footman, a gardener paid by the week and lodged abroad, and three maidservants. She kept her coach and pair of horses. Her table was genteel and she had frequent company at it. . . . Their behaviour and conversation was gentleman-like, with much respect at all times, and much friendship subsisted between them.' Amongst these friends were some of the town gentry of Rochester and Chatham, professional families like that of Pelham Johnson, a well-known local doctor, and Rochester cathedral families like the Soans.[34]

This pleasant interlude in Mrs Hasted's life was a brief one, however, and was rudely shattered in 1742. At her husband's death in 1740, only two of her seven children were still living, five of her six sons having died in infancy. Anne, her eldest child, was only twelve years of age and Edward, the future historian, no more than eight. Two years later, at the tender age of fourteen, Anne suddenly eloped with a marine named James Archer, whom she had met at Chatham and who came of a poor family in or near Kettering, 'little above common labourers'. The two were married in Exeter and eventually Mrs Hasted purchased a commission for Archer in the army. He turned out a thoroughly bad lot, however, and in the end his wretched wife had to separate from him, returning to live obscurely with her mother in London, and dying in her thirty-fifth year, without issue, in 1762.[35] The elopement was a terrible blow to anyone of Mrs Hasted's pride. The historian's account graphically describes the social humiliation that such a solecism brought upon families like the Hasteds in the eighteenth century. The famous elopement scene of Lydia Bennet in *Pride and Prejudice* was evidently by no means overdrawn. 'The distress of sorrow it brought upon [Mrs Hasted], and the uproar of scandal which the knowledge of her [daughter's] elopement caused throughout the neighbourhood, determined her to quit Chatham immediately.'[36] Thereafter she lived in or near London until about 1770, when she moved to Canterbury to be nearer her son and his family, who by that time were also living there.

THE HISTORIAN AND HIS FAMILY[37]

The tragedies regarding her daughter can have been slight compared with those of her son Edward to a woman of Mrs Hasted's temperament. The historian's life has been described elsewhere by the present author and only a summary of the facts can be given here. After an early childhood spent at Hawley, he was educated at the King's School, Rochester, at Eton, and at a private school in Surrey. The Eton education was a characteristic idea of his mother's. It took him well beyond the limited circle of his Kentish forebears, all of whom, like the vast majority of Kentish gentry, were educated locally. More important than his formal education, however, were the links he formed as a young man with the antiquaries of his time. Eton left no permanent impression on him and he remained completely Kentish throughout his life. Characteristically, he showed no interest at all in the history and antiquities of other areas when he visited them in the 1790s. His work on the history of Kent began in the 1750s and continued almost without intermission for nearly fifty years. It was in every sense a life work, and the whole of the monumental task was undertaken by the historian himself. The first edition was published in four folio volumes between 1778 and 1799; the second, a heavily revised version, was published in twelve octavo volumes between 1797 and 1801. The research behind it was enormous: by 1774 his manuscript notes already extended to more than 100 volumes and a further twenty-five years' research stretched in front of him before the work was completed.

On this work, between about 1755 and 1790, Hasted expended much of his family fortune. At his father's death in 1740 this had amounted to nearly £1,000 a year in freehold and leasehold property. The *History* itself records from time to time how the scattered properties acquired by his frugal grandfather were gradually sold off to meet his mounting embarrassments. The *History*, it is true, was not the only cause of his difficulties. Like many antiquaries he was devoid of business sense and in his early married life he clearly lived well beyond his means. Then about the year 1760 he first resorted to the unwise expedient of borrowing money from his lawyer friend, Thomas Williams of Dartford. Little by little the debts and the mortgages mounted up. Eventually, by 1791, the plausible attorney had involved the unsuspecting antiquary in such legal entanglements that he was compelled to sell the whole of his remaining property at a considerable undervaluation. The estates were then worth £11,500, but Williams forced Hasted into a position where he had to sell them to him for no more than £8,685. The Hasteds were not the only local family whom Thomas Williams ruined in this way. Like so many lawyers, he was a thoroughly odious man.

The collapse of Hasted's fortunes was accompanied by the equally tragic breakdown of his marriage. In 1755, at the age of twenty-three, he had married a local girl, Anne Dorman, the daughter of his friends and neighbours John and Dorothy Dorman of Sutton-at-Hone. The Dormans were a substantial family at Sutton, where many of them lie buried beneath a fine series of eighteenth-century tombstones. They belonged broadly speaking to the same class of pseudo-gentry as the Hasteds themselves; but they were not of armigerous descent, and they were perhaps a degree or two below Edward in the social scale. Anne Dorman, moreover, brought her husband no dowry, and the marriage was deeply resented by his ambitious mother. Old Mrs Hasted's tiresome sensibility where class distinctions of this kind were concerned was in part a merely personal peculiarity; but it was also rather more than that. It was an indication of the ambiguous social position still occupied by the new pseudo-gentry. In the class-ridden world of Hanoverian England families like the Hasteds could not afford to lose caste: their origins were too recent for them to live down a *mésalliance*.

Despite the rift with his mother, however, Hasted's marriage seems for many years to have been a happy one. Between 1760 and 1774 Anne Dorman bore him six sons and three daughters, all but two of whom – the two youngest – reached maturity. The bonds of affection clearly ran deep in this large family and the breach that eventually developed, after thirty years of married life, is not altogether easy to account for. Basically, however, it was due to a certain strain of weakness in the historian's character. In 1785 he 'unfortunately became acquainted with Mary Jane Town', and in the following year Miss Town became his mistress. Nothing is known of her origins, though to judge from her surname she must have been a local girl. For the next eleven years, through every conceivable vicissitude, she and Hasted remained together: in rented houses at Sheldwich and Boughton-under-Blean, in obscure lodgings in London, and then at Dover and Canterbury. In 1791, when Hasted was forced to fly to France to escape his creditors, Mary Jane Town accompanied him. The outbreak of war in 1793 compelled them to return to England incognito and eventually, after many wanderings, they settled in Camden Town in 1795. A few months later they were discovered, and the historian was imprisoned for debt in the King's Bench. Extraordinary thought it may seem, Mary Jane Town accompanied him to jail, and they remained together, in virtual destitution, for the next two years. It was not until 1797 that their liaison came to an end, when Hasted 'parted with her for infamy and wickedness' – a phrase whose meaning it is not difficult to interpret. In the following year he was reconciled with his wife, but he himself remained in prison for another five years, until 1802. It was during this period, when his only source of livelihood was the charity of a few friends, that the whole of the second edition of his *History* was revised and rewritten.

After Hasted's release, the suit in Chancery which had been instituted on his behalf against Thomas Williams' heir was concluded, and eventually the historian regained what little was left of his family property. It was several years before his financial worries were over; but the last five years of his life were passed in more genial circumstances, when his old friend, Lord Radnor, presented him to the mastership of Lady Hungerford's Hospital at Corsham in Wiltshire. It was there that he died, in 1812, in his eightieth year. As far as the present writer can discover he had never revisited the county which owed him so much, and which he loved so deeply, since he left it twenty years earlier in 1791.

Quite as revealing as the historian's own response to these adversities was that of his family. At the time when he left his wife, in 1785 or 1786, the eldest of his seven surviving children, Edward, was only twenty-five years of age and the youngest, John Septimus, no more than seventeen. There were three other sons, Francis Dingley, George, and Charles, and two daughters, Anne and Katherine, all aged between nineteen and twenty-three.[38] For the next few years the whole family must have lived in very straitened circumstances and virtually nothing is known about them. The care of the younger children as well as Hasted's wife and mother, who was then aged eighty-three or eighty-four, seems to have fallen on the unfortunate Edward, the eldest son. Edward had been educated at Oriel College, Oxford, and was the only member of the family to receive a university education; but at this time he had no benefice and apparently no curacy, though in 1786 he was officiating occasionally in various churches in Canterbury.[39] Owing to the obscurity that enveloped the family at this time, the only fact generally known about the historian's descendants is that in 1790 this son, Edward, became vicar of Hollingbourne with Hucking, a joint living which he held from 1790 until his death sixty-five years later, at the age of ninety-four, in 1855.[40] It was one of the longest incumbencies in Kentish history, and during this period Edward was also a local magistrate for upwards of fifty years.

Some further information about the historian's descendants is to be found in the Hasted papers in the Eastgate House Museum at Rochester. As already explained, these papers consist chiefly of legal and estate documents, a diary and account book for the year 1851, and letters to the vicar at Hollingbourne. Three general points of interest mark this concluding phase in the history of the Hasteds: first, their intense sense of family pride and their dread of losing caste, a dread that was highly characteristic of decayed gentlefolk in this period; secondly, the means which they adopted to earn a respectable livelihood without compromising their social standing; and thirdly, the association of several of them with the Evangelical Movement of the period. This Movement powerfully affected the whole of England, of course, but it was exceptionally strong in Kent, where many of the leading families of the county, such as the Earls of Darnley at Cobham Hall, as well as the local gentry, became strong Evangelicals.

Of the historian's sons apart from the vicar of Hollingbourne, George, the third, was educated at King's, Canterbury, where he shewed 'great talents' and was considered the most able member of the family. He was destined for the law and put into a London attorney's office, but he died in 1787 at the age of twenty-four and was buried in the family vault at Newington near Sittingbourne.[41] John Septimus, the youngest son to survive childhood, was born in 1768 and became a naval surgeon, probably about the year 1794 when his brother Francis spoke of his recent 'good fortune'.[42] He married a Miss Notley, who died in 1834 leaving him a small property which she had inherited from her mother and which he invested in an annuity which added £150 a year to his meagre naval pension. Like his father and grandmother before him, and like his eldest brother, John lived to a great age, dying in 1853 in his eighty-fifth or eighty-sixth year. (Nearly all the Hasteds either died young, like George, or lived to a great age.) Charles, the fourth son, was born in 1764 and became a brewer, first apparently at Sheerness and then near Chatham.[43] From a letter of his to his brother Edward in 1828, one suspects that he inherited something of his father's fatal incapacity for business. At any rate he had by then had to give up the Chatham brewery and had moved with his wife to Shadwell in east London, where he became a seller of 'intermediate beer in Johnson Street, St George-in-the-East'. The date of his death is not known; he may have lived on into the 1840s, but he certainly died before 1851 and so predeceased both Edward and John Septimus.

Of the two daughters, Anne, the elder, was born in 1765 and was certainly still living in 1834, when she was left a legacy of £20 a year in the will of her brother John. Anne seems to have been her father's favourite child, for in his will he left her, amongst other bequests, five guineas for a ring or locket to keep 'in remembrance of her father, whose affection is great towards her': a touching little comment since it was possibly more than ten years since he had seen her.[44] The second daughter, Katherine, was a year younger than Anne and spent most of her life with her brother Edward, for whom she apparently kept house at Hollingbourne, where she died unmarried in 1842 in her seventy-seventh year.[45]

Of these six children of the historian, only two, Charles and John Septimus, married, and neither of them had any children. The historian's only grandchildren were the sons and daughters of the remaining son, Francis Dingley Hasted, who was a year younger than Edward. It is of Francis and his family that the Hasted papers at Rochester are most informative, and with him the family history takes its most surprising turn. Francis had been born in 1762 and at some time before 1794 he left England and sailed to India in the hope of making his fortune as an indigo merchant. One wonders what suggested the idea of an Indian fortune to him; but his was a sanguine, expansive temperament like his grandfather's, and in December 1794 he wrote back in high hopes to his brother Edward. Although Edward had now been presented to the living of Hollingbourne, he and his mother were still living in very straitened circumstances. The two sisters, Anne and Katherine, had been taken under the wing of their mother's sister, Mary Dorman of Barming, near Maidstone; but this Aunt Dorman, who was now an old lady of seventy, was seriously ill and their future was uncertain. It must have seemed a cruel world to these unhappy girls, brought up to a leisured upper-class existence but now no longer youthful and no longer wanted. Their father was living with a mistress, a fugitive from justice, about to be arrested and imprisoned; they themselves had no money of their own, and no one was likely to court them. Their aunt, who had given them a home, was thought to be dying;[46] and now, at the age of nearly thirty, it seemed they might have to go out to work, presumably as governesses or companions.

It was this humiliating necessity that Francis wrote about, from Malda in Bengal. His letter is an interesting document in several respects.[47] It illustrates the social prejudices of a family of impoverished gentlefolk in the late eighteenth century. Its strain of sensibility reveals the intense affections of a family to whom the sorrows and separations they were called upon to bear seemed peculiarly bitter. (It was during this same decade that their distant kinswoman, Jane Austen, was writing her first draft of *Sense and Sensibility*.) The letter also illustrates the influence of the new Evangelical piety of the period: not the masculine, militant Evangelicalism of a Wilberforce, but rather that of the tender, submissive, quietist tradition of Philip Doddridge and John Newton. 'You write, my dear Ned, very despondingly,' Francis wrote;

> wait but a little and I will help you all in my power. I would earlier have remitted you and our dear mother some money but really it has not been attainable; it will now very soon, and be assured I will not let slip the very earliest opportunity. You are already acquainted with the concern I am engaged in with two gentlemen residing near Malda. This is the second year and it has been productive beyond all expectation. We have this year, by moderate computation, cleared a net profit of thirty thousand rupees, or three thousand pounds sterling, one third of which is mine. I have great hopes of doing still better this coming year.

What he dreaded, however, was their

> dear sisters' being forced to go abroad into the world to seek their living. I shall do everything in my power to prevent so sad a calamity befalling them. Men may bustle through life, but women, brought up too as they have been, with far better prospects, are hardly capable of bearing up against the trouble and contumely usually attendant upon menial stations. I entreat therefore, my dearest brother, your best interest and exertions with our friends, if any we have, in the behalf of our dear sisters, only for a while, perhaps a very short time, when they might either live comfortably at home, or if they approve it better, one or both come out to me. I never can consent to their being sent out into a wide, uncertain, and unfeeling world to make their own way through it, a task to which, it seems to me, on many accounts they are so very incompetent. I am persuaded they have a father in you, poor dear girls! How I lament their case, but I forebear; there is a ruling providence, and those words 'it is the Lord' should . . . silence our complaints.

The plight of his father, now living in obscurity with Mary Jane Town near Tottenham Court Road, was Francis's other worry.

Our poor father, I am always fearing you will fall into distress, besides
should his person remain unmolested, yet having, as I suppose, no
certain or annual subsistence, the source must at length fail. You have
not hitherto said anything particular on that head; it is undoubtedly,
should such an hour come, our duty to render him necessary help;
pray tell me more about this in your next letter.

The rest of Francis's long letter was more cheerful: it announced
his recent marriage to Miss Sarah Powell. The Evangelical pro-
clivities of this generation of the family, which Edward as well as
Francis seems to have shared, were also reflected in this marriage; for
Sarah Powell was a Baptist with missionary connections. Her
father, Benjamin Powell, was a well-off London cabinetmaker of St
John's Street, Clerkenwell. The family was a well-known one in
Baptist circles and friendly with Dr William Carey, the celebrated
orientalist and founder of the Baptist Missionary Society. Sarah
apparently went out to India with her brother Samuel, who, like
his mother's brother the Rev. Thomas of Fairford, was probably a
missionary. She was clearly a woman of charm and character, and
the marriage seems to have been an ideally happy one. Between 1795
and 1808 she bore her husband five sons and one daughter – the
historian's only grandchildren.

Whether Francis was ever able to afford his mother and sisters the
financial relief he promised is not recorded, but on the face of it it
seems unlikely. He was not the kind of man that Indian nabobs were
made of, and with his rapidly growing family and his lavish mode of
life he can never have had much to spare. His mother died in 1803,
within a few months of her husband's release from the King's
Bench.[48] Katherine, as we have seen, eventually found a home with
her brother at Hollingbourne, presumably after her Aunt Dorman's
death in 1800. Anne may have had to earn her own living and
certainly in her later years she was living at Lambeth, possibly as a
companion or governess. By the time the historian died in 1812,
however, there had at last been some improvement in the family fortunes of those in England. In the codicil to his will of 1812, the
historian had left virtually the whole of his property to his eldest
son, the vicar, 'knowing that he will of his goodness assist his
brothers and sisters with as much as he sees necessary of it from time
to time'.[49] Accordingly, what remained of the family property was
sold, after Edward died, apparently for a little more than £7,000.[50]
With this modest patrimony to fall back on, and with their occupation in the church, in the medical profession, and in wholesale trade,
the three sons and two daughters in England were able to maintain

their standing as gentlefolk with respectability at least, if in somewhat uninspiring circumstances and certainly without any *éclat*.

Meanwhile the history of the Indian branch of the family, if more colourful, had also been more chequered. Though they clearly lived in considerable style, Francis's sanguine hopes of a rapid fortune proved ill-founded, and one by one his family was struck down by disease in the cruel climate of Bengal. His deeply-loved wife Sarah died in 1809, leaving six young children between one and fourteen years of age. In 1815 the third son Jonathan died, apparently of fever, at the age of seventeen, and in 1818 the fifth son Edward at the same age. In the following summer of 1819 Francis himself died, aged fifty-seven, and exactly a month later, on 22 June, his only daughter, Sarah Anne, at the age of twenty-three.

The three remaining sons were left alone and practically destitute in the vast subcontinent. Their father's business enterprises had been on an extensive scale, but must have been insecurely based, and at his death he was found to be insolvent. Of the three orphans, Francis, the eldest son was only twenty-four, George was twenty, and John, poor boy, no more than eleven. They had never been out of India and had never seen any of their English relatives; but their Aunt Anne had kept in touch with them, and they had recently received a letter from their uncle the vicar. They knew that their grandfather's estates had been sold and that their father might have looked for some share in the proceeds from them. Accordingly, although the posts from India were notoriously unreliable, all their hopes, they said, were for help from England. On 26 July 1819 Francis therefore sent a desperate appeal to his Uncle Edward at Hollingbourne.

His letter, written with all his father's sensibility and enthusiasm, and in a racy copperplate hand that curiously parodied his father's, must speak for itself.[51] It was an emotional kind of letter that his grandfather the historian could never have written and his rather frigid uncle probably did not appreciate. 'My dear Uncle,' Francis wrote,

> My mind shudders at taking up my pen for the first time that I am writing to you, it should be to communicate the most melancholy and afflicting of news, the deaths of my very dear Father, sister, and brother!!! Oh how shall I explain to you the heavy afflictions that have fallen upon us, and of our forlorn state, my poor Father's insolvency has left us penniless in the world, the factories are entirely at the agent's disposal, and will certainly be put up to sale soon, when we shall be cast upon the wide world without the means of support: finding employment in this country is become a matter of the

greatest difficulty. I beg, my dear Uncle, you will take our state into
consideration and have compassion upon us; any sum that you may
be able to remit from what might have fallen to my poor Father's
share, from the sale of the estate, or otherwise, will prove of the
utmost consequence . . . I beg to be kindly remembered to my uncles
and aunts in England. Will providence ever grant that we shall meet?
I see no likelihood of it, God's will be done. My mind is in a very
confused state at present, and I hope you will forgive the shortness of
this, I have just got over a severe attack of fever.

The fever had been caused by a hunting accident, when his servant's
gun had accidentally gone off and the contents lodged in his leg, leaving him lame for life.

This letter was succeeded by an enigmatic silence on Edward
Hasted's part, and in March 1820 his nephew wrote again, in much
the same vein.[52] The three young men had now been turned out of
their home; and although George Hasted had been taken on as a
clerk by Messrs Palmer and Co. at Calcutta, his salary was barely
sufficient to provide them with the necessities of life. Edward
Hasted received this letter in the following September; he did not
reply to it till the last day of March 1821. Possibly he did not quite
believe in his nephews' 'indefatigable exertions' to try and support
themselves; but surely he might have been a little more prompt in
responding to the orphans' appeal. Whether he sent them anything
from the £7,000 arising from the estates it is impossible to say; but
his reply does not seem to have encouraged them to maintain the
correspondence. It is possible that they wrote and their letters were
lost at sea; but certainly Edward received no letters from them and
there was no further communication with them till 1828.

The correspondence of 1828 between the two branches of the
family arose indirectly out of the terms of the will of Benjamin
Powell, the maternal grandfather of the three young men in India.[53]
Powell had died in 1819, leaving his estate to his surviving children
and, after their death, to his Hasted grandchildren. By 1828 the
death of the last surviving son was imminently expected and
Powell's executor set himself to discover the whereabouts of the
grandchildren. The task did not prove an easy one owing to the
complete obscurity in which the Hasted family had shrouded itself
since their father's misfortunes. Eventually, however, and quite by
chance, a friend of the executor's came across Charles Hasted, the
former brewer, at his business premises in St George-in-the-East.
Charles got in touch with his brother at Hollingbourne, and after
various legal delays, the Indian nephews were informed of their

good fortune.

Belated though it was, and modest in scale, the bequest of the Powell estate – which amounted to about £2,500 – must have played its part in the success of Francis and George in eventually establishing themselves as indigo planters. (The third nephew, John, had died in 1823.) When their uncle Edward Hasted enquired after them in 1831, through his friend Henry Lushington of Boxley, whose brother Colonel James Lushington was in the India Office, they were reported to be 'respectable and worthy men', deserving of their uncle's countenance, and carrying on their own business in the Benares district.[54] Perhaps, one may hope, a little of the business acumen of their great-grandfather Joseph Hasted, the founder of the family fortunes, had reappeared in them. Beyond this date it is impossible to trace anything further about them except the year of their death. Neither of them appears to have married or at any rate to have left any descendants, so that with the death of Francis at Goruckpore in 1844 and George at Doolepore in 1850 the Indian branch of the family apparently came to an end.[55]

THE LAST YEARS AT HOLLINGBOURNE

Meanwhile, far away across the world, the rest of the family still lived on in Kent within a few miles of Highsted, where their fore-bears had originated nearly 700 years earlier. Despite the circum-stances that had separated them since the 1790s, the sense of kinship they had inherited was still powerful amongst them. Nowhere is this feeling more clearly expressed than in their father's will. The will was drawn up at Corsham in 1808, with a codicil added in 1810; it was written in Edward Hasted's own hand and couched in his homely yet telling language. It was nearly twenty years since he had left Kent and nearly twenty-five since he had lived with his family. Yet the will demonstrated that the welfare of his children, the credit of the Hasted family, and the history of the county were still the only matters that interested him.[56] His abiding preoccupation with the history of Kent is illustrated in the bequest of his historical collections to a fellow-antiquary in the county. These had originally been left to the British Museum; but in the event this bequest was cancelled and they were left instead to his 'much respected friend William Boteler of Eastry, Esquire, as a small mark, the only one in my power, of my grateful remembrance of the many favours I have received from him.' The British Museum, the historian seems to have thought, was no longer sufficiently private. The bequest to

Boteler was virtually the only one in the will outside the family circle. Almost everything else was left to the eldest son Edward. What survived of the family property was to be sold and the proceeds retained by Edward as a kind of trustee for his brothers and sisters. His father believed that he would assist his brothers and sisters from it, and entreated 'that he will at his death consider his brother Francis's children by giving and leaving them a good portion of it, my other children being all independently provided for and having none of them issue'. Edward was also left all the family furniture, plate and books in his possession at Hollingbourne Vicarage; the pedigrees his father had compiled of the Hasteds, Dormans, and Dingleys; the 'large folio Bible, printed in Henry the 8th's time, in which are inserted the births, marriages, and deaths of my family and children'; the 'Anecdotes of the Hasted Family' which his father had written in 1800; the historian's portrait, which was 'to continue with my family pictures now in [Edward's] possession at Hollingbourne'; and finally 'my old-fashioned gold ring set with pearls, being the wedding ring of my great-grandmother Walker [of Chatham], and my late wife's gold wedding ring, my steel seal with my arms on it and my silver seal ring with my crest on it, all which are now in my possession'.

In all these bequests there was a clear determination on the part of the historian to maintain inviolable the sacred privacy of the family. Above all, its frailties must not be exposed to the world. The increasing emphasis on the sanctity of the home and the growing tendency of gentlefolk to draw further apart from the common run of mankind were pronounced developments in provincial society in the late eighteenth and early nineteenth centuries: it was a time when divisions between class and class were clearly becoming deeper. In the original will of 1808 the executor had been instructed to examine Hasted's historical collections very thoroughly, to remove the pedigrees of Hasted, Dingley, and Dorman, and such of the rest 'as shall be judged by him improper to be made public [shall be] taken from them and destroyed'. All the historian's private papers were also to be scrutinised by the executor; those that were judged unnecessary to be retained were to be destroyed, and the rest were to 'remain in his possession and not to be inspected or given up to any one else'. If, after Edward's death, Francis and Charles Hasted should refuse to accept the bequest of the family portraits, these also were to be 'destroyed to prevent their coming into the hands of brokers and exposed to sale for a few shillings'.

What kind of a man was Edward Hasted, the vicar of Holling-bourne, who figured so prominently in his father's will and who succeeded him as the family head? His character is an enigmatic one. There are few personal records relating to him apart from his diary and account book for the year 1851. We know him almost solely through the letters he received, and it is possible that the impression these convey of a rather limited man, careful to the verge of meanness in money matters, may be a somewhat unjust one.[57] Yet the impression cannot be altogether gainsaid. His only surviving personal letter, relating to a tithe dispute with his parishioners in which he promised to take no further services in the church and to 'interfere in no parish business whatsoever', certainly shews him in rather an odd light.[58] His apparent lack of energy in coming to his unfortunate father's aid when in prison in the 1790s and to his young nephews' in the 1820s is also, to say the least, difficult to understand. And surely, since he inherited most of the family property, he might have ful-filled his father's modest request that a monument should be erected to his memory in Corsham church. As it was, there was no monument at all to the historian, in Wiltshire or Kent, until 1929, when Dr F. W. Cock of Appledore placed a memorial tablet to him in Corsham church: a graceful act of homage by a fellow-antiquary to a faulty yet remarkable man.[59]

These lapses of Edward's were perhaps due to a dislike of dis-turbance and a dilatory habit of mind rather than to conscious un-kindness. Yet the impression of a certain nearness in money matters is more difficult to discount.[60] In 1851, when his total income amounted to nearly £650 a year, or probably as much as his father ever received from the family estates in the eighteenth century,[61] he was spending less than half of it and devoting very little to charity. When the village girls came round a-maying he gave them a mere eighteen pence when they called at the vicarage. At the annual tithe feast, after receiving more than £200 from the Hollingbourne farmers, he spent less than £3 on dinner for them and gave his servants a miserly two shillings. His curate Mr Spurgin, who performed nearly all the aged vicar's duties, in both Hollingbourne and Hucking, received the pitiful stipend of £75 a year.

What does the vicar's solitary personal record, his diary for 1851, tell us about the man? The most obvious fact is that it tells us so little. It is the dull, laconic record of an unimaginative man. Yet for the local historian it has one real point of interest. Day by day throughout the year it faithfully records his visitors. During the course of 1851 there were about forty families in the neighbourhood who called on him at more or less regular intervals, so that the diary precisely describes the social circle of a Victorian country parson. Nearly all these families came from parishes within six or seven miles of Hollingbourne: a distance, no doubt, that marked the limit for afternoon calls by the local 'carriage families' of the period, particularly if they had to negotiate the narrow lanes and wooded, broken countryside of the Kentish downs and chartlands.

Who, then, were these visitors? Several were parsons of nearby parishes, like Mr Burney of Thurnham and Mr Riddell of Harrietsham. Quite a number were town gentry from Maidstone, like the Readers and Beales, and a few were local military men like Major Waytts. A further group, perhaps the most numerous, comprised the landless village gentry and the gentleman farmers of the area, like the Cobbs of Bredgar and the Robinses of Borden. Then there were the numerous local squires of the parishes around Hollingbourne: the Bests of Boxley Lodge, the Baldwins of Stede Hill, the Thomases of Eyhorne House, the Duppas of Hollingbourne House, the Wykeham-Martins of Leeds Castle, the Savages of St Leonards in Malling, and the Crofts of Doddington Place. All of these were well-established local gentry, but none of them, except the Wykeham-Martins, were important county families. Their estates ranged in scale from the Savages' very modest 550 acres and the Thomases' 710 acres to the Bests' 1,830, the Baldwins' 2,120, the Duppas' 2,300, and the Wykeham-Martins' 3,320.[62] Twice in the year, in July and September, the aged vicar was visited by a more august neighbour, when the Earl of Romney came to see him from Mote Park. There was only one other visitor, throughout the period covered by the diary, with a handle to his name – Sir John Croft. Yet there was no one in the list, on the other hand, who would not have been quite definitely thought of as a 'gentleman'. By 1851 the social barrier between gentry and commonalty in rural England was distinct and inflexible: and this barrier is as clearly evidenced in the pedestrian pages of Edward Hasted's diary as in the Court List of a contemporary directory.

By 1850 Hollingbourne Vicarage had been regarded as the family home of the Hasteds for nearly sixty years. Thither in the summertime the other branches of the family sometimes used to come and spend their vacations with the vicar and his sister. Charles used to drive over from Chatham, and on fine afternoons he and his wife sat out on the vicarage lawn with Edward and Katherine, underneath the great quince tree, in the shadow of the downs. '[I] should very much like to be sitting under your quince tree,' Charles wrote with a touch of nostalgia in 1828, after he had parted with his Chatham business and moved to London; 'but that cannot be this summer.'[63]

Hollingbourne with its vicarage is still a lovely, peaceful spot, girdled with trees, watered with springs, the great Elizabethan manor house on one hand, on the other the church where Edward ministered so long, with its noble Culpeper tombs. As we have seen, Katherine remained with her brother at Hollingbourne till her death in 1842 at the age of seventy-six. Charles and Anne appear to have predeceased her, and John Septimus died in 1853. Edward, the eldest of the family, lived on alone in the vicarage for another thirteen years after Katherine's death, dying in 1855 at the age of ninety-four, the last of the line. 'They were son and daughter of Edward Hasted, esquire, Historian of Kent,' says the simple memorial to him and his sister in Hollingbourne church: 'Blessed are the dead which die in the Lord from henceforth; yea, saith the Spirit, that they may rest from their labours, and their works do follow them.'[64]

NOTES AND REFERENCES

1. They are listed as 'Private Residents' under the town and village entries. The 'Court Directory' is a cumulative list of all the 'private residents' in the county. It follows the village and town entries and precedes the 'Trades Directory', which comprises all occupational categories in the county. There are minor discrepancies between the Court Directory and the Private Residents listed under villages and towns, but these do not affect the general picture.

2. The average household size in Kent in 1861 was 5·8 persons, i.e. 734,000 inhabitants (including those in the Greater London parishes of Kent) in 126,221 inhabited houses.

3. The figure for Kent excludes the Greater London parishes in the county.

4. See 'Three Devon families', in *Old Devon*, (David and Charles, 1966) reprinted from W. G. Hoskins and H. P. R. Finberg, *Devonshire Studies*, (Jonathan Cape 1952). The third family in this study, the Galsworthys, is a good example in its later generations of a 'pseudogentry' family: see pp. 118–20.

5. All but four of these 24 are in Kent. The four Sussex examples occur close to the Kentish border, in Hastings and St. Leonards.

6. Edward Hasted, *The History and Topographical Survey of the County of Kent* (2nd edn, Canterbury 1797–1801; facsimile reprint 1972), i, 'Introduction', pp. v–xlix.

7. I am much indebted to Mr Michael Moad, the curator, for drawing my attention to this collection and facilitating the use of it.

8. I am much indebted to Mr L. R. A. Grove, the curator, for drawing my attention to this collection and facilitating the use of it.

9. This correspondence was printed in *Archaeologia Cantiana*, [*AC*] xxvii (1905).

10. Apart from these records, the principal sources for the history of the family include the following: ten or eleven wills and an administration amongst the probate records of the dioceses of Canterbury and Rochester, in the Kent Archives Office; the historian's own will in the Public Record Office [PRO] (Prob. 11/ 1530/2682); the baptismal registers of several Canterbury churches, particularly those of St Alphege, St Dunstan, St George, St Peter, and the Cathedral; *Canterbury Marriage Licences*, 2nd and 3rd series, ed. J. M. Cowper, (Canterbury 1894 and 1896); and *The Roll of the Freemen of the City of Canterbury, from A.D. 1392 to 1800*, ed. J. M. Cowper, (Canterbury 1903).

11. Hasted, *op cit.,* vi, 430–31; *AC*, xxvii, (1905), 139. The editorial footnote to the latter page is incorrect in stating that Hasted's great grandfather, Moses Hasted, was a yeoman in the neighbourhood of Canterbury in or about 1628. Moses was a tailor in Canterbury, not a yeoman. The date of his birth not known, but since he did not marry his first wife till 1657 ('Anecdotes' of the Hasted family', *AC,* xxvi (1904) (hereafter cited as 'Anecdotes'), 271) and married his third after May 1679 (see note 22 below), he is unlikely to have been born much earlier than 1628.

12. 'Anecdotes', 267–8. The original manuscript of these 'Anecdotes' is in the Maidstone Museum. The printed version is the one usually cited in this essay, except where errors of transcription have been noted, when the original is cited.

13. Cf. *AC*, xxvii (1905), 139. At an earlier period the Hampshire Hausteds were connected with Kent. Their arms appeared in the medieval armorial glass of Mereworth church, and Humphrey de Hausted held lands in Pluckley which in 8 Edward II came to the important medieval Kentish family of Malmain of Mereworth (*AC*, lxxvii (1962) 61, 62). Their surname may therefore be of Kentish origin, but philologically the invariable spelling of it with a 'u' suggests a connection with Halstead rather than Highsted, from which the Hasteds derived.

14. The historian and the anonymous editor of the 'Anecdotes' (271n) incorrectly state that the marriage took place in St Peter's; it is recorded in the St Alphege register – *The Regyster Booke . . .of the Parish of St Alphage . . . 1558–1800*, ed. J. M. Cowper (Canterbury, 1889), p. 124. Both parties were resident in St Peter's parish, however.

15. *The Roll of the Freemen of the City of Canterbury . . .*, ed. J. M. Cowper (1903), col. 274.

16. *The Register Booke of the Parish of St George the Martyr . . .*, ed. J. M. Cowper (Canterbury, 1891), p. 4.

17. The anonymous editor of the 'Anecdotes' (268n) says the name was sometimes spelt *Harsted,* but I have not myself seen this form; in the only case he actually cites (*ibid.*, 271n) he has mistaken the spelling. The name *Harste* occurs in Canterbury wills, but philologically it is unlikely to have been a variant of Hasted. If the surname *Harsted* in fact occurs, it is more likely to have been a variant of *Horsted,* the name of another Kentish family quite distinct from the Hasteds. Another local surname, *Hal(l)ste(a)d*, is found chiefly in West Kent and

probably derives from the parish of Halstead in that part of the county.

18. *AC*, lxvi (1953), 174.

19. There is another place named Highsted in Kent, in Chislet parish; but the early distribution of the surname suggests that Highsted near Sittingbourne is the more likely place of origin for the family.

20. I am much indebted to Mr Norman Scarfe for this information. Curiously enough one of the Suffolk family, Rev. Henry Hasted (1771–1852), was also an antiquarian and took a leading part in the founding of the Bury and West Suffolk Archaeological Institute in 1848.

21. Hasted MSS, Eastgate House Museum, Rochester: MS entries in Rev. Edward Hasted's copy of *The Kentish Companion and Almanack for 1851*.

22. His first wife, Mary Goslin, was buried in May 1678 (*The Register Booke of the Parish of St George the Martyr*, p. 195). His second wife Mary Edwards, buried in May 1679 (*ibid.*), was the daughter of a minor gentleman of Faversham, and left a son Nathaniel whose descendants were the historian's only known relatives on his father's side. Moses' third wife, Mary —, is recorded in the St. George's registers as bearing him a son Thomas in 1680 (*loc. cit.,* p. 47). I have not been able to discover her maiden name, and Edward Hasted the historian does not mention her in the 'Anecdotes'. Of her son nothing further is known, unless he was the Thomas Hasted who in 1709 was in the navy at Chatham and made his will leaving his goods to his wife Elizabeth (Kent Archives Office [KAO], DRb/Pw 52). Since this Thomas was illiterate (he signed his will with a mark), it seems unlikely he was a brother of Joseph Hasted and a son of Moses.

23. 'Anecdotes ', 271–2 and n.

24. *Ibid.*, 272n.

25. *Ibid.*, 272–3 and n; Hasted MSS, rentals and miscellaneous estate documents.

26. 'Anecdotes', 273n.

27. *Ibid.*, 272n, 273n. Elderberry wine was a common drink in Kent in the eighteenth century amongst the yeoman and gentry.

28. *Ibid.*, 278 and n.

29. *Ibid.*, 282n.

30. *Ibid.*, 276 and n.

31. *Ibid.*, 281. The historian also gives a minute description of his father's dress and of the family coach.

32. *Ibid.*, 276; Hasted, History, xi, 514. Hasted here says his mother died in 1792, but her burial is recorded under 10 March 1791 in *The Register Book . . . of the Cathedral and Metropolitical Church of Christe of Canterbury,* ed. R. Hovenden (1878), p. 151.

33. 'Anecdotes', 289.

34. *Ibid.*, 282–4.

35. *Ibid.*, 277–9.

36. *Ibid.*, 284.

37. The following account of the historian's life is a summary of the present author's 'Introduction' to Hasted, *History,* I, pp. v–xlix. The reader is referred to this Introduction for further details and references.

38. 'Anecdotes', 293–4.
39. *The Booke of Regester of the Parish of St Peter in Canterbury* . . ., ed. J. M. Cowper (Canterbury 1888), p. ix; *The Register Booke of Christeninges* . . . *in St Dunstan's, Canterbury* . . ., ed. J. M. Cowper (Canterbury 1887), p. vii. Cowper incorrectly identifies the Edward Hasted referred to as the historian.
40. Monumental inscription in Hollingbourne church.
41. Hasted, *History*, vi, 65; Sir Egerton Brydges, *The Autobiography, Times, Opinions, and Contemporaries* . . . (1834), i, 51. Unless otherwise stated, the biographical facts in this and the following paragraphs are based on scattered references in uncatalogued letters and papers in Hasted MSS. The dates of birth of the historian's children are given in 'Anecdotes', pp. 293–4.
42. Hasted MSS, letter of Francis Dingley Hasted, 16 December 1794.
43. Cf. also *AC*, xv (1883), 375.
44. PRO, Prob. 11/1530/2682.
45. Monumental inscription in Hollingbourne church.
46. In fact she lived till 1800, when she died in her seventy-sixth year and was buried at Sutton-at-Hone (monumental inscription in Sutton churchyard).
47. Hasted MSS, letter of Francis Dingley Hasted, 16 December 1794.
48. *The Gentleman's Magazine*, lxxxii, pt i (1812), 190.
49. PRO, Prob. 11/1530/2682.
50. A note of Charles Hasted of 26 September 1812 (in Hasted MSS) appears to relate to this sale and records the disposal of fifteen lots for a total of £7,155.
51. Hasted MSS, letter of Francis Hasted, jr, from Serasing, 26 July 1819. The punctuation in the above quotation is mainly Francis Hasted's.
52. Hasted MSS, letter of Francis Hasted, jr, from Calcutta, 1 March 1820.
53. This correspondence and other papers relating to this matter are in Hasted MSS. This and the two following paragraphs are based upon these documents.
54. Hasted MSS, letter of J. S. Brownrigg to Colonel J. L. Lushington, 12 November 1831.
55. Hasted MSS, copies of two newspaper advertisements of 8 August 1856, pursuant to an order in the High Court of Chancery requiring the next of kin and creditors of John, Francis, and George Hasted to prove their claims before the Master of the Rolls.
56. PRO. Prob. 11/1530/2682.
57. These documents are principally in Hasted MSS.
58. KAO, U.1142.C.1.
59. *AC*, xlii (1930), xlv; *AC*, xliii (1931), 295. Curiously enough, the historian's age is incorrectly given as eighty in both the monumental inscription and the parish register. Since he was born on the last day of December 1732, he was only just seventy-nine when he died in January 1812.
60. This and the following paragraphs are based on entries in his copy of *The Kentish Companion and Almanack for 1851* in Hasted MSS. This publication was a kind of annual diary or pocket book, containing a good deal of information for the clergy, for whom, it was principally intended, together with blank spaces for memorandum and accounts. The volume for 1851 is the only one of the vicar's diaries to have survived.

61. The family property at the death of the historian's father in 1740 had been worth nearly £950 a year. But the father had died intestate, so that his estate became subject to the Kentish law of gavelkind. The freehold land (worth about £650 a year) was therefore equally divided between the son and his mother during her life; the leasehold land (about £270 a year) was shared between the son, his mother, and his sister. (See 'Anecdotes', p. 278. The details as described by the historian on this page are broadly confirmed by the legal and estate papers in EHM.) The sister died in 1762 but old Mrs Hasted lived on till 1791. She and her son should in theory have then been receiving half the income each, or about £460 a year. In fact the historian admitted that he rarely paid his mother her full share. Moreover the estate had not been well-managed by the historian, and by 1791 it had mostly been mortgaged or sold.

62. *Return of Owners of Land, 1873*, (1875), i, Kent.

63. Hasted MSS, letter to Charles Hasted from Shadwell, 2 July 1828.

64. Monumental inscription to Edward and Katherine Hasted in Hollingbourne church. The verse is quoted from the Apocalypse; it was a favourite text amongst Victorian Evangelicals.

URBAN GROWTH

8

The Cumbrian Town
Between 1600 and 1800

Through a quarter of a century of writing about the English land-scape and its history W. G. Hoskins has explored and analysed the relationships between the elements of the countryside and the great economic and social movements that have shaped the life of Britain. Farmsteads, hedgerows, the shapes of fields and footpaths, the build-ing stones and styles of parish churches are all evidence, obscure as it may seem at times, of the abstract pattern of history. Both in the East Midlands and Devon, two tracts of the English landscape that have yielded many of his fruitful ideas, W. G. Hoskins has recognised the importance of the two and a half centuries after the Norman Conquest in the topographical development of England. The Great Rebuilding of churches in the stone belt of Rutland and east Leicestershire between 1160 and 1260 is a symptom and symbol of that period of prosperity when the population of many parts of England seems to have trebled within the space of two hundred years.[1] In Cumbria, the area covered by the counties of Cumberland, Westmorland and Lancashire north of the Sands, the same themes may be discerned but with a different emphasis. There the twelfth and thirteenth centuries saw the creation of fresh farms and hamlets out of the wilderness, a more effective organisation of the natural resources of the region with the foundation of several important monasteries, and the establishment of the first towns. But in com-parison with lowland England the north-west displayed many of the characteristics of a pioneer region, a frontier land. The making of the Cumbrian landscape was only brought to fruition in a later period of economic and social resurgence from the beginning of the seventeenth century to the end of the first quarter of the nineteenth. The dissolution of the northern march came with the Union of the Crowns in 1603 and the revolution in transport and marketing

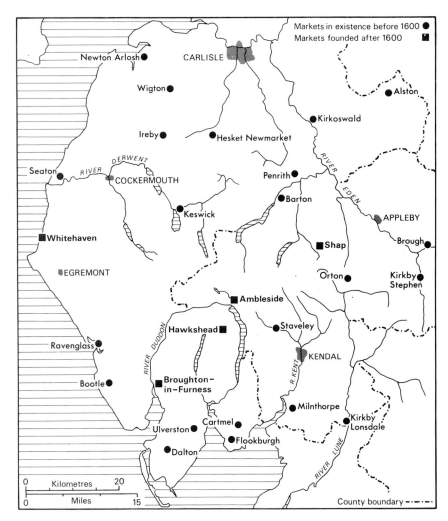

Fig. 8.1 Cumbrian markets and boroughs.

that was engineered by the railways mark two important boundaries in the regional history of Cumbria. It is proposed to discuss this later period of growth in the north-west as it is reflected in the urban history of the region, in the attempts to found new market towns, and in the topographical and social changes that overtook the old-established centres. The evolution of the medieval town into its Georgian successor represented changes as revolutionary as any imposed by the Victorians on the urban face of England. These changes can be studied with great clarity in some of the small towns of Cumbria whose cycle of growth was all but complete by the middle of the nineteenth century.

THE FIRST TOWNS OF CUMBRIA

Cumbria formed the western flank of the northern marches. It was not until 1092 that the Normans, under William II, extended the power of the English crown to the Solway Firth and across the wild moorlands of the northern Pennines into the country of the Roman Wall. The twelfth century, apart from two decades of reoccupation by the Scots, diverted the Lake District and its enveloping lowland from an agelong involvement with the Celtic world. During this formative period political power was focused on the marcher lordships, and it was the Norman marcher lords and their organisation of territory that sketched the ground plan for the urban geography of Cumbria. A succession of castle towns planted at the hearts of the Norman baronies provided the foundations for a continuous urban history in the north-west. As far as one can tell, trade and urban ways of life had long since and totally vanished from settlements of Roman origin, such as Papcastle and Old Carlisle, by the time that William Rufus (1087–1100) brought his troops and bands of colonists to establish the northern frontier.[2] Only at Carlisle is it possible that some kind of urban life survived from the days of the Roman frontier settlement to the time of the Norman reorganisation of the northern border. Even so, the few scraps of evidence about Carlisle in the centuries before the Norman Conquest argue against the continuity of urban life and institutions there. The monastery was destroyed early in the tenth century by Scandinavian raiders, and tradition claims that woodland once more colonised the site of the Roman town on the neck of land between the Eden and the Caldew. The Anglo-Saxon Chronicle as it relates the events of the year 1092 suggests that William II reoccupied a deserted site when he 'marched north to Carlisle with a large army, and re-established the fortress, and built the castle . . . and garrisoned the castle with his men'. Within half a century the foundations for an unbroken urban history had been established at Carlisle. A medieval fortress town obliterated the foundations of the Roman settlement.

At the time when the crown was engaged in the reestablishment of Carlisle as the urban focus of its territories in Cumbria, the marcher lords were busy building castles, encouraging trade and markets and bringing urban communities into being to serve their baronies. At Appleby, where Ranulph de Meschines had built a castle on a completely unoccupied site within a meander loop of the Eden, a new borough had come into existence by 1110.[3] William de Meschines, the brother of Ranulph and lord of the Barony of Copeland, created a new town at Egremont, a name that means 'the castle mound by the Eden'. The wide, gently curving market street that still forms the focus of this attractive little West Cumberland town was probably laid out between 1130 and 1140 at the time of the building of the castle. One of the most successful towns of the north-west, Kendal, was set upon its urban career in the closing years of the twelfth century when Gilbert fitz Reinfred obtained the grant of a market charter in 1189.[4] In the exposed border territory of north-east Cumberland the lords of Gilsland determined that Brampton should be the chief centre of markets and fairs in their little domain. In its evolution Brampton followed the classic topographical pattern of the seignorial town where a spacious market street is overlooked by the vast green mound of a Norman castle. Another new town, Cockermouth, slowly emerged in the middle of the thirteen century nestling beneath the walls of a castle that occupied the narrow tongue of land between the rivers Derwent and Cocker. Penrith, whose markets are first put on record in 1123, seems to have been an active rural settlement before the Norman Conquest.[5] Its evolution into a small twelfth-century market town was encouraged by its position as the centre of the honor of Penrith – a medieval territorial unit that stretched for some miles into Inglewood Forest and eastward into the Eden valley.

The fourteenth century brought to an end this long medieval experiment in the making of towns and markets in England. In the north-west a ground plan of urban settlement that can still be recognised had been firmly laid. But if some topographer of Cumbria had been able to speculate in the closing years of the fourteenth century about the future details of the urban map of his region, he might have gone wildly astray in his extrapolations.

Could any medieval surveyor of the urban scene have identified all
the towns that would succeed over the following six centuries?
Would he have foreseen those settlements endowed with all the
rights to hold markets and fairs that failed to maintain their purpose
in the long run? Among these places, the failed market towns, we
find Hesket Newmarket, Ravenglass, Barton that lies at the foot of
Ullswater, Bootle, Ireby and Staveley.[6] The abbey of Holm Cul-
tram was driven to an ambitious scheme of urban planning in the
early years of the fourteen century after a great storm in the Solway
Firth had destroyed its port and market centre of Skinburness in
1301. Four years later the abbot received a charter to establish
markets and set up a new town at Newton Arlosh. Even today
Newton Arlosh has nothing more to show than a handful of widely
scattered farms along two parallel lanes and a little church with a
dark, stifling pele tower that speaks of raids by armies and ill-
organised bands of moss-troopers out of Scotland. The understanding of the failure of the proposed towns and markets in the
north-west is as important as an appreciation of the factors that
gave success to some of the competitors in the centuries of urban
evolution. The key to some of the questions of uneven urban
development lies in a study of the next phase of growth during the
seventeenth and eighteenth centuries.

FACTORS IN URBAN GROWTH AFTER 1600

The first years of the seventeenth century in Cumbria announce a
period of urban expansion that is as important in the history of the
region as 'the golden age' that followed the Norman Conquest.

The urban network of the north-west in 1600 was based on the
coastal plain and the lowland corridor of the Eden that encircled
the Lake District. Only three places had reached full borough
status – Carlisle, Appleby and Kendal. Cockermouth and Egremont
functioned as seignorial boroughs. For the rest Cumbria was served
by a number of market towns. Some such as Penrith were long
established and successful, others weak and failing. In the eastern
parts of Cumbria we find regular markets at Brampton and Alston,
the latter focusing the life of the flourishing lead-mining communities of the northern Pennines. In the Vale of Eden, close to the
ancient trade-route into the north-west from the Stainmore gap,
there were markets at Brough, Kirkby Stephen and Kirkoswald.
Westward of Carlisle, in the Solway plain, Wigton and Ireby had
market charters, while further south Ravenglass, Bootle and Seaton

competed with the towns of Egremont and Cockermouth for the organisation of the trade of West Cumberland. On the southern fringe of the Lake District two rival markets fed on the traffic of Furness, the declining town of Dalton that had been founded by the monks of Furness Abbey and the upstart Ulverston. The latter was part of the estates of the Duchy of Lancaster and had been granted a market charter in 1280. Further east, in the lowlands that run down to the head of Morecambe Bay, the busy and expanding wool and cloth town of Kendal dominated over all. Its closest rivals were the markets of Milnthorpe, Westmorland's only port, Kirkby Lonsdale and Cartmel. Other late medieval rivals that failed to throw off their rural chrysalis within the ambit of Kendal's influence were Orton, Staveley and Flookburgh. The only market town that truly belonged to the mountainous heart of the Lake District was Keswick, whose charter had been obtained by Thomas de Derwent-water in 1276.

The seventeenth century opens with a political event of no less consequence than William II's advance on Carlisle and the succeeding creation of the baronies and their castle towns. In 1603 the Union of the Crowns transformed the political and social character of the northern march. A long peace descended on the region broken only briefly and at long rare intervals by the marching troops from across the border. For instance, in 1645 the mayor of Kendal complained of the exactions made by Scottish soldiers from the tradesmen of his town. Again, at the time of the Jacobite Rebellion of 1715 there were complaints of money exacted from the burgesses of Kendal by troops from the north. The changed political geography of the north-west in the seventeenth century opened up the possibility of expanding trade in the tiny market towns. Places such as Appleby, Penrith or Brampton, whose very survival had been threatened by armies and spasmodic raiders following the roads from the north, now stood to benefit most from the rising summer traffic of cattle from the Highlands that followed the same roads through northern England to the markets of the south-east at St Ives, Cambridge, Norwich and, chief goal of all, London.

The seventeenth century also witnessed deep changes in the social structure of the north-west that were to have profound effects upon the prosperity and growth of towns. The most important was the emergence of a rural middle class, known as the *statesmen*, which had been shaping throughout the Tudor period. The destruction of the monasteries in 1537 provided the background to the rise of the statesmen. But the birth of the yeoman farmer, as a stratum of Cumbrian society, took more than a generation and involved much litigation. Now in Elizabeth I's reign the prospect was opened up of gain, and improvement in social position, through the exchange and buying-up of land. In the countryside the improving lot of the statesmen is recorded in the steady and undocumented enclosure of the open fields that went on through the seventeenth century. But the practice of dealing in land, as it became more common in the countryside, was reflected in an increasing instability of the social structure. Some statesmen families were able to pass into the gentry largely through the active and successful buying-up of land, but for others the process of social change worked in the opposite direction. Many, through the sale of land, seem to have lost their stake in the countryside. Such families of yeomen farmers passed into the labouring classes and, as the process accelerated in the eighteenth and early nineteenth centuries, many contributed to the rising population of the towns.

The emergence of the statesmen provided a double stimulus to the expansion of urban life in the north-west in the seventeenth and eighteenth centuries. Sheep rearing played a dominant part in the economy of the statesman's farm, especially on the Furness Fells and among the deep valleys of the Lake District; and the secondary occupations of spinning, weaving and fulling that employed every member of a farmer's household found an outlet for their products in the market towns. The traffic of Hawkshead, Kendal, Penrith and Kirkby Stephen – to mention only a few of the wool markets – steadily expanded through the seventeenth century at the time when the statesmen diverted a part of a modestly increasing prosperity to a widespread rebuilding of their farmsteads in stone. As C. M. L. Bouch and G. P. Jones have written in their important study of the economic history of the Lake counties, 'it may well be that the seventeenth century was a not unfavourable period for the prosperity of the yeoman or, at any rate, that it was better for them than for some of the gentry'. Again, they sum up the same period in a sentence: 'There can be no doubt that by the seventeenth century a market in the economic sense had developed.'[7] The functions of this economic abstraction, the market, were focused on the towns and market villages that had been created out of the strategic necessities and trade demands of that earlier period of economic expansion in the Middle Ages.

The second stimulus that the countryside gave to the expansion of the towns of north-west England came from its surplus population, a surplus that was created among those who fell on hard days and were forced out of the statesman class by the sale of land and which also reflected the expansion of population that can be traced throughout Western Europe in the eighteenth century. The seventeenth century was already a time of population growth in the marcher counties. Bouch and Jones in their calculations of population changes in a group of Cumberland parishes between 1563 and 1688 reckon that there was an increase of 46 per cent. Over a similar period in Westmorland, for which they used the Bishop of Carlisle's Survey of 1563 and the hearth tax returns of 1669–71, they estimate a population growth of some 9 per cent, adding that 'growth may have been much more rapid in Kendal'.

The expansion of population was greatly accelerated in the eighteenth century. In 1688 the total population of Cumberland probably stood close to 60,000; by the time of the first census in 1801 it had reached 117,230.[8] Over the same period the population of Westmorland had climbed from less than 30,000, in the last quarter of the seventeenth century, to 40,805 in the first year of the nineteenth century. Fascinating local trends have been revealed by studies of population in the north-west over this period. For instance, Cumberland's population grew at twice the rate of that of Westmorland, a fact that seems to be explained by the opening up of its west-coast coalfield and the exploitation of the mineral resources of the northern Pennines in the eighteenth century. The pace of population change differed from parish to parish. For instance, some parishes were declining; in all some thirty-six Cumberland parishes lost population between 1700 and 1800. Towns, on the other hand, revealed a remarkable expansion of their numbers. Penrith, for example, had a population of little more than 1,000 in 1688; by 1801 it was approaching 4,000. Over the same time Workington showed an increase of 581·5 per cent climbing from 945 in the year 1688 to 6,440 at the time of the first census. Behind these bare facts we can glimpse the revolution that was taking place in English society and its economic organisation during the eighteenth century. Here was the chrysalis from which the Victorian world was to be born. By the close of the first decade of the nineteenth century twelve of Cumberland's towns counted populations of more than 1,000 and, perhaps even more striking, 40 per cent of the county's population was by that time living in towns. Even in the more rural Westmorland, we find that a fifth of the county's population in 1811 was living in Kendal. The revolution that was reshaping Cumbrian landscapes and society in the eighteenth century did not pass without notice from the untrained observer of the times. A popular article that appeared in *The Gentleman's Magazine* in 1790 records in unstatistical terms the deep social changes in the Lake District. 'But things are now assuming a new appearance. The rust of poverty and ignorance is gradually wearing off. Estates are bought up into fewer hands; and the poorer sort of people remove into towns, to gain a livelihood by handicrafts and commerce.'[9]

NEW MARKETS AND TOWNS

The beginning of the seventeenth century marks a period of modest commercial and urban expansion that forms a prelude to the revolutionary changes of the Victorian age. In several English counties one can point to attempts to establish fresh markets; the new town was a much rarer phenomenon. More often than not, as at Westerham in Kent, a seventeenth-century market charter marks the revival of a medieval trading centre. But among the newly founded markets we find Earith, Huntingdonshire, in 1623 and Stevenage, Hertfordshire, in 1624. New markets, some of which were to evolve into thriving industrial towns, appeared in Lancashire at Blackburn, Colne, Haslingden, Leigh and Padiham. In Lancashire, too, the grant of a royal charter to Thomas Fleetwood in 1700 to hold a market at Marton Mere shows that this second phase of economic expansion could suffer its casualties like the earlier post-Norman period of urban growth.

On the whole this period of expansion is not characterised by the exuberant and prolific experiments of the medieval epoch of town-making. The explanation lies in the fact that the medieval town-makers had already created a web of markets and fairs across the face of England that was ready to serve the slowly expanding commerce of the decades following the Tudor period. Again, society and the way it organised its affairs had changed deeply between 1400 and 1600. The monasteries had been swept away. They had played an active role in developing markets, the grand monastic buildings themselves often providing the focus for a tiny urban community. The medieval baronies and regional lordships were now shadows of their former selves. The incentive to found towns, at least as expressions of political power, had vanished. Even so, in Cumbria, where urban development had started so late, we find a number of interesting experiments in the two centuries after 1600. Hawkshead started its official transformation into a market town with the granting of a charter to Adam Sandys in 1608.

Ambleside, Shap and Broughton-in-Furness belong to the other newly founded markets of the period, but the most exciting and successful venture of all was the creation of a new town, port and industrial centre on the Lowther estates at Whitehaven.

Hawkshead, the first of the new markets, illustrates perfectly the history of the town in Cumbria in the period of urban expansion between 1600 and 1800. It was brought into being by the forces for growth that were most active in those times and it became 'fossilised' because it stood aside from the changed currents of development in the Victorian age. Cowper in his classic study of the local history of High Furness,[10] published in 1899, could look back in his own lifetime to the extinction of Hawkshead as a local market centre. He remarks that by the 1890s markets had ceased and that the fairs were 'only nominal'. The trade of the little town that had come into existence scarcely two centuries earlier had been 'killed by machinery, railways and auction marts'. Cowper also regretted the decline of the inns in the nineteenth century 'from places where farmers carried on business to tourists' hostelries and village idlers' haunts'.

The beginning of Hawkshead as the most important wool market of Furness in the years about 1600 had been very different. Hawkshead played an important role in the economy of Furness Abbey. Hawkshead Hall was the centre from which the monks of Furness organised the wool trade of the outlying sheep farms in the fells between lakes Windermere and Coniston. A fragment of medieval Hawkshead still survives in the gatehouse, a fifteenth-century building close by the hall where the manor courts were once held. The rental of Abbot Roger, the last head of the monastic community of Furness before the dissolution on 1537, hints at the value of the manor of Hawkshead and the extent of its wool trade. Although only a chapelry in the vast medieval parish of Dalton, Hawkshead was valued at three times that of the mother church; similarly it was reckoned at four times the value of Great Urswick, an ancient primary parish in Low Furness. The wealth of Hawkshead came from its flocks of sheep and the annual harvest of wool that passed through the abbots' market town at Dalton. The survey of the resources of Furness Abbey made at the time of the dissolution leaves no doubt about this. There the chapel tithes at Hawkshead included lambs valued at £90. Cowper calculated that 4,000 lambs were born each year in the chapelry of Hawkshead. They probably represented a flock of 10,000 sheep there in the late Middle Ages. The monastic settlement of Hawkshead consisted of a handful of farms gathered in the bowl of lowland that opened on to the shore of Esthwaite Water. There lay the strips of a common field shared by the monks at the grange farm, on the site of Hawkshead Hall, and their tenants. A chapel stood on a rocky knoll above this scattered settlement of sheep farms.

The destruction of Furness Abbey and the confiscation of its extensive territories by the Crown set in train the events that changed the status and the very landscape of Hawkshead. The economic structure of the abbey's wool trade, focused on the monastic market town of Dalton, was destroyed. At the same time the structure of rural society in High Furness was transformed by Elizabeth I's reign when the tenants of the crown lands succeeded in defining their rights and establishing their independence of the control of manorial law. At Hawkshead these changes resulted in the diversion of the wool trade from Dalton to Kendal. Hawkshead now became a collecting centre for raw material that was handed on to the wool-merchants and clothiers of Kendal – business men whose trade stretched far across England, to London and Southampton among other places. The statesmen families of High Furness were above all responsible for the emergence of Hawkshead as a regional centre. The Sandys family who had long been associated with Graythwaite as tenants of Furness Abbey were the driving force behind the transformation of Hawkshead. In 1578 Hawkshead was cut off from Dalton and established as a separate parish. It served most of the long corridor of broken fells between Windermere and Coniston until Colton was set up as an independent parish in 1676. The raising of Hawkshead to parish status is indelibly recorded in the architecture of the church on the knoll. A south aisle was added in 1578 and the work was paid for by Edwin Sandys, a member of the Graythwaite family who became Archbishop of York. The extension of the church in that year might point to the growing importance of Hawkshead and the need to find more accommodation for its parishioners. On the other hand, it may suggest nothing more than Hawkshead's new position at the heart of a large parish in the Furness Fells. Seven years later Edwin Sandys gave another impetus to the growth of Hawkshead when he obtained letters patent for the foundation of a grammar school in 1585.

Hawkshead's rights as a market centre were legally enshrined in the charter obtained in 1608 by another member of the Sandys family, Adam Sandys. It was allowed to hold a weekly market on Monday and two fairs in the year. During the next two centuries a little town grew at the foot of the knoll that is the site of the parish church. With its contrasting moods of dark grey slate and white-washed roughcast Hawkshead has remained one of the most attractive settlements of the Lake District. The haphazard arrangement of its cottages and the little squares and yards connected by narrow alleys present a comfortable feeling of disorder that is suddenly resolved by the fact that everything leads to the little market place with the town hall that was completed in the last decade of the eighteenth century. Hawkshead is the perfect eighteenth-century market town of the northern hill country that has escaped most of the technological and economic changes of the nineteenth century. Alas, the mid-twentieth century and the age of the motor-car has rudely awakened the former wool market town from its hundred-year-old sleep. Tourism with all its repulsive concomitants – cafés, gift shops, phoney antiques and parking grounds that begin to take on the dimensions of air-strips – threaten this little seventeenth-century town far more than the distant railways and auction marts that Cowper found so obnoxious.

Three other attempts to establish market towns in Cumbria before the end of the eighteenth century either ended in failure or were ultimately diverted along a different path of development. In 1650 the Countess of Pembroke secured a market charter for Ambleside. It provided for a weekly market on Wednesdays as well as two fairs. Ambleside in the middle of the seventeenth century consisted of a cluster of dark grey slate farmsteads and a little chapel gathered on the summit of a knoll above the precipitous densely wooded gorge of the Stock Ghyll. The new market site was located on smoother ground below the medieval hamlet, but still above the level of the flood-threatened plain of the Rothay where the Romans had planted their fortress on a rocky outcrop. Ambleside seems to have developed satisfactorily through the eighteenth century. Soon after its establishment as a market centre, it achieved the status of a parish in 1675. Again, in 1721 a grammar school was founded there by John Kelswick. By the 1760s Ambleside's success as a growing market centre seemed to be secured when it lay on the route of the new turnpike that joined Kendal to Keswick and Cockermouth. The eighteenth century was the formative period in the topographical development of Ambleside – a time as important as the first decades of the twelfth century in the shaping of Appleby. The market square, now scarcely noticed by the summer motorists driving bumper-to-bumper through the little town along the choked and overburdened road to Keswick, became the focus of

Ambleside's life before 1800. Here the inns were built whose heyday came with building of the turnpike across Dunmail Raise. The back streets and lanes behind the market place still have many slate cottages built in this period of prosperity, late in the eighteenth century, when Ambleside was a true regional centre, famous for its wool sales and the great sheep fair that was held each year on October 13th.

When P. J. Mannex published his trade directory of Westmorland in 1849 Ambleside's market was faring no better than its neighbour Hawkshead.[11] He reported that the weekly market had become extinct and that the autumn sheep fair was in 'a declining state'. Mannex explained the collapse of local and regional trade at Ambleside in a somewhat different way from Cowper, whose view of the degeneration of Hawkshead was taken a generation later from the end of the nineteenth century. He claimed that Ambleside's markets were destroyed by 'the general introduction of machinery' and 'the system of hawking provisions and goods from door to door'. The vagueness of the former phrase hardly supplies an adequate explanation of the extinction of a market day in a new and busy little town at the head of Windermere. No doubt the Victorians were liable to ascribe the particular ills and changes in their society to the obvious technological changes that were going on in their daily lives. An increase in the practice of door-to-door hawking might have had some effect on the prosperity of Ambleside's market-place just as changes in our own shopping habits in the second half of the twentieth century are beginning to have profound influences on the detailed topography of our towns. The truth is that Ambleside could not intrude itself successfully into the web of long established market towns in the north-west, particularly after the building of several turnpike roads between 1750 and 1770 had started a revolution in the communications of the region. The provision of regular coaching services and carriers' wagons running to daily timetables, the opening of inns to supply food, accommodation, and to act as depositories for parcels and packages helped to increase the catchment areas of the old market towns. Even though Ambleside was more favourably placed than Hawkshead on the trunk road across the Lake District, it failed to compete with Kendal for the organisation of the trade of southern Westmorland.

Chance plays an important role in the fortunes of towns. One can only speculate on what might have happened at Ambleside if the railway had reached the head of Windermere instead of stopping at Windermere village, five miles south of Ambleside. It so happened

that as Ambleside failed to fulfil its destined role as a market centre
in the first decades of the nineteenth century, the physical advantages of its site were to make the town, after Keswick, a main focus
of the Victorian tourist industry. Its hotels and boarding houses
stretched along the road towards Waterhead and in the 1850s a new
quarter with its streets of opulent middle-class villas – all dominated
by the discordant tall broach spire of Sir Giles Gilbert Scott's church
– grew to the west of the market-place. The sleep of a century fell
upon Hawkshead with the coming of the railway age. Ambleside
entered the century of the motor-car as a successful tourist resort and
today the character of this eighteenth-century market town is
distorted out of all recognition by an unbroken stream of cars and
heavy lorries and an intolerable crush of tourists.

Later still two other markets were founded in Cumbria. In 1687
Lord Wharton was granted the rights to establish a Wednesday
market at Shap, as well as three annual fairs. In this bleak, cloud-
swept trough of moorland a new market town would help to replace
the tasks that had been performed by Shap Abbey before 1540. In
1753 a further impetus was given to the growth of Shap with the
building of the turnpike road from Kendal to Eamont Bridge and
Penrith. Shap seemed well placed to benefit from the growing
traffic of a western turnpike route to Carlisle and the border. But
Shap, despite the intention of Lord Wharton, failed to establish
itself as a market town. And it was not the railway that caused its
death. Even at the beginning of the nineteenth century, long before
the triumphant threading of the Lune gorge by the railway builders,
the fairs were no longer held there and the weekly market had
become obsolete. Perhaps Shap's intolerably exposed site had something to do with its failure. A severe handicap was its location in
one of the most thinly populated tracts of the north-west on a
watershed whose flanks turned to the ancient and firmly established
regional markets at Kendal and Penrith. Shap, in the seventies of
the twentieth century, is a quieter place than it has been for more
than a hundred years now that the motorway to Carlisle has drained
the traffic from the former turnpike. One object of its forlorn
landscape recalls the seventeenth-century attempt to make a
market town there; half way along the street of cafés, pubs, farms
and quarrymen's cottages stands the little market hall that was
built about 1690 at the time of the charter.

On the south-western edge of the Lake District, at the head of
the Duddon estuary, some features of an interesting experiment in
town-making late in the eighteenth century survive at Broughton-

in-Furness. There had been a settlement at Broughton for centuries before the Gilpin-Sawrey family embarked on the reshaping of the village. Broughton had long been important as the centre of a large parish that reached far into the Furness Fells. A manor court was regularly held there and in the sixteenth century it was a centre of cloth making, the equal to Hawkshead or Cartmel. Some visual evidence of medieval Broughton still survives in the Late Norman south doorway of the parish church and the considerable parts of the building that date from the early sixteenth century, suggesting a total reshaping of the church at that time. The estate that presses on the northern fringe of the little market town, Broughton Tower, is centred on one of those relics of the unquiet decades of the late Middle Ages, a fourteenth-century pele tower.

Broughton-in-Furness already held markets in the seventeenth century for John Adams includes it in his *Index Villaris*, published in 1690. It was in the second half of the eighteenth century that the lords of the manor, the Gilpins, set about the transformation of the settlement. Between 1750 and 1780 their manor house, Broughton Tower, was largely rebuilt and extended. A spacious mansion was built round the fourteenth-century pele tower. At the same time John Gilpin gave a piece of land for the laying out of a market-place.[12] A handsome square with stone-built terraces and a late eighteenth-century town hall, the whole completely urban in character, was added to a village of slate and roughcast cottages. Broughton was planned to serve the economic needs of the years about 1800. Ships sailed far up the Duddon estuary to within a stone's throw of the market town, and it gathered woollen yarns from a wide hinterland of mountain farms to supply the hungry needs of the Yorkshire manufacturers. The deep changes in the economic geography of the north-west that took place in the nineteenth century have left Broughton fossilised in the first stage of its trans-formation from a village into a town. The urban revolution of the Victorian age was not destined to be worked out at Broughton with its coppice woods, slate quarries and sheep pastures, but close to the rich ironfields of Low Furness and West Cumberland at Barrow and Millom.

The most successful of the new towns of the seventeenth century was undoubtedly Whitehaven. The history of the town, its streets and its buildings, illustrate so many of the important themes in the development of Cumbria between 1600 and 1800.[13] The laying out of the new town at Whitehaven on a strictly gridiron plan in the years after 1680, the exploitation of the coal seams that stretched under the bed of the Irish Sea, and the giddy rise of its port until it briefly achieved second place among all the harbours of the United Kingdom, all may be closely ascribed to the energy and investments of the Lowther family. In this period, and over most of England, the theme of the lord and the landscape is mostly concerned with the building of splendid country mansions, the landscaping of the acres of former open fields, and the laying out of those painfully neat estate villages that sheltered the retainers of the aristocratic families of Georgian England. The Lowthers conform to this pattern in their role as landlords in the countryside to the south of Penrith. There another Sir John Lowther, in the very years that his cousin was directing the development of the new town at Whitehaven, engaged in the making of a vast estate and deer park on the limestone fells above the Lowther valley. The old settlement of Lowther was destroyed in 1682 to open up the prospect of Sir John's mansion, and a freshly planned estate village, Newtown, was brought into being. The same ability to reshape a whole landscape and express the purposes of an individual landowner was achieved with even greater success and more dramatic effect at Whitehaven. The Lowthers climbed in the Tudor period to an important position among the gentry of Cumbria. Their success is explained by the gradual acquisition of estates that had started in the fifteenth century and was much accelerated in the more fluid land market that emerged after the destruction of the monasteries. Whitehaven had been part of the properties of St Bees Abbey before the dissolution of the monasteries. It reached the hands of the Lowther family through those complex processes of marriage and mortgage that helped in the accumulation of rich estates. Christopher Lowther took over the Whitehaven property in 1630. Four years later, at the south end of the open bay, where there was a handful of fishermen's cottages, he built a pier for the shipping that was using the port.

The development of Whitehaven depended, above all, on Sir Christopher Lowther's son, Sir John, and on his successor, Sir James Lowther, who inherited the estate in 1705 and directed its growth for another half-century. The 1660s, when the young Sir John Lowther was still in his twenties, proved to be an important decade in the expansion of the settlement. In 1660 he secured the right to hold markets and fairs at Whitehaven. Even more important for the growth of the coal trade and the exploitation of its mines was Charles II's grant to Sir John Lowther in 1666 'of all the derelict land at this place'. Derelict land in seventeenth-century Cumberland meant wasteland to which ownership could not be attached. An-

other important victory in Sir John Lowther's struggle to consolidate his interests was achieved in 1678 when, after a struggle involving three other claimants, he gained all rights to the foreshore
between high and low water marks for two miles to the northward
of Whitehaven. At the same time Sir John Lowther aimed to extend
and rationalise his mining interests around Whitehaven through
the purchase of land or the acquisition of leases on coal-bearing
lands that bordered his estate. For instance, in 1675 he leased from
his neighbouring land-owner, Henry Fletcher, the mines of Disting-
ton. Three years later the gain over the control of rights on the foreshore at Whitehaven placed the loading of ships there in the hands
of the Lowther family.

   Such was the background against which the new town of Whitehaven was to emerge in the 1680s. The concentration of landownership and all the rights of access and movement that went with
it on this rich and easily worked coalfield of West Cumberland
gave the Lowther properties a head start in the industrial revolution
in the north-west. By the closing decade of the seventeenth century
the coalpits around Whitehaven were yielding almost 20,000 tons
per year. The chief market for the coal was Ireland and, as a consequence, the port owned a fleet of fifty-five ships by the end of
the 1680s. Sir John Lowther's new town was successfully planted in
this economic setting of an expanding coal trade and a flourishing
port. During the 1680s a spacious rectangular grid of streets was
sketched out north-east of the original nucleus of the fishing village,
a place of scarcely fifty houses in 1660. The new town spread itself
over the meadows and hedged fields between the Pow Beck and
the boundary of Sir John Lowther's estate, the Flatt. Within a
decade the population of Whitehaven had passed 2,000, and by
the beginning of the eighteenth century it had reached almost 3,000.

   Sir John Lowther's energy and initiative in the creation of what
must be considered as the first planned town of the Industrial Revolution was carried on through another half-century from 1705 until
1755 by his son, Sir James Lowther. In 1708 he engineered a private
Act of Parliament that created the Town and Harbour Trustees, a
body that was to guide the development of Whitehaven until the
achievement of full borough status in 1894. Between 1700 and 1760
the population of Whitehaven had risen to a little more than 9,000.
By the time of the first census in 1801 the population of the township
together with the working-class hamlets of the Ginns and Mount
Pleasant that lay beyond its immediate boundary had reached
12,000. Whitehaven's success was secured by the rising output of

its coal-mines through the eighteenth century. In the latter part of the eighteenth century the average annual output of coal was 150,000 tons and by the 1830s this had increased further to almost a quarter of a million tons a year. Another important economic stimulus in the first decades of the town's expansion between 1700 and 1750 was the tobacco trade with Virginia. Imports there quadrupled to almost five million pounds in weight between 1710 and 1740. Against this background of trade the new town of the Lowthers took shape. Sir John Lowther had in mind a town of wide streets with substantial houses set in spacious gardens – an urban counterpart to the elegant planning of his country estate at Lowther. Planned towns rarely follow the pattern imagined by their founders. The forces of growth impose their own shapes and the original plan becomes distorted or buried under the bricks and mortar of later decades. The rapid growth of population, particularly in the last quarter of the eighteenth century, was largely housed by building over the gardens that belonged to the large mansions in the centre of the town. The dark courtyards and narrow alleys that came to occupy the blocks between the wide streets of Sir John Lowther's primary plan for Whitehaven degenerated into the slums of the twentieth century, slums whose clearance and improvement has given rise to the most radical piece of town-planning at Whitehaven since the new town first began to take shape about 1690. Unfortunately the ruthlessness of contemporary redevelopment has swept away or threatens much of the visual evidence of Whitehaven's history. Even so, as one comes across the sight of Whitehaven, its chequer-board plan suddenly revealed from some viewpoint on the surrounding hills, one cannot fail to be moved by the prospect of a place whose outlines were shaped by the idea of the bastide towns of that earlier medieval age of urban expansion. One can still enjoy that view of Whitehaven from the north-east so vividly set down by Cumberland's great eighteenth-century historian and topographer, Hutchinson:

> As you descend to the town from the northern road, it has a most singular appearance, the buildings lie so deep in the creek, and the eminence you descend is so much superior, that you see nothing but the slated roofs of the houses. This singularity is an advantage to the traveller's surprise, when he enters the town, consisting of wide and elegant streets; the houses built in a modern style and good taste.[14]

The success of the Lowther family in the creation of Whitehaven was not to be repeated in Cumbria, although it was imitated at

Maryport and in a modest way at Workington. A brief comparison of the history of these two places with that of Whitehaven illustrates the complex forces that have operated in the shaping of the English landscape. Any observer of the geography of Cumbria in the seventeenth century would have expected Workington to emerge as the focus of the West Cumberland plain. In Elizabeth I's reign it was already 'the chief haven of the county of Cumberland'. During the first half of the seventeenth century most of the exports of coal from Cumberland had gone through Workington. In the sheltered estuary of the Derwent Nature seemed to have given the place so much advantage over Whitehaven's open bay. The disadvantages that hampered its expansion in the seventeenth century were of human making. There were disagreements among the freeholders working the coal pits around Workington, the multiple ownership of land created obstructions in the way of carting coal to the harbour, and in his time as lord of the manor of Workington Sir Patrick Curwen demanded such high payments from the working of collieries and use of the harbour that the exports declined. Although the production of coal at Workington, where the Curwen family owned nine pits, increased in the eighteenth century, the district around the mouth of the Derwent was no match for the highly organised properties of the Lowther family a few miles to the south. For instance, the Whitehaven pits, like most early mining operations, suffered badly from flooding. As early as 1717 Sir James Lowther had installed a Newcomen engine to speed the drainage of water from the Howgill mine. It was not until the close of the eighteenth century that the same technical improvements appeared at the coal-pits on the Curwen properties at Workington. Hutchinson, writing in 1794, reported that 'within these few years Mr Curwen has erected six fire-engines, which are employed both in winding up coals and pumping water. The fire engines have greatly lessened the number of horses used'. Perhaps the least investigated cause of the impetuous development of Whitehaven in the eighteenth century and the sluggish growth of Workington lies in the attitudes of the two landlords, the Lowther and Curwen families. All the evidence points to the Curwens of Workington Hall as a family whose interests were directed towards agriculture rather than industry. Sir Patrick Curwen, as we have noticed, regarded coal as a by-product of his properties that was to be taxed to the hilt. In the eighteenth century, John Christian Curwen played a part in the agrarian revolution in Cumberland that achieved as much notice as the role of the Lowthers and their agents – obscure men such as John

Spedding – in the industrial revolution. John Christian Curwen was the peer among the improving landlords of the north-west. His pedigree herds on the Workington Hall farms and his experiments 'with every plausible compost or agency that the theory of chemistry, or the reasoning of practical men could suggest' earned him the title of 'father of Cumbrian farming'. In the years about 1800 John Christian Curwen invested large sums in the enclosure, fencing and draining of poor land.[15] Perhaps the economic and urban development of Workington suffered because the Curwens conceived of the farmer as the true exploiter of Nature's gifts. Even so the little port on the Derwent estuary that had reached a population of 6,440 by the first census of 1801, was the object of improvements in the 1780s. The quays were extended and a tiny newly planned quarter, focused on Portland Square, formed the core of the upper town above the cluster of older cottages that stretched along the estuary between the parish church and Workington Hall, the chief mansion of the Curwens.

Further north, where the Ellen empties into the sea, another experiment in town-planning followed the pattern that had been laid down at Whitehaven. In 1749 Humphrey Senhouse whose estates were at Netherhall set about the capitalisation of his properties by the building of a coal dock within the arc of the Ellen's curving estuary. On the gentle slope to the north of the river Humphrey Senhouse's new town, Maryport, was established with a grid-iron network of streets. For a century Maryport's economic prospect looked pleasing. By the 1770s it had an ironworks and three shipyards, and the coal trade seemed to be firmly rooted because between seventy and eighty ships used the harbour each year. In 1840 the construction of the Maryport and Carlisle railway provided a temporary impetus to the northern fringe of the Cumberland coalfield. But Maryport entered the competitive race between the towns of West Cumberland late in time. It failed to assume the role of a minor regional capital that fell to Whitehaven.

CHANGES IN THE TOPOGRAPHY OF THE ESTABLISHED TOWNS

The decades that elapsed between the Union of the Crowns at the beginning of the seventeenth century and the passing of the Reform Bill, an event that opens up the epoch of the Victorian town, witnessed some fundamental changes in the topography and society of the long established towns of Cumbria. For instance, the accelerating growth of urban populations was reflected in extensions to the built-up areas of places like Appleby, Cockermouth and Kendal. Cockermouth, a late foundation in the series of medieval towns in the north-west, seems to have survived with considerable difficulty until the years of the seventeenth century introduced a more favourable period of prosperity and growth. Ever since the grant of a market charter in 1221 Cockermouth's trading activities had been confined to a local Monday market. In 1638 a fresh charter from Charles I to the earl of Northumberland expanded the trade of Cockermouth with the permission 'to keep a fair in his town of Cockermouth every Wednesday from the first week of May till Michaelmas'. These weekly horse and cattle fairs, introduced at the time when the trade in livestock between the hill-lands of northern Britain and the south was becoming an important part of the nation's economy, helped to change the shape and extent of the little market town that had been confined between the castle and the church. The weekly cattle fairs took place outside the built-up area of the medieval town along the lane that led towards Brigham. By the beginning of the eighteenth century a new quarter had come into existence, centred on the wide street where the cattle dealers and horse traders gathered for their Wednesday fair. A hundred years later Main Street, as the cattle market was now called, had taken over from the medieval market-place beneath the castle as the chief focus of Cockermouth.

The seventeenth century saw the first important extension of Appleby. For more than five hundred years this Norman castle-town had existed within a huge meander of the Eden, guarded by the river on three sides and dominated by its castle from the south. Towards the close of the seventeenth century a tiny suburb had been established on the east bank of the river, facing the bridge that leads into the market-place.[16] Of all the towns of Cumbria, Kendal illustrates most clearly the themes of urban change between the end of the Tudor period and the threshold of Victoria's reign. In this modest Westmorland industrial town and regional market centre we can trace the social and topographical transformations that link the Middle Ages with our own times. Kendal received its first market charter before the end of the twelfth century. In 1575 a royal charter established this busy wool market and cloth-making town as a borough. Two glimpses of the appearance and layout of this newly recognised borough are contained in documents from the period. The borough records of December 1577 show great concern about the haphazard and uncontrolled character of building that was beginning to encroach on the market-place and streets. A record of

5 December says that

> the Alderman and Burgesses of this borough of Kirkbiekendall at this present not only being and thoroughly perceiving by sundry examples the manifest hurt and inconvenience already come to this Borough by the great 'streitninge' of the market places within the same, by reason chiefly of Dyers houses, shops, taverns, galleries, stairs and buildings heretofore being suffered to be set up.

It was then decreed that further development could only take place with the permission of the alderman and burgesses. The new and expanding borough that was already suffering the problems of congestion we can see in Speed's map of Kendal published in 1614. The simple plan of the town was focused on two roads, roads that still form the skeleton of modern Kendal. From the bridge across the river Kent, close to the parish church, a long street ran northwards for almost a mile as Highgate and Stricklandgate. From the market-place, on a flattened spur where Highgate passes into Stricklandgate, another primary road in Kendal's town plan, Stramongate, ran down to a second bridge across the Kent. On the further side of this bridge, to the east of the river among the meadows and town fields, a tiny outlying suburb was already in being along Wildman's Gate.

The two centuries that followed the making of Speed's map saw the gradual disappearance of most of the open land within the town. The long gardens and orchards that ran down to the river from the houses, shops and industrial premises that faced on to Highgate were gradually built over with cottages and workshops. Access to this slowly expanding honeycomb of new buildings was by narrow alleys or through tortuous courtyards. The results of this process are plainly visible when we compare the plan of Kendal drawn by John Todd in 1787 with the earlier survey of Speed. The land on either side of the two axial roads has been covered with a mass of buildings and narrow lanes that conform to the lines of the ancient burgage plots. Kendal, towards the end of the eighteenth century, still remains substantially within its medieval bounds; its sharply rising population has been accommodated within the area of the old town. The 'Order for buyldinge within this Boroughe' which the alderman and burgesses of Kendal enacted in 1577 might have restrained the encroachment of buildings on to the public highways, but it hardly achieved an orderly development of the town, if one is to judge from the accounts of the first topographers and tourists in Cumbria. Thomas Gray's *Journal in the Lakes*, published in 1769, was the result of a hectic fortnight's sightseeing that was to bring

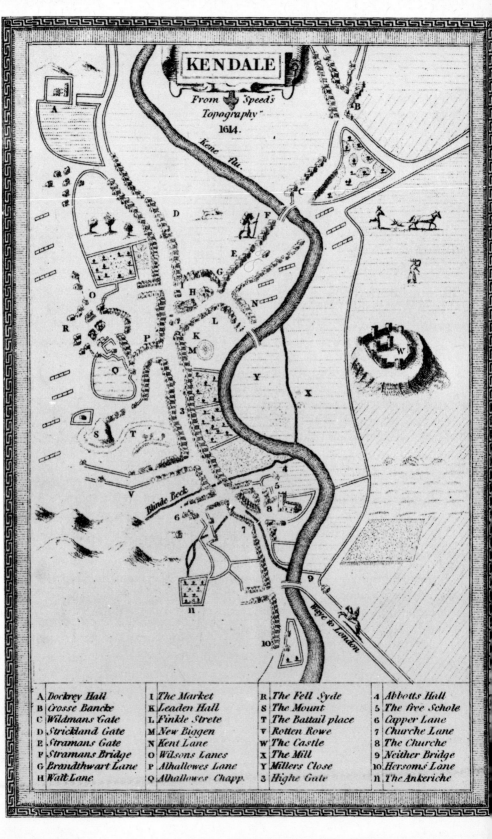

KENDALE

From Speed's Topography
1614.

A	*Dockrey Hall*	I	*The Market*
B	*Crosse Bancke*	K	*Leaden Hall*
C	*Wildmans Gate*	L	*Finkle Strete*
D	*Strickland Gate*	M	*New Biggen*
E	*Stramans Gate*	N	*Kent Lane*
F	*Stramans Bridge*	O	*Wilsons Lanes*
G	*Brandthwart Lane*	P	*Alhallowes Lane*
H	*Walt Lane*	Q	*Alhallowes Chapp.*

R	*The Fell Syde*	4	*Abbotts Hall*
S	*The Mount*	5	*The free Schole*
T	*The Battail place*	6	*Capper Lane*
V	*Rotten Rowe*	7	*Churche Lane*
W	*The Castle*	8	*The Churche*
X	*The Mill*	9	*Neither Bridge*
Y	*Millers Close*	10	*Hersoms Lane*
3	*Highe Gate*	11	*The Ankeriche*

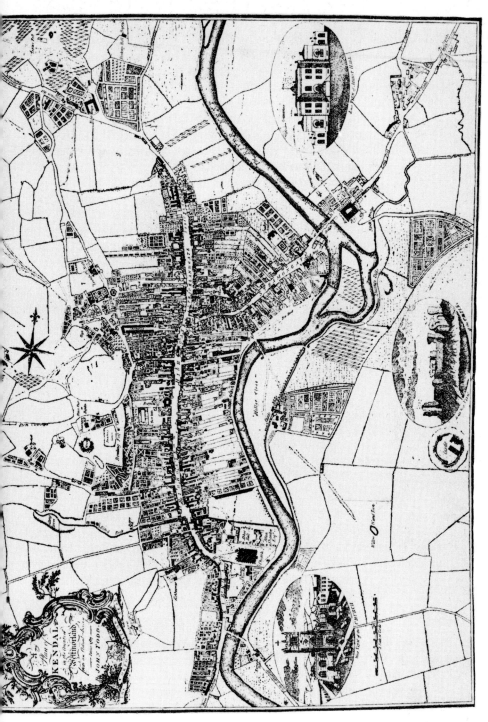

thousands of tourists in its train by the end of the eighteenth century. His memory of Kendal was of a town 'where, excepting the two principal streets, all the houses seem as if they had been dancing a country dance, and were out; there they stand, back to back, corner to corner, some up hill, some down, without intent or meaning'.

After 1750 the revolution in communications that came with the construction of the turnpike roads increased the nodal qualities of Kendal and extended the range of the town's influence over the surrounding country. In a single decade between 1752 and 1763 six different turnpike roads were constructed from Kendal linking it with the West Riding, the Eden valley, north Cumberland, Lancashire and Furness. The first regular mail coach to run from Manchester to Glasgow began in 1786; it made Kendal one of its chief calling places. By the beginning of the nineteenth century twelve different stage coach services left the town's inns every day. Kendal's overwhelming traffic problems of the twentieth century were already foreshadowed in the new role that the town had acquired as a transport centre by 1800. *The Beauties of England and Wales*, a long series of volumes that appeared in 1814 to serve the rising interest in travel and topographical history, expressed clearly the economic and social revolution that the new roads had brought to the north-west.

> The press of commerce towards Carlisle and Glasgow and the numerous visitors to the Lakes, introduced a constant stream of travellers from the metropolis, and with them new ideas of human life. The Mail began to run along the Kendal and Shap road in 1786. After this the revolution in buildings, dress, furniture, food, manners, and literature, soon attained its height, and the peculiarities of this county are now verging fast into oblivion.[17]

The changes of this period are still written into the topography of Kendal; several were the result of the need to accommodate the rising stream of traffic through the town. To this end the Market Cross was removed in 1765. The bridges over the Kent had to be widened – Nether Bridge at the southern approach to Kendal in 1772 and again in 1822, the northern exit across Stramongate Bridge in 1794. In 1781 a new street, Lowther Street, was cut from Highgate directly to the river, providing a bypass along the water-front that avoided the market-place and the upper part of Stramongate. Gardens disappeared to make way for the new road and an inn, the Black Bull, had to be demolished. *The Cumberland Pacquet*, a Whitehaven newspaper, reported these changes on 27 February

1781. 'The ground for building a new street in Kendal is let off, and a great part of it will be done in the course of the summer.' The new road opened in 1782, the building plots on the land of the former gardens were rapidly taken up and an historian of Kendal, a century later, was able to write 'what might have been an open sunny thoroughfare, became a narrow path of gloom'.[18] Two years after the opening of Lowther Street the *Cumberland Pacquet* was able to strike a more practical note than J. C. Curwen in his history. 'The new street lately opened in Kendal is almost built up and is found of great convenience, not only by opening a way to the river, but by taking carriages, etc., by the outside of the town and thereby avoiding a great part of the pavement in passing through the place'. Kendal was already struggling with its traffic problems almost two centuries ago.

The decades about 1800 gave to Kendal the face that is still familiar to us today. Houses and shops along the two axial streets were largely rebuilt in stone – the pale grey limestone that came from the quarries outside the town on Kendal Fell. The urbane ideas that filtered into the north-west with the building of the turnpikes produced a style of town architecture that for the first time was cut off from the modes and methods of the countryside. Behind the Georgian façades of modern Kendal we can still find traces of that earlier period of building in the seventeenth century that followed the vernacular design and techniques used in the great wave of rebuilding in the 'statesman' farms – round chimneys, heavy slate roofs, projecting spinning galleries.

The years about 1800 not only gave Kendal and the other market towns of Cumbria a physiognomy that is still recognisable, but at this time many elements of modern urban society were to take root. Two banks were founded in Kendal in 1788 – Wakefield's in Stricklandgate and Maud, Wilson and Crewdson in Highgate. A subscription library appeared in 1794, and by 1820 Kendal was able to publish two newspapers – the *Kendal Chronicle* expressed a Whig point of view and the *Kendal Gazette* was Tory in outlook. The theatre was less successful in Kendal where playhouses were founded and failed on several occasions. Perhaps a town whose streets and immediate surroundings in Westmorland contained the largest concentration of Quakers in the country was hardly likely to be a profitable ground for the establishment of a theatre. It is estimated that in the late eighteenth century between 10 and 12 per cent of the population of Kendal belonged to the Society of Friends. But if theatres failed in Kendal, the foundation of a Natural History

Society in 1817 seemed a suitable recreation for the more austere members of its society.

The seventeenth and eighteenth centuries form a transition period in the history of the English town. The structure of medieval society was dissolved and these changes were reflected in the topography of the town. From the earlier centuries only the street-plans and a scatter of buildings in our urban cores have survived into the present age. The Victorian decades were another formative epoch in the urban history of England, wiping away so much of the past in the great conurbations. The changes of this later time, particularly those belonging to the industrial revolution, touched the north-west only lightly. It is our good fortune that we can examine in Cumbria the lineaments of the town without the deep undergrowth of urban development in the nineteenth century.

REFERENCES

1. W. G. Hoskins, *Midland England*, (Batsford, 1949).
2. E. Birley, 'Roman Papcastle', *Transactions of the Cumberland and Westmorland Antiquarian and Archaeological Society* [Trans. *CWAAS*], lxiii, new ser. (1963), 96–125.
3. W. D. Simpson, 'The town and castle of Appleby: a morphological study', *Trans. CWAAS*, xlix, new ser. (1950), 118–33.
4. C. Nicholson, *The Annals of Kendal* (1861).
5. W. Furness, *History of Penrith* (Penrith, 1894).
6. C. Caine, 'The fair at Ravenglass', *Trans. CWAAS*, xi, new ser. (1921), 237–52.
7. C. M. L. Bouch and G. P. Jones, *A Short Economic and Social History of the Lake Counties, 1500–1830* (Manchester University Press, 1961).
8. Bouch and Jones, *op. cit.*
9. *Gentleman's Magazine*, lx, pt 1 (1790), 506.
10. H. S. Cowper, *Hawkshead: its history, antiquities and folklore* (1899).
11. P. J. Mannex, *History, topography and Directory of Westmorland* (1849).
12. W. Whellan, *The History and Topography of the Counties of Cumberland and Westmorland* (Pontefract, 1860).
13. D. Hay, *Whitehaven, a short history* (Whitehaven Public Library, 1966).
14. W. Hutchinson, *The History of the County of Cumberland*, 2 vols (Carlisle, 1794).
15. T. H. Bainbridge, 'Eighteenth century agriculture in Cumbria', *Trans. CWAAS*, xlii, new ser. (1942), 56–66.
16. M. W. Holdgate, *A History of Appleby* (Appleby, J. Whitehead, 1956).
17. J. Britton *et al.*, *The Beauties of England and Wales: Westmorland*, vol. xv (1814).
18. J. F. Curwen, *Kirkbie-Kendall* (Kendal, 1900).

9

The making of some new towns, c. 1600–1720[1]

There has been very little historical study of the people and capital involved in town building. Both geographers and historians have examined the morphology of urban development, students of architecture and building construction their appearance and the structure of surviving houses and public buildings. But this is only part of the story. Professor Hoskins has emphasised this point repeatedly. In his book *Fieldwork in Local History* he remarked: 'Men are as important in town development as geography. . . . One should therefore ask continually: "Who planned these streets? Who financed the development?" and so on.' More recently he has said that 'who built the needed houses, laid out the streets, financed the work, is still largely a mystery before the nineteenth century, above all in our provincial towns'.[2] Although several excellent monographs on the history of individual towns have been written in the past ten or fifteen years this theme has been largely overlooked. As a contribution to this neglected topic this paper is concerned with the creation of four new towns: Whitehaven in Cumberland, Deal and Tunbridge Wells in Kent, and Portsea in Hampshire, between about 1660 and 1720. Because the initial growth of a successful new town is rapid, the planning of the streets and building plots, the provision of public buildings and the erection of the houses are specially interesting. This essay discusses particularly the types of people who were responsible and, so far as the sources allow, the money they spent.

Most urban building in the seventeenth and eighteenth centuries took place in established centres. Indeed the new town has played a relatively minor role in the gradual urbanisation of England since the Middle Ages. It is estimated that in 1700 between 1 million and 1·5 million people in England and Wales lived in towns and that by 1911 the figure was almost 29 million,[3] yet nearly all towndwellers live today in centres already existing before the seventeenth century. The basic reason is that England in the early modern period was well endowed with towns, mostly founded in the Middle Ages. According to how one defines an urban centre, there were between 500 and 800 towns reasonably well spread over the landscape of England and Wales.[4] Even the smaller English counties, such as Bedfordshire, Oxfordshire and Huntingdonshire, had their handful of market towns. Though the great majority were tiny, with between 100 and 250 households, their strategic position and existing services made them a suitable centre for further economic development in the district from the seventeenth century onwards. Even the industrial regions of the North and the Midlands were largely dependent on the traditional trading centres for the services required during the rapid industrialisation of the eighteenth and nineteenth centuries. There were of course some exceptions: Merthyr Tydfil and the Five Towns of the Potteries were created during the Industrial Revolution, Crewe and Middlesbrough in the mid-nineteenth century, but the majority of the larger manufacturing centres of today were in existence, though by modern standards on a minute scale, in the seventeenth century.

The later decades of the seventeenth century were a period of considerable economic growth. Foreign trade expanded, industry diversified, and agricultural production is believed to have grown, helped by the spread of new techniques. It is still understandable in view of the existing urban endowment that development should have been mostly based on the traditional commercial nuclei. For example, despite its expansion of agricultural output and the flourishing growth of its textile industries no new town is known to have emerged in East Anglia in these years. Yet certainly some new English towns appeared in consequence of industrial development. The export of coal from the Cumberland coast created Whitehaven, the largest of the new towns at the beginning of the eighteenth century. Wednesbury, in the Black Country, which combined coal and iron-ore mining with nail making and the distribution of nail rod, was granted a market in 1709, but its growth during the whole of the seventeenth century had been fairly slow and it was a settlement of some size in the 1660s and 1670s.[5] It is thus difficult to regard it as entirely the creation of the later seventeenth century. Some of the most important new settlements which appeared between about 1650 and 1720 were not created by normal commercial development or manufacturing industry. The pressures of naval warfare and defence in the sixteenth century had led to the foundation of Chatham in the sixteenth century; now the great expansion of the Navy in the Nine Years War under William III and the War of the Spanish Succession led to the creation of the new towns of Dock, near Plymouth, and Portsea, near Portsmouth, both based on the respective naval dockyards. A settlement at Deal on the East Kent coast emerged more gradually during the seventeenth century because of the importance of the Downs as a naval station, its growth accelerating towards the end of the century. Tunbridge Wells appeared as a small town in the 1680s and 1690s on account of the growing popularity of spas as resorts. Enthusiasm among Englishmen to take the waters had originated in the late sixteenth century. It was developed by the advocacy of spa waters for medical purposes by the doctors, and by the expansion in the wealth and leisure of at least part of the landowning and trading classes.

The estate of St Bees at Whitehaven, on which the town was later built, was bought by Sir John Lowther, a member of a prominent Cumberland gentry family, at the beginning of the seventeenth century. Coal was probably first dug for sale about 1620. As Dr Millward says elsewhere in the volume, the port facilities were begun with a pier constructed by Sir Christopher Lowther in the 1630s: presumably the existence of a little creek at Whitehaven with a few cottages led to its choice as a port.[6] It was another Sir John Lowther (d.1705) commissioner of the Admiralty between 1689 and 1696, who established the prosperity of the settlement on a firm footing. The ways in which this was done are described in Dr Millward's essay on Cumbrian towns.

The dependence of the origin of the town of Whitehaven on the export of coal and the enterprise of the Lowther family is shown by its prior existence as a mere seaside hamlet doing a trifling seaborne trade and some fishing. In 1566 'there were but six houses and no shipping except one small Picakard of eight or nine ton . . . no mariners except a few fishermen, nothing exported besides a small quantity of herrings and codfish, nor anything imported but salt'.[7] The depositions of several old inhabitants in two Exchequer lawsuits in 1680 reveal the growth earlier in the seventeenth century. David Hamilton, who had lived in Whitehaven for forty-eight years, said that when he first knew the town (i.e. in the early 1630s) there were twelve vessels belonging to Whitehaven varying between twenty-eight and 8–10 tons, and forty-one dwellings occupied by salters, colliers, fishermen and other tradesmen. These inhabitants obtained the right to hold a market during the Interregnum. Another deponent implied that there had been considerable house building since the Restoration, and two agreed that at present there were about 132 houses, suggesting a population of about 650 to 800. There were thirty-three vessels (seventy-five down to 10 tons) owned in the port.[8] The great expansion came in the next thirty years. As was said in 1705

> great numbers of people have been drawn to bring their effects, settle
> their families, and build houses at Whitehaven to carry on a trade
> there. And the town has now advanced to that degree as to own about
> eighty sail of ships of a considerable burthen, many of them are
> employed in the plantations and other foreign trades.[9]

In 1693 there were 2,222 inhabitants and in 1713 there were 4,000.[10]

The medieval parish of Deal had been centred on the village (later known as Upper Deal) a mile from the sea, with a church and manor house. There may have been a few buildings adjoining or on the sea beach by the 1530s, at the site of the future town, later known as Lower Deal. While Deal fishermen and pilots serving vessels passing through the Downs were presumably the first to use the shore, the almost annual assembly of warships in the Downs from the beginning of the reign of Henry VIII and the building of three local castles in 1539 and 1540 providing employment for local people were probably additional incentives to building by the shore.[11] However the settlement was no more than a village in the early seventeenth century: speaking in 1694 Jane Barrow said that when she first came to Deal in the 1620s there were about forty houses, suggesting a probable population of only about 200 or 250.[12] One reason for the slow growth of the settlement may have been the fear of the military authorities that building on the shore would interrupt cannon fire from the castles against an enemy landing, and the possible prohibition of construction in the period of intermittent threat of invasion from the Continent between the 1530s and 1604: a survey of the manor of Court Ash in Deal in 1616 refers to the existence of cottages on the beach, and that the Lord Warden of the Cinque Ports was to decide whether they 'shall stand or be demolished as noisome to the Castles there'. Again the freeholders of the manor were anxious to keep open access to the seashore and may have tried to prevent building on the pretext of holding rights of common on the beach: in 1623 a Deal pilot named Andrew Rand who was a freeholder tried forcibly to stop the construction of a house on the beach by a baker. However there are other indications that the number of dwellings was growing in the early part and middle of the seventeenth century both from increasing services to shipping and on account of convenience to the military staff of the castles.[13]

In the later seventeenth century the settlement became a small town. The population rose considerably between 1640 and the 1670s, and development continued in the next two decades.[14] In 1694 James Farrer, a tailor, who had lived in Deal for twenty-seven years, said that during this period 'a great many houses had been built in the Middle Street and Beach Street in Deal to wit neer as many as were standing there when this deponent first knew the same'.[15] The growing quantity of shipping using the Downs remained the basis of the town's economy, as its own trading and fishing were still tiny. As the settlement grew the livelihood of the inhabitants widened beyond that of the occupations of pilots, seamen, victuallers and suppliers of ships' provisions and stores to the general crafts and trades needed to serve these occupations and the farmers of the surrounding agricultural district. As one inhabitant remarked in 1694, the streets 'are and were inhabited by people of all or most sorts of callings'. The settlement formally received urban status in 1699 with a grant of a charter of incorporation and the right to hold a market, ending the dependence in this respect on Sandwich, five miles away.

The history of Tunbridge Wells as a resort begins about 1606, when some iron-impregnated waters in the parish of Speldhurst in southwest Kent, only a few yards from the Sussex parish of Frant and the Kentish parish of Tonbridge, were found to be of medical value. Their popularity was almost immediate. In 1619 John Chamberlain could write that 'the waters at Tunbridge . . . for these three or foure yeares have been much frequented, especially this summer by many great persons'.[16] The publication by a doctor of a long treatise entitled *The Queenes Wells, or the Nature and Virtue of Tunbridge Water* in 1632 is evidence of its continued importance. [17]After the Restoration, as the numbers attending for diversion began to exceed those coming for health reasons, it grew even more popular. By then the Wells ranked second only to Bath as a health resort, and probably almost equalled it as a fashionable rendezvous.[18]

The history of Tunbridge Wells as a settlement begins about seventy years after the start of its history as a spa. Up to 1680 it was a remote and barren spot: the nearest market town was Tonbridge, six miles to the north, and the nearest hamlet, Rusthall, over a mile away. Only a lane between Tonbridge and the Sussex village of Frant ran near the main spring, which lay in a valley at the bottom of a common (Bishops Down) belonging to the manor of Rusthall. The surrounding hills were covered with forest and heath. As late as 1680 there was no more than the principal well surrounded by a pavement and railings, a shaded walk, two or three public rooms and several tradesmen's booths.[19] No lodging houses had been erected, and in the 1670s visitors stayed in the neighbouring hamlets in Southborough and Rusthall, the former being two and a half miles away, or with local gentry.

When at last building began the settlement grew rapidly. In 1680 the first lodging houses were erected on the north side of Bishops Down in Culverden Wood on the hill later known as Mount Ephraim. After 1682 shops were built on 'The Walks' near the well; and finally, after 1685, lodging houses were built on the hill, to be known as Mount Sion, a few hundred yards to the east. By the beginning of the eighteenth century, when a long lull in the physical development of the town began, there were about 150 houses (see Plate 11).[20] The chief source of income for the property owners or their tenants were the lodging houses, shops and public rooms. When Celia Fiennes visited the town in 1697 she found that 'they have made the Wells very commodious by the many good buildings all about it and two or three mile around, which are lodgings for the company that drinke the waters'.[21] The shops, principally on the Walks, were 'full of all sorts of toys, silver, and china'. She also found 'two large coffee houses for tea, chocolate, etc., and two rooms for the Lottery and Hazard board', and there were bowling greens and assembly rooms for dancing. Many of the tradespeople lived at the Wells for the whole year. It is true that several Londoners owned shops which were only open in the summer, and that farmers and tradespeople living and working elsewhere in the neighbourhood owned lodging houses. Yet from the first there were tradespeople as permanent residents at the Wells for whom the service of the company in the summer was the chief source of livelihood. Like hotel keepers and shopkeepers at seaside resorts today, the income of these earliest inhabitants came mainly from the summer visitors; but they might add to their livelihood by following a trade or craft of use to local people. Like many craftsmen in country villages some of them farmed a few acres on the edge of the town.

The construction at Portsea with which we are concerned took

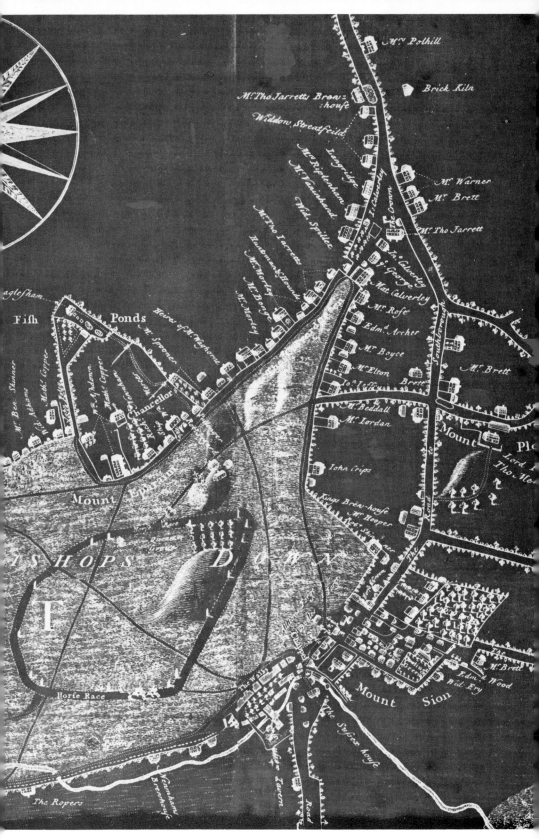

Plate 11   Tunbridge Wells in 1738.

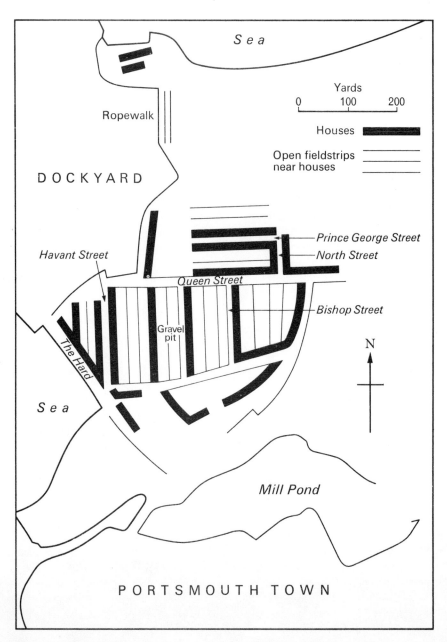

Fig. 9.1   Portsea in 1720.

place in the War of the Spanish Succession and the years immediately
following, that is, in the first two decades of the eighteenth century.
About 1670 most of the inhabitants of Portsea Island, numbering
between about 3,500 and 4,000,[22] lived in the town of Portsmouth,
covering about 110 acres at the south-west corner of the Island and
encircled by fortifications. Most of the remainder were farmers
living in three or four hamlets scattered over the Island. The Dockyard was situated half a mile north of the town, from which it was
separated first (and nearer the town) by an inlet known as the Mill
Pond and then by some Corporation waste and open field strips in
West Dock Field (see Fig. 9.1). The work of the Dockyard was
expanding in the later seventeenth century, and in the 1680s and
1690s there was some house building on the southern edge of the
Field and probably on the waste, that is, several hundred yards from
the Dockyard. However, the Portsea ratebook of 1700 records only
fifty-two property holders in this part of Portsea (excluding thirteen
staff resident in the Yard).[23] Building immediately adjoining the
Yard, the most natural spot for the dwellings of employees, may have
been prevented in the last two decades of the seventeenth century by
the refusal of the Governor of Portsmouth Garrison to allow building here because it would weaken the defence of the Yard in the
case of attack on the landward side. In a memorial in May 1702 the
Lieutenant-Governor represented the danger of allowing construction between the town and Yard and mentioned his previous
attempts to prevent them.[24] According to tradition, Prince George
visited Portsmouth in 1702 with Queen Anne, and 'it was owing to
his good offices that consent was obtained for the men employed in
the Dockyard to build at Portsea. . . . Colonel Gibson, who was in
command of the Garrison, had threatened to turn the guns of the
fortress upon the men if they dared to place one brick upon another'.[25]

Whatever the truth about the influence of Prince George, the
year 1702 marked the beginning of more than a decade of heavy
building activity. By 1710 the Portsea ratebook names nearly 250
property holders, and there were over 350 in 1720, suggesting a
minimum population in the settlement at that date of 1500 or 1600.
When Defoe visited Portsmouth he found that though 'the town of
Portsmouth is a well inhabited, thriving, prosperous Corporation;
and hath been greatly enriched of late', yet

> since the encrease of business at this place, the confluence of people has
> been so great, that the town not admitting any enlargement for
> buildings, a kind of suburb, or rather a new town, has been built on

the heathy ground adjoining . . . [which is so considerable, that] it threatens to outdo, for numbers of inhabitants, and beauty of buildings, even the town itself.[26]

The history of urban development in the later eighteenth and nineteenth centuries suggests the great importance of the pattern of landholding and the attitude of owners in influencing the way building land is used. If the land was held by many people, or if owners were relatively few but there were no compact holdings, then the layout of the streets and even perhaps of the building plots tended to be determined by existing property boundaries, and large-scale planning was unlikely. If the land was held by one person, or in two or three large blocks, owners had the opportunity to plan streets and plots in a regular manner. From financial motives, to attract more builders or to obtain a higher price for land, and perhaps from an interest in town planning, for its own sake, the owner might be inspired to take an interest in the provision of some basic amenities. He might lay out at least some wide streets, provide sites (and possibly the money) for public buildings such as a church. Particularly if substantial housing for well-to-do residents was intended, attempts might be made to control the quality of the houses to be erected by the use of building covenants. The building of houses by the original landlord in any number has tended to be more exceptional, though examples are of course well known. To what extent do these features appear in the new towns which are the subject of this paper, bearing in mind that they precede by at least 100 years the larger and more familiar urban growth of the period since the Industrial Revolution?

In the case of Whitehaven and Deal the pattern of land ownership was simple. Almost the whole of the site of Whitehaven was the property of the Lowther family; most of the houses erected in the later seventeenth and early eighteenth centuries were built on waste used by coal-dealers and fishermen.[27] Most of the site of Deal was waste, mainly just beach, largely owned by the Archbishop of Canterbury.[28]

At Tunbridge Wells and Portsea the ownership was more complicated. In the case of the spa the Walks and the principal well lay as we have seen at the bottom of a common known as Bishops Down (now Tunbridge Wells Common), belonging to the manor of Rusthall. The manor was owned by Lord Muskerry of Somerhill near Tonbridge until his death in 1664, and then by his wife Viscountess Purbeck, who sold it to a Londoner, Thomas Neale, a later

Master of the Mint, about 1680. In view of what is known about his
career as a building land speculator in the West End of London and
promoter of the National Land Bank in the 1690s, the purchase can
be assumed to have been a speculation. Viscountess Purbeck continued to own the forest and heath of Southfrith to the north and
east of the Walks. The land immediately to the south-east of the
Walks was part of the Eridge Estate of the Earl of Abergavenny.
Beyond the top and north-west side of Bishops Down almost half a
mile from the Walks the Culverden Wood was owned by Sir
Charles Bickerstaffe of Sevenoaks, over ten miles away. There were
thus four landowners involved in the development of the town in
the 1680s.

Finally the site of Portsea was principally the open-field strips
making up West Dock Field. While two or three of the owners held
together a considerable proportion of the strips they were inter-
mixed with other properties and there were no compact holdings.
Nothing is known about possible common rights in the field. If they
did exist they were no impediment to the release of land to builders.[29]
The possessors of the strips were a social cross-section of English
property owners in the seventeenth and eighteenth centuries,
including a peer, two corporate bodies (Winchester College and
Portsmouth Corporation), several professional men, and at least one
farmer, brewer and shipwright.[30]

At Whitehaven the original village to the south of Whitehaven
Beck reveals no obvious overall plan. This is understandable on
account of the slow growth before the middle of the seventeenth
century and the fact that not all the land here appears to have
belonged to the Lowther family.[31] Probably about 1680 or possibly
a few years earlier Sir John Lowther began the disposal of sites
according to a regular scheme on the waste to the north of the
beck[32] (see Fig. 9.3). The layout of the first street, King Street
parallel to the shore may have preceded the working-out of a
general scheme, but a map drawn about 1690 shows a gridiron of
streets, either in use or projected, covering about 18 acres. The
thoroughfares nearer the waterfront were already lined with some
dwellings; those further away were only gradually used over the
next thirty years, and a few lots were sold as late as the early 1740s.[33]
The plots followed the normal rectangular tadpole shape allowing
for a house with a street frontage and space for a yard and garden in
the rear.

Lowther laid out most of the streets to the relatively narrow
width of approximately 10 yards. This included King Street, which

attracted many of the merchants' houses because of its proximity to the waterfront, and should have been an obvious choice for more spacious layout. However, one main street, Lowther Street, was laid out with a width of about 16 yards running through the middle of the whole scheme, from King Street to the Lowther residence several hundred yards beyond the main group of projected streets. It

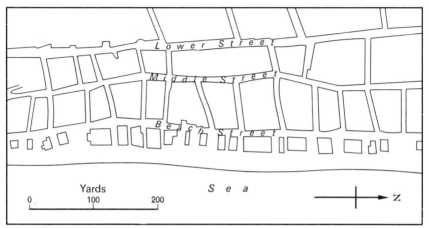

Fig. 9.2   Deal in 1819.

involved the demolition of the old Whitehaven chapel lying in its path, and the construction of a larger church. For this Sir John gave the site and according to a nineteenth-century local historian 'a considerable donation of money'. He also provided a site for a Presbyterian chapel several years later in 1694. According to the same source he used the materials from the old chapel in the erection of a schoolhouse.[34] A market had been obtained by the inhabitants during the Interregnum, but Sir John obtained a confirmation of the grant at the Restoration.

Of even greater interest than his contribution to amenities were Sir John's attempts to control the quality of the buildings erected as part of his scheme 'of building a regular town'. In his own words, probably in the later 1690s:

> [My] chief care being to have the streets laid out regularly, and that the houses in each street should be made uniform so far as it could be, and carryed on in the same range, and built contiguous to each other, and for that end the builders were commonly obliged that they should not build their fronts under such a hight, and that they should make their doors, windows, and other ornaments conformable to a rule that was given them.[35]

The fact that these remarks were made in the course of legal proceedings against a prominent local merchant to prevent an infringe-
ment of one aspect of these building regulations shows the extent to
which Sir John was prepared to go to secure enforcement, even if it
also suggests that he may not have been successful in every particular.

Lowther appears to have been a paternalist landlord of the best
type. Clearly his financial interest was a dominant motive in the
development of the town. Initially at least, and almost certainly
until the end of his life, his chief income came from the collieries,
and his interest in the development of the community lay partly in
its provision of traders and seamen to handle the coal trade. Further,
the conveyance of building sites was profitable for its own sake. In
the lawsuit Lowther claimed that he did

> from time to time grant estates of inheritance to such persons who were
> desirous to build houses, of such parcells and plots of his wast and other
> ground . . . as were proper for that purpose, for very small and
> inconsiderable ground rents and upon such easie terms, as might make
> it appear that your orator preferred the growth and flourishing
> condition of the place and the common good of the inhabitants thereof
> to his owne private interest.

However the fact that the site was previously waste made it well
worth development, even if Sir John was at pains to keep his
charges moderate.

His interest in the development of Whitehaven was not purely
economic. His concern for local schooling suggests an interest in the
general welfare of the community. Apart from his contribution to a
school building, in his absence from Whitehaven Sir John wanted to
be informed of the progress of the school. On 29 September 1696
he wrote to his agent: 'I desire you to send me ye state of ye school at
Whitehaven. No. of boys, how many classes, and wh they learn.'[36]
The layout of an avenue from his house to the waterfront through
the middle of the town and the efforts to control house building
suggest an interest in urban creation for its own sake and in Whitehaven in particular as a monument to his wealth and unchallenge-
able local social pre-eminence.

At Deal, where most of the site was waste and much of it held in
one property, the principal landlord showed an almost complete
lack of interest in development (see Fig. 9.2). According to depositions by witnesses in a lawsuit in 1694, the early settlers built their
houses on the waste where they chose, presumably enclosing a
small parcel for a yard, and only years later were summoned to the

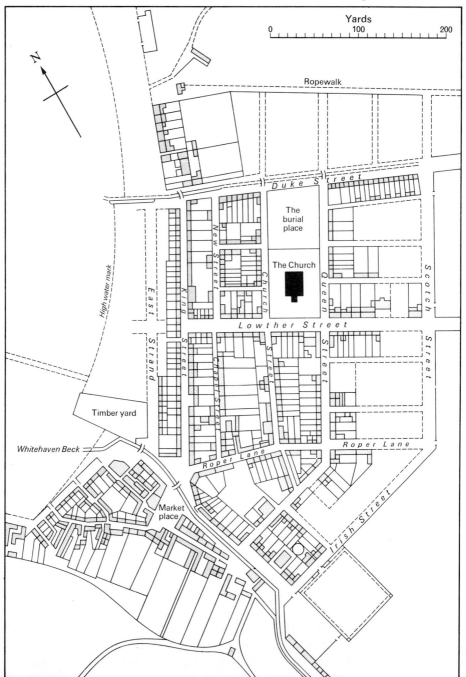

Fig. 9.3 Whitehaven in the early eighteenth century.

archbishop's manorial court to pay some acknowledgment. Jane Barrow, who claimed to be at least eighty-four, said that the inhabitants of the early and mid-seventeenth century never 'paid any rent to any person, but when they had built a house they looked on it to be their owne'. Her first husband had taken a piece of ground in Lower Street and built a smith's shop and paid no rent all his life; after his death her present husband had been called to the court to pay some money.[37] The archbishop was letting property on the waste on twenty-one-year leases from 1660, and the Restoration of the Church may have meant the beginning of the regular granting of sites on such leases.[38] But presumably by this date the rough line of the three original principal streets of Deal had been established. It thus would have owed nothing to estate planning. The innermost road, or Lower Street, emerged along the boundary of the freehold manorial lands with the waste; Beach Street naturally ran parallel to the shore, which runs roughly on a due north–south line. The lack of planning is still visible today in the case of Middle Street which also runs north to south, between Lower and Beach Streets. Apart from lacking a straight line its width alters constantly, varying between five and seven yards. Lower Street (now High Street) was bigger but even it varied in width from point to point.

The effect of the absence of control over building is observable in contemporary and later comments about the piecemeal use of the site and the mixed types of structure erected. Thomas Dunkin, mariner, born in Deal about 1617, said in 1694 that 'there were scattering houses here and there standing on the ground Lower Deal is now built on ever since this deponent can remember, but it was not soe built into streets as now it is'. Some of the earlier houses were built of timber, others of brick, and many were 'sorry poor cottages and inhabited by poore people', which led naturally to considerable rebuilding as the town grew by the 1690s.[39] At the end of the eighteenth century Hasted referred to it as 'built like most other sea-faring towns very irregularly'.[40] Naturally, too, amenities were secured by the efforts of the inhabitants. The move to obtain a charter of incorporation and to hold a market was based on the initiative and financial subscriptions of the inhabitants. Even the move for building a chapel of ease in the town came from the inhabitants, though the Archbishop when asked for his support contributed £100 towards a total expenditure of £2,559 12s 5d.[41]

At Tunbridge Wells the most natural area for building would have been in the immediate neighbourhood of the Walks and the well, the centre of attraction for the visitors. It has been seen that the land on the north-west of the Walks was common belonging to the manor of Rusthall, and the freeholders of the manor, several of whom held lodging houses in the hamlets of Southborough and Rusthall, refused to surrender their common rights except in a strip of land immediately adjoining the Walks, and this only on condition that no lodging houses were erected. Thus the building of houses continued in Culverden Wood on the far side of the Common, and for nearly a mile to the north of the Walks on the Southfrith Estate. Thus the attitude of the freeholders of the manor of Rusthall not only affected the character of property development on their own estate but also that of the neighbouring landowners.

There is no evidence that Bickerstaffe imposed any building control over the leaseholders on his estate in the Culverden Wood on Mount Ephraim, and houses were naturally erected lining the crest of the hill where the Estate bounded the Common looking down at the Walks.[42] On the Southfrith Estate no attempt was made to influence the nature of the construction, but at least on Mount Sion there was careful planning with regard to the allocation of the sites. In a chancery suit in 1707 Thomas Weller, a Tonbridge attorney, formerly Lady Purbeck's steward, said that she had employed him to treat with several people about letting land, between November 1684 and the beginning of 1690. According to him most of the leases comprised two or three parcels, each from a fraction of an acre up to twelve acres in size. Those for building were normally an acre or less, and lay near the Walks and the Common. The larger allotments were sections of the vast tract of heath to the north and east, almost certainly intended for conversion into meadow or pasture to be occupied with the newly built houses.[43] Further, as an encouragement to potential builders there four acres were set aside to be preserved as a Grove, for the use of visitors and the inhabitants. Finally Lady Purbeck gave some land on the edge of the Estate near the Walks as a site for a chapel, which was built by 1686.[44]

Particular care was taken in the leasing of sites adjoining the Walks which the freeholders released to Neale in 1682. Plots for building were laid out in two main rows, running south-westwards from the well for about 175 yards. The lessees were required to cover their buildings with slate and tile (thatch was regarded as inferior because it was a fire risk), and not to build so high as to prejudice the air of the Walks. A sewer was dug on one side of the Walks into which the houses might drain. Thus some elementary attempt was made to ensure that the Walks did not suffer from building which might discourage its continued use by visitors as a promenade.[45]

The division of landownership in Portsea understandably resulted in the absence of a uniform plan for building development. With one exception the role of the landowners was passive, since they were content to sell their strips to local tradesmen and craftsmen who acted as land developers, staking out the building plots and a roadway to provide access. For example, Thomas Seymour, brewer, bought a strip 85 feet broad and about 160 yards long in Seamill Furlong from Viscount Powerscourt, laid out a 15 foot track on the west side and divided the rest into tadpole-shaped plots 70 feet deep, which he was selling by builders in 1705 and 1706.[46] Often the road was widened subsequently by the development of the adjoining strip and the reservation of a narrow parcel on it alongside the existing road to widen it. The regularity in the general street pattern in West Dockfield came not from any overall scheme but from the fact that the strips in each furlong were roughly parallel, and as we have seen, their layout dictated the street pattern. However all the roads were narrow, the main road through the West Dockfield, Queen Street, which had divided the furlongs, being only 10 yards wide.

The spread of ownership was also reflected in the piecemeal use of the strips: many of those lying intermingled with the parcels used for building, including several particularly suitable for the dwellings of dockyard workers, were converted to ropewalks, market gardens or gravel pits, and were only gradually released to builders during the course of the eighteenth century, the last becoming available in the early 1790s. It is also reflected in the lack of interest on the part of the landlords in the provision of amenities. Apart from the parish church over a mile away a chapel in the Dockyard had to supply the needs of the inhabitants of Portsea until a church was erected in the town in the early 1750s, on the initiative of the inhabitants. Throughout the century there was no regular market in Portsea, the inhabitants using that of Portsmouth.[47] Further with the exception of one street facing the Dockyard no attempt was made by landlords or developers to control the character of the houses by the insertion of building covenants in the deeds conveying the sites.

The absence of any interest by the landlords at Portsea is understandable on account of the scattered nature of their property. At Tunbridge Wells no single plan for the development of the town was likely with ownership of the site in several hands, and particularly with a crucial section being subject to common rights. Most of the properties were still of sufficient size to allow some planning. The

Southfrith Estate at least went so far as to allocate the land carefully, while the lord of the manor of Rusthall took steps to protect the character of the Walks, which was essential if their place as the centre of the spa was to be preserved. However the large size of many of the lodging houses and a few of the places of amusement which were erected in the 1680s and 1690s was basically a reflection of the capital which builders were willing to invest in real estate at the Wells in response to the demand for suitable facilities by the well-to-do visitors.

Further, the contrast between the attitude of the archbishops at Deal and the Lowther family at Whitehaven is particularly interesting on account of the large area in their respective ownerships. The lack of a positive interest on the part of the archbishops in the development of Deal is possibly explicable on several grounds. Lowther lived in Whitehaven, while the archibishops resided in London. Their right of ownership to at least part of the site was challenged more than once during the seventeenth century, and building on the beach early in the century was discouraged by the military authorities of the castles. Again, the development of Deal was not linked to any commercial exploitation in the neighbourhood in which the archbishops had an interest. Nor did the quality of the demand for dwellings – for modest habitations for pilots, seamen, victuallers and other tradesmen and craftsmen – require any special amenities. Perhaps the outstanding factor in the contrast between the development of Deal and Whitehaven in the later seventeenth century was the character of Sir John Lowther himself, whose interest in the creation of Whitehaven went beyond that of financial gain.

The cost of building a house for most tradesmen, craftsmen and artisans – for all that is, except the few wealthy inhabitants – was modest in the later seventeenth and early eighteenth centuries. Some evidence on new house prices survives for Portsea, relating to the 1700s and 1710s. The dwellings erected for shipwrights and other tradesmen sold for between about £50 and £150 each. Those fetching between £100 and £150 consisted of terraced houses with a frontage of about 14 feet, two storeys with two rooms per floor, garrets and possibly a kitchen in the yard. Houses selling for £50 or £60 may have just consisted of a ground floor and attics in the roof, but one cannot be certain on this point.[48]

Because of the number of houses constructed total expenditure on dwellings in Portsea during the War of the Spanish Succession, or in Whitehaven or Tunbridge Wells in the 1680s and 1690s, was large in the financial terms of the time. For Portsea the aggregate size of building investment in the twenty years from 1702 may be indicated approximately. The rate books suggest that about 300 dwellings were erected. Most houses sold when new for between £50 and £120, with a few costing as much as £150. On a hypothetical average of £100 the total value of new house property would have been £30,000. As the available evidence does not represent a statistical sample it is safer to suggest merely that the true figure lay between £20,000 and £40,000.

The big outlay on construction in the new towns was found through numerous small investments by a wide occupational range of townsmen. They acted either as building undertakers or lent money on mortgage. The typical sums used were between, say £50 or £100 and £300 or £400. On the other hand none of the land-owners, some of whom would have had the financial resources to build on a much bigger scale, undertook house building. The one small exception is significant. Sir John Lowther at an early stage in the development of his project built eleven or twelve stone dwellings and six brick houses in one quarter of Whitehaven (in the words of his agent) 'for accommodating workmen of his collieries (which was at that time necessary) and were let to several colliers at twenty shillings per annum a piece', but these were sold in the early eighteenth century, because 'being slightly built, and ye repairs great, and ye rents ill paid, and ye occasion for accommodating workmen less, by reason of a great number of little houses which by this time were built elsewhere'.[49] Thus Lowther's one tiny building contribution was primarily in the interests of his collieries rather than an integral part of his scheme for the building development of Whitehaven. As the agent remarked, house ownership increased the admin-istrative burden on the estate from the point of view of rent collec-tion and repairs, and further, any house building added to the expenditure of estate development. As elsewhere building was undertaken by numerous settlers: one contemporary described them as 'most seafaring men', to which contemporary deeds suggest should be added traders and professional men.[50]

In the case of Portsea it is possible to study the builders in detail.[51] A few of the undertakers were inhabitants of the town of Portsmouth and several builders in Havant Street were tradesmen in the market town of Havant eight miles from Portsmouth. However most were inhabitants of Portsea, often almost new arrivals. Typically erecting one, two, or three adjoining houses in a speculation, they were either craftsmen-builders or dockyard workers. For example, the twenty purchasers of lots for one or two houses each staked out of an acre on the north side of Queen Street in 1703 comprised seven house carpenters, a glazier, four bricklayers (who either worked in the dockyard or on houses), a wheelwright, caulker, shipwright and five other dockyard workers.[52] Loan capital came from craftsmen, traders, professional and leisured people: some of them lived in the older towns of Portsmouth and Gosport, but even in this case much was found in the new settlement.

Construction at Tunbridge Wells revealed several special features. There were at least three or four builders whose outlay was in thousands of pounds rather than in the £100, £200 or £300 usual in other provincial towns. They took leases of several large parcels either on the Walks, or on Mount Sion or Mount Ephraim, built on them extensively, and perhaps sub-leased the remaining land. On the Walks Thomas Ashenhurst, of Lambeth, gentleman, built several amusement rooms and at least seventeen shops. He also built or leased lodging houses on the hills.[53] Sir Thomas Janson, baronet, of St Martin in the Fields early in the 1680s paid 'a considerable sum' for the lease of four acres and the houses recently erected in the Culverden Wood, and by November 1684 he had spent £1500 on additional buildings.[54] Clearly considerable capital was available to these men. Such people were not prominent in building in the typical provincial town. They may have been attracted by the exceptional possibilities of profit in a new settlement, particularly if the property was directly managed: thus Ashenhurst's sister ran three of his lodging houses on his behalf.[55]

Most of the builders were content with erecting two or three houses. On the Walks in 1685 and 1686 Thomas Neale let 12 small plots, mostly intended as sites for a single shop, and all to different people. Some built as a speculation with little or no capital behind them, and raised mortgages locally or less often in London to finish the work. A local bricklayer, Gabriel Tonkin, took a building lease of four acres, probably on Mount Sion, in 1686. To start work he borrowed £50 from a local farmer. This was insufficient, and in February 1689 he obtained £100 from a Londoner, Thomas Heywood. But by Michaelmas 1689 the house was still unfinished, no interest had been paid, and Heywood obtained a writ of ejectment. Finally new mortgagees were found who paid both the ground rent and the cost of completion.[56] Despite the presence of Janson and Ashenhust as builders, and of several Londoners among the smaller undertakers, the majority were local tradesmen and craftsmen. Some of them built shops and lodging houses for personal management.

The influx of London capital was a special feature in the building of

Tunbridge Wells. Another contemporary spa in the Home Counties, the village of Epsom, was also developed with the help of London financiers.[57] In general terms the use of London capital may be seen as just one of many investment activities in the Home Counties by Londoners in the seventeenth century, of which the purchase of land and industrial undertakings are other examples. However special factors clearly influenced the flow of capital into the spas. Tunbridge Wells and Epsom were the leisure resorts for the inhabitants of the capital: they were therefore personally familiar to many potential investors and well-known by report to a much greater number. For some building was a means to the provision of lucrative services to visitors: apart from Ashenhurst the builders on the Walks included a milliner in the Strand and an apothecary in Lombard Street. For the same reasons the introduction of London capital was to be repeated a century or more later in the construction of some of the seaside resorts in the Home Counties.[58] But London finance is not a typical feature of the building of English new towns in general.

With regard to the nature of the houses erected in the four towns, the principal influence was the attitude of the numerous builders. This was naturally governed by the character of the demand for accommodation in the town, based on the social structure of the community. Original landowners did not build, and attempts to control the structure of the houses erected on their land was the exception rather than the rule. Regulation of building in some of the main streets of Whitehaven was the result of the special interest of Lowther in town planning. On the Walks at Tunbridge Wells the covenant regarding the height of the shops was an endeavour to preserve the attractiveness of the main promenade of the company, on whom the livelihood of the inhabitants depended. It was more usual for builders to be left to their own devices.

In other aspects of urban development the attitude of the original landowners was sometimes crucial. At Tunbridge Wells the refusal of the freeholders of the manor of Rusthall to lease the Common had a permanent influence on the shape of the physical growth of the town. Other land was available, but building was much more widely dispersed than elsewhere. However the refusal of owners to release land was exceptional, because of the profitability of the leasing or the sale of sites for building. More important in its effect was the existence or absence of an interest among owners in the character of urban development on their lands. Since at Portsea the site of the town was held in small parcels by a number of owners it was natural that they were sold without thought being given to the general development of the town. Elsewhere, ownership of large blocks of property offered the opportunity for general planning. At Whitehaven and to a less extent at Tunbridge Wells it led to the regular layout of streets and plots and the landowner helped to provide public buildings and amenities. For various possible reasons, the chance to influence the creation of Deal was not taken by the archbishops, and its emergence was haphazard and piecemeal. Much of the form and character taken by Whitehaven and Tunbridge Wells was determined by the degree of interest possessed by the original landlords.

NOTES AND REFERENCES

1. I am very grateful to Professor Beresford and Mr Havinden for their helpful comments on a draft of this paper. Study in the Cumberland Record·Office and at the Portsmouth Record Office was facilitated by grants from the University of Reading Research Board.
2. In *Crisis and Order in English Towns 1500–1700*, ed. P. Clark and P. Slack (Routledge, 1972), p. vii.
3. Chalklin, *The Provincial Towns of Georgian England: a study of the building process, 1740–1820* (Edward Arnold, 1974). p. 16.
4. In *Index Villaris or an Alphabetical List of all Cities, Market Towns, Parishes, Villages and Private Seats in England and Wales* (1680), John Adams implied the existence of 788 market 'towns', but some of the markets were decayed or discontinued, and the contemporary hearth tax assessments reveal that many of these settlements had only a few dozen inhabitants, and their classification as urban is thus doubtful.
5. J. F. Ede, *History of Wednesbury* (Wednesbury Corporation, 1962), pp. 117–38, 147.
6. I. Fletcher, 'The archaeology of the West Cumberland coal trade', *Transactions of the Cumberland and Westmorland Antiquarian and Archaeological Society* [*Trans. CWAAS*], iii (1877–88), 270; Public Record Office [PRO] E134/31 and 32 Chas. 2 Hil. 26.
7. Fletcher, *op. cit.*, 271.
8. PRO E134/31 Chas. 2 Mich. 28 and E134/31 and 32 Chas. 2 Hil. 26.
9. Fletcher, *op. cit.*, 172.
10. D. Hay, 'Whitehaven in the eighteenth century', *Whitehaven News*, 29 Dec. 1938.
11. J. Laker, *History of Deal* (T. F. Pain and Sons, Deal, 1917), ch. 5.
12. PRO E134/6 Wm and Mary East. 36.
13. Laker, *op. cit.*, pp. 45–71.
14. This is suggested by a comparison of the number of communicants in the parish in 1640 with the number of inhabitants over 16 in the Compton Census of

1676: while in the surrounding wholly rural parishes the figures for 1640 and 1676 are roughly comparable, Deal parish had 500 communicants in 1640 and 1500 inhabitants over 16 in 1676: E. Hasted, *The History and Topographical Survey of the County of Kent* (Canterbury, 1799), iv, 145–200; *A Seventeenth Century Miscellany*, Kent Records, xvii, Chalklin, 'the Compton Census . . .', pp. 161, 168.

15. PRO E/134/6 Wm and Mary East. 36.

16. *The Letters of John Chamberlain* (American Philosophical Society, Philadelphia, 1939), ii, 261.

17. The author was L. Rowzee.

18. R. Lennard, 'The watering places', in R. Lennard, ed., *Englishmen at Work and Play: some phases of English leisure* (Clarendon Press, 1931), pp. 46–7.

19. J. Radford Thomson, *Pelton's Illustrated Guide to Tunbridge Wells* (1881), p. 12; Kent Archives Office [KAO] U749 M1; PRO C11/2318/2.

20. J. Bowra, *A Survey of Tunbridge Wells* (1738).

21. *The Journeys of Celia Fiennes*, ed. C. Morris (Cresset Press, 1947), p. 133.

22. PRO E179/247/30 (1674 hearth tax).

23. Portsmouth Record Office: Parish of Portsea rate book 1700–25.

24. *Calendar of State Papers Deomestic, 1702–3*, p. 414.

25. W. G. Gates, *Naval History of Portsmouth* (Evening News and Hampshire Telegraph Co., Portsmouth, 1931), p. 102.

26. Daniel Defoe, *A Tour through England and Wales* (1724), (Dent, 1928 edn), vol. i, p. 139.

27. W. Jackson, 'Whitehaven: its streets, its principal houses and their inhabitants', *Trans. CWAAS* (1878), 356.

28. Hasted, *op. cit.*, iv, 162; Laker, *op. cit.*, p. 32. The rest of the waste, attached to the manor of Chamberlains Fee, was owned by the Gookin family of Harbledown, Canterbury, in the later seventeenth century.

29. The fact that the area was known to contemporaries as 'the Common' suggests that grazing rights over the strips had once existed.

30. Portsmouth Record Office: deeds re Bishop St, Queen St, Havant St, Union St, Prince George St, etc.

31. Jackson, 'Streets', *loc. cit.,* 364.

32. This suggested dating of the origin of Lowther's project is based on the following facts: (*a*) it was clearly some years prior to the map made *c.* 1690, which shows several streets lined with houses; (*b*) Sir John was particularly involved in consolidating Whitehaven's position as a port in 1680 and 1681; (*c*) one of the depositions taken in 1680 refers to the existence of only 20 houses north of the beck on ground allotted by Sir John, and these may not have been part of the scheme under discussion.

33. Cumberland Record Office: Lowther MSS: property register.

34. Jackson, 'Streets', *loc. cit.*, 354, 360, 355.

35. Cumberland Record Office: Lowther MSS, complaint of Sir John Lowther to the Lord Keeper of the Great Seal: Sir John refers to the alleged encroachments of the defendant Addison as occurring after 1688, and as being done while he was in London for several years, presumably during his tenure of office at the

Admiralty until 1694.

36. Lowther MSS: LW2/D13.

37. PRO E134/6 Wm and Mary East. 36.

38. Kent Archives Office U47/11 T232 and U313 T3: the latter refers to lawsuits between the Archbishop and William Rand regarding the ownership of twelve houses on the waste, in and prior to Nov. 1664, suggesting that the archbishop's rights as owner were contested.

39. E134/6 Wm and Mary East. 36.

40. Hasted, *op. cit.*, p. 164.

41. Laker, *op. cit.*, pp. 236–40, ch. 14.

42. The one surviving building lease, to Samuel Cooke of Speldhurst, pailmaker, 1 Jan. 1680 merely imposes a condition that £100 be spent on building a 'substantial new messuage'.

43. PRO C6/100/7.

44. KAO U38 T2.

45. KAO U38 T32.

46. Portsmouth Record Office: deeds re Havant St.

47. *The History of Portsmouth, Portsea, Gosport and their Environs* (Gosport, 1800), p. 51.

48. No probate inventories survive for Portsea for these years, and nearly all the dwellings have been demolished; the prices are derived from contemporary deeds (which are numerous), and an indication of the types of houses constructed may be obtained from later newspaper advertisements.

49. Lowther MSS: property register and LW2/A4.

50. Lowther MSS: complaint of Thomas Addison to the Lord Chancellor, and register of deeds vol. 2; Jackson MSS in Carlisle Public Library: I am grateful to Mr Phillips for drawing my attention to these MSS.

51. Portsmouth Record Office: deeds as above; on the other hand the earliest deeds surviving for Deal do not identify the builders.

52. Portsmouth RO D1/729.

53. KAO U749; PRO C5/222/22.

54. PRO C8/400/34.

55. PRO C5/222/22.

56. PRO C10/511/114.

57. For example, C5/277/22.

58. For example, at Brighton and Bognor Regis.

Society, belief, and the building of Bath, 1700–1793

'Tis neither Town nor City', wrote a visitor to Bath in 1700, 'yet goes by the name of both: five months in the year 'tis as populous as London, the other seven as desolate as a wilderness.' It is, he added, 'a Valley of Pleasure, yet a sink of Iniquity; nor is there any intrigues or debauch acted in London, but is mimicked here'.[1] To supply these pleasures the freemen of Bath provided a rude hospitality, kept aliens from trading or working in their midst and apprenticed their sons to occupations serving the needs of these visitors: shoe-making, tailoring, barbering and wig-making, victualling, shop-keeping, and building.[2] The town, with a population of about 3,000, was of modest size. This, coupled with its provincial standards of accommodation and attitudes to development,[3] meant that neighbouring rural parishes seemed to have received from it all the stimulus to change and develop they were likely to get. These parishes remained sparsely populated. All were enclosed and divided into small fields, gardens and orchards owned or farmed by numerous small freeholders or by tenants with lifehold leases for ninety-nine years or three lives. Many of the freeholders must have been absentees and many were citizens of Bath. On the western side of the city, however, there were three areas of ground owned in large consolidated blocks. These were the town common on which freemen had common rights, some ground in Kingsmead belonging to Lovelace Haynes, a landlord resident in Berkshire, and the eighty-five acre Barton Estate in the possession of Robert Gay, a successful barber-surgeon in London. This estate appears to have been let in small parcels but on leases that were easily extinguished.[4] Thus Bath was a small urban island surrounded by a sea of small fields, gardens and orchards. It was easily approached only in dry weather and only from the London side. Popular prejudice among sophisticated people was not too wide of the mark in dubbing Bath 'a place standing in a hole; on a quagmire; impenetrable to the very beams of the sun; and so confined by almost inaccessible hills, that people have scarce room to breathe in the town, or to come at it without danger to their lives'.[5]

Yet the country and the countryside were changing. In the forty years before 1700 developments in agriculture had produced some increase in productivity as well as in output, which, accompanied by a slowing in the rate of population growth, provided the basis for improvements in living standards for a growing proportion of English society. Some of this increased real income was consumed in Bath – one measure is that from 1712 to 1725 expenditure on cards and dice increased threefold,[6] with the result that rustic Bath was transformed into a sophisticated provincial town so that by 1750 it was the 'Atlantic City' of the eighteenth century. In this year it probably had a population of over 10,000 and was capable of entertaining upwards of 12,000 visitors during its spring and autumn seasons. John Wood's testimony about this increase and shift in demand points to the stimulating effect they must have had on a wide range of manufacturing industries as well as on building.[7]

Although an increase and a shift in demand were the first and necessary conditions for the emergence of Bath as the premier place of resort in the country, they were far from sufficient to account for nearly a century of supremacy in the face of competition from other resorts. Also needed were innovators able to spot the opportunities, and competent, flexible and adventurous enough to respond to them in ways which would give Bath an edge over its rivals. In this respect historians of Bath generally concentrate their attentions on the activities of three men, all immigrants to the city; Richard [Beau] Nash (1674–1761), Ralph Allen (1694–1764), and John Wood (1704–54). Between them, it is said, they carried Bath triumphant into the eighteenth century. There is some truth in this. But each was able to make his contribution only because the milieu into which he moved was already congenial. This was particularly true of Wood. That building to meet the new and growing demand at Bath had already begun under the direction of other builders and was likely to continue was a necessary condition for his setting up as an architect-developer in Bath in 1728.

Some of the earliest developers of real estate in Bath in the period 1700–28 included large landowners like the Duke of Chandos, as well as other more modest landholders like Lovelace Haynes and George Trymme. Other developers were William Brewer, a Bath cordwainer, and John Hobbs, a Bristol timber merchant. But, whatever their origin, they all built on a small scale, either rebuilding within the city or adding a few houses and the occasional new street outside the medieval walls. Although we cannot be sure, it seems likely that they were restricted in their activities by the small size of the market and the difficulty of obtaining capital. This latter was certainly Wood's problem when he first arrived in Bath in 1726 or 1727. He had great schemes for developing the whole of Bath but was compelled to spend his first few years there working for others as subcontractor for building and digging. Lacking capital he could not acquire land, nor had he been able to acquire any, could he have financed its development. Indeed, it is doubtful whether he could ever have purchased land to the amount he wanted. Corporation property in and around the city was mostly let in small parcels on leases for three lives and would have been expensive and difficult to acquire even if the Corporation had been willing to sell; and occupiers of large estates were either reluctant or unable to sell land since it was too prestigious or too heavily entailed and the responsibility of several trustees. Acquiring land belonging to small freeholders was also out of the question since their holdings were too small and fragmented and too distant from the baths and assembly rooms to be worth considering for the projects he had in mind.

Fortunately for Wood and the Bath townscape the Barton Estate, lying on the north-western edge of the town, had been in the sole occupation of Robert Gay and his descendants since 1699. Throughout our period and although none of the family had any wish to set up as a developer himself, the Gays were vitally interested in increasing the income from their estate. Consequently, between 1728 and 1766, the Gay family leased some forty acres or ninety-nine-year leases to John Wood and his son for an annual rent of £560.[8] The Gays thus gained an eightfold increase in the annual value of their land coupled with its reversion to the family after ninety-nine years. Indeed, building so increased the value of the Gays' land that in 1765 they were able to lease five acres of the original estate to three other builders for £20 an acre.[9]

Armed with these leases the Woods were enabled to carry out

their projects with relatively little capital of their own. They sublet building plots, mostly to other builders and building craftsmen, and wrote conditions into the subleases specifying what was to be built, the materials to be used, the subcontractors' responsibility in regard to digging sewers, pitching, paving and lighting, and placing limitations on heights of walls and outhouses,. and on occupancy. The difference between the rent paid to the landowner and the ground rents received under these subleases provided the main source of the Woods' profit on their undertakings. These subleases also had other purposes. Through them the developers spread the responsibility and cost of raising capital over many more individuals. Since it must have cost something like £100,000 to build the King's Circus and the Royal Crescent this device was of considerable importance. On the security of their subleases builders raised funds on mortgage and obtained credit from suppliers of raw materials.

This was not the end of the matter. Once Wood had completed his first project, Queen Square, he was able to use the titles to the ground rents due to him as mortgage security in order to raise capital to meet the expenses of his share of preparing further sites; digging sewers, providing water and access, and laying out the open spaces which were an important feature of each of his building schemes. The importance of this for the Woods is indicated by the fact that when John Wood the elder began building in 1728 he was compelled to economise; for the want of £4,000 he had to build Queen Square on its natural slope instead of levelling the site, and, because he could not raise funds in order to build houses himself, he was forced to accept modifications to his original plans in some of the subleases he made.[10] On the other hand, in the 1770s and early 1780s, his son was able to command substantial resources through his ownership of ground rents with a capital value of some £50,000.[11] He was to find that even that was not enough. Almost all other developers in Bath financed their projects in similar fashion.

Thus the initial decision of a landowner to lease ground for building was vital. It not only provided the site and placed control of it in the hands of one man or one firm, it also placed first-class collateral and the key to outside sources of capital in the hands of the developer, who in his turn allocated some part of the collateral to the working builder so that he in turn could raise funds. Clearly, in the matter of private building in Bath, the key to capital accumulation was legal title to land, although in the case of a mortgage raised on fee farm rents or ground rents it was legal title to the income from land rather than the land itself that was mortgaged. These aids to development presuppose a society in which private property and a sophisticated system of law relating to property and mortgage were understood and accepted as a matter of course.[12] Without such a legal system and without commercially minded landowners Wood's schemes would have been truly chimerical.

Since the key to capital in building lay in legal titles to land it came, as it were, out of the past. But the capital it unlocked and attracted into building had more diverse origins. In these early years some came from landowners but most came from professional men, prospering tradesmen and successful craftsmen, or from the widows and sisters of all sorts of men. Thus John Wood the elder borrowed £3,000 from the widow of a Hertfordshire landowner, £1,000 from a Bath doctor, and a further £1,600 from a Bath widow. Contrary to popular belief, however, there is no record of financial dealings between Wood and Ralph Allen.[13] On the other hand, the building of Bath generated such a growth in demand for capital that some of its citizens early on became specialists in financing developers as well as lending to working builders. The careers of two of these men, both closely associated with the Woods, are worth outlining since they do show how much developers like the Woods were dependent on the expertise of others and how fortunate Bath was, not only in regard to its landowners, but also in producing native sons who responded enthusiastically to the demands made upon them.

The first was Richard Marchant, Quaker (1702–73).[14] Although Richard Marchant was apprenticed as a merchant taylor to his father in 1714, he never seems to have practised as a merchant taylor on his own account. But by 1727 he was sufficiently well known in the local world of real estate development to be employed by the Duke of Chandos as his financial intermediary and agent in Chandos's first venture into building development in Bath. Marchant subsequently advanced £1,000 to the Duke of Kingston, became agent for the Sun Fire Office, acquired property in the city, built Marchant's Court, and put out considerable sums on mortgage. He made his first recorded loan to John Wood the younger in 1757 during the building of the King's Circus. By 1771 his outstanding advances on mortgage to Wood totalled £4,115 and, by way of outright purchase of ground rents, he had supplied him with a further £1,500. During the early stages of building the Royal Crescent, which represented a capital investment of at least £60,000, Wood settled his outstanding debt with Marchant and renegotiated a loan of £8,000 from Marchant and Harford Lloyd, a partner in the Bristol Old Bank. When Richard Marchant died (1773) he must have possessed assets worth at least £30,000 including all his property in Bath, his loans to Wood, and a £6,000 share in the Bristol Brass Company. My impression is that Marchant's career was not an unusual one. In another branch of the Marchant family Edward Marchant, son of a very successful rough mason, grew wealthy out of distilling and lending on mortgage, whilst other leading eighteenth-century Bath families with origins in the seventeenth-century company of Merchant Taylors included the Attwoods, Collibees, Chapmans, Wiltshires, Cogwells, Harfords, and Ditchers.

The other man closely involved in financial dealings with John Wood the younger was John Jeffreys, Attorney-at-law.[15] In all probability Jeffreys was an immigrant attracted to Bath during the early 1750s. Among his first customers were Richard Marchant and Harford Lloyd for whom he acted in drawing up mortgages and negotiating purchases of land. From experience in this kind of work it was but a short step to acting as an intermediary putting lenders in touch with borrowers. Between 1752 and 1767, he succeeded in this fashion in arranging loans totalling some £11,000. Jeffreys also made direct loans himself and negotiated bills of exchange. By the early 1770s he was acting as banker to Wood negotiating loans, providing credit to pay wages and other small accounts, and making long term advances on mortgage. Thus he negotiated the ending of the Marchant-Harford loan in 1779 and by 1781 had himself advanced £3,000 to Wood. Wood's death (1781) ended Jeffreys's connection with him, but by that time Jeffreys was town clerk (1776–1800) and his fortunes were tied to the affairs of the Corporation which was embarking on a massive programme of public works that was to increase the corporate debt from a mere £10,000 in 1775 to nearly £60,000 by the end of the century. Jeffreys, like Marchant, was not unique. One of his clerks, John Cogswell, having learnt his trade well in Jeffreys's office played the banker to John Eveleigh during his building extravaganza of the 1790s – but that is another story.

The main point is that the building of Bath required a great proliferation of decision-making and repeated ongoing responses from wide sections of society, natives as well as immigrants. The fact that these responses were forthcoming tells a good deal about the rising expectations and the dynamism of English provincial life in the south-west of England in the first half of the eighteenth century; the country was overflowing with entrepreneurs on the lookout for opportunity. As well as building Bath – an innovation in itself – they early on took steps to reduce transaction costs through establishing a turnpike trust in 1707, which had an accumulated debt of £19,000 and some fifty miles of road by 1758. They canalised the Avon from Bristol to Bath in 1727 and experimented with railways for hauling stone before 1731. To avert risk they cooperated in forming the first provincial fire office, The Bristol Crown, in 1718 and, after the Bubble Act of 1720, were the first to establish a further insurance company, the Bath Fire Office, 1767. Subsequently they resorted to a variety of devices to raise large capital and reduce the risk of failure; they tried tontines, joint stock companies, and the equitable trust.[16]

The physical product of this multitude of separate decisions made over more than a hundred years was the unique urban landscape which today sets Bath apart as the most complete and compact example of an eighteenth-century town in the United Kingdom. But, distinctive though Bath's architecture, architect builders, entrepreneurs, and the long-term demand for their services were, there is the intriguing question whether the timing and sequence of building in Bath was uniquely determined by the interrelationships of these elements at a purely local level. That is, whether, given the long-term demand for the pleasures of Bath, the economy of the city was so self-contained that the ebb and flow of building activity was determined by local decisions about the state of demand or need for building, or whether general constraints in the national economy in regard to the supply of capital and materials were more important factors determining the level of activity.

One problem in endeavouring to answer this question for the first half of the eighteenth century is that those historians who argue that there were long swings in building in the national economy use snippets of evidence from Bath as pointers to upturns and peaks in national building activity.[17] Insofar as these historians have selected the 'right' snippets it would not be surprising to find some symmetry between the experience of Bath and generalisations in part based on that experience. A second problem is that there is no agreement as to the timing of the national peaks and troughs. Since the answer to the question of turning points cannot be found in logic nor yet in mathematics, it is necessary to fall back on the evidence. Since, too, the building of Bath can throw some light on changes in expenditure for consumption purposes by the ruling elite and by the upwardly mobile, it is also worth attempting to identify these turning points with some precision.

II

Fluctuations in the general level of economic activity and in building in particular in Bath can be tentatively traced in time series, isolated figures, and estimates based on a number of local records.[18] Before 1730 the only continuous series are those for expenditure and borrowing (mostly for building purposes) by Bath Corporation. These series suggest three distinct high points in corporate economic activity: 1704–06, 1715–18 and 1729–30. Other piecemeal evidence tends to increase the probability that these high points were peak years or close to peak years in building activity in the city. Thus in the first period, 1704–06, a theatre and a row of houses in the Gravel Walks were built, in 1707 Trymme Street was started, a new Pump Room was built, and Bath got its first Turnpike Act authorising the making of thirteen miles of road. Since the amount of building begun in 1707 seems to have been greater than that in the previous two years it seems safe to suggest that 1707 was the peak year for building. The next peak in the corporation series, 1715–18, shows a big jump in expenditure in 1715/16 followed by an increase in net borrowing to 1718. Evidence of renewed building in 1718 in Trymme Street and of new starts in 1719 in the Bristol Road and in Broad Street, all suggest that the peak was closer to 1718 than to 1715.

It is not until the third high point in the corporation series (1729–30) that the documentation about building activity becomes much clearer. The rise to this high point seems to have been well under way in the bad harvest years of 1727–28 when the Duke of Chandos built five houses in Chandos Court and the Avon Navigation Company completed its work with the 600 yard cut at Twerton, a large warehouse on the quay, and a 100 ft long quay wall. By 1729–1730 corporation expenditure reached an all time high of nearly £3,000 and the corporation debt at £4,500 was the highest it had ever been or was to be again until 1766. In the next year the tolls and dividend of the Avon Navigation were higher than they were to be again until 1743. Queen Square, started in 1729, was still being built in 1730 when John Strahan began Beaufort Buildings and Mr Thayer opened his newly built Assembly Rooms. Judging by the Avon Navigation Tolls, which were only marginally lower in 1732–33 than in 1730–31, economic activity remained high throughout the early 1730s. Indeed the demand for housing, the key to the whole expansion, was so buoyant at the start of 1731, when Wood announced his intention to build a chapel in Queen Square, that he was inundated with requests for building sites in adjacent streets.[19]

According to Wood building went on vigorously until 1736. However, the dates of his subleases for the whole of the Queen Square development suggest that the peak of activity was past by 1732.[20]

After this surge of activity building slowed down until the industry was sunk in a deep depression from 1740–41. The Avon Navigation tolls sank to their lowest level in 1739–40 since 1731 and the company paid no dividend for two years running. In the same period corporation expenditure fell to two-thirds of average expenditure over the preceding four years, and, by 1743 lenders had recalled half their loans to the Corporation. To make matters worse building on the Mineral Water Hospital came to an end in the winter of 1740 and Wood, who had hopefully signed subleases to begin building seventeen houses on the North Parade in May of that year, found it impossible to complete any further subleases for the project until the end of 1741. Even then recovery was sluggish until January 1743. Every economic indicator points to the fact of a deep depression in the building industry in 1740–41.

It also seems that it was not until the early or mid 1750s that a real recovery was under way. It is true that the Avon Navigation tolls reached a new peak in 1742–43 but they fell again to a record low level in 1745–46 and the Corporation so reduced its contribution to the economic life of Bath that its debt of £1,000 in 1751–52 was lower than at any time since 1704. Moreover, the only difference between Thorp's map of 1740 and a survey of 1750 is in the addition of Wood's development in the Parades, which had come to an end in 1749, and Galloway's Buildings begun and finished in 1749–50. After the completion of these projects there were no new major starts until 1754–55 when Wood began the King's Circus and Prince's Building projects and Thomas Jelly started Bladud's Buildings. As materials were brought in in anticipation of this new work the Avon Navigation tolls reached a new high in 1753–54 and the company paid out its highest dividend since 1732–33. Whether these new starts were delayed by the panic associated with the start of the war against the French in America and exactly when after 1755 the peak was reached, is difficult to say. If, for example, the Avon Navigation tolls are anything to go by, building could have peaked as late as 1758–59.

The peaks in building so far noted – 1707, 1718, 1732, possibly 1743–44, and 1755–56 – approximate more closely to peaks identified in the national economy by T. S. Ashton than they do to those more recently calculated by Parry Lewis. However, the fact that

now a House for the Master of St John's Hospital. 23 Presbyterian Meeting House. 24 Quakers Meeting House. 25 Bell Tree House. 26 St John's Hospital. 27 St Catherines Hospital. 28 Bellots Hospital. 29 Lepers Hospital. 30 An Hospital intended for 60 Poor Strangers. 31 A House for the Poor of the City. 32 Charity School. 33 Mr Leake's Shop. 34 Lindseys Great Room and Theatre. 35 Harrisons Great Room and Theatre. 36 Old Theatre. 37 Ives Court, an Elegant Room of 100 feet long, 40 feet wide, and 40 feet high. 38 Cold Bath. 39 An Obelisk erected by Mr Nash in the Year 1734, to perpetuate the Vertue of the Bath Water in the Recovery of the Prince of Orange from a very dangerous Indisposition. 40 A Lock intended to be made to extend the Navigation from Bath into Wiltshire. 41 A Crane for Loading of Barges with Free Stone, the Motion of lowering the Stone is the most Expeditious of any thing of its kind, and allowed by the Curious to be a Master piece

of Mechanism; to which Crane if Stone in large Blocks seldom less than 5 or 6 Tun at a time, descends from the Quarries, at least a Mile and a half, by Machines contrived at the great Charge & Expence of Mr Allen the Proprietor of it, on which Account the Stone is Sold for a fourth part less than heretofore, to the great Advantage of the Publick & Gentlemen that use it. 42 Turnpikes. N.B. The Government of the City, with the Description of it and its Antiquities, are particularly recited in Dr Guidots Treatise of the City and Waters of Bath, sold by T. Leake Bookseller in Bath, where likewise this Plan may be had. Advertisement. For the Convenience of Builders, Mr Wood intends very soon, to set up a Deal Yard in BATH, in which Persons may be supply'd with the best of Norway Goods for ready Money at the most reasonable Rates, and for their Encouragement, shall be directed in the Use & Choice of their Materials, from whence great Advantages will arise (at least 10 Pounds in every hundred) to the Buyer.

Published by J. Leake October 27, 1736 according to Act of Parliament

of BATH
merset.

QUEEN
SQUARE

Barton Fields

Barton Street

Town Acre

CITY ARMS

NORTH

Bath-wick

Meadows

Mr John Wood

50   100   150 yards

the last three peaks show lags of two, four, and two to three years respectively behind Ashton's peaks indicates that strong local factors as well as influences from the national economy were at work. Clearly supplies of capital and timber were essential to building but it is difficult to avoid the impression that it was the availability rather than the price of these essential components that mattered. Thus the Corporation was able to borrow on long-term bonds at 4 per cent from its chief creditor from 1704 to 1739. Further, although it sometimes paid 5 per cent to some creditors early in the century and 4·5 per cent to others in 1721–22 and 1727–28, it generally paid most of them 4 per cent from 1732 to 1753. It borrowed, therefore, at 4 per cent throughout most of the period 1704–53 and it was not until 1753 that it was able to take up its first loan at 3·5 per cent. However, by 1756 this corporation rate was back to 4 per cent, where it remained until the mid 1780s. On the other hand the Bath Turnpike Commissioners seemed to have had to borrow at the legal rate from 1707 to 1757 i.e. 6 per cent to 1714 and 5 per cent thereafter. This was reduced to 4 per cent in 1757, raised to 4·5 per cent at the end of 1760, and reduced again to 4 per cent in 1764. It remained at 4 per cent from then until 1778. Private borrowers borrowing on mortgage almost always paid the legal rate for their loans and continued to pay 5 per cent until the mid 1760s. For example, Wood took up his first loan at 5 per cent in 1735 and his 'firm' paid 4 per cent for the first time in 1757, but then only if the half-yearly payments were met within forty days of the date they were due. In 1765 the effective rate for Wood was raised to 4·5 per cent. A comparison of these local interest rates with Ashton's index of the yield on consols provides no empirical basis for the notion that rates of interest were 'moving freely' in steps of one-half per cent and there is no reason to suppose that the yield on consols is an adequate indication of the level of building activity in the City.[21] Thus the slowdown in building after 1732 was accompanied by a fall in the yield on consols from 3·1 per cent to 2·8 per cent in 1737, and the ensuing long period of low interest on consols was insufficient to stimulate building before 1740 at which date there was the false start mentioned earlier.

There are many reasons why developers responded only sluggishly to changes in national interest rates. One is that the market for capital was largely a local one. Another and perhaps more important reason is that many of the building projects had long

Plate 12 (*pp. 262–3*) Bath in 1735

periods of gestation and the value of each part was a function of the completed whole. Consequently developers and builders looked closely at the state of the local market for houses before deciding to build. Thus in the first big boom, 1727–32, the relative backwardness of Bath's provincial standard of accommodation meant that returns to investment in building were potentially very great, particularly for those first in the field. As the Duke of Chandos, John Wood, and John Hobbs realised, visitors were demanding quality accommodation, seemingly in unlimited quantities. In this situation builders and others were as eager for property development as gamesters for the game. Provided they could get capital at all they were prepared to pay the maximum interest the law allowed. By 1739, however, many of the deficiencies in accommodation had been made good while the Gaming Act of that year and the harvest failure of 1740 damped expectations of high returns on the investment already undertaken. Consequently the low yield on consols of the late 1730s and early 1740s failed to excite local developers and builders. This was because it seemed for the moment as if the attraction of Bath as an international centre for gambling was gone. Government revenue on cards and dice fell 14 per cent from 1740 to 1741 and as one gambler breaking into verse put it,

> Farewell Bath, and hie for Scarborough;
> Bath's as dull as Market Harborough.[22]

These factors probably explain John Wood's false start on the Parade development in 1740.

After the invention of games not covered by the Gaming Act revived the prospects of gambling and gamblers, Wood was encouraged to sign further building subleases in 1742 and 1743, but in 1744 a further Gaming Act put paid to all games of chance. In the next year Charles Edward Stuart marched towards London and government revenue from cards and dice tumbled a further 20 per cent. It was probably no accident that the Avon Navigation tolls fell to the lowest level in the history of the company in 1745–46, or that Wood signed no new subleases on the Parade development for two years, or that it took him ten years to complete.

The role of developers' expectations about growth in demand in relation to the existing stock of houses and other facilities in fixing the timing of peaks and troughs in the level of building activity is also well illustrated by developments in the twenty years after the peak of 1755–56 or 1758–59. Although there is uncertainty about the timing of this peak there is less doubt that 1760 was a year of little building in Bath. The Avon Navigation tolls were at their lowest for seven years, corporation expenditure had declined since 1753–54, lenders were withdrawing loans to the Corporation, and there had been no new major starts since those of 1754–55. Moreover, the Corporation, which had developed an interest in building schemes in 1753, was still finding difficulty in starting the Milsom Street project in 1760. They also took no immediate steps to follow up their 1760 decision to build a new Town Hall. This stagnation may have been brought about by wartime rises in interest rates and costs of materials. However, as far as the Corporation was concerned, the main stumbling block in the Milsom Street development was the agreement to be negotiated with the sitting tenant of the ground, Charles Milsom.[23] When suitable terms were finally agreed in September 1761 subleases for building Edgar Buildings were granted immediately.[24] Nevertheless, subleases for the main development in Milsom Street were not signed until December 1763, by which time the war was over and national interest rates had started to fall. Yet the case for the crucial role of national interest rates in this recovery is by no means certain. Thus, in April 1762, when consols yielded 4·2 per cent, their highest yield for thirty years, Messrs Jelly and Fisher in conjunction with the Duke of Kingston began a large private development including three new streets and a new bath in the centre of the old town.[25]

By the mid-1760s the local boom, coinciding with boom conditions elsewhere, was well under way. The Corporation increased its expenditure and began borrowing heavily in preparation for the new Town Hall. They also began work in the Paragon and sold off the town hall at one shilling per foot to facilitate building in Westgate Buildings and the Ambury; here Messrs Jelly and Fisher began sixty houses on a five-acre site while John Wood the younger entered into an agreement to build the thirty houses of the Royal Crescent on 19 acres. Between 1766 and 1771 over 300 houses were built to produce such a rise in land values that William Johnstone Pulteney thought fit to initiate the development of the Bathwick side of the Avon.[26] To carry this project through he was obliged to obtain three Acts of Parliament, borrow £12,000 and employ two architects. In the course of building he also ruined two builders. Other public buildings erected during this boom included The Countess of Huntingdon's Chapel, The Octagon, and the New Rooms, built at a cost of £20,000 from 1769–71.

If one is to judge by the Avon Navigation tolls and dividends this boom reached its peak as early as 1769–70. There was, however, a downward revision of toll rates in September 1770 and other evidence suggests that the boom did not break until 1770–71. Thus a count of houses in the rate books suggests that houses were still being added at the rate of about one hundred each year until that year. Thereafter the annual rate of addition fell to fifty or less until 1776. Furthermore there was a slight drop in the takings of the Bath Turnpike from 1770–71 to 1772–73, and a continuing sharp drop in the Avon Navigation tolls after 1770–71. Finally, a 1770 map shows the completion of all the schemes begun in the 1760s with the exception of the half-built Royal Crescent, the western approach to Pulteney's bridge, and the bridge itself. All in all it is difficult to avoid the conclusion that there was a decline in building after a peak in 1770–71 and that this peak preceded the national peak by as much as five years.

The downturn after 1771 cannot be attributed to the effects of war, the yield on consols, or a scarcity of timber. The most plausible explanation is that developers in Bath had overestimated the growth in demand for houses, and, carried away by the rage of the moment, had overbuilt. One badly hit developer was William Pulteney. Starting late in the boom he had been faced with the problem of mounting costs which led to the adoption of modifications aimed at reducing costs and raising income; modifications which today make the bridge a striking feature of the townscape. Nevertheless, when the bridge was finished and the roadway to the Bathwick side completed, shops built on the bridge to raise income remained unlet for at least nine months[27] and no builders were willing to take sub-leases on the Bathwick side. Indeed, Pulteney's attempts to divert traffic through the Bathwick estate failed, and local evaluation of the likely state of the market for housing was so low that no house building took place on the Bathwick side until 1788. No doubt the outbreak of war in 1776 served to depress demand still further but it was not the first cause of the downturn.[28] In any case the Corporation's decision to proceed with the new Town Hall in 1775 and to increase its debt by some £15,000 between 1775 and 1778 went some way to counteract any effects of war and afforded relief to local builders and building workers. In spite of such relief the Avon Navigation tolls continued to fall until 1779–80 when they rose slightly at the same time as a handful of new starts by a new generation of developers gave a temporary boost to building activity.

It was not until 1785 that building activity really began to revive to produce an explosive boom in the years 1788–93. The timing of this boom and the subsequent slump show that Bath was once more caught up in the national ebb and flow of economic activity. In these years something like a thousand houses were added to the town. These included small units in new areas of high density working class housing as well as four new crescents, two of which were built with exquisite adaptation of architectural style to terrain. Also built were: an enclosed tennis court, a pleasure garden and hotel, a new town across the river in Bathwick as reward for Pulteney's foresight, and several new streets and a pump room as part of a scheme of massive urban renewal in the town centre. All this was greatly assisted by a rapid proliferation of credit facilities including, by 1791, six banks and at least two quasi-banks, and, by 1794, an equitable trust. The end result by the early 1790s was that at least one million pounds had been invested in house property alone in the city, and its population, close to 30,000, made it one of the largest cities in the country, fit, it was said, to be the capital of a small kingdom.

III

In spite of the recurring fever of building activity, the unlocking of land, the entrepreneurial drive not all of Bath responded vigorously to the new opportunities. For, until this final explosive growth Bath was still a rather old-fashioned country town responding to the demands being made upon it within a framework of attitudes and beliefs rooted in the past. Control of the city still rested with a Corporation rendered cautious by its limited income as well as by tradition and choice. In social matters its members welcomed and used Beau Nash to spread conformity to the conventions of London society. In economic matters they used their powers to protect their private interests and investments. Until the mid-1760s they sought with some success to prohibit immigrant workmen and tradesmen from practising within the city, and early in the century manipulated the rates charged by chairmen in an attempt to keep building development within the city walls.[29] Only when this failed did they become developers themselves. Even then the Corporation refused to allow the town commons to be used for building, and as late as the 1770s, with support from the Turnpike interest, they used their parliamentary influence to prevent William Pulteney diverting the main traffic from London through his Bathwick properties and across his new bridge.[30] It is true that in 1789 the Corporation initiated an impressive redevelopment scheme for the old or lower town but this was mainly for fear that the focus of attraction, wealth, and power would shift permanently to the upper town. On this occasion the 'conservative' opposition came from other centres of interest; the Turnpike Commissioners and their creditors, and agricultural and mining interests outside the city who feared they would be adversely affected by increases in tolls to meet charges on a debt of £25,000.[31] These 'conservative' responses, arising out of wishes to preserve existing interests, helped to reinforce the traditional side of the milieu of eighteenth century Bath and many of them had such effect on the urban environment that they still influence profoundly the townscape in the twentieth century. Thus, Victoria Park, established in the 1830s on the site of the town commons, is a happy accident. Similarly the peacefulness of Pulteney Street and the survival of Pulteney Bridge flow from the Corporation's self interested objection to Pulteney's grandiose plans for the development of Bathwick.

This relationship between development and non-development, between innovation and conservatism, in eighteenth-century Bath is one that can be traced out in innumerable instances in the surviving townscape – it poses a good many problems for those who like to think of eighteenth-century Bath pre-eminently as a planned and ordered city composed of a sequence of interlinked streets.[32] But it is through another kind of contradiction that I wish to seek to unravel the ways in which the surviving townscape can tell us lessons about Bath and the society it mirrored and lessons about the strength and creativity of tradition even in the midst of the onward press of seemingly impersonal forces and inevitable change.

The work of John Wood the elder must have first place in any discussion of the building of Bath and must have a place of importance in the history of eighteenth-century architecture and building. So far I have focused attention on him as a remarkably successful entrepreneur. His architectural work is also generally regarded as wholly innovatory in the field of town building and town planning. His major development projects are regarded as representative of the tastes, values and attitudes of the people and society for whom he built; the rich, the powerful, the libertine and the gambler, members of a leisured and pleasure loving society. No doubt, in these circumstances, economists would like to claim Wood as an autocentred, profit-motivated entrepreneur. But I would like to try to show that he was driven by a religious–aesthetic vision of a world different from the real one in which he was condemned to live and work and that his contribution to the Bath townscape is a statement about a system of religious belief and of a social order threatened by the people who 'demanded' Bath and by those dynamic entre-

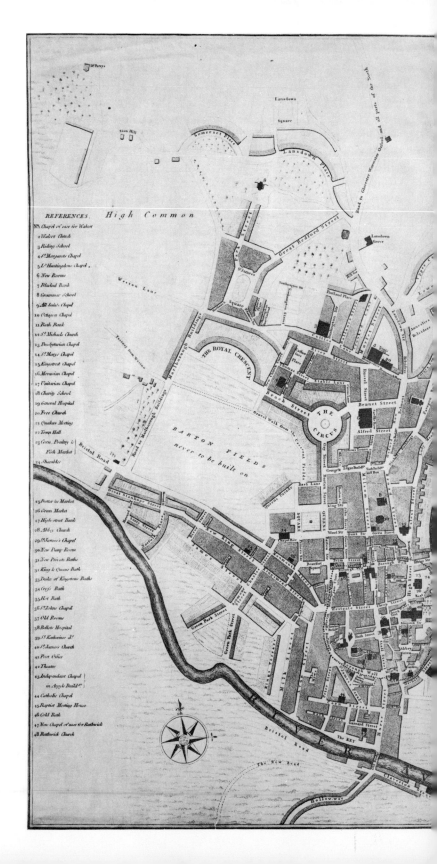

A NEW and ACCURATE
Plan
of the CITY of
BATH
to the present Year.
1796

Published by
A. Taylor
and
W. Meyler

NB The intended Buildings are included in this Plan
and are marked with fine single lines
The Boundary of the Old City of Bath
is marked with a black dotted line thus.........

Scale of Feet

Scale of Yards or One Furlong

preneurs, including Wood, who supplied it.

Most of the writers who have written about Wood and eighteenth-century Bath have been aware that Wood hoped to create there a replica of a Roman city complete with Forum, Circus, and Gymnasium. They have also emphasised his 'planning' as if he were some modern town planner. Other writers like to think of him as a precursor of the Romantics.[33] There is truth in all these views, but in none of them is there any sign of awareness of the contemporary meaning of Wood's work. Perhaps it is because his motives in building have been for so long taken at their face value that they have never been as closely scrutinised as the buildings themselves. Yet, for a provincial architect and successful entrepreneur, Wood was unusually given to explaining his objectives in writing. As well as declaring his dream of a Roman city he also published, in 1741, a remarkable book called, *The Origins of Building, or the Plagiarism of the Heathens Detected*. The argument of the book suggests that he was troubled by the way he was called on to exercise his talents almost exclusively on secular building and by the fact that the Palladian style in which he worked was derived from pagan art forms. He solved these problems to his own satisfaction by proving a divine origin for Palladian architecture. But it seems to me that it was the contradiction between his Christian desire to glorify God and the work he had to do and the forms in which he worked which was the source of that energy and creativity which led him to initiate and carry through his development projects, frequently in the face of adverse economic conditions.

According to Wood beauty in building and classical architecture were expressions of divine wisdom brought into the world at God's command at the time of the building of the Tabernacle. God, the Divine Architect, worked only with 'perfect harmony, and the most delightful proportion'. Above all he preferred the circular form, universally constituted of three principal parts representing Use, Strength, and Beauty 'to illustrate which, the figure of a man, created in the image of God, is the most notable example'.[34] Wood also preferred the circular form and considered that man made in God's image, 'is a complete figure and the perfection of order'. 'Man', he wrote, 'consists of three principal parts, namely, the head, the trunk, and the limbs; all the parts in their utmost extent, are comprehended in a square, or in a circle; and so exact is the mechanism of his whole structure, that all the parts mutually assist each

Plate 13 (*pp. 270–1*) Bath in 1796

other, and contribute to the strength of the whole.'[35] The symbolic representation of this notion of the omniscience, essence, uniformity, and justice of God, and of Man as his most perfect work, is the Vitruvian figure. This is a naked man, arms and legs diagonally outsretched with the points of his feet and hands touching the circumference of a circle and the perimeter of a square. Palladio's religious architecture derived from this notion and he employed abstracted versions of its symbol in their construction.[36] Wood, as a disciple of Palladio, also worked with the notion in the forefront of his mind and used versions of the symbol in his secular architecture. He also believed that classical architectural forms, such as proportion and the orders of columns, derived direct from God.[37] In his architecture in the 'Valley of Pleasure' Wood used a wealth of religious symbolism and contrived to put a frame around the urban environment that would enhance man's awareness of God and of Man in his image. Look at his plans for Queen Square.[38] This square was a novelty in Bath; it let far more light and air get to its surrounding houses than reached those in Chandos Court or Beauford Square, or those in the courts of early eighteenth-century Edinburgh. But the enlargement of the space enclosed does not alter the fact that what Wood planned was an enclosure and not a street or an isolated block of houses. The central area of this enclosure was designed as a perfect square – it was also intended to be perfectly level. At the centre of the square was to be a perfect circle radiating four diagonals each ending in smaller circles. The final geometrical design looks like an abstract Vitruvian figure. This visual impression should be borne in mind when one reads what Wood wrote about the purpose of the enclosure, which he persisted with in spite of the heavy expense involved. He wrote:

> I preferred an inclosed square to an open one, to make this as useful as possible. For the intention of a square in a city is for people to assemble together, *and the spot whereon they meet ought to be separated from the ground common to men and beasts, and even to mankind in general, if decency and good order are necessary to be observed in such places of Assembly, of which I think there can be no doubt.*[39]

Clearly Wood intended the enclosure as an environmental determinant of good order. It was to be a place in which a chosen few would be able to assemble apart from the bustle of everyday things, the animal kingdom, and the generality of men. Therefore nature, except in the shape of a green turf and formal shrubs, was expressly excluded. There were to be no forest trees in the square, only low stone walls and espaliers of elm and lime. The fact that the chapel he intended to build as an integral part of the whole development attracted the demand for building sites already noted suggests that many of his customers, even in the midst of iniquity, fancied the form – if not the substance of his own religious notions.

When Wood moved to begin his next development in the Parades in May 1739 he planned to turn the square inside out.[40] The houses of the Grand and South Parades became the central square form whilst the surrounding places of assembly were opened up to the country across the Avon. Nevertheless, his main concern was to create large open paved areas for the practice of public walking and talking; activities which distinguish men from beasts. In the South Parade he hoped to render these activities more congenial by letting in the winter sunshine. He also interposed circular forms and the geometry of a formal garden between the central mass of building and the natural landscape which he kept at a safe distance. Indeed, Wood's original intention was that the Grand Parade should be viewed *across* a formal garden to be called St James' Triangle.[41] As far as Wood was concerned nature was still only a very pale background to his man centred buildings and derived any aesthetic appeal it may have had from its religious associations; thus the principal natural feature to be seen from the Grand Parade was Solsbury Hill which, in Wood's mythology, had been the site of the Temple of Apollo. 'If those works had still existed', he wrote, 'their tremendous look, from the Grand Parade, must have inspired Mankind with a religious awe as often as they should consider that the Great God of Heaven and Earth was adored by them.'[42] For good measure and for those who did not share his mythology Wood incorporated a portico into the west side of Pierrepoint Street and made Orchard Street into a convenient way to St James' Church. Subsequently two other developments in the town included enclosed and wholly paved streets and excluded from them all animals and wheeled traffic in order to elevate the importance of men and the public life; William Galloway built Galloway Buildings in 1749, and Henry Fisher, Thomas Jelly, and Richard Jones built Thomas Street in 1765.

But it is in the design of the King's Circus that Wood gave full expression to the ideas he set forth in his book of 1741. The King's Circus is planned around two perfect circles one inside the other. The design also embodies a threefold expression of his notion of the trinity and of the three parts of man. Thus he cut the outer of the two circles into three equal segments, made three approaches to the

Plate 14 The Royal Crescent and the King's Circus, Bath

centre circle, and piled the three principal orders of pillars one on top of the other. This piling of the orders had further symbolic meaning. The three orders, Doric, Ionic, and Corinthian were at one and the same time symbolic trees and symbolic men. According to Wood one

> may, with Vitruvius, see in them the most lively symbols of the Robust Man, of the Grave Matron, and of the Sprightly Young Girl; and when they are placed upon one another, a Harmony, will in many cases attend the composition beyond anything that can be produced by columns of unequal altitudes sustaining one another. However, by making the shafts of the columns of each order of one and the same diameter at bottom . . . the delicacy and stateliness of one entire column above the other becomes still more conspicuous. *For as the orders advance towards virginal beauty and elegance, the columns increase in their altitude, and thereby one order receives a majesty above the other, even in miniature upon paper, which words can scarcely describe.*[43]

Who can doubt that Wood the entrepreneur was driven by something more than profit maximisation or that one extra half per cent on loan capital was unlikely to deter him from building?

Since a circle of buildings throws the eye more towards the centre and seems to enclose the space within more effectively than a square of buildings, so the King's Circus, enclosing a smaller area than Queen Square, was even more inward looking. Moreover the King's Circus was also built on a level ledge cut into the hillside and was designed to be totally devoid of natural vegetation. Only its southernmost entrance let in the sun and a distant view of Beechen Cliff. It was pure space enclosed by three equal segments of a perfect circle. Since, as I have argued, Wood's architecture sprang from his sense of the awefulness and omniscience of God this austerity of the King's Circus and the deliberate exclusion of forest trees and of all nature would appear to have a religious significance. He could be content with symbolic trees and men and uninterested in integrating town and country since his deepest purpose in building was to glorify God. Thus in the King's Circus Wood wrote *The Whole Duty of Man* in stone and his son financed it with the aid of loans from local Quakers. His own conclusion to his work on the origin of building also seems a fitting comment on his own building. 'The pagans', he said, 'forgot the divine origin of architecture and claimed it as their own invention.' The Jews, too, forgot the

> symbolical (meaning) nor could they tell to what divine matters the various parts of the sacred edifices referred. This we have sufficiently made appear in the preceding sheets, in which we had no other

hypothesis in view, nor have we any other now, but that of rendering unto Caesar, the things which are Caesars: and unto God, the things which are God's.[44]

Since Wood built within the context of supplying comfortable lodgings as bases for the pursuit of self indulgence by those rich in earthly things, and for the profit of himself and his fellow builders the King's Circus stands as a monument to the contradictions of the age. Unfortunately the finished work, impressive though it is, neither soars nor uplifts. Consequently contemporaries missed the point. Tobias Smollett, another eighteenth-century moralist, made Matthew Bramble, whom he created as an old man of the old school of almost perfect rectitude, find the King's Circus inconvenient, exposed to the elements, and difficult and dangerous to approach. He dismissed it as 'a pretty bauble, contrived for show'.[45] Lydia Melford, Smollett's lovesick modern miss, delighted in it as a sumptuous palace in an earthly paradise.[46] Those modern historians who choose to think of the King's Circus as an instance of the 'English Garden' applied to urban development or as a precursor of the Romantic Movement have also missed the point.[47]

Wood was a religiously quixotic conservative using the place and the fashion of his time to protest against both. In so doing he was led to innovate and to encourage and assist the spread of innovation. He also accumulated ground rents with a capital value of £20,000 and became himself representative of the new men of his time. He died in 1754 even as the King's Circus was begun and well before Bath entered its second great wave of expansion – an expansion that would have made it as unrecognisable in the 1770s to John Wood, had he lived, as it was to his fellow moralist Matthew Bramble. The Bath of 1793 was different again; becoming a location for manufacturing as well as an expanding centre for self-employed tradesmen and artisans in the service and building industries, Bath became a threat to its own existence as a place of resort, and, as a breeding ground for new Radical ideologies it became a threat to the class whose pleasures had brought it into being.[48] In their turn, the Radical tradesmen and artisans of Bath passed out of popular memory and all that remains are fragments of the urban landscape they knew and inhabited. To understand the story these fragments can tell we must cease looking at them through the spectacles of accepted opinion and seek out and brush the dust off the records – and read them.

NOTES AND REFERENCES

1. Anon, *A Step to the Bath with a Character of the Place* (1700).
2. Guildhall Archives, Bath [GAB] Merchant Taylors of Bath, 1666–1878, *Inrolment of Apprentices Book, 1706–1776.*
3. See for example: C. H. Collins Baker and Muriel Baker, *James Brydges, First Duke of Chandos 1674–1744* (Clarendon Press, 1949), p. 299, and John Wood, *An Essay Towards a Descriptign of Bath* (second edition London, 1765), preface.
4. Reference Library, Bath [RLB], A Plan of The Parish of Walcot in the County of Somerset, surveyed for Gay Esq. by Thomas Thorp, 1740; Index to the plan in Walcot Estate Papers, M.S. 516/B912. Somerset County Archives, Taunton [SCA], B.R./Sb.N68, Surveys of Walcot Manor, 1623 and 1638. British Museum [BM], *K37.29a*/P27527 Bathwick Survey, 1727. RLB, Pulteney Estate Papers.
5. Wood, *op. cit.*, (1st edition, Bath, 1742), preface.
6. T. S. Ashton, *Economic Fluctuations in England 1700–1800* (Clarendon Press, 1959), Statistical Table 23.
7. Wood, *op. cit.* (second edition), preface.
8. GAB, Wood Box, Particulars of Fee Farm Rents and Leasehold Ground Rents, 1787, and Indenture 1.11.1754. SCA, DD/BR/PY BX4, Indenture 30.4.1768. RLB, Wood Bundle, Indenture, 20.12.1766.
9. SCA, DD/X/STU Indenture, 29.10.1767.
10. Wood, *op. cit* (second edition), Part III, pp. 343–7.
11. GAB, Wood Box, Particulars of Fee Farm Rents and Leasehold Ground Rents, 1787, and Draft Agreement, 21.8.1770.
12. A. W. B. Simpson, *An Introduction to the History of The Land Law* (Oxford University Press, 1961), D. E. C. Yale ed., *Lord Nottingham's Chancery Cases*, Selden Society (Bernard Quertch, 1961).
13. Benjamin Boyce, *The Benevolent Man* (Harvard University Press, 1967), p. 46. RLB, Ralph Allen and Buckeridge MSS. p. 14. GAB, Wood Box, Indentures, 29.10.1747 and 11.8.1748. I am also indebted to C. W. Chalklin for his analysis of the financiers of 226 houses built in Bath 1736–80 which shows that 65 per cent were built by men in the building trades, 27 per cent by men in other trades and crafts, and 8 per cent by the leisured class and professional men.
14. The principal sources for Marchant's life and activities are: GAB, *Inrolment of Apprentices Book, 1706–1776*; *Minute and Record Book of Merchant Taylors, 1666–1735*; *Freeman's Book, 1697–1775*; *Lunatics Estate Account*; *John Jeffreys' Account Books, 1751–1762.* BM, Egerton MS. 3647, fol. 136–7. *Bath Chronicle*, 4 August 1774. Boyce, *op. cit.*
15. The main source of Jeffreys' activities is his Account Book, 1751–62, *loc. cit.* But see also, RLB, Walcot Estate Papers, and GAB, Box 1780.
16. *An Act for Repairing, Amending, and Enlarging the Highways between the top of Kingsdown, and the City of Bath*, 6. Anne, 1707. Other Acts extending the powers of the trust were: 7. George I, 12. George II, 30. George II, 32. George II. Arthur Elton, 'The prehistory of railways', *Somersetshire Archeological and Natural History Society Proceedings*, cvii–cviii (1963–64), 36–52. F. B. Relton, *Fire Insurance Companies* (1793), p. 114 and 204, also, E. Nugent Linaker, 'A History of the

Bath Fire Office', *Sun Alliance and London Group Gazette* (Autumn 1971), 10–11. R. S. Neale, 'An equitable Trust in the Building Industry in 1794', *Business History*, vii, no. 2 (July 1965), 94–6.

17. Ashton, *op. cit.* J. Parry Lewis, *Building Cycles and Britain's Growth* (Macmillan, 1965). The peaks in building identified by these authors are: Ashton: 1701, 1707, 1716–18, 1730, 1739, 1753, 1760, 1776; Lewis: 1705, 1724, 1736, 1753, 1776.

18. The location of the main sources are: GAB, Bath Corporation Accounts and Improvement Commissioners, Box [1789], Summary of Accounts of Improvement Commissioners. RLB, Bath City Rate Books, 1766–1800, and Walcot Poor Rate Books, 1777–1800. British Transport Historical Records, London, The Avon Navigation Accounts, AN23/7, 8, 9, 10. BM, Egerton MS. 3648, Kingston ground and property rents. In this section I have sought to keep footnotes to a minimum since the time series on which the narrative is based are buried in the above records. I hope to make them generally available in a later publication.

19. Wood, *op. cit.* (second edition), p. 312.

20. GAB, Wood Box, Particulars of Fee Farm Rents and Leasehold Ground Rents, 1787.

21. Ashton, *op. cit.*, pp. 85–8; Lewis, *op. cit.*, pp. 12–13.

22. Quoted in John Walters, *Splendour and Scandal in the Reign of Beau Nash* (Jarrolds, 1968).

23. GAB, Minute Books Bath Corporation: 1 October 1753, 31 December 1753, 1 April 1754, 4 May 1754, 19 May 1760, 30 September 1761.

24. GAB, Corporation Leases, Box, 1754–1761, Indenture 29.9.1761.

25. BM, Egerton MS. 3647, Fol. 113, Indenture 10.4.1762.

26. RLB, MS. 1809, Pulteney Estate Papers. Act of Parliament 9. George II, 1769.

27. An advertisement for letting, 'several shops on the New Bridge, fit for any genteel business; and at the end of the bridge, some exceeding good stables and warehouses, etc. fit for carpenters shops, or any business that requires room', first appeared in the *Bath Chronicle* 13 January 1774. It reappeared regularly until 8 September 1774.

28. 'From the year 1778 to the year 1783 by reason of our dispute with America, our army and navy being then on service, the seasons at Bath were so little frequented that houses in Bath were greatly reduced in value' (Public Record Office Exchequer K.R. Depositions taken by Commission E 134, 34 George III Mich. 14, quoted in J. R. Ward, 'Investment in Canals and House-building in England, 1760–1815' (unpublished D.Phil. thesis, Oxford, 1970).

29. This is amply illustrated by the records in GAB, The Merchant Taylors of Bath, 1666–1878, particularly the case of the Merchant Taylors v Glazby, 1764. For restrictive practices by other trades, see Bundle 114 in same location; J. Jeffreys's Account Book, 1751–62; and RLB, MS. 1602.

30. GAB, Minute Books Bath Corporation: 2 February 1771, 28 February 1774. SCA, D/T/ba7, Minute Books Bath Turnpike, 1770–76; 1 January 1771, 21 January 1774, 26 February 1774, 3 March 1774. *Bath Chronicle*, 17 March 1774.

Anon, *A View of Bath, Historical, Political, Chronological* (Bath, 1813).

31. SCA, Minute Books Bath Turnpike, 1776–93: 14 March 1789, 11 May 1789. *Bath Journal*, 6 April 1789. *Bath Chronicle*, 9 April 1789, 21 May 1789.

32. Colin Buchanan and Partners, *Bath – a planning and transport study* (London, 1965).

33. See, for example, John Fleming, Hugh Honour and Nikolaus Pevsner, *The Penguin Dictionary of Architecture* (Penguin Books, 1966), p. 242, and the extravagant claims in Bruce Allsopp, *A History of Renaissance Architecture* (Pitman, 1959), p. 185, and in Sacheverell Sitwell, *British Architects and Craftsmen* (Batsford, 1945), p. 137, in which it is claimed that Wood was responsible for Lansdowne Crescent. Nikolaus Pevsner, *An Outline of European Architecture* (Penguin Books, 1960), p. 581 claims in reference to Wood, that in 'Bath nature was close at hand and willingly admitted'. Fritz Baumgart, *A History of Architectural Styles* (Pall Mall Press, 1970), p. 255, makes even more extravagant claims when he says that in the King's Circus as well as in the Royal Crescent, 'the town was opened up to draw its natural surroundings unto itself. Nature is no longer the servant of architecture. The two are equals. The Romantic Movement is at hand.'

34. John Wood, *The Origin of Building or The Plagiarism of The Heathens Detected* (Bath, 1741), p. 71.

35. *Ibid.*, p. 71.

36. Rudolf Wittkower, *Architectural Principles in the Age of Humanism* (second edition, Tiranti, 1952), pp. 1–32, 70–100; see also Edward MacCurdy, *The Notebooks of Leonardo Da Vinci* (Cape, 1954) vol. i, plate 13 and p. 204, vol. ii, plate 26; and Rudolf Wittkower, *Art and Architecture in Italy 1600–1750* (Penguin Books, 1958), pp. 116–21.

37. Wood, *op. cit.*, pp. 68–73, and John Wood, *A Dissertation Upon the Orders of Columns* (1750).

38. John Wood, *An Essay Towards a Description of Bath* (second edition), plate 12, and pp. 343–349.

39. *Ibid.*, p. 345. My italics.

40. *Ibid.*, plate 14.

41. *Ibid.*, p. 349.

42. *Ibid.*, p. 351

43. John Wood, *A Dissertation Upon The Orders of Columns* (1750), p. 27. My italics.

44. Wood, *The Origin of Building*, p. 235.

45. Tobias Smollett, *Humphry Clinker*, 1721 (New York, Signet Edition, 1960), pp. 44–5.

46. *Ibid.*, p. 48.

47. Above, note 33.

48. R. S. Neale, *Class and Ideology in the Nineteenth Century* (Routledge, 1972), pp. 41–74.

11

The making of a townscape: Richard Paley in the east end of Leeds, 1771–1803

For his first book, published in 1935, William Hoskins chose a long title but one which brought together a past topography, a past society, and a past economy, a fusion of subject matter that was to characterise all his later writing. The essay which follows, written a generation after *Industry, Trade and People in Exeter, 1688–1800*, also happens to have a long title with a similar mixture of elements (as is appropriate for a tribute volume) in its study of a leading figure in an early but formative stage in the transformation of the urban environment when industrialisation came to Leeds and its region.

Among modern urban historians the informative use of studies on a scale large enough to embrace the individual house and street was pioneered by Professor Dyos.[1] *Victorian Suburb* was published in 1961, and the history of townscapes will never be the same again. Alongside work on the local contribution of building to the overall level of the English economy, initiated by Weber in 1955, some beginning has now been made on the no less intricate but wholly local problem of the timing, the motives, the movers, and the strategy of urban housing development in terms of the size, shape, and social standing of particular houses and particular streets. Here, rather than with aggregates, are the foundations of historical explanation.[2]

As with the builders of factories, the history of domestic housing cannot be written wholly in terms of the giants. Recent studies of insurance inventories have shown that new mill building in industrial areas of the Midlands and the North could involve the raising of a capital sum very different from the expenditure of a Gott, a Strutt or an Arkwright. Estate development did have its giants, and we now know something of their strategies from Sir John Summerson and Professor Olsen's work on Georgian London, and from Mr Chalklin's survey of the provinces: but the characteristic protagonists, who sold and purchased fields and then built speculatively upon them, were far from giants. Initial development on this small scale within the yards, gardens, and burgage plots of old towns had been indicated by Dr Kellett, among others, in his study of Glasgow from 1780 (published in 1961), and it will be found as a reiterated theme in the studies of the early years of industrial housing in England brought together in the symposium, *The History of Working-class Housing*, edited by Dr Chapman. It is odd that Manchester, where the transformation began earliest and most rapidly, has so far failed to stimulate academic curiosity of the kind that gave rise to Mr Taylor's study 'The eighteenth-century origin of the Liverpool slum'. If the word *slum* did indeed come into English use in the 1820s, the houses that it described in the industrial North were then no more than a generation old. It was therefore their character, their density and their setting, rather than their aged dilapidation, which marked them out: and these attributes (in Leeds at least) arose from entrepreneurial decisions made no earlier than Richard Paley's land purchases on the eastern edge of Leeds in 1787, and the first promotion of a terminating building society in the town in the same year.[3]

I

No new street of houses was built in Leeds between 1634 and 1767. The inactivity is remarkable. In 1634 John Harrison had built New Street at the North End of Leeds as an adjunct to the new church of St John's, the new vicarage, and the new almshouses with which he endowed that fashionable and expanding quarter of the town centre. On the best estimates, the population of the in-township had risen between 1634 and 1767 from 5,000 to 16,000. This additional population was absorbed in traditional ways: by tenementing of large houses near the centre; by new infill building in the burgage plots of Briggate, and in the crofts and garths of the five other old streets that made up the clothing town; and by infill of farmyards or *folds* along Marsh Lane, the arterial road towards York.[4]

Nor was the tardy resumption of street building in 1767 an East End matter. While a tentative but eventually unsuccessful attempt was made to create a West End[5] of new streets and squares from 1767 onwards, no new streets were built in the north or east quarters of the town, whether for artisans or labourers, until twenty years later when the population was nearly 22,000. There can be no doubt. Quite apart from the positive dating evidence from the conveyances, placing no street before this date, there is the cartographic evidence: John Tuke's map of 1781 shows no street[6] (other than in the West End) that was not already there in John Cossins' map of 1725.

The working-class cottages[7] that eventually made up most of the East End did not come in a single wave of speculative building. The first were built by several near-contemporary terminating building clubs, and it was not until the advent of Richard Paley that one can discern an organised attempt to meet the new need by speculative development of streets and courts in high density, back-to-back housing. Significant as this development was in the long run for the sanitary history of Leeds, it must be noted that its early vigour was no more successful than the West End development in achieving a rapid completion. When Paley was bankrupted in 1803 there were vacant building plots in every street that he had essayed, and four of the large fields that he had acquired on the edge of the East End were bare of streets, even though one of them contained the first two steam-powered cotton mills in the town. In his two most developed closes, McAndrews Garden and Forster's Close, there were nearly three acres of unsold building ground in 1809. Nor was the position much better in 1815, as the first large-scale plan of the town shows; and it was 1823 before the assignees of the Paley estate succeeded in disposing of the final acres.

Thus for the whole of the first generation of steam-power in Leeds, from 1790 to 1820, there was abundant land near the factories, half-developed and certainly available as 'building ground' although Fowler's map of 1821 was the first printed map to sketch in hypothetical street-lines with such a caption. The demand for new houses was limited by population increase and influx, the acceptable average level (judging from the ratios both in 1771 and 1801) being not far from one house for every additional 4·5 persons. Demand was also limited by income so that the working-class 'cottage' was typically the back-to-back house, one room up, one room down, the whole needing a ground area of some 30 square yards. In the not untypical area of streets and courts developed by Paley (Fig.

Plate 15 The East End of Leeds, I. Dufton's Yard, looking north (1901). From a series of photographs taken for the Commons Committee hearing property-owners' objections to designation as an *Insanitary Area*. The Yard is a court at

the rear of back-to-back houses, entered from Somerset St. by a tunnel (left).
The principal open sewer of the town was 25 yards away. It is conceivable
that some of the young children shown could still be living in 1974.

11.4b), where there were 272 dwellings on the 12,500 square yards of McAndrews Garden, the extra ground needed for access by streets and courts reduced the overall density from 46 to 30 square yards per house, or about 105 houses to the acre.

Since by 1793 Paley had accumulated some 38 acres of potential building ground in the East and North Divisions of the in-township, demand would have had to increase by some 3,800 houses for all the plots to be taken up, assuming 100 houses to the acre. In the event, the average annual increase for the whole in-township between 1772 and 1801 was about 112 houses, and the average was certainly no more than 120 between 1801 and 1811 when the Census figures are available. Paley's hopes, which proved fatally optimistic, may have been inflated by seeing 200 new houses a year from 1790 to 1795 and 180 a year from 1800 to 1805. Yet even if that rate had been maintained through every year of the trade cycle, it would have taken nearly twenty years to drain the reservoir that he held. Even had Paley been able to build more factories, there would still have been much vacant land. The four factories that he did build (Bank Low, Bank Top, Cawood's Foundry and Marsh Lane Flax Mill) covered 2,700, 1,570, 1,800 and 250 square yards respectively, or 1·3 acres in all. By 1831 the total number of new industrial establishments in the whole East End was no more than 29, many of them smaller than the Paley mills.[8]

The assignees of his bankrupt estate after 1803 were only a little better placed, for the annual average for 1811–21 was 320 new houses. Even set against the greatest rate of increase for the whole nineteenth century, that of 540 per year between 1821 and 1831, Paley's building ground was extensive, and of course there were at all times fringes of the old built-up area where other developers were bringing land on to the market. Paley's ground was well placed, as Fig. 11.1 shows, but he did not enjoy a monopoly of strategic sites.

In the economic history of nineteenth-century Leeds the decade 1821–31 was perhaps the most critical. It was the decade of the first passenger railway, the first gas works, the first significant public buildings programme, the first smoke abatement cases, and the first invasion of the West End by working-class streets. This rapid and massive accumulation of houses where there had once been fields, and of sewers where there had once been streams, was to culminate, a year after the 1831 census, in a cholera epidemic. Intermixed high-density industrial and building development on this scale may have been within Paley's vision and ambition forty years earlier, but in fact the local economy of his day, although on the move, could not yet achieve movement of that magnitude.

A critical editorial in the *Leeds Mercury*, noting the contribution of piecemeal development to sanitary problems, once commented that in Leeds the whole street plan 'looked as if the town had used an earthquake for an architect'.[9] Paley's original plans had nothing as fortuitous as this. He did not want to be bounded by the limits of small fields and small purchases, and his initial streets, yards, and courts were designed as coherently for his clientele as the West End was for another part of the social spectrum. He could hardly have anticipated that in the 1930s more of the original East End would survive than the West End, nor that some of his working-class cottages would still be occupied in 1955, that is 122 years after Robert Baker had condemned them in his cholera report to the Leeds Board of Health in 1833.[10]

II

Whether in East End or West End, coherence and strategy in street development were difficult to achieve without owning several adjoining fields, for the enclosure of the common fields of Leeds on the north and east of the town had characteristically produced small fields of no more than two or three acres, while the former manorial park on the west, which had once possessed the unity of demesne ownership, had been broken up at disparking. Physical division of the old park was accompanied by multiple ownership, no single proprietor in Leeds being wealthy enough to take on the whole of the demesnes. The assembly of selions into the long, narrow fields of the north and east was indeed a step in building up a compact property but it went no further: at enclosure (the post-medieval date of which is unknown) there must have been many proprietors to be satisfied, for the characteristic pattern discernible from the late seventeenth century onwards was of the one-field owner. Why was there not the agglomeration which elsewhere in England went alongside farming developments of the seventeenth and eighteenth centuries? It is probable that the single-field ownership was retained in Leeds because fields of the in-township were an annexe to industry: they were of particular value to freeholders who were occupied in the finishing trades, needing tenter grounds with light and air away from the confined yards of their town centre workshops. Any field plan on a scale large enough to show detail is likely to have tenters sketched in.[11] By the late eighteenth century even the large vestigial grass common, the Moor, was prized by the freeholders as much for its tenter rights as for its grazing.

Singly-owned fields of this size were appropriate to small-scale development, and indeed in the 1820s and 1830s they were to succumb one by one to small-scale developers,[12] producing some of the worst features of insanitation for the 1840s. But, in the 1780s, when the first developers were hoping to achieve large-scale projects, it was necessary to find willing sellers who would dispose of something larger than the tenter garths. In 1755 the Ibbetson estates at the Leylands had been freed from entail and put on the market, but they were made up of scattered fields. ' So situated that there is now a Fair Prospect and Opportunity by granting Building Leases, to make a great Improvement of the same', claimed the preamble to the Estate Act,[13] but the Leylands – a notorious slum name at the end of the nineteenth century – were not developed in fact until after 1815. Yet, as it happened, there were two other medium-sized settled estates, one in the East and one in the West, which had achieved a measure of agglomeration and which were not unwilling to sell building ground at the key moment.

The Wilsons' project, in the West End, was possible only because from 1717 Richard Wilson I invested the proceeds of legal office and a good marriage in a deliberate but slow accumulation of land, restoring the former unity of the Park estate and going beyond it.[14] His motive was probably not a building development but to make a fit setting to the west of the old Manor House were he lived, and which his son rebuilt as a residence in 1765. But building leases began to be granted on the town edge of the accumulated estate by Richard Wilson II in 1767; in the next year a large plot for the building of the Infirmary; and just before his death in 1792 Richard II had contracted to sell a plot of land near Bean Ing for the Gott mill. The family had abandoned the Manor House for Bristol.

In the East End also, the first developers found an estate, only a little smaller than the Park estate of the West End, that was ready to sell off building ground which included quite large fields at the very edge of Vicar Lane, Kirkgate, and Lady Lane, the three streets to the east of Briggate, the old central market street of the town (Fig. 11.1). This estate, by coincidence also a Wilson estate (although of a quite different family), was sub-manorial, being based on North Hall near the bridge that took Lady Lane over Timble Beck towards Quarry Hill and York. It lay on both sides of the Beck, where water fulling mills and dye houses were already sited, even in 1715 when landscape engravings emphasised the sylvan nature of

Plate 16 The East End of Leeds, II. Back York Street, looking west (1901). On the left is the chimney and wall of a saw-mill: across the narrow street the doors and windows of six pairs of back-to-backs, Goulden's Buildings, insured with the Sun by William Goulden, 'bricklayer', for £200 as 'twelve new tenements' in May, 1797. Paley sold the land in January 1797. (See arrow at 11a on Fig. 11.1, p. 294, below.)

Leeds as viewed from the east.[15] These settled estates of Ann Wilson had been freed from entail by Act of Parliament[16] as early as 1765. There were no takers for twenty-two years after the Act until in 1787 the Crackenthorpe Gardens Building Society bought enough ground to allow an interconnected group of three streets to be laid out north of Kirkgate and east of Vicar Lane.[17]

This first development by a terminating building society was quickly followed by four others, all in the East End. But the major and further development of the East End for working-class cottages was to be undertaken by private speculative building, virtually all of it by one man, Richard Paley, 'soap boiler and chapman', in an elaborate ambition that ended with his bankruptcy in 1803 and the transfer of his estate by the Commissioners of Bankruptcy to assignees who were to sell it piecemeal in the interests of Paley's creditors.

My first apprehension of Paley's role in the development of the East End of Leeds arose from frequent encounters with his name and those of his assignees when I was working over the deeds of the properties in the York Street Unhealthy Area, purchased for clearance by the Corporation in 1892. Some of the bundles included manuscript and printed *Abstracts of Title to Lands to be sold by Richard Paley*, and his name frequently occurred at the beginning of *Schedules* even when there was no actual statement of title surviving from the late eighteenth century. Soon after, I began to meet his name in the Town Rate Books where I was tracking down the owners of cottage properties in the 1790s, and by good fortune this was the very time when the City Archivist was taking a further consignment of documents from a Leeds solicitor's collection, including the papers of Paley's assignees in bankruptcy.[18] I am grateful to the City Archivist, Mr Collinson, for permission to work over these papers in advance of their cataloguing. The papers include many deeds and mortgages from the years when Paley was accumulating his estate, and other transactions are documented in the West Riding Registry of Deeds. The property advertisements in the *Mercury* and the *Intelligencer*, the two Leeds newspapers, afford further evidence; the clearances of recent years and the accompanying purchases have now brought other property deeds of that period into the hands of the Corporation, including maps of Paley's Skinner Lane project; three other maps, two manuscript and one printed, have also been found in the miscellanea of the solicitor's collection mentioned above.

Richard Paley's progress towards the first purchases of 1787 must now be charted. Apart from brief references to his partnership in the Bowling Iron Works, his name will not be found among the chronicles of the industrial revolution, although he may fairly lay claim to that often mis-used adjective of historians, 'neglected', since he was not only the pioneer of speculative building for the working classes of Leeds, but also the builder of the town's two first steam-powered cotton mills, earlier than the woollen mill of Gott or the flax mill of Marshall. These, and his provision of a new foundry for the Leeds engineer, Cawood, lie beyond this essay, and the loss of all accounting records makes it impossible to disentangle Paley's business affairs.[19] Which of his ventures provided capital for which we shall never know. But his biography, as far as contemporary newspaper notices go, begins with an infusion of capital from an endowment of worldly goods openly celebrated and published in every marriage service.

III

In June 1771, at the age of twenty-five, already a soap-boiler and already in Leeds, he was married, and the *Leeds Intelligencer* noted the fact tersely:[20] 'last Monday was married at Otley Mr Paley Soap Boiler of this town, to Miss (Mary) Preston of Merebeck nigh Settle, an agreeable lady with a fortune of £1,000', and in June 1772 the *Intelligencer* reported that his first child, a daughter, was christened at Leeds Parish Church.[21]

Richard Paley himself was born at Langcliffe near Settle in the Craven limestone area of the West Riding, where his father, Thomas, inherited a small estate centred on Langcliffe Scar Farm. Born in 1746 and dying in 1808, Richard was almost an exact contemporary of his celebrated cousin, the theologian William Paley (1743–1805). As a younger son, William's father had left the family estate in Craven for a career in the Church, becoming a minor canon of Peterborough and only returning to the Settle area to become headmaster of Giggleswick School. As a younger son also, Richard Paley left Settle some time before 1771 to become a soap boiler in Leeds. In July 1772 the Poor Law apprenticeship register shows him taking Elizabeth Frances.[22]

No record of any property transactions by Paley has been found earlier than a house purchase at the industrial village of Hunslet, south of the river, in November 1773. In April 1775 he leased an extensive property at Kirk Ings, next to Leeds parish churchyard, (15 on Fig. 11.1) and running south from Kirkgate to a riverside wharf in the basin above the Navigation locks.[23] By that time Leeds had become a merchanting and finishing centre for cloth rather than a place of manufacture, with a plentiful use of soap in the finishing processes.[24] The Kirk Ings property had a house on Kirkgate, built by the old Leeds merchanting family, the Cooksons. It was from a widow Cookson that Paley took the forty-year lease, and began to improve the warehouses, malthouses and soaphouses. In February 1776 the improved property formed the security for a loan from his father, redeemed in March 1779 but mortgaged again in May 1779 'with buildings erected and about to be erected'.[25]

If his wife's dowry had helped him to come to Kirk Ings, so centrally situated, this second dip into the family purse enabled him to move his manufacturing to a country site, purchasing some fields at Knostrop in November 1780. Here he built a house, and after massive purchases of further land in 1787 he built the soap works that were to be known as *Gibraltar*,[26] although retaining the Kirk Ings base where the firm's counting house stood 'containing every requisite Convenience for a large family; with the compleat Warehouses, Dressing-Shops, Drying-house, and Tenter Ground'.[27] In the same year, 1787, his investment interests significantly widened: besides his Knostrop purchase, he took a quarter share of £700 with the Sturges in the Bowling Iron Works partnership; bought a riverside mill at Wakefield for the associated Fall Ings works;[28] and – taking on for the first time the role that stimulated this essay – he re-entered the property market in the East End of Leeds, not to extend his work premises nor to build his family a town house, but to participate in the building of new streets of working-class houses.

If Leeds did not have a true West End before the developments on the Wilson's Park estate, it had long had essential elements of an East End, like all industrial towns situated on rivers bringing traffic westwards from the sea. Additionally, Leeds Bridge posed a barrier to further westward movement of traffic larger than barges, and the head of the Navigation was built east of the Bridge in 1699. The south bank was low and marshy at the Navigation terminus, and wharfside development was initially restricted to the north bank. Apart from wharves, warehouses and the processing industries, the north bank eastward of the Bridge was the site for important water-mills, both corn and fulling; while only a few yards east of the parish church the Timble (or Adel) Beck joined the Aire. For more than four miles from the higher ground north of Leeds this Beck was lined with mills – Marshall's first flax mill lay on it in Adel – and in its last mile the dyehouses began to accumulate on either bank. A plan of 1772 shows further dyehouses crowded around the junction of

Beck and river between Leeds and the weaving hamlet of Hill House.[29]

The Timble Beck, crucial to the development of the first industrial East End, flowed north and south before joining the Aire, and no roads followed its bank: the two arterial roads going east to York and Pontefract crossed it at Lady Bridge and Timble Bridge. These two bridges lay at the eastern end of the Headrow and Kirkgate respectively, and from bridge to bridge there was still open ground on either side of the Beck; south of Timble Bridge there was also open ground to the east where the causeway carried a road to the hamlet of Hill House (22 on Fig. 11.1).

Within two years, 1787–89, all this open land between the bridges,[30] east and west of the Beck, was owned either by one of the building clubs or by Paley. A military occupation could hardly have been better planned, although the diverse membership of the Clubs and the different composition of their trustees make collusion unlikely. If there was a unifying factor, apart from the attraction of the proximity to existing streets, it lay with the trustees of the Ann Wilson settled estates to whom much of this land belonged; Paley's own purchase of three houses in St Peter's Square (5 on Fig. 11.1),[31] products of the Greater Building Society, was probably no more than an ordinary investment, although it is true that he laid out his streets to link with Duke Street and St Peter's Square, and to the west of the Beck he took from the Wilson trustees the spare land that the Crackenthorpe Gardens Society was not using for its three parallel streets, an area on which Paley built before April 1791 'twelve several cottages . . . with the cellars under the same on the said piece of Ground bounded on the north by a New Street late other part of the Said Crackenthorpe Garden called Ebenezer St'.[32]

The chronology of Paley's purchases, re-sales, mortgages and redemptions is reserved for Appendix I. A summary of sales in Table 11.1 shows that between 1788 and his bankruptcy he sold more than ten acres in parcels of varying size. After 1803 his former estate provided the chief reservoir of land for development in the East End of Leeds, and his assignees conveyed some 32 acres before they wound up his affairs in July 1823, fifteen years after his death.[33]

These figures include the Knostrop estate, purchased between 1780 and 1787 for the Gibraltar soap works; this property lay well east of Leeds in open country and will not be considered further here. Apart from the domestic and industrial base at Kirk Ings, Paley's building developments can be said to begin with the contract in October 1786 for the purchase *inter alia* of a close at Black Bank and a close at

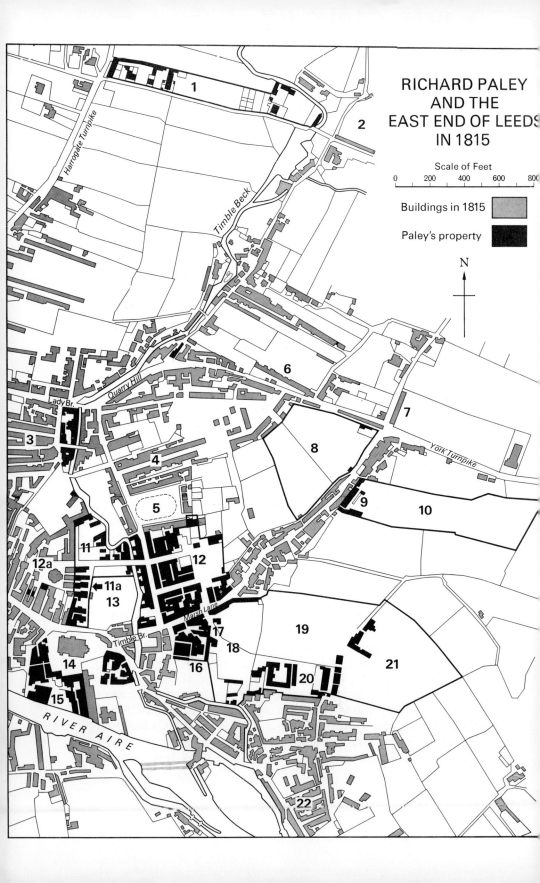

RICHARD PALEY
AND THE
EAST END OF LEEDS
IN 1815

Scale of Feet

0   200   400   600   800

Buildings in 1815

Paley's property

N

Harrogate Turnpike

Timble Beck

Quarry Hill

Lady Br.

York Turnpike

Marsh Lane

Timble Br.

RIVER AIRE

1
2
3
4
5
6
7
8
9
10
11
11a
12
12a
13
14
15
16
17
18
19
20
21
22

TABLE 11.1   *Summary of Paley's and assignees' sales, 1788–1823*

	Number	Area sq yd	Houses thereon
1788	2	346	—
1789	—	—	—
1790	2	2,115	—
1791	—	—	—
1792	3	2,744	1
1793	6	14,130	2
1794	1	423	—
1795	6	5,756	—
1796	8	7,777	15
1797	7	3,927	4
1798	2	714	6
1799	2	1,433	—
1800	8	8,159	2
1801	6	3,831	5
1802	1	424	14
1803	—	—	—
Total	54	10·7 acres	49
1803–23 (Assignees)	110	32 acres	356

Coneyshaws.[34] It may be significant that the former had recently been advertised as suitable for purchase by a building club,[35] and that the first terminating building societies in Leeds were being formed at this time (Fig. 11.1 nos. 3, 12 and 22).

The chronology of purchases can be followed in Appendix 1, but the most significant in terms of the building styles discussed below were those of Forster's Close (1787), McAndrews Garden (1787) and White Cross Close (1792). For the industrial developments near Marsh Lane the crucial purchases were those of Skinner's Croft (1789) and Well Houses (1789).[36]

Early experience at Kirk Ings would have taught Paley the advantages of leasing, improving and mortgaging, but since there

Fig. 11.1   The East End of Leeds, 1815, with Richard Paley's developments, 1775–1803. Base: Francis and Netlam Giles' plan of 1815; Paley's closes and houses located from deeds and houses cited in the text.
1 Skinner Lane (White Cross Close); 2 Mabgate Green and Cotton Mill; 3 Crackenthorpe Gardens Building Society; 4 Lesser Building Society (High St.); 5 Greater Building Society (St. Peter's Sq.); 6 Union Row Building Society; 7 Union Place Building Society; 8 Ridsdale Purchase, 1792, (north); 9 Paley's Galleries; 10 Coney Shaw; 11 Forster's Close; 11a Goulden's Buildings (see pl. 13, p. 289); 12 McAndrews Garden; 12a St James' Church; 13 New Burial Ground; 14 Parish Church and Yard; 15 Kirk Ings and Wharf; 16 Cawood's Foundry; 17 Marsh Lane Flax Mill; 18 Ridsdale Purchase, 1792, (south); 19 Sigston's Closes; 20 Skinner's Close with Bank Top and Bank Low Cotton Mills; 21 Low Cavalier Close with Well Houses; 22 Hillhouse Building Club (East King St., and East Queen St.)

was virtually no leasehold land available in Leeds his estate development had to take the form of purchases, improvement and resale of
freeholds. He was also a landlord of house property, as Table 11.2
shows, and the 'To Let' advertisements are too consistent for this
role simply to have been forced upon him by difficulties in selling.
Indeed the reverse, since 'For Sale' advertisements of houses did not
appear in any quantity until his financial difficulties on the eve of
bankruptcy in 1803.

The last year for extensive sales of plots was 1801: in 1802 he had
sold only one plot,[37] and at this time he was still carrying the two
large mortgages,[38] totalling £15,000, renewed in February 1800. In
February or March 1803 he remitted £5,000 to London for the local
collector of Excise but failed to find acceptance for his bill;[39] he
publicly disowned agreements made by one of his servants;[40] his
former partner Dade, died at this time;[41] large mortgages were
obtained from bankers at Malton, Huddersfield, and Pontefract in
March, and despite another mortgage and a public offer of sale for the
Knostrop estate in April,[42] he became bankrupt on 21 May 1803 at
the suit of the Huddersfield and Pontefract mortgagees.[43]

In the absence of any general business records it is not known which
of his enterprises forced him into a crisis of liquidity; the soap-
making firm certainly continued to function after the bankruptcy,
directed by his son, and there had been no massive land purchases
since 1793. The dissolution of the cotton-making partnership with
the Wilkinsons in 1795 had been followed by a group of mortgages[44]
totalling £17,425; at that time also the cotton mill was put up to let,
and interested parties were invited to seek details of building ground
for sale. Ironically, the last two acquisitions before Paley's own
bankruptcy were the result of the insolvency of others: in 1799 a
house in York as a result of the default of a grocer; and in 1798 closes
at Richmond Hill and cottages at Hillhouse from the bankruptcy of
his former associate at Kirk Ings, the brewer Thomas Appleyard.[45]

                                        IV
So far in this essay a purposive purchase plan has been assumed. It
can be documented. The premeditated yet casual nature of Paley's
first partnership with Thomas Dade, a timber merchant also from
Knostrop, is set out in a note which the assignees' solicitor prepared
for the instruction of counsel in 1807 when the interest of Dade's heir,
Edmund Maude, was being extinguished in a cash-and-land
compensation payment.[46]

Mr Paley long previous to his Bankruptcy and Mr Dade in his
lifetime [i.e. also before 1803] became Joint Purchasers of Sundry
Estates in Leeds which were Conveyed to them as to an undivided
Moiety to Mr Paley and his Heirs and the other Moiety to Mr Dade
and his Heirs. Mr Dade's Moiety was between himself and his
Partner Mr Maude although conveyed solely to Mr Dade.
Mr Paley and Mr Dade purchased the above Estates with the sole
View of parcelling them out in Building Lots, and from time to time
proceeded to sales of sundry parts thereof, sometimes dividing the
purchase Monies equally and at other times the whole received by
each without ever coming to an account with each other. Mr Paley
agreed verbally to become the Purchaser of a Plot of Ground part of
the Joint Estate and has proceeded to erect Sundry Buildings upon it
without any conveyance from Mr Dade, and Mr Paley has also
erected Sundry Buildings upon other parts of the Joint Estate.
Mr Paley is indebted to Dade and Maude [Dade's sole legatee] by
Trade and by the Sales of the Joint Estate, even excluding those parts
built on without contract. Mr Maude is willing to convey the unsold
part of the Joint Estate and the other parts built on by Mr Paley if he
is given the balance of the Trade Account.

The Paley-Dade joint (or indistinguishable) property formed only
a small part of the estate which the assignees were then endeavouring
to sell off, but the survey and valuation that were made for them are
most useful evidence of Paley's intentions, for this area lay nearest
to the town, and by 1803 its street development had been taken
further than anywhere else in the whole Paley estate. The fortunate
survival of maps[47] from the partition of 1807 and from 1809 enable
the incomplete development to be shown in detail (Fig. 11.4a and b),
and its housing character will be discussed in a later section.

Away from the two beckside fields (Forster's Close and Mc-
Andrews Garden) where the Paley-Dade purchases lay, Appendix I
shows further housing development on land bought solely by Paley,
mainly between Marsh Lane and the industrial hamlet of Hill House
but with three other fields near the junction of Marsh Lane and York
Road. The accumulation of houses on the whole Paley estate can be
seen in the surviving town Rate Books, where owners and occupiers
were distinguished, and these data make-up Table 11.2.

By 1790 Paley, whose town properties in 1787 did not extend
beyond the soap-house, maltkilns, and residence at Kirk Ings, owned
forty houses, virtually all in the East Division and rated so low that
they must have been working class cottages. In the Rate Book of
1795 he was assessed on twice that number, and by 1800 on treble;
and these were the houses that he had retained – others, not appearing
against his name in the Rate Books, had been built for immediate

resale; and most of those who bought building plots from him had also built on them. The period of greatest development shown in

TABLE 11.2   *Paley in the rate assessments, 1790–1805: number of houses*

	Total Number	Kirkgate Division	East Division	North-east Division	Elsewhere
1790	40	2	35	3	0
1795	83	16	57	10	0
1800	123	25	71	26	1
1805	262	18	172★	71	1

★13 others had already been sold by the assignees, 1803–5.

Table 11.2 was between the Rate Books of 1800 and 1805, and everything attributed to Paley or his assignees in the 1805 Book must have been built before the bankruptcy of May 1803. Indeed, between 1803 and 1805 the assignees had already disposed of thirteen cottages and nearly three quarters of an acre of building ground not assessed to them in 1805. The Census of 1811 shows that 136 houses were built since 1801 in the East Division of the town; that is, the area between Marsh Lane and the river. From our evidence, 114 of these had been built by Paley in the first two years of that decade.

Paley was also rated on his commercial and industrial properties, and on the vacant ground that he had accumulated but not yet developed. Four surviving Rate Books between 1790 and 1805 allow us to take stock of the overall situation.[48] As might be expected, the total value of the building ground fell over time as it was converted into buildings, more than compensated for by the steady rise in the assessed value of the new buildings. The overall values rose fastest between 1790 and 1795 although the peak was reached in the 1800 assessment: the lower assessment of 1805 is a result of the sales of some assets by Paley himself on the eve of the bankruptcy, and by the asignees after November 1803 (Appendix 1 and Table 11.3).

More striking than this absolute growth is the place that Paley swiftly took among the property owners of the town. Even in 1790, after only three years of property development, his total assessment of £164 ranked fourth among the property owners of Leeds, out-done only by three families, Nevile, Wilson, and Denison, who then had nearly a century of merchanting or the professions behind them. (The high assessments on the Aire-Calder Navigation and on the Town Charities estates are excluded from these rankings.) In the

TABLE 11.3 *Paley in the rate books; 1790–1805.*

	DIVISIONS												
	Kirkgate		East		South		North East		Mill Hill		Total Land	Total Buildings	Total
	Land	Buildings	Land	Buildings	Land	Buildings	Land	Buildings	Land	Buildings			
As Owner													
1790	10.10.0	17.19.0	55.10.0	57.14.0	—	3.10.0	20. 0.0	8.15.0	—	—	86. 0.0	87.18.0	173.18.0
1795	9. 0.0	121.10.0	79. 0.0	209. 2.0	—	3.10.0	22.10.0	148.18.0	—	—	110.10.0	483. 0.0	593.10.0
1800	3. 0.0	82.13.0	72. 0.0	270. 5.0	—	3.10.0	17. 0.0	183. 3.0	—	—	92.10.0	539.11.0	632. 1.0
1805	—	56. 0.0	26.17.0	299.15.0	—	—	13.10.0	137.10.0	—	5. 5.0	40. 7.0	498. 0.0	538. 7.0
Rented													
1790	—	33. 8.0	7. 0.0	5. 0.0	—	—	15. 0.0	—	—	—	7. 0.0	38. 8.0	45. 8.0
1795	—	32.15.0	48.10.0	5. 0.0	—	—	15. 0.0	10. 0.0	—	—	63.10.0	47.15.0	111. 5.0
1800	—	32. 5.0	24.10.0	1.10.0	—	—	10. 0.0	—	—	—	39.10.0	33.15.0	73. 5.0
1805	—	57.15.0	29.13.0	—	—	—	10. 0.0	—	—	—	39.13.0	57.15.0	97. 8.0

Source: LCA, LOR B 34–7: Rateable value in £.s.d.
Largest single industrial rating for comparison:
Nevile, King's Mill (corn and oil) (1790) 400 5 0
Wormald and Gott, Bean Ing Mill (cloth) (1795) 133 0 0
"   "   "   (1800) 207 0 0
"   "   "   (1805) 217 0 0

assessment of 1800 Paley had climbed to second place, falling short of
Nevile by a mere £49. In the 1805 Rate Book the entries for Paley's
assignees give a total only £34 less than Nevile's, and there had been
disposal of land and buildings by the assignees in the two years since
the bankruptcy.

The Rate Book evidence effectively displays the cottage property
accumulated by Paley; although the undeveloped building ground is
itemised in the Rate Books, the best view of its extent is obtained on
a map such as Fig. 11.1, based partly on conveyances and partly on the
maps of the central area made for the assignees in 1807, 1809 and 1810.
Its base, drawn from the Giles's map of 1815 indicates the contribution of Paley to the total East End, and shows not only his ambitious
strategy of purchase but also the small proportion that had been
taken up for high density building by 1803, and the relatively small
further development between 1803 and 1815 resulting from the
assignees' sales. Fig. 11.1 also shows his important industrial buildings:
the two steam-powered cotton mills at Bank Low and Bank Top, the
Marsh Lane Flax Mill, and Cawood's New Leeds Foundry.

A third view of the semi-developed estate is afforded by the
topographical detail in the massive mortgages of 1795–96, the
renewals of 1800 and the final mortgages of March 1803 (Table
11.4). Like the Rate Book entries, these descriptions often located a
property by naming the earlier owners, so that the names of Ridsdale, Wilson, Elsworth, Eamonson and Rogerson still haunted the
documents. The solicitors acting for the assignees continued to
preserve their documents in parcels corresponding to these names,
and this system of filing had a practical point when it was necessary

TABLE 11.4   *The Paley mortgages, 1795–1803*

	Location	Origin of land	Composition
(b) (c)	Timble Bridge	ex Hall	Four messuages near the Calls and Old Church Yard.
(b) (c)	Kirkgate	ex Wild	Royal Oak Yard.
	Marsh Lane	ex Lee	Messuages; newly erected but vacant flax mill with steam engine and 1½ acres adjoining; messuages and gardens on north side of Marsh Lane, bottom.
(a) (c)	Marsh Lane	ex Ridsdale	Dryhouse with tenters, ware-house; tenter ground and ropery,

			$2\frac{3}{4}$ acres adjoining; messuage with carpenter's shop on north side; stable and cowhouse.
(a) (b)	Marsh Lane	ex Ridsdale	6 acres, north side of Marsh Lane, top.
(c)	Marsh Lane	ex Elsworth and Eamonson	Brickyard, $6\frac{1}{2}$ acres, on east and south-east side of Marsh Lane and 62 newly erected messuages.
	Hill House Bank	ex Baynes	Two newly erected cotton mills with steam engines; nineteen newly erected messuages and $\frac{3}{4}$ acre adjoining.
	Hill House Bank	ex Wilkinson	Thirty-four newly erected messuages and 4 acres adjoining.
(b) (c)	Northall Bridge	ex Mrs Wilson	Messuages, warehouse and shops.
(b) (c)	Hill House Bank	ex Mrs Wilson	Sigston Close, 5 acres.
(b)	Well Houses	ex Rogerson	Nineteen messuages and $3\frac{1}{2}$ acres adjoining.
(b) (c)	Sheepscar (Skinner Lane)	ex Denison	Ten newly erected messuages with workshops, warehouses, stables, and garden, with 4 acres adjoining.
(b) (c)	St Peter's Square	ex Sykes	Messuages with stables and gardens on east and south side of Square, with shares in communal central garden.
	York Street	ex Sykes	Eleven messuages.
	Marsh Lane	ex Goulden	Four newly erected messuages; thirteen messuages.
	Mabgate	ex Elsworth	Three cottages.
(a)	Marsh Lane	ex Hudson	Messuages.
	Timble Bridge	ex Dade	Forty-one messuages.
(a)	Kirk Ings	ex Cookson	Remainder of lease, made 1775.
	Fall Ing, Wakefield	?	$6\frac{1}{2}$ acres and messuages, lease of 1792.
	Bristol	?	Potash manufactory, newly erected.

(a) Items re-mortgaged between February 1803 and the bankruptcy. The Knostrop properties were mortgaged to Lumb 18 April 1803 for £5,000; see also Appendix 2 for industrial premises mortgaged 8 March 1803.

(b) Items mortgaged and redeemed in the £15,000 mortgage of 1 March 1796–24 September 1796, which also included the Knostrop properties.

(c) Items mortgaged and redeemed in the £10,200 mortgage of 17 May 1793–26 September 1795.

to draw up Abstracts of Title for the information of prospective purchasers and of conveyancers. Summaries of the content of all the mortgages[49] will be found in Appendix 2.

V

After this brief aggregate view we now pass to consider in more detail the characteristic houses erected by Paley on land that he developed between 1788 and 1803. A number of his cottages were packed into the *Folds* of Marsh Lane but there were two areas particularly worthy of consideration that show him introducing the interior court form of development to the East End. One of these lay on the Harrogate turnpike near to Sheepscar and Mabgate water-mills (Figs. 11.2 and 11.3) and the other occupied most of Mc-Andrews Garden, between Marsh Lane and St Peter's Square (Figs. 11.4a and 4b).

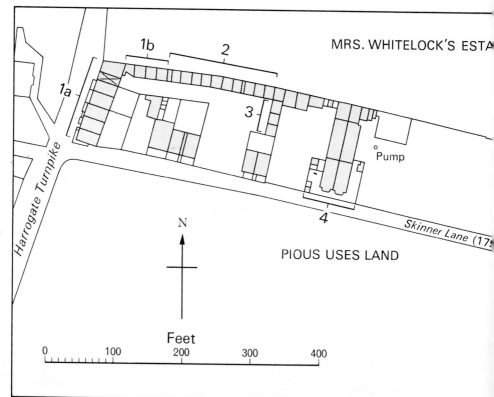

Fig. 11.2   White Cross and Fish Pond Closes, developed by Paley, 1792–6. Houses and shops facing Harrogate Turnpike with entrance passage to Brown's Yard (1a); twin bay-windowed merchants' houses and workshops (1792) (4);

The axis of building club development in Leeds was usually a new street frontage. In only two cases, Union Row and Union Place, both small-scale terraces, was this street frontage an existing road. The clubs who required a greater area took up closes into which they had to drive their own roads, thus creating Nelson Street, Ebenezer Street, George's Street, High Street, King Street, Queen Street, and St Peter's Square. These streets formed frontages for terraces of back-to-back houses, sometimes with cellar dwellings below.

Interior courts are found only occasionally, where streets did not run exactly parallel and there was room to spare behind the terraces for an infill of small groups of similar houses, back-to-back or blind-back, facing into an interior court and reached from the street by a tunnel or series of tunnels. If we are thinking of standards customarily acceptable to incomers, it should be remembered that

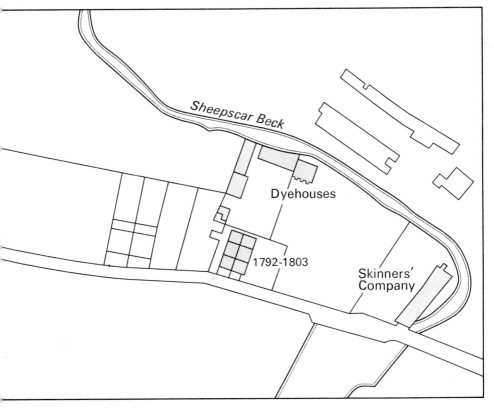

Skinner Lane (created 1793); blind-back houses in Brown's Yard (from 1796) (1b, 2 and 3). Industrial premises leased by the Skinners' Company lay between the Beck and Skinner Lane. Base: plans in LCD 12929 (1803) and 8899 (1815).

interior-facing courtyard housing of this kind was exactly what had
been produced during the previous generation of infill in the burgage
plots and innyards of Briggate and Kirkgate; and it was already the
style of Birmingham and Liverpool streets.[50]

Indeed, since only its first stage was reached in his lifetime, the
courtyard developments by Paley after 1793 at the newly purchased
White Cross Close (Fig. 11.2) could easily be mistaken for such a
burgage infill, entered through a tunnel beneath a pair of superior
houses erected on the east side of the Harrogate turnpike, were
they not too far from the town to be on a burgage plot, and the
circumstances of their origin so well documented. It is clear that
Paley intended to build a set of interior courts accommodated to the
long, narrow shape of the Close, just as he was filling up the more
rectilinear shape of McAndrews Garden with interior tunnel courts
between the south side of St Peter's Square and Marsh Lane (Figs.
11.4a and b).

In White Cross Close each of the fourteen houses built between
1792 and 1803 had one room only on their ground and first floors.[51]
They were blind-back, that is without entrances on their north sides,
and had their only door facing southwards into a common yard since
the next close northward was not in Paley's possession and, indeed,
was still undeveloped in 1815. The whole group of houses was later

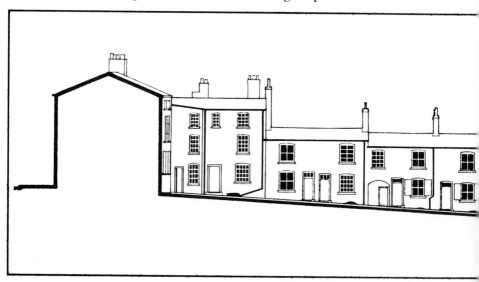

Fig. 11.3   Brown's Yard: elevation of blind-back houses, 1796–1803. Scale
drawing by R. Stuart Fell, from photographs before demolition in 1956.

known as Brown's Yard (Fig. 11.3) but its original name, as the 1815 map shows, was New Row; the few houses that had then been achieved on the southernmost side of the close were then called South Row. The length of this close and its neighbour, Fish Pond Close, some thousand feet, made it impossible to continue a yard indefinitely eastwards, and for access to the eastern part of the close it was necessary for Paley to create his own road all along the southern edge of the close and to build a bridge giving access to Mabgate at the eastern end of it. Thus was Skinner Lane born.[52]

Earlier than the White Cross Close development, the conjunction of the Greater and the Lesser Building Society's houses at St Peter's Square and High Street shows that (in 1787 at least) there was as yet nothing deterrent for those buying quite large houses if they had back-to-back houses (and even cellar dwellings) close by them.[53] Similarly at Skinner Lane, the non-repellent character of the blind-back houses designed for New Row is shown by the fact that from their earliest days they were neighbours to a superior pair of houses erected by Paley himself and offered to let in 1793 as 'Convenient and New-built . . . with Warehouses, Dressing-Shops, and Tenter Ground adjoining, pleasantly situated at Sheepscar near Leeds, and very suitable for a Merchant or Cloth-Dresser',[54] while further east Paley was offering to sell building land from the adjacent

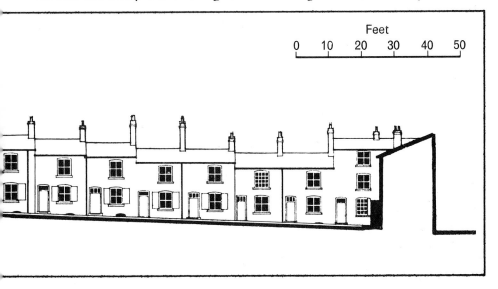

Feet

0 10 20 30 40 50

Fish Pond Close, 'eligibly situated'. A plan in a conveyance of 1815 shows that this pair of houses had ornamental gardens and orchards on their eastern side[55] (Fig. 11.2, no. 4).

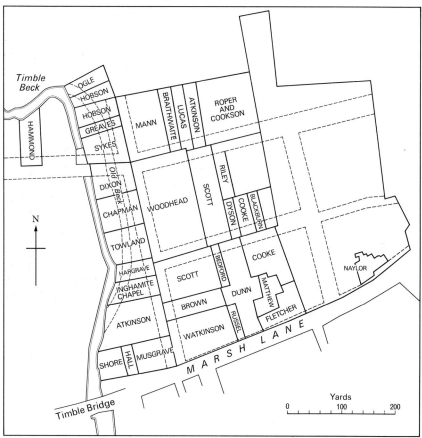

Fig. 11.4a   McAndrews Garden: Paley's Purchase (1787) and division into building plots (1788–1801). The names of purchasers are shown on each plot. Source: plans of 1807 (LCA, DB 233) and 1809 (DB Map 119).

The Paley development of courtyards in Marsh Lane began earlier than at Skinner Lane, and Fig. 11.4a shows the building plots into which Paley divided McAndrews Garden for the sales that began[56] in January 1788 and were still incomplete at the bankruptcy. The last recorded sale[57] was more than two years before the bankruptcy, and, as Fig. 11.4a shows, there had been no takers for the eastern part of the York Street–Off Street block nor for what one would have thought would have been two attractive corner sites at Brick Street–Marsh Lane and Duke Street–Off Street. Although so much nearer the centre of the town than Skinner Lane, the York Street and Off Street development shows the same hesitant development. Incomplete in the partition and sale plans of 1807 and 1809, it had gone very little further by the time that the 1815 map was drawn.

If the first Figure (11.4a) shows the varied sizes of plot for which takers were forthcoming, the second Figure (11.4b) in contrast shows the virtually standard house-size with which the thirty-five plots were filled, each five by five yards, the same area as the cottages of the building club streets. It also shows, facing each other across York Street, two completed examples of the long interior court with a tunnel entrance; two others, incomplete, on the north side of York Street; and shorter courts between Duke Street and the diverted course of the Timble Beck. The longer courts had from fourteen to eighteen houses within them, and the shorter courts, two or three.

Along the main frontages of Off Street, Duke Street, and Marsh Lane the standard back-to-backs were built two deep, and any remaining land within the plot was filled up with an appropriate number of blind-backs. Immediately north of the land in this Figure, it will be remembered, Paley himself owned three superior houses built at the south-east corner of St Peter's Square and included in Fig. 11.4b; on a plot in York Street bought in 1796 by Roper, Cookson and Co. the partners had erected another superior house together with a warehouse; the other non-cottage development was the small chapel of the Inghamite connection in Duke Street, built on land purchased from Paley in 1797.

Of a third type of Paley building we unfortunately know very little. On the Ordnance Survey map of 1850 'Paley's Galleries' appear on the south side of Marsh Lane; they were later absorbed by the goods yard extensions to Marsh Lane station and their deeds are not available for study.[58] Yet their name and hints in other conveyances suggest that they were built by Paley,[59] and they certainly appear on the assignees' sale plan of 1809. They were taken over by the railway too early for photographs, but from photographs of other Leeds properties the 'galleries' were probably wooden platforms giving access to first-floor, single-room, houses back-to-back.[60] Two- and three-storey single-room back-to-backs with interior tunnel-staircase entrances were certainly built here-and-there in Leeds in the 1820s, although disparaging comment on London model building schemes shows that Leeds shared the usual provincial distaste for multi-storey tenements, perhaps from their similarity to barrack and prison styles.[61]

By a later development that Paley could not have envisaged, the tunnel character of the courts between York Street and Off Street was accentuated when the extension of the railway station westwards from the old terminus at Marsh Lane to a central station thrust an embankment across the courts by neatly excising two houses from either side of each yard and further enclosing the courts by the archway that carried the tracks across the yard of each court.[62] Built in 1796 and 1797 at an overall density of 138 houses to the acre but then no more than 80 yards from grass fields, these working-class cottages in their triply tunnelled courtyard were to be a central issue in the long debate on slum clearance that divided informed opinion in Leeds during the last quarter of the nineteenth century.

VI

A complete entrepeneur of his day, Richard Paley was also the pioneer of foundry and mill building in Leeds earlier than Gott or Marshall, a fact that has escaped attention hitherto, probably because he was building for cotton and flax and not for wool. The absence of fame has been fortunate in one respect, for Gott's Bean Ing mill was recently swept away by a Corporation anxious to demonstrate that the 'Motorway City of the North' was truly in the second half of some century or other: yet three Paley mills were still standing un-noticed at Whitsun 1974. Paley's industrial activity can be treated only briefly in this essay, for it was not significant as an influence on housing location until nearly a decade after his bankruptcy and death. When James Watt junior came to spy out patent infringements[63] at Paley's mill in 1796 he had to approach on three sides over open ground (18, 19 and 20 on Fig. 11.1) like a raider on a medieval town, and even in 1815 working class streets on Paley land were no nearer Bank Low and Bank Top Mills (20 on Fig. 11.1) than they were to Bean Ing; the development by 1815 south of the Bank mills was not on Paley land.

It was Paley who brought the steam engine to the East End of Leeds, thus giving it a conjunction of mill chimney, mill effluvients, back-to-back courts, cellar dwellings, burial grounds, inadequate water, inadequate sewerage and inadequate drainage that was to figure large in the criticisms of the East End of Leeds made by Robert Baker and others in 1833, 1839 and 1842. It was to be an ugly and deadly conjunction of streets and steampower but it must be stressed that there was no actual conjunction in Paley's lifetime. Paley had owned the land, and could have built streets cheek by jowl with the mills.[64] No doubt he would have done so in time, but his first choice lay with more conservative sites adjacent to Marsh Lane, Timble Beck and the new housing of the Building Clubs, and in 1803, after fifteen years of property development, he had not built streets alongside the two Bank Mills. Mill Street did not come for twelve years more until the assignees in bankruptcy succeeded in selling

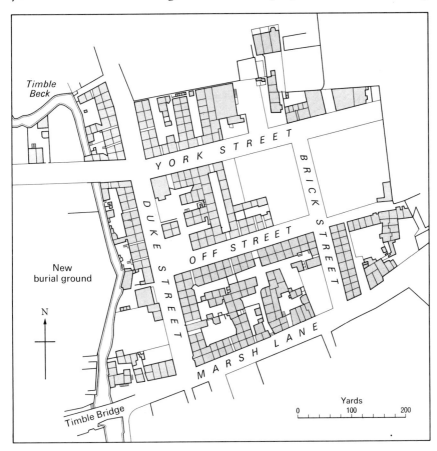

Fig. 11.4b Building plots as developed with back–to–back houses and interior courts (1788–1803). Source: as for Fig. 11.4a, and 1850 O.S. 5 feet = 1 mile plan.

part of the building ground in November 1815. Thenceforward there was an East End with houses and mill chimneys thoroughly inter-mixed, and St Peter's Square stood among them as incongruously as the incomplete Park Square in the West End. The unhappy conjunction was finalised when the gas works (1818) and the first railway station (1834) were sited in the same group of fields, to which other mills had meanwhile come.

It was an essential feature of deteriorating working-class housing standards in the 1830s and 1840s that the properties were simultaneously accumulating and ageing. Each of these processes, products of the passage of time and of urban development, brought their contribution to urban deterioration and to the Sanitary Question. The significance of Paley's East End development, therefore, is not so much that he filled the greater part of two closes with high density working-class housing but that he set a pattern for speculative development in Leeds which contemporaries accepted and which later generations followed. As we have seen, the state of demand for this type of property by 1815 did not extend this pattern very far, even where employment in the new mills was close at hand: but after that date, and especially in the 1820s, it was the pattern to be followed by those who developed the remaining parts of Quarry Hill, north of High Street and east of St Peter's Square; by the developers of the southern end of the Leylands, north of Lady Lane; and by some of those who eventually took up the parcels of ex-Paley land put on the market piecemeal by the assignees in bankruptcy between 1803 and 1823.

Paley did not originate the back-to-back house in Leeds although it was the form of working-class housing with which he and his sub-developers peopled the East End. The first back-to-backs were being built by members of at least three different Building Societies while Paley was acquiring Forster's Close and MacAndrews Garden. The Building Societies did, however, align their front houses along streets. Within McAndrews Garden and Forster's Close Paley and his sub-developers built back-to-backs but on plots shaped so as to exploit every square yard of the interior space between the grid of streets (Figs. 11.4a, 11.4b). As a result, whole lines of houses were set end-on to the street just as Brown's Yard was set end-on and not frontaging Skinner's Lane. Interior courtyards with only a tunnel entrance to the street had been created, the Paley pattern, high density housing with additional sanitary hazards.

In the first half of the nineteenth century it was common to name streets as well as courts and yards after the landowner or the speculative builder who had developed them. Many of those who had purchased plots from Paley or his assignees were so commemorated on the large-scale OS plans of 1850. After the bankruptcy there seems to have been an understandable wish to forget Paley himself, and Leeds has never had a Paley Street. However the 1850 OS plan did bear his name. A row of thirteen back-to-back houses with 97 inhabitants on the south side of Marsh Lane near the railway terminus was then called Paley's Galleries. They were soon to be demolished to make way for railway sidings so that we have no photographs, but from a description of them in 1848 they were back-to-backs piled vertically as tenements with wooden galleries serving the upper storey and cellar dwellings beneath.[65] For one who had tried so hard to maximise the density of housing in the East End of Leeds the survival of his name at the Galleries was not an inappropriate memorial.

APPENDIX 1 *Outline chronology of Richard Paley 1746–1808 and his assignees in bankruptcy, 1803–1823.*

1746		Born at Langcliffe, Settle.
1771	June	Marriage to Mary Preston of Merebeck, Settle.
1775	April	Takes forty-year lease of Kirk Ings and wharves from *Cookson*.
1776	Feb.	Mortgage on improved Kirk Ings properties from father for four years.
1780	Nov.	First purchases at Knostrop.
1782	July	Purchases two houses at Low Bank.
	July	Leases a brewery in the Calls to Appleyard and shares wharves with him.
1786	Oct.	Contracts to purchase cottages, a close at Black Bank, cottages at Mabgate, and Coneyshaws Close.
1787	Jan.	Large purchases at Knostrop from *Lucas*.
	Feb.	Purchase, with Dade, from *Eamonson*: 4 acres and 41 cottages, Marsh Lane.
	Feb.	Purchase from *Hall*: $4\frac{1}{4}$ acres of Forster's Close for £1,050.
	April	Purchase from *Elsworth*: 3 acres at Coneyshaws and one messuage in Mabgate for £255.
	Aug.	Purchase of McAndrews Garden from *Ann Wilson* settled estate.
	Dec.	Contributed £700 to £2,800 capital of Bowling Iron Works; purchase of Fall Ings, Wakefield.
1788	Jan.	Plot of 238 sq yd from McAndrews Garden to Hartley.
	May	Plot of 108 sq yd from McAndrews Garden to Hall.
	June	Purchase of remainder of Crackenthorpe Gardens from *Ann Wilson* settled estate.
	June	Mortgage for five years of Eamonson and Elsworth purchases for £900.
1789	April	Mortgage for four years of Forster's Close for £800.
	May	Purchase from *Baynes* of Skinner's Croft, 2 acres, dyehouse etc. for £445.

	June	Purchase from *Rogerson* of close and workshops at Well Houses, Hill House Bank. Elected to Corporation, Sept.
1790	May	Purchase from *Goodall* of 286 sq yd and nine messuages in Marsh Lane.
	May	Purchase from *Wild* of Royal Oak, Kirkgate.
	July	Plot of 975 sq yd from a close near Marsh Lane to Atkinson.
	Oct.	Plot of 1,040 sq yd from McAndrews Garden to Mann.
	Dec.	Purchase from Barnes of Lots xv and xxx from Greater Building Society, St Peter's Square, for £200.
	—	Paley builds two cotton mills with steam engines, one for Wilkinson, Holdforth and Paley, on land purchased from *Baynes.*
1791	Feb.	Purchase from *Hudson* of five cottages north of Marsh Lane for £130.
1792	Feb.	Purchase from *Ridsdale* (Ann Wilson) of two closes, 4 acres Tenter Close), dyehouses etc. south of Marsh Lane.
	Feb.	Purchase of two Yards in Kirkgate.
	May	Mortgage on Knostrop properties of £8,000 for three years.
	July	Purchase from *Denison* of White Cross and Fish Pond Closes for £2,200.
	Aug.	Plot of 106 sq yd to Maude.
	Sept.	Plot of 2,530 sq yd and house in Marsh Lane Close, to Dunn.
	Nov.	Mortgage on White Cross Closes and houses in St Peter's Square for £2,500.
	Nov.	Plot of 108 sq yd from Crackenthorpe Gardens to Goodall.
	Nov.	Purchase from *Lister* of three closes of 7 acres in Marsh Lane, north side.
	Nov.	Fall Ings partnership dissolved; lends ex-partner £1,000 at 5 per cent.
1793	Jan.	Purchase from *Lee* of croft and 41 messuages in Marsh Lane south side, Dufton's Yard.
	Jan.	Plot of 373 sq yd Marsh Lane, south side, Appleyard.
	Feb.	Plot of 1,335 sq yd near Kirkgate. Ministers and Zion chapel trustees (eventually St James).
	April	Mortgage of Hall, Wild and Ridsdale purchases for £8,000 for three years.
	April	Plot of 240 sq yd from Marsh Lane woodyard to Wilkinson.
	May	Mortgage on most of remaining properties for £10,200.
	May	Mortgage of Lady Lane properties for £2,585 for two years.
	May	Takes lease of Harper's water-frizing mill, Mill Garth, for twenty-five years.
	May	Purchase from *Ann Wilson estate* of Sigston Closes for £2,950.
	May	Purchase from *Ann Wilson estate* of Lady Bridge cottages and workshops.
	May	Purchase from *Lucas* of Green End Croft, Mabgate, for £2,000.

	May	Plot of 37 sq yd and two houses from Marsh Lane, north side to Naylor.
	June	Plot of 275 sq yd from Ridsdale's Close to Joy.
	Aug.	Plot of 11,870 sq yd in Mabgate to Wilkinson.
	Nov.	First press advertisement of property to let at Sheepscar (Skinner Lane) and elsewhere.
1793	?n.d.	Mortgage of Well House properties for £2,000.
1794	Jan.	Plot of 423 sq yd from Crackenthorpe Gardens to Smith.
1795	March	Plot of 424 sq yd from McAndrews Gardens to Goodall.
	June	Partnership of J., and J. J. Wilkinson, and Paley dissolved.
	Aug.	Plot of 355 sq yd near Lady Bridge to Simpson.
	Sept.	Mortgage on Eamonson and Elsworth properties for £2,425.
	Sept.	Buys £100 share in Leeds Waterworks Co.
	Sept.	Plot of 80 sq yd in Marsh Lane, Tenter Garth to Tomlinson ex *Green*.
	Oct.	Plot of 236 sq yd from McAndrews Garden to Towland.
	Oct.	Plot of 2,009 sq yd on Kirkgate, north side to Wright.
	Nov.	Plot of 2,652 sq yd near Lady Bridge to Bootham.
		Watt complains of Paley's breach of steam engine patent.
1796	Jan.	Plot of 4,015 sq yd at Skinner Lane to Brown and Sayer.
	Feb.	Plot of 135 sq yd and two houses from McAndrews Garden to Cooke.
	Feb.	Plot of 1,307 sq yd with warehouses at McAndrews Garden to Roper and Cookson.
	Feb.	Plot of 885 sq yd and thirteen houses from McAndrews Garden to Salt.
	March	Plot of 136 sq yd south-west of St Peter's Square to Baistow.
	March	Mortgage on Well House, two cotton mills and thirty other properties of £15,000.
	April	Plot of 144 sq yd from Dunn's Garden to Dyson.
	April	Plot of 867 sq yd to Scott.
	May	Plot of 288 sq yd from McAndrews Garden to Atkinson.
	May	Cotton Mill to let; sale of building ground envisaged.
1797	Jan.	Plot of 288 sq yd from McAndrews Garden to Lucas and Atkinson.
	Feb.	Plot of 514 sq yd in Marsh Lane to Lee.
	April	Plot of 392 sq yd from McAndrews Garden to Braithwaite.
	May	Four houses in St Peter's Square to Rathmell.
	June	Plot of 2,147 sq yd in Marsh Lane, bottom to Woodhead.
	July	Plot of 496 sq yd in Marsh Lane, bottom to Ingham.
	Sept.	Plot of 90 sq yd from Tenter Garth ex *Green*, Marsh Lane, east side to Gledhill.
	—	Holdforth, Wilkinson and Paley purchase a Watt engine from Soho.
1798	Feb.	Acquires from bankrupt *Appleyard*, closes at Richmond Hill and cottages at Hillhouse.

	Sept.	Plot of 466 sq yd in St Peter's Square to Smithies.
	Nov.	Plot of 248 sq yd and six houses in Marsh Lane bottom to Bell.
	Nov.	Paley contracts to build flax mill with steam engine in Marsh Lane for G. and J. Wright.
1799	March	Plot of 1,057 sq yd in Close adj. Sheepscar Beck to Richardson.
	Sept.	Obtains houses in York from trade debt by Johnson (£3,300).
	Oct.	Plot of 376 sq yd on Quarry Hill, north side to Clarkson.
1800	Feb.	Mortgage on remaining estate for £13,000.
	Feb.	Mortgage on Wilson purchases for £2,000.
	March	Plot of 923 sq yd to Goulden.
	April	Plot of 420 sq yd from Forster's Close to Hammond.
	May	Plot of 129 sq yd from McAndrews Garden to Simpson.
	May	Plot of 174 sq yd from McAndrews Garden to Wilkinson.
	June	Plot of 166 sq yd and two houses from McAndrews Garden to Lee.
	Aug.	Plot of 284 sq yd from Forster's Close to Sykes.
	Oct.	Plot of 1,360 sq yd in a Marsh Lane croft, and maltkiln to Musgrave.
	Dec.	Plot of 4,481 sq yd from Forster's Close sold for Burial Ground.
	Dec.	Plot of 222 sq yd in a close, Marsh Lane to Mennill.
1801	Jan.	Plot of 166 sq yd from McAndrews Garden to Wilkinson.
	June	Plot of 953½ sq yd near Lady Bridge woodyard to Woodhead.
	Sept.	Plot of 338 sq yd and five houses from Forster's Close to Schofield.
	Sept.	Plot of 4,491 sq yd from Forster's Close to Blayds and others.
	Dec.	Plot of 553 sq yd in St Peter's Square to Sherbrock.
		Plot of 1,809 sq yd from McAndrews Garden to Watkinson.
1802	April	Plot of 424 sq yd and fourteen houses from Forster's Close to Sykes.
1803	Jan.	First press advertisement for sale of Sheepscar, Mabgate, Lady Bridge, St Peter's Square and Kirk Ings properties.
	March	Malton Bank mortgage.
	March	Huddersfield and Pontefract bankers' mortgage.
	April	Lumb mortgage; Knostrop estate advertised for sale.
	May 11	Probate of Thomas Dade's will.
	May 21	Commission of Bankruptcy; assignment of personal goods; Bank Upper Mill and building lots advertised.
	June 11	First meeting of creditors; some dividends paid.
	Sept.	Further sale advertised.
	Nov. 28	Richard Paley subscribed 10 guineas for relief of poor.
	Nov. 29	First conveyance by assignees: 179 sq yd to Asquith.
1804	Jan.	Further sale advertised.
		Twelve conveyances from assignees.
1805	Feb.	Further sale advertised.
	Nov.	Creditors agitate for change of policy by assignees.
		Nine conveyances from assignees. Paley resigns from Corporation in Sept.

1806	Jan.	Further sale advertised.
	Feb.	Further sale advertised.
	May	Further sale advertised.
	Oct.	Creditors again agitate.
	Oct.	Further sale advertised.
		Eighteen conveyances by assignees.
1807	Jan.	Creditors yet again agitate.
	Mar.	Partition of the Dade moiety in favour of legatee, Edmund Maude.
		Sixteen conveyances by assignees.
1808		Four conveyances by assignees.
	Nov. 24	Paley dies at Knostrop, leaving widow Agnes, and son George as heir.
1809		Plan of central section of estate made for assignees; no conveyances this year.
1810	Dec.	Printed Sale-plan of estate by Oastler for assignees' sale; three conveyances this year.
1811		Six conveyances by assignees.
1812		No sales by assignees.
1813		No sales by assignees.
1814	Dec.	Original Clapham group of assignees replaced by Ikin group.
1814		Six conveyances by assignees.
1815	June	Further sale advertised.
1815		Eleven conveyances by assignees.
1816	Nov.	Further dividend to creditors.
1816		Seven conveyances by assignees.
1817		No sales by assignees.
1818	Feb.	Remaining part of estate advertised for sale.
1818		Three conveyances by assignees.
1819		One conveyance by assignees.
1820		One conveyance by assignees.
1821		Two conveyances by assignees.
1822		Three conveyances by assignees.
1823	Jan.	One conveyance by assignees.
	Mar.	One conveyance by assignees.
	April 12	Last five conveyances by assignees.
	July	Final dividend paid.

* The values of purchases and mortgages are incompletely known since the enrolments at WRRD always omitted this confidential fact; original deeds in LCA and LCD do not survive for all transactions.

APPENDIX 2 *Paley's mortgages, 1776–1803*

Date	Location	Origin of land	Mortgaged to	£	Redemption
4.2.1776	Kirk Ings	Cookson, 1775	T. Paley	?	6.3.1779
1.4.1779	Kirk Ings	Cookson, 1775	J. Crofts	?	?
30.1.1787	Knostrop	Lucas, 1780	J. Lucas	?	?
3.6.1788	Coneyshaws Close and Mabgate	Elsworth, 1787	C. Davison	900	26.8.1793
14.5.1789	Forster's Close	Hall, 1787	W. Hey	800	14.1.1793
25.11.1789	Knostrop	Lucas, 1780	J. Lucas	?	?
27.5.1792	Knostrop	Lucas, 1780	Beckett, Calverley & Co.	8,000	17.12.1795
22.11.1792	White Cross Close	Denison, 1792	} Townend	2,500	assignees, 1807
	St Peter's Square	Barnes, 1790			
11.4.1793	Timble Bridge	Ridsdale, 1792			
	Royal Oak, Kirkgate	Wild, 1730	} Glover	8,000	5.12.1799
	Forster's Close	Hall, 1787			
	Marsh Lane, 4 closes, of 9 acres	Ridsdale?			
3.5.1793	Northall	Mrs Wilson, 1793	Beckett & Duncombe	2,585	6.4.1795
17.5.1793	Timble Bridge	Ridsdale, 1792			
	Royal Oak Yard	Wild, 1790			
	Forster's Close	Hall, 1787			
	St Peter's Square	Barnes, 1790			
	St Peter's Square	Stephenson, 1793			
	White Cross Close	Denison, 1792	} T. Paley	10,200	26.9.1795
	New buildings	Elsworth, 1787			
	New Buildings	Eamonson, 1787			
	New buildings	Goodall & Cookson, 1790–1			
	Kirk Ings	Cookson, 1775			
	Fall Ing, Wakefield	—			
11.6.1793	Marsh Lane	?	E. Wetherhead	?	10.12.1799
23.11.1793	Cavalier Hill Close	Wilkinson, 1792	S. Harvey	2,000	7.2.1800
	Low Bottom Close				
?.5.1793	Marsh Lane,	Mrs Wilson, 1788	} H. Duncombe	?	6.4.1795
	Sigston Closes	Rogerson, 1788			
	Well House Close				
28.9.1795	Coneyshaws Close and Mabgate	Elsworth, 1787	R. Goddard	2,310	assignees, 1807
1.3.1796	see Table 11.4, item (b)		W. Dawson	15,000	24.9.1796
12.3.1796	all in 28.9.1795 and 1.3.1796 mortgages		T. Paley	?	22.9.1796
18.4.1796	Hill House and two cotton mills	Baynes, 1789	T. Wilson	1,000	?
28.9.1796	Knostrop	Lucas *et al.*, 1780	J. Armitage	?	?
7.2.1800	Cavalier Hill Close	Wilkinson, 1792	J. Armitage & W. Cookson	1,300	
	Low Bottom Close				
15.4.1800	See Table 11.4	Ridsdale, 1792	Cookson *et al.*	?	19.2.1803
22.4.1800	Northall	Mrs Wilson, 1793	Rhodes	2,000	1.2.1803
	Well House Close	Rogerson, 1788			
15.9.1801	Forster's Close	Hall, 1787	Blayds *et al*	?	?
8.3.1803	Marsh Lane Closes, Wright's Flax Mill, Farmery's Whitesmithy, and Cawood's Iron & Brass Foundry	} Ridsdale, 1792	Malton Bank	?	?
12.3.1803	Kirk Ings lease	Cookson, 1775	Seaton, Seaton & Seaton	?	?

Date	Location	Origin of land	Mortgaged to	£	Redemption
18.4.1803	Knostrop	Lucas *et al.*	Lumb	2,000	?
18.4.1803	Marsh Lane, closes Marsh Lane, cottages	Ridsdale, 1792 Hudson, 1791 }	Lumb	3,000	?

Sources: 4.2.76:WRRD, BZ35; 1.4.79: CE546; 30.1.87: CU193; 3.6.88: CX35; 14.5.89: DA186; 25.11.89: DB243; 27.5.92: DI428; 22.11.92: DK449; 11.4.93: LCA, DB233; 3.5.93:WRRD, DN119; 17.5.93: DM256; 11.6.93: DM662; 23.11.93: DN178; 5.1793: DR150: 28.9.95: DS187; 1.3.96: DT251 and LCD 359; 12.3.96: DT306; 18.4.96: DU9; 28.9.96: DW103; 7.2.00: EC55; 15.4.00: ED339; 22.4.00: ED550; 15.9.01: EK118; 8.3.03: EM 462; 12.3.03: EM590: 18.4.03: EN575; 18.4.03: EN623.
WRRD; West Riding Registry of Deeds. LCA; Leeds City Archives. LCD; Leeds Corporation Deeds, Civic Hall.

NOTES AND REFERENCES

Maps. Printed maps are those of John Cossins (1725), John Tuke (1781), and Netlam and Francis Giles (1815); those of Thomas Jeffreys (1770) and John Heaton (1806) are less useful.

1. H. J. Dyos, *Victorian Suburb* (Leicester University Press, 1961).

2. For a recent bibliographical essay, see A. Sutcliffe, 'Working-class housing in nineteenth century Britain', *Bulletin of the Society for the Study of Labour History*, no. 24 (1972), 40–51. An early study of the local strategy of development in Leeds was the M.A. thesis of David (now Professor) Ward, part of which appeared as 'The pre-urban cadaster and the urban pattern of Leeds', *Annals of the Assocn. of American Geographers, lii* (1962), 150–66. B. Weber, 'A New Index of Residential Construction', *Scottish Journal of Political Economy*, ii (1955), 104–132.

3. Sir John Summerson, *Georgian London* (2nd edn, rev. Barrie & Jenkins, 1962; Penguin Books); D. J. Olsen, *Town Planning in London: the Eighteenth and Nineteenth Centuries* (Yale University Press, 1964); C. W. Chalklin, *The Provincial Towns of Georgian England: a study of the Building Process, 1740–1820* (Edward Arnold, 1974); J. R. Kellett, *Glasgow* (Blond Educational, 1961); S. D. Chapman, ed., *The History of Working-class Housing* (David & Charles, 1971); I. C. Taylor, 'The eighteenth-century origin of the Liverpool slum', *Trans. Hist. Soc. Lancs. and Cheshire*, cxxii (1970), 67–90.

4. Illustrated in M. W. Beresford, 'The back-to-back house in Leeds, 1787–1937' in Chapman, ed. *The History of Working-Class Housing*, figs. 3.1 and 3.2.

5. Illustrated in M. W. Beresford, 'Prosperity Street and others', in M. W. Beresford and G. R. J. Jones, eds, *Leeds and Its Region* (British Association for the Advancement of Science, 1967), figs. 41–3.

6. In the transpontine South Division of the in-township the development was similar: infill of yards on Meadow Lane and Hunslet Lane until the building of Kendall Street (1793) and Camp Field (1805–6). Beyond the in-township on the south bank were the industrial villages of Hunslet and Holbeck.

7. 'Cottage' was the contemporary term: see W. G. Rimmer, 'Working men's cottages in Leeds, 1770–1840', *Thoresby Society*, xlvi (1961), 165–99. The usage arose not from neo-rustic romanticism but probably from the unbroken tradition of infill at the farming *Folds* on the town edge; see also maps cited in note, above.

8. Houses in the in-township: 1772: 3,345 (*Publns of the Thoresby Society*, xxiv (1919), 34); 1801: 6,694; 1811: 7,854; 1821: 11,160; 1831: 16,580 (Census); rates of building in the 1790's from Rimmer, *loc. cit.*, p. 187; number of factories *ex inf.* Dr. M. J. Ward.

9. *Leeds Mercury* [*LM*], 25 September 1852.

10. Robert Baker, *Report of the Leeds Board of Health* (1833).

11. For example, the plan of Crackenthorpe Gardens before its sale to the Building Society trustees: Leeds City Archives [LCA], DB Map 373 (1784).

12. As late as the Tithe Award of 1847 (LCA) the average size of the 54 fields designated as 'building ground' was only just over $1\frac{1}{4}$ acres.

13. 28 Geo. II cap. 10.

14. R. G. Wilson, *Gentlemen Merchants* (Manchester University Press, 1971), pp. 193–203; but it is wrongly stated there (p. 198) that Richard Wilson I inherited the Parks estate intact; purchases of many closes 'part of the Ancient Park' will be found in 1717, 1729 and 1748: West Riding Registry of Deeds (Wakefield) [WRRD], M19/26; AA326/422; AC169/237.

15. The second of W. Lodge's *Prospects* of 1715, with the southern part of the town in the foreground, has a less idyllic view of the town with a line of dye-house chimneys on the eastern skyline.

16. 5 Geo. III, Acts Private.

17. Leeds Corporation Deeds [LCD], 320, 334, 423 and 435.

18. LCA, DB 233.

19. Creditors claimed that from £15,000 to £20,000 capital was locked in the soap works and the cotton mill; one assignee declared hopefully that after meeting creditors' claims in full there would be £50,000 to distribute: *Leeds Intelligencer* [*LI*], 13 February 1804. For descriptions of the cotton mills see *LI*, 24 October 1796 and LCD, 1615; for the flax mill, *LI*, 19 October 1801; the foundry, *LI*, 11 July 1805.

20. *LI*, 25 June 1771; Paley's partner, Thomas Dade (note 41, below), came from Otley; perhaps Paley had connnections there. In 1800 a Mrs *Agnes* Paley joined Richard in a conveyance: Borthwick Institute, York, R. IV. K57; R. I. 38, f. 356; WRRD EK 118/166.

21. *LI*, 3 September 1772.

22. LCA, DW 514 and 685 for the Langcliffe connections; LO/AR1 for the apprentice.

23. WRRD, BX71/111. Breviates of most of the WRRD deeds appear also in LCA, DB 233.

24. Wilson, *op. cit.*, pp. 37–62.

25. WRRD, BZ35/51; CE545/686; CE546/688.

26. WRRD, CU192/236; DB98/125; DB243/296.

27. *LI*, 28 March 1808 and 18 November 1816 for the Paley offices and home.

28. WRRD, DF596/769; DH491/622; DK613/758; DS185/199; DM256/306; Hilary Long, 'The Bowling Ironworks', *Industrial Archaeology*, v (1968), 171–7; W. L. Norman, 'Fall Ings', *ibid.*, vi (1969), 1.

29. Plan *penes* British Waterways Board, Dock Street, Leeds.

30. Most of it was in use as allotment gardens, as the field names show: McAndrews Garden; Dunn's Garden; Crackenthorpe Gardens; Forster's Close was also known as Old Garden; the conveyance of Ridsdale's Tenter Close in 1792 describes it as part gardens: WRRD, DH455/569; DL692/815.

31. WRRD, DF7/6.

32. WRRD, DG72/106.

33. Assignees' sales: WRRD, EP329/426 (29 November 1803) to HX510/507 (2 November 1823).

34. WRRD, CW85/108.

35. *LI*, 5 December 1786.

36. WRRD, CT417/546; CW441/568; DI603/839; DB143/174; DI464/662.

37. WRRD, EM16/21: 424 square yards and fourteen newly erected houses on part of Forster's Close.

38. WRRD, EC55/860; DN178/238; also LCD5063.

39. LCA, DB 233, 'Counsel's Opinion' 1804: the sheriff was in possession of Paley's property 'to a large amount'.

40. *LI*, 7 February 1803.

41. Dade's will was proved on 3 November 1803: WRRD, EW742/853: it provided for a division of the Paley-Dade joint purchases but this was not achieved until March 1807 (WRRD, FD14/15). On 18 February 1803 Paley conveyed his share to trustees for his heirs, the origin of the 'private estate' of 2 acres remaining to his son in 1809: LCA, DB Map 119.

42. WRRD, EM462/612; EM590/807; EN575/773; EN623/835.

43. 'indebted in the course of trade, for £3,062 2s 3d to 'Seatons', four of whom were still shareholders in Richard Paley and Co. six years later. The Paley files in the Court of Bankruptcy records are not among the small sample undestroyed; Public Record Office B6/11, f. 131 but see C13/57 (ii) no 50.

44. 'Mr Paley having an unusual occasion for a large sum of money' took a loan in the form of £15,000 of 3 per cent Consols (LCD 359: 1.3.1796).

45. Appleyard: WRRD, EA35/36 and EB779/1045; also LCA, DB233; York: WRRD, EB1/1043.

46. LCA, DB 233: 'Note for Counsel', undated.

47. 1807: LCA, DB 233, map with partition deed; 1809: LCA, DB Map 119. A printed map by Oastler was published by the assignees in 1810, showing all the East End properties; there are several copies in DB 233.

48. Rate Books, LCA, LO/RB 34–7.

49. 1795–6: WRRD DS187/201; DT251/289; DT306/360; DU9/10; DW103/109; 1800: EC555/860; ED 339/445; ED 550/744; 1803: EM462/612; EM590/807; EN575/773; EN623/835.

50. Birmingham: *Victoria County History: Warwickshire*, vii (1964), 52–4; Liverpool: I. C. Taylor, *loc. cit.* (see note 3 above), 67–90, esp. fig. 9.

51. LCD 83, 8596, 8879, 10864, 12356.

52. WRRD, DM691/826; 692/827; 693/828; LCD, 83.

53. High Street was for 'the Sons of Labour' and St Peter's Square for 'Persons in the Middle Road' according to the *Leeds Guide* (1808); for the physical contiguity of these classes, see Beresford, *art. cit.*, inf.n.4, fig. 3.3.

54. *LI*, 4 January 1793.

55. LCD 8899: as fig. 11.2 shows, there was a block of six back-to-backs immediately east of the orchard; these were also built by Paley (LCA, DB97: Wild's Title); north of them were premises leased to the Skinners' Company.

56. WRRD, CX111/146.

57. WRRD, EH205/260; twenty messuages were 'unfinished' at the time of the Malton Bank mortgage, 8 March 1803: WRRD, EM462/612.

58. Being in the custody of Eastern Region, British Rail, and not the British Transport Historical Record Office, York.

59. LCD, 92.

60. Line Fold is the classic photograph (Leeds City Library, Local History Room). The Census of 1851 shows twenty-one separate dwellings in the Galleries; matched with the 1850 OS plan, two storeys are suggested.

61. *LM*, 22 July 1848.

62. Illustrated in Beresford, *art. cit.*, p. 84.

63. Birmingham Reference Library, Boulton and Watt MSS: in-letters, 20 June 1797; out-letters to Paley, 7 December 1795 and 7 February 1796; 'Catalogue of Old Engines', July 1796, p. 102.

64. A few houses had been built by Paley near Bank Mills and Cawood's foundry, but no streets created: see nos. 20 and 21, Fig. 11.1.

65. *LM*, 22 July 1848; for the 97 inhabitants of 1851 see PRO, HO 107/2319/4/5.

12

The rationale
of traditional building

The studies in recent years of local history to which Professor Hoskins has made so fine a contribution, enable us to see our British terrain as an exhibition ground of long term experiments in design and in good durable buildings, in the arts and crafts, and in degrees of hygiene and comfortable living. Traditional building reflects two enduring things – the richness of our varied raw materials and the disciplines of our climate. We take our unique climate for granted, but familiarity hides some significant facts. It has been praised for its contribution to human health and energy,[1] but its effect on house construction is less advantageous. The alternation of wet and dry, and hot and cold conditions at frequent intervals, together with pollution by sulphates in air and in rain, can cause serious decay to exposed building surfaces. Therefore it is important to design for maintenance, particularly with regard to the roof. House property has often to stand for twenty years in the open air without any attention. And in this respect common house building is in a category of its own, different from the design and servicing of all the transient objects of use, and objects of fashion, sheltered for us under the immense exhibition roof of modern commerce and advertisement. Common building is also in a different category from engineering structure such as bridges kept always under careful inspection. And there is the homely economic aspect that a well-built house with low maintenance charge has, unlike a motor car, probably paid for itself several times over in the course of a century.

In architects' offices fifty years ago, and on the site with good country builders, many were the long, slow, cautious discussions as to a particular building element on a particularly exposed part of the site. And so the relationships of shape to function, as argued by architect and craftsman, in the matter of roof shapes, overhangs, drip-moulds, good valleys etc., were learned. Aesthetic styles thus helped to maintain and hand on useful techniques.

Further, the aesthetics of fine building must also recognise another aspect of climate, namely the degree and kind of daylighting. This is relevant because, in addition to providing primal shelter, architecture is also an art of large cubic shapes well lit and achieving harmonies of its own which if seen, can give aesthetic satisfaction. But in daily life we are poor observers. I have heard an architect say: 'In this country those who look do not think, and those who think do not look.' This is partly on account of poor daylighting, and the lack of visual impact by objects in the open air. It is interesting to compare measurements of daylight in cities in this country and abroad. Over the whole year London averages 4 hours per day of bright sunshine while Rome has as much as 6·4 hours, and Manchester has only 2·7.[2]

I recall on an early visit to Rome experiencing the Italian blue sky relatively pale and neutral, and realising that the bright source of light was from sunlight beamed on to walls and ground surfaces and reflected upwards. The change was from the diffused light which comes from the large white cloud areas we have in Britain to the intense footlighting from bright pavements, terraces, steps and stylobates. The effect was to give a *presence* to buildings and specially to the porticos and colonnades.

In our climate we experience occasionally something approaching Italian light. When this happens the Greek portico of St Pancras Church, London, for example, is illumined from ground reflections and we can understand its aesthetic intention.

We also know that there is another aesthetic tradition and another architecture. It happens that St Pancras railway station is not far away, and in a good light this vast building with its multiplicity of features is bewildering; but in a mist or a pearl-pale London fog, its terminal gable-end, roof peaks, and clock-tower, distantly seen ending the long roof lines, seem to epitomise the genius of the Gothic.

A full analysis of architecture must therefore recognise both the functional and the aesthetic aspects and their interactions. It was in 1921 that systematic research began, at the newly organised Building Research Station, on common building materials under English skies. Materials were tested, samples exposed to the weather for long periods, building failures systematically visited and investigated. The work soon pointed to special regions of enquiry, namely to the efficiency of roofs, also to surface decay, cracks in the walls, and specially to thermal and moisture movements of materials caused by the frequent repetitions in the British Isles of wet and dry, frost and thaw, as noted above. It became clear that certain parts of a building under relentless climatic attack were more vulnerable than others.

Thus in my view the elaborate Gothic style provides, in fact, one of the most functional and efficient roofing systems yet devised. In our climate exposed roof structure like parapets and tops of party walls, are our eternal liabilities, but when they are rapidly drained and dried on a good slope, frost action is reduced and life prolonged. We find that developed Gothic detail with its overhangs, and its throatings forming water checks under projecting surfaces, and drips to hood moulds, and its splayed projecting splash-plinth below throwing the drip clear of the footings, forms a whole watershedding system. Also aesthetically the horizontal lines of the watershedding mouldings can be used to contrast with the powerful uprights of the buttress. A close analysis of function contributed to the style.[3]

This thorough water-shedding technique of the medieval builders was lost sight of by architects in Renaissance and Modern times. For instance Georgian parapets, wet on both sides and with flat narrow copings were, and are, a frequent cause of complaint. Before the introduction of the principle of the inserted damp-proof course (about 1880) parapets easily became reservoirs of moisture able to penetrate downwards, and in brick buildings generally showed the increased weather action by a slight change in tone colour. The classic cornice as a type did not give as efficient an overhang as the Gothic, but our country and small-town builders improved matters in the eighteenth century by developing the English 'cove cornice', giving greater projection.

It happens that our coastal resorts and their seafronts have provided useful testing grounds for common building materials. They can show us bricks and lime mortar, and various lime-plaster renderings, now 200 years old and more, and demonstrate what they can stand up to. The characteristic attacks are driving rain, wind erosion, sand-scouring and salt spray giving to sand a hygroscopic quality. The extreme case is often seen in a recent slate-hanging now covering an old exposed brick gable. But some bricks have stood the test. There are old Kentish stock bricks to be seen at Margate facing towards the sea front well over 150 years old; and at Rye there are old Sussex bricks on the very exposed position known as the Gun Garden. There is a still older example in the little red brick church at Small-hythe, which stands on the Rother estuary once navigable and providing shipbuilding yards in the sixteenth century. The church has stepped gables and is dated 1514. In these conditions of severe exposure research has shown that traditional handmade bricks will stand the strain better than modern machinemade ones – again stressing the point that traditional styles, evolved over a long period, seem specially adapted to the vagaries of regional conditions.

THE INFLUENCE OF BRICKS

There is an important factor in the history of building often ignored namely fire-risks in cities and its influence on building materials. Well on into the eighteenth century the narrow streets of cities were lined with 'half timber' and whole timber buildings, often projecting one storey above another and frequently roofed with thatch. It is not difficult to realise the risks of fire involved. The Great Fire of London was only one of innumerable conflagrations in cities all over the country during many centuries. London had been partly burnt three times in the century after the Norman Conquest.[4] Thus bricks and mortar, tiles and slates, had a real advantage over the old timber and thatch techniques and their increasing use led to the development of new variations in traditional building styles, related to their new functions.

It was of course the Great Fire of 1666 that produced the scenic change from the London of Shakespeare and his Globe theatre in half-timber work, and the succeeding Georgian London in brick. The instrument of change was the code of new building laws insist-ing on fire-proof party walls and brick street fronts. The practical-minded builder and writer Joseph Moxon who was writing his text-book *Mechanick Exercises* during the last years of the seventeenth century refers to the Act of Parliament for re-building the City of London as follows:

> And because the Act of Parliament may not be in every builder's
> hand I will insert so much of it as relates to Bricklayers Work to wit
> the heights and number of stories, and the thickness of Walls of the
> several sorts of Building . . . [He notes that] the Cellars thereof 6-ft.

and a half high, if the springs of water hinder not. [Walls shall be –]
First Story 9-ft. from floor to Seeling, and the Second Story 9-ft., . . .
that all Walls in front and rear, as high as the First Story, shall be of
the full thickness of the length of Two Bricks and thence upwards to
the garrats of the thickness of one brick and a half.[5]

There was probably some experimenting with brick sizes at
the period of formulating the new building regulations: Moxon
(c. 1678) states that common English bricks were as much as $11\frac{1}{2}$ inches
long, 9 inches wide and $2\frac{1}{2}$ to $3\frac{1}{2}$ inches thick. These dimensions
must have been experimental, for the normal 9 by $4\frac{1}{2}$ by 2 inches are
often quoted before and after the date 1700; bricks were not noticeably enlarged until the brick taxes in the later eighteenth century.

A famous brick contributing to our history, is the 'London Stock'
evolved during the eighteenth century from the 'brick earth' of
the Thames valley gravels. The term is derived from the fact that
handmade bricks were moulded on a special board called a 'stock'.
Washed chalk was added to the local material, but something else
worthy of note, was also added. The expansion of London in the
eighteenth century led to serious problems, not only of food supply
and water, and wet building sites as noted by Moxon, but also of the
removal of refuse. Every day the high basket grates of Georgian
London, with their wide bars, spilt out ashes and cinders. Tons of
material had to be removed. Part was sold to the brickmakers.[6]

What was added from London ash-bins was a useful silica in-
gredient to the local brick-earth, which resulted providentially in a
remarkably frost-resisting brick. The proof is seen in the eighteenth-
and nineteenth-century party walls coming above the roofs. Some
party-walls have copings but many are merely 'bricks on edge'. Old
London Stocks are also to be seen in garden walls, and in the retaining
walls under the pavements forming the old Bloomsbury coal cellars,
that is to say in those wall surfaces distinguished by building research
as giving maximum exposure to attack. They have gone the dark
colour characteristic of the Bloomsbury squares, but have stood up
to frost and also to acid rain caused by smoke pollution.

The good London Stock was also the result of hand-picking.
It was a 'common brick' divided into classes with peculiar names.
The fine record of performance in London walling is that of the
first quality stock brick taken from the best placings in the clamp.
What then became of the others – the milds, commons, place
bricks, shippers? They were no doubt used for partitions, interior
walls and backings. But as soon as a cheap external plaster rendering
or 'stucco' had been evolved, a market was ready for the use of

poorer quality bricks on external walls protected by stucco from weather attack, as seen in the Regency terraces.

TRADITIONAL ROOFS AND CLADDINGS

Equally important on the point of reducing fire risk was the use of tiles instead of thatch. The term 'thack tile' had become generalised from the early universal employment of thatch. Again fire-risk plays a decisive part historically. Roofs caught fire easily. In 1212 building regulations were issued by which no roofs in London 'were in future to be covered with reeds, sedge, straw or stubble, but only with tile,

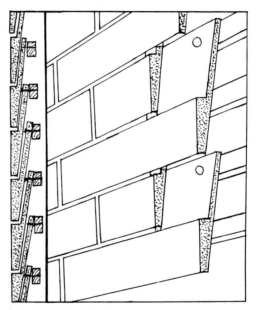

Fig. 12.1   Mathematical tiles.

shingles, boards or lead or plastered straw (*estra detorchiato*)'. Also 'all existing reed or sedge roofs were at once to be plastered, and if this were not done they might be pulled down'.[7] As the use of roof tiles increased, and tile-making became an industry, some standardising of sizes was found necessary, and also some standard specifying of materials. In the fifteenth century complaints were made of the lack of uniformity and also of the poor quality of roofing tiles. We learn that many of the roofing tiles on farm buildings of that date would last for only four or five years instead of forty or fifty.[8]

Plate 17 Tile hanging giving a simple pattern.

In 1477 an Act was passed regulating the manufacture and also the standard size.

Tile-hanging on walling is a thoroughly useful waterproofing practice – obstinately surviving in all periods on gable-ends and at bay windows. It is light in weight. The external angles can be made waterproof by using purpose-made angle tiles. The good 'lap' or overlying of one course upon the course below, in vertical tiling, ensures a good seal against driving rain. Tiling of walls can give a pleasant pattern by using the round-ended units, as can be seen in traditional buildings along the Kent and Sussex country roads. It is a rural craft of considerable value, and has been used by Edwardian architects (see plate 17). Taxes on bricks in the eighteenth century certainly encouraged the tile-making and tile-hanging as an industry. The tile courses could be 'pointed' with mortar and this later contributed to the deliberate arranging of hung tiles to imitate Georgian brickwork. In country towns it became the fashion (especially in Kent and Sussex) to build a classical facade to an old town house, and this could be done by *masking* the half-timber structure by a 'front' in brick concealing the medieval gables behind it and exhibiting to the street a cornice and tall Georgian windows. In some market squares a side view of the old gables behind the Georgian fronts can often be discovered.

But brickwork was comparatively expensive, and made more so by the brick taxes noted above, so that there was a real urge to imitate bricks in a light-weight technique. The result was to develop further the early 'mathematical tile' which had been hung on battens and could be used to imitate brick courses in stretcher bond (Fig. 12.1). In Canterbury and other Kentish towns the tile areas can only be located by tapping the wall on a street front. Being lighter in weight they evaded the tax. The economic aspect is seen in the fact that mathematical tiles appear to have been used on important buildings during the eighteenth century. Thus Holland used some for Brighton Pavilion in 1788; also Wyatt at Belmont, Kent, in 1792; and Soane in Sidney Lodge, Hamble, in 1786. But they were known before the brick taxes. Nathaniel Lloyd records their use at Lamb House, Rye in about 1755.[9]

An interesting sequel to the mathematical tile technique occurred after 1945 when wall units in concrete were being tried out as a useful substitute for bricks which were in short supply. It was obvious that mathematical tiles, however wrong in aesthetic principle, did in fact keep the water out. Could not the principle of the tile lap be applied to a concrete cladding unit as with the common wood weatherboard? But with concrete units there was always the risk of thermal expansion and contraction. But this was out-weighed by the recognised useful waterproofing performance of relatively small concrete roofing tiles. The size of slab decided on, after technical trials, was a 3 feet nominal length fixed on concrete 'studs' (upright posts), spaced at 18 inches. The system is well represented by the 'Airey Rural House'. Several thousands have been erected on postwar housing estates. The maintenance over some twenty-five years has been on the whole satisfactory.

Another postwar building technique has ancient precedents. This is the steel frame able to carry aloft a tiled roof before the walls were built. The suggestion was made that by building a good roof first various claddings could be tried out and also that the floors, partitions, linings etc. could be kept fairly dry during erection and thus be more rapidly completed. The design point is that the umbrella function of the roof is of importance in our climate, but that the walls could be regarded as screen units. The ancient method of building on crucks was, in fact, a *roof first* technique. Innocent says that he had always found that wherever, in any region, cruck building was known and recognised 'there was also a tradition among the old people that the walls were put up after the roof'.[10] I have also once or twice noted that old village tradition.

The ancient building term 'beam-filling' refers to filling in the gaps in the timber framework of a house between beams and up-rights. Thus the church wardens of St Mary at Hill in London in 1488 'paid James Dawber for walling, flooring and beam-filling'.[11] The 'walling' here refers probably to a base or to a gable wall. For 'beam-filling' between the half-timber work, there was always at hand the ancient weaving or wattling technique making use of straw, withies, rushes, ling or bracken. They were used from the earliest times with hazel rods for making hurdles for fencings, and for field sheds, and also for making cotes and cottages. It was a universal craft known variously as wattle and daub, stud and mud, ruddle and dab. And any crofter who had 'common rights' could gather these useful building materials from the waste or the common to build an addition to his house. William Horman writing in 1519 notes, in his treatise *Vulgaria*: 'Some men will have their wallys plastered, some pergetted and whytlymed, some roughcaste, some pricked,[12] some wrought with playster of Paris'.

The later economy in timber caused wider interspaces between the timber framings, and also called attention to the waterproofing value of different beam fillings. The wider fillings bring in the term 'panel'. Harrison in 1586 writes 'the claie wherewith our houses are empanelled is either white, red loam, or blue'.[13] It is likely that the rougher treatments such as daubing or torching were mostly for outside surfaces exposed to the weather, and the lime-plastered areas were for both outside and inside.

The development of external plastering is also connected with the ever present problem of waterproofing. In half-timber buildings the rain runs down the plaster panels and is delivered over the low level wood sill. The sills tend to rot, and the practice of the lead aproning of lower sills is fairly common. A later practice then was to plaster

Plate 18 Combing and pargetting, Hertford (Martin Coombs)

over the whole timber framing and interspaces together, and then to line out the interspaces, giving a deliberate large panel effect. But large plaster surfaces have an imperfection of their own: they can *craze* and display small surface cracks. Then the craftsmen discovered that by 'combing' – that is just breaking the plaster surface, while soft, with small furrows – the crazing effect is reduced, and a coat of whitewash will usefully improve the rainproofing. At first a pointed stick was used, but later a strong comb. And it was clear that the light furrowing of the plaster surface could make patterns out of contrasting units. A wave pattern could be given: also the comb could be rotated to give a pattern by means of a series of half circles within a moulded panel. And this in turn led on to the elaborate 'pargetting' in fairly strong relief characteristic of East Anglian buildings, both in town and country. The art extended into Hertfordshire. In Hertford on a row of houses, Nos 3 to 13 Fore Street, there are good examples dating from the seventeenth century of both combed panels and pargetted panels (Plate 18).

CRUCKS AND RIGGIN TREES

Turning to rural crafts an early activity was to free pasture by removing the field stones and building them into high fence walls in dry stone walling. An extreme case is found on Aran Mor, off the coast of Galway, where numbers of very small fields have walls 6 feet high to protect crops and livestock from gales, and also to free the valuable pasture from stones. An early step was to make use

Plate 19 Field shed in Newtondale, Yorkshire

of an angle of wall to make a small cote with a primitive roof. This use of field stones lasted in the Yorkshire Dales until the present century. The field shed, recent in date, in Newtondale (Plate 19) has forked posts in a row, and the 'gavel fork' at one end comes on the outer side of the gable wall.[14] It is in fact a repeating in modern times of an age-old building mode. The rafters are not fixed to the wall-plate but are lashed to the ridge tree and merely rest on the wall plate and could be pushed up here and there. But that means that the whole roof was held up from above by the 'riggin tree' and did not thrust on the walls. The term enters folk-lore in the Yorkshire designation 'the man astride the riggin tree' for the man who holds a mortgage on the property. The open gable ends were filled in with straw or heather.

But before posts in a straight row there was an earlier house type, namely posts in irregular rows. A valuable study by Lady Fox takes us back to the Iron Age in Glamorgan in Wales, and to a building designated 'the Lower House' at Dinas Noddfa, Gellygaer Common, and reconstituted by her after excavating.[15] The cross section is illustrated in Fig. 12.2, taken from interesting drawings by the late

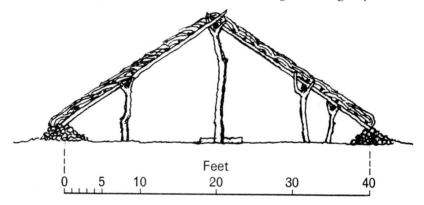

Fig. 12.2   Irregular post rows (suggested reconstruction, after Fox).

Sir Cyril Fox. It is a 'long house' of primitive type. The interior dimensions are width approximately some 20 to 40 feet and length approximately 58 feet. A wide low-pitched roof appears to be supported by irregular rows of posts. The centre row was on stout posts (post holes diameter about 10 to 12 inches). Some 12 feet away approximately on each side there is a row of posts of lesser diameter. It is conjectured that the stouter centre row carried a ridge tree at a high level, and that the side posts with spars and thack formed a very rough three-aisled interior. Also some random post-holes suggest subsidiary proppings. The thatched roof comes down to the ground or on to low turf walls or on to piles of stones. A paved central area may mark a chair of authority. The large 'internal slope', roofed over at the east end, could have provided some kind of seating for a tribal council. The scale of the plan and its three entrances suggest a community use.

This early house having irregular posts propping the roof developed into the more regular posts in a straight row carrying the ridge tree and giving more head room. But there is here a design point, namely that the older type, with low side roofing, gave some buttressing and would be less easily overturned by side gales. We tend to forget gale havoc in folk building although it is reflected in 'he huffed and he puffed and he blew the house down'. Gales causing destruction of church towers in stone, and the unroofing of town houses occurred in the Middle Ages. What then must have been the destruction of peasant houses built of 'clam, stave and daub'? This weakness no doubt contributed to the remedial method of the two intermediate rows of posts forming couples on the ground and inclined towards each other, meeting at the apex to take the ridge tree. Its origin in wind resistance is noted by Innocent, referring to Danish building on the windswept islands and shores of Jutland and Zealand: 'Experience has shown that gales which blew down the buildings with centre-posts (skraa-suler) left those with inclined posts (strid-suler) standing.'[16] (Fig. 12.3).

Here is design by trial and error leading to the recognition of stresses. The evocative Danish term 'strid-suler', as of heavy timbers striding the floor space, conveys this recognition, namely the recognition of buttressing by wooden 'shores', or 'struts'. It is likely that they were often brought into an existing house and fixed to the ridge tree in an intermediate inclined position, first as a safety precaution, and later in Denmark as an accepted insurance against gales.[17] (Fig. 12.3, example 2.)

But the answer in England is the 'curved tree' giving the principal couples, derived from our oak forests. No doubt in Jutland straight fir timber was often to hand: and in England occasionally the early 'couples' are straight.[18] But the gift of our pedunculate oak, slow growing, giving massive curved boughs, angle branches, crooks, knees and natural brackets, has helped our building crafts continuously.

The early 'couples' or pairs of crucks must often have been made from two different trees, but the term 'couple' suggests an exact reciprocal, only to be got by the considerable labour of sawing a tree down the centre, and this apparently became later a regional practice. The building mode is well illustrated in the Yorkshire barns – noble structures which, with their 'out-shuts', can span some 30 feet (see Fig. 12.3, example 5). Their special interest as buildings is that they can provide for all the farming activities of the region under one roof – cow byre (mistal), stacking space, threshing floor, and can even include a one bay cottage. James Walton has shown a Pennine plan on which the living space shares the same 'threshold' with the threshing floor – giving to 'threshold' its true connotation. The entrance to the living space off the barn was screened by a 'speer' or light-weight partition.[19]

The heavy Yorkshire crucks carried a stout rooftree at the apex and side trees or wavers (purlins) one on each side. The usual kind of dimensions were a span width between the cruck feet of 18 feet approximately, and a height to the fork of about 20 feet. A well chosen 'tree' could be nearly upright for 4 feet before the curve began to encroach. By increasing the width the height is reduced. By increasing the height (for headroom in a cottage) the width tends to be reduced. But in North Country districts in barn or byre or long-house it is the sense of the riggin tree out of the forest – a powerful key member holding up the whole structure as from above – which seems to linger on and give essential character.

The development of crucks from early times to their re-emergence in modern architecture is illustrated in Fig. 12.3.

Fig. 12.3   Cruck types. Some cruck types drawn roughly to scale. Example 1 shows the field shed. Example 2 is the Danish 'stridsuler' with intermediate raking struts, providing protection against side gales. Example 3 is a Scottish cruck house from Aberfeldy with a hump roof of turves (divots) covered by thatch. This roof is heavy, and when the thatch gets wet, exerts thrust, but in nearly all Scottish roofing the thick rubble walls help to buttress the roof. Example 4 is found in Wales and Yorkshire but is probably an age-old wood-land universal prototype. Example 5 is the Yorkshire curved cruck often used in barns – note the holes left in the foot of each for lifting and placing heavy units on the site. Example 6 is the Monmouth type, a refined version in which the line of the upper arm is straight to the apex. The cruck shape is so useful that it has now reappeared in concrete as the 'Portal frame'. The modern reinforced concrete units (example 7) are made deepest at the elbow, like the developed Monmouth unit, for strength against bending stress. Concrete crucks are used mainly for workshops and stores, but in recent years crucks have also been made out of laminated wood (example 8) and used by architects for modern churches and halls. (I am indebted to *Monmouthshire Houses* by the late Sir Cyril Fox and Lord Raglan, published by the National Museum of Wales.)

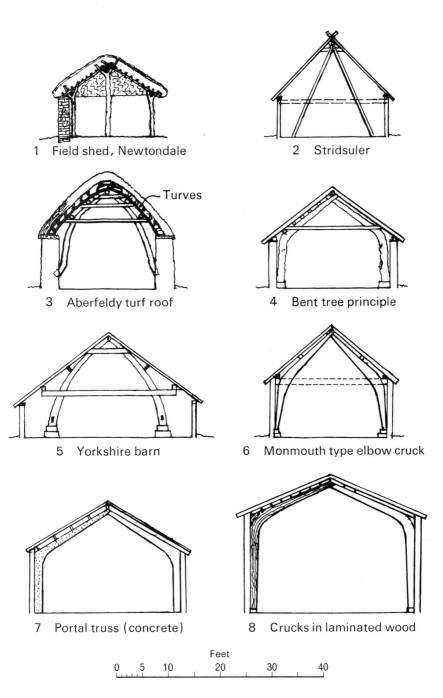

1   Field shed, Newtondale

2   Stridsuler

— Turves

3   Aberfeldy turf roof

4   Bent tree principle

5   Yorkshire barn

6   Monmouth type elbow cruck

7   Portal truss (concrete)

8   Crucks in laminated wood

Feet

0   5   10   20   30   40

Plate 20
A weaver's cottage;
Ainly Place, Slaithwaite

In a stone wall region however there is the continuous temptation to increase interior height by lifting the crucks to higher and higher levels in the walls. There is then real risk of thrust and of overturning. I have noted old neglected barns that have collapsed for that reason.

In the matter of length, cruck structure can give a 'bay' of 16 feet between the couples, and bays can be added. The term *bay* (origin disputed) came to mean a unit of length subdividing a building. At the bay, in town dwellings, it was convenient to locate partition walls, also fire-places with chimney 'tunnels', new hearths, etc. We find in Shakespeare the curious statement by Pompey in *Measure for Measure* that – 'if this [unpopular] law holds in Vienna ten years, I'll rent the fairest house in it for three pence a bay' (II, 1–245). For 'bay' the alternate term 'Severy' was employed in some agreements with builders. In 1512 at the vaulting of Henry VIth's chapel at Kings College, Cambridge in Weldon stone the builders John Wastell and Henry Semark 'shall make their bargains for stone, so that they be evenly paid with £100 at the performing of every severy'.[20]

THE INFLUENCE OF STONE ON TRADITIONAL STYLES

Traditional building sought not only to solve the basic housing needs of the inhabitants of each region by means of utilising the local raw materials, but also to extract the special characteristics from each material to add an aesthetic element to housing construction. Some examples of different styles arising from diverse materials such as timber-frame building and pargetting have already been given, but it is in the areas of stone construction that the influence of the

Plate 21 Eldwick Old Hall
Mediaeval mullioned windows were deliberately retained, while the pitch of the roof was lowered by heavy stone slates replacing thatch. The hipped roof is now rare; the wide low gable-end can, in Yorkshire, easily become a Classic pediment. Another characteristic is the ornamenting in a light relief of the massive door lintel over the main entrance. The roof finials are also peculiar to the West Riding, giving points of ornament, namely the stone lantern and the stone pine cone. Eldwick Old Hall illustrates the serious *dignity-of-office* which the style conveys. Later a more refined Classic is reached simply by using the genius of the stone. (Plate 22).

building material on the traditional style can be most clearly seen. Many possible examples could have been chosen to illustrate this, but lack of space obliges us to concentrate on one good regional example, that of Yorkshire.

One such style was developed in the West Riding where the 'putting-out system' of cloth production affected house layouts in the seventeenth and eighteen centuries. The homes were stone built and had low-pitched roofs of thackstones, thick enough to project as 'drips' some inches at the eaves. There were two rooms on the ground floor – a 'house' and a parlour: and on the upper floor, reached at first by a ladder, there was often a single workroom stretching the full length of the building, but sometimes divided into a larger and a smaller room. Furnishings were simple. An inventory

Plate 22 Houses near Halifax. These moderate street fronts show the Geological Classic. The eaves are strengthened into a simple cornice, the three-light windows are just formalised, the long stone units give sills and surrounds, and the natural stone slabs provide hoods over doors and brackets to support them. Some of the large early factories (nineteenth century) of the West Riding, untouched by Ruskin, and before the concrete era, are structural *monuments* derived directly from the geology, and worth study.

of 1779 giving the possessions of Joseph Broadbent of Honley records that the 'house' was also the kitchen and contained the table and chairs, a dresser, a pewter case and pewter, and kitchen utensils.

In the 'parlour' was the best bed, also a small table, nine chairs, and on the table a 'large bibell'. On the upper floor there were two rooms. The 'great chamber' which had a bed but was essentially a carding and spinning room, and the 'little chamber' which was a loom shop. Two 'arks' are mentioned in the great chamber to hold oatmeal. 'Outside in the tenter croft were the thirty odd yards of tenter; in the stable was a galloway; in the mistal two cows.'[21]

There was a development in the eighteenth century when the weaving of coarse fabrics was succeeded by finer spinning and closer weave patterns. This needed better daylighting for the handloom weavers, and produced long rows of windows between narrow stone mullions on the upper floors. Ainly Place in the Upper Colne Valley was a whole handloom community – a rock-built citadel – developed round the clothier's home and his 'take-in door'. Plate 17 illustrates the long mullion windows of the workroom on the upper floor. Mr Bernard Wood quotes the diary of Cornelius Ashworth, a weaver of Wheatley near Halifax in the year 1782: 'A fine frosty morning but was overcast and was dull. Went with my Piece [of cloth] to Halifax and loomed a Warp. . . . Shower in the forenoon. Droughty in the Afternoon. I worked outside till 3 o'clock. Wove two yards before Sunset.'[22] This stresses the significance of the long windows on the upper floor.

The bigger Yorkshire hall house also responded to industrial use. By the seventeenth century the practice was to add weaving rooms and weaving galleries to the old massive structure, or to add a third floor. A special 'take-in' door was planned with a landing on stone brackets above, for hauling up wool to the store rooms. At Clegg Hall, Rochdale, the ground floor and the third floor were weaving and store rooms, the family occupying the first and second floors.

Of course, architecture is never purely functional, and the use of stone provided an opportunity for the elaboration of local styles. A good example is provided by Eldwick Old Hall at Baildon (Plate 21), using the genius of the stone. This Geological Classic is well seen in some moderate street fronts near Halifax (Plate 22).

Another Yorkshire region showing a building art of its own is the North Riding. Here is the north-east end of the great diagonal band of Jurassic rocks that began on the Isle of Portland and has given us our limestone cathedrals, at Filey Brigg it disappears again under the sea. But in the north-east the rocks include sandstones as well as limestones. Also the Vale of Pickering was once a lake in which alluvial clay was deposited, now giving us red and brown pantiles. These materials can be seen in the vernacular building. The

strong monolithic sandstone lintels and jamb stones show us the
Classic doorway in unlikely situations, as in back walls of random
rubble. The general character of the houses is given by the stone

Feet

0   5   10   20   30   40

Fig. 12.4   Pickering town house. Note the 'haunch lintels' over the ground
floor windows. These are theoretically wrong but there is evidence that they
resist fracture from settlement better than the normal beam on its bearings.

walls capped by red pantiles, and by the Yorkshire sliding casements.

In Pickering the walls of the older houses are in a random masonry
2 feet 3 inches thick but there is a dual tradition of roofing. One
type has stone walling, with heavy bearer beams carrying the roof
load, and another has normal crucks supporting the 'roof tree',
which in turn holds up the roof from above. Pickering town houses
are often of neat dressed stone in a vernacular Classic. A curious trait
is the absence of dormer windows in tile roofs and often noticeable
shortness of window breasting to bedroom windows (Fig. 12.4)
probably caused by inserting a floor at a low height.

With these examples of Yorkshire stone building we have moved
away from the purely functional and practical aspects of traditional
resources to observe how over the years the disparate elements of
building structure – roofs, walls, windows and doors – have been
transmuted, through local materials, into distinctive vernacular
styles. They are only a few of the many which came to maturity

between the fifteenth and nineteenth centuries all over England, and demonstrate that the ordinary needs of daily living could be blended with an aesthetic sense to produce a perfectly functional yet distinctively attractive series of architectural styles.

NOTES AND REFERENCES

1. C. E. P. Brooks, *Climate in Everyday Life* (Benn, 1950), p. 30.
2. *Ibid.*, Table 10.
3. In respect of ground moisture there is some recent evidence of an early damp-proof course formed of oyster shells running under the projecting plinth mould of King's College Chapel, Cambridge, begun in 1446. This was discovered by Mr E. A. Gee of the Royal Commission for Ancient Monuments. Oyster shells were sold by the bushel for lime in early times, and the idea of lapping whole shells could easily follow.
4. L. F. Salzman, *Building in England down to 1540: a documentary history* (Clarendon Press, 1952), p. 223.
5. Joseph Moxon, *Mechanick Exercises* (3rd edn., 1703), pp. 262–3.
6. H. Ardern, 'Disposal of London rubbish', *Journal of the London Society* (July 1961), 14–19.
7. Salzman, *op. cit.*, p. 223; see also C. F. Innocent, *Development of English Building Construction* (Cambridge University Press, 1916), p. 190.
8. Salzman, *op. cit.*, p. 230.
9. N. Davey, *A History of Building Materials* (Phoenix House, 1961), p. 8; also N. Lloyd, *A History of English Brickwork* (Granville Montgomery, 1925), pp. 12–14.
10. Innocent, *op. cit.*, p. 113.
11. Salzman, *op. cit.*, p. 192.
12. The term 'pricking' probably means filling the interspaces with narrow timbers called 'prick-posts', to make a stronger panel structure. Alternative terms seem to be stothes (later studs), and puncheons.
13. W. Harrison, *The Description and Historie of England*, in *Holinshed's Chronicles* (1807), i, 315.
14. H. Bagenal, 'Some Yorkshire studies', *RIBA Journal* (1938), 616.
15. Sir Cyril and Lady Fox, Dinas Noddfa, 'Gellygaer Common', *Archaeologia Cambrensis*, xcii (1937), Part A.
16. Innocent, *op. cit.*, p. 23.
17. See also the excellent *Guide Book* (in English) to the Netherlands Open-air Museum at Arnhem.
18. See the interesting cruck barn, a framing only, at the West Yorkshire Folk Museum, Shibden Hall, Halifax.
19. J. Walton, *Homesteads of the Yorkshire Dales* (Dalesman Publishing Co., 1947), plan 288.
20. R. Willis and J. W. Clark, *Architectural History of the University of Cambridge* (Cambridge, 1886), i, p. 608 (appendix).
21. J. Walton, 'Pennine weaving hamlets', *Country Life*, 16 May 1957, 995.
22. G. B. Wood, 'A forgotten regional style', *Country Life*, 18 February 1960, 316.

W. G. Hoskins: a Bibliography

The aim of this bibliography is to include all Professor Hoskins's academic writings with the exception of very short notes and reviews. Because of the wide range of his interests and writings this has not been an easy task and has necessitated the omission of some articles and reviews in journals like *The Listener*, which in the editors' judgment did not come under the rubric of academic. Thus it is hoped that the bibliography includes all the writings of academic interest, even if it is not a complete list of all his publications.

Abbreviations: *Ag.HR*   *Agricultural History Review*
               DCNQ   *Devon and Cornwall Notes and Queries*
               Econ.HR   *Economic History Review*
               EHR   *English Historical Review*
               HT   *History Today*
               TLAS   *Transactions of the Leicestershire Archaeological Society*

1929   'Woollen industry', *DCNQ*, xv, 154.
       M. A. thesis: The Rise and Decline of the Serge Industry in the South West of England (University of London).

1933   'Formation of parishes in Devon', *DCNQ*, xvii, 212–14.

1935   *Industry, Trade and People in Exeter, 1688–1800 with special reference to the Serge Industry*, Manchester University Press. History of Exeter Research Group monograph no. 6. Second edition, University of Exeter, 1968.

'The Anglian and Scandinavian settlements of Leicestershire', *TLAS*, xviii, 110–47.

1936   Ph.D. thesis: The Ownership and Occupation of Land in Devonshire, 1650–1800 (University of London)

1937   'Further notes on the Anglian and Scandinavian settlements of Leicestershire', *TLAS*, xix, 93–111.
'The fields of Wigston Magna', *TLAS*, xix, 163–9.
'The Baring family', *DCNQ*, xix, 173.
'Banking in Exeter', *DCNQ*, xix, 175.

1939   'Wigston Magna lay subsidies, 1327–1599', *TLAS*, xx, 55–65.
'A history of the Humbersone family', *TLAS*, xx, 241–89.
'Burrow farm in Stoke Cannon', *DCNQ*, xx, 27–8.
'Farway subsidies', *DCNQ*, xx, 32–4.
'Cadbury and Thorverton subsidies', *DCNQ*, 74–6.
'No man's land', *DCNQ*, xx, 87.
'Devonshire trade in the early eighteenth century', *DCNQ*, xx, 151–4.
'"Cross" place names near Silverton', *DCNQ*, xx, 184–5.
'Population of Exeter', *DCNQ*, xx, 242–7.
Reviews: *John Tregagle of Trevorder: man and ghost* by B. C. Spooner, *DCNQ*, xx, 143–4; *Cornish Crosses: Christian and Pagan* by T. F. C. Dexter and H. Dexter, *DCNQ*, xx, 189–90; *Proceedings of the West Cornwall Field Club (Archaeological) DCNQ*, xx, 237; *The Changing Village* by F. G. Thomas, and *The Material of English History* by F. J. Weaver, *DCNQ*, xx, 332–4.

1940   'The Leicestershire country parson in the sixteenth century', *TLAS*, xxi, 89–115; reprinted in *Essays in Leicestershire History* 1950.
'Murder and sudden death in Medieval Wigston', *TLAS*, xxi, 175–87.

1941   'The occupation of land in Devonshire, 1650–1800', *DCNQ*, xxi, 2–12.
'Mol's coffee house', *DCNQ*, xxi, 25.
'Exeter bookseller's stock in 1615', *DCNQ*, xxi, 36–8.
'Earthwork in Cruwys Morchard', *DCNQ*, xxi, 164–6.
'East Devon yeoman', *DCNQ*, xxi, 241–8.

1943   'The reclamation of waste in Devon 1550–1800', *Econ.HR* (first ser.) xiii, 80–92.

1944   Review: *The English Yeoman under Elizabeth and the Early Stuarts* by M. Campbell, *Econ.HR* (first ser.), xiv, 193–6.

1945   'The Leicestershire farmer in the sixteenth century', *TLAS*, xxii, 33–95; reprinted and revised in *Essays in Leicestershire History*, 1950.
'Galby and Frisby', *TLAS*, xxii, 173–211; reprinted in *Essays in Leicestershire History*, 1950.
'The deserted villages of Leicestershire' *TLAS*, xxii, 241–265; reprinted and revised in *Essays in Leicestershire History*, 1950.

1946   *The Heritage of Leicester*, Leicester, Edgar Backus; second edition, City of

Leicester Publicity and Development Department, Information Bureau 1950, third edition 1972.

'A Devon yeoman in 1648', *DCNQ*, xxii, 162–4.

'Courtenay Pole's account book', *DCNQ*, xxii, 239–40, 251–2.

'Devonshire Gentry in Carolean times', *DCNQ*, xxii, 317–27, 353–62.

Review: *Farming Systems from Elizabethan to Victorian days in the North and East Ridings of Yorkshire* by G. E. Fussell, *Econ.HR* (first ser.), xvi, 79.

1947   'Leicestershire yeoman families and their pedigrees', *TLAS*, xxiii, 29–63.

1948   *Touring Leicester*, City of Leicester Publicity and Development Department, Information Bureau.

Introduction to 'Studies in Leicestershire agrarian history', *TLAS*, xxiv, 11–15.

'The Leicestershire crop returns of 1801', *TLAS*, xxiv, 127–53.

1949   *Midland England: a survey of the country between the Chilterns and the Trent*, B. T. Batsford 'Face of Britain Series'.

Rutland, City of Leicester Publicity and Development Department, Information Bureau.

'The origins and rise of Market Harborough', *TLAS*, xxv, 56–68; reprinted in *Provincial England* 1963.

'Devonshire gentry in Carolean times', *DCNQ*, xxiii, 1–10.

'Chagford and Moreton markets', *DCNQ*, xxiii, 21–2.

'Feodaries' surveys', *DCNQ*, xxiii, 54–5.

'The meaning of Barton', *DCNQ*, xxiii, 273–7.

Reviews: *Bedfordshire Historical Record Society Publications*, xxv, *Econ.HR* (second ser.) ii, 104; *The Population and Epidemics of Exeter in Pre-Census times* by Ransom Pickard, *DCNQ*, xxiii, 124–7; *The Story of Woodbury* by Rev. A. W. Leyland, *DCNQ*, xxiii, 127–8; *The Raleigh Country* by E. R. Delderfield, *DCNQ*, xxiii, 399–400.

1950   *Essays in Leicestershire History*, Liverpool University Press.

Introduction to Devon, in *Devon and Cornwall in Pictures*, Odhams Press.

'Croft hill', *TLAS*, xxvi, 83–92; reprinted in *Provincial England*, 1963.

Reviews: *Leicestershire Abbey*, by Levi Fox, *TLAS*, xxvi, 142–3; *The Guildhall, Leicester* by Philip Stevens, *ibid.*, 142–3; *Roman Forum, Leicester* by Philip Stevens, *ibid.*, 142–3.

1951   *Chilterns to the Black Country*, Collins, 'About Britain Series' no. 5.

East Midlands and the Peak etc., Collins, 'About Britain Series' no. 8.

'The Leicestershire farmer in the seventeenth century', *Agricultural History*, xxv, 9–20; reprinted in *Provincial England*, 1963.

'British towns and cities, IV: Exeter', *HT*, May, 28–37.

'British towns and cities, VII: Leicester', *HT*, September, 48–56.

'Stone farm, Thorverton', *DCNQ*, xxiv, 145–7.

'Devon hearth tax returns', *DCNQ*, xxiv, 211–12.

'A Domesday identification (Leigh Barton, Silverton)', *DCNQ*, xxiv, 111–12.

Review: *More old English farming books from Tull to the Board of Agriculture* by G. E. Fussell, *Econ.HR* (second ser.), iii, 397–8.

1952 *Devonshire Studies* (with H. P. R. Finberg), Jonathan Cape.
Old Exeter: a description of its growth and old buildings illustrated with photographs, plans and a map, London, Compton Dando.
'The writing of local history', *HT*, July, 487–91.
'The landscape of towns, I. The planned town'; 'II. The open-field town'; 'III. The market town', *The Listener*, xlviii, 457–8, 499–500, 539–40, 555.

1953 'The rebuilding of rural England 1570–1640', *Past and Present*, iv, 44–59: reprinted in *Provincial England*, 1963.
'Annals of the Parish', *The Listener*, l, 496–8.
Reviews: *An Inventory of the Historical Monuments in Dorset*, I, *EHR*, lxviii, 424–6; *Andrews and Dury's Map of Wiltshire, 1773*, *EHR*, lxviii, 487–8; *Guild Stewards' Book of the Borough of Calne, 1561–1688*, ed. A. W. Mabbs, *EHR*, lxviii, 640–1. *A Handbook of Local History: Dorset* by Robert Douch, *EHR*, lxviii, 668–9.

1954 *The Making of the English Landscape*, Hodder & Stoughton.
Devon, Collins, 'A New Survey of England', ed. Jack Simmons, no. 2; reprinted 1964; second revised edition, Newton Abbot, David and Charles, 1972.
'Regional farming in England', *Ag.HR*, ii, 3–11.
1. 'The anatomy of the English countryside' (the first of five talks under this general title); 2. 'A hand-made world'; 3. 'The road between'; 4. 'The "Rash Assault"'; 5. 'The house through the trees', *The Listener*, li, 732–4, 772–4, 819–20, 864–6, 917–18.
Reviews: *Stratford upon Avon* by Levi Fox, *EHR*, lxix, 141–2; *The Manor of Etchingham cum Salehurst*, ed. Sir Sylvanus P. Vivian, Sussex Record Society, *EHR*, lxix, 150; *Victoria County History of Sussex*, iv, ed. L. F. Salzman, and *Victoria History of the County of Cambridge and the Isle of Ely*, iv, ed. R. B. Pugh, *EHR*, lxix, 350–1; *Victoria County History of Wiltshire*, vii, ed. R. B. Pugh. *EHR*, lxix, 511; *Miscellanea of the Yorkshire Archaeological Society*, ed. C. E. Whiting, *EHR*, lxix, 691; *The Making of our Towns* by Sir William Savage, *History*, xxxix, 292–3; *Yorkshire Archaeological Journal*, part 148 (1951), *History*, xxxix, 312.

1955 *Sheep Farming in Saxon and Medieval England*, a lecture to the Royal Society of Arts, London, 3 November 1955. Department of Education of the International Wool Secretariat, London.
'An Elizabethan provincial town: Leicester', in *Studies in Social History: a tribute to G. M. Trevelyan*, Ed. J. H. Plumb, Longmans, pp. 33–67; reprinted in *Provincial England*, 1963.
'English agriculture in the seventeenth and eighteenth centuries', *Relazioni del X Congresso Internazionale di Scienze Storiche, Roma, 1955*, v, Firenze, Sansoni, pp. 205–26.
'The great rebuilding', *HT*, May 1955, 104–11.

'George Wightwick and John Foulston', *DCNQ*, xxvi, 40–1.

'Devon parish notes', *DCNQ*, xxvi, 101–2, 132–4.

'Butcher Row, Exeter', *DCNQ*, xxvi, 109.

Reviews: *The City and County of Bristol: Study in Atlantic Civilisation* by Bryan Little, *EHR*, lxx, 473–4; *A History of the City of Oxford* by Ruth Fasnacht, *EHR*, lxx, 474–5; *Medieval Cornwall* by L. E. Elliott-Binns, *EHR*, lxx, 659–60.

1956   'English provincial towns in the early sixteenth century', *Transactions of the Royal Historical Society* (5th ser.), vi, 1–19; reprinted in *Provincial England*, 1963.

'Seven deserted village sites in Leicestershire', *TLAS*, xxxii, 38–53; reprinted in *Provincial England*, 1963.

'Fieldwork in local history', *Amateur Historian*, iii, 1–8.

Review: *The Leicestershire Archaeological Society, 1855–1955, EHR*, lxxi, 682–3.

1957   *The Midland Peasant: an economic and social history of a Leicestershire village* [Wigston Magna], Macmillan; reprinted Papermac no. 107, 1965.

Exeter in the Seventeenth Century: tax and rate assessments, 1602–1699, edited and introduced by W. G. Hoskins for the Devon and Cornwall Record Society, new series, vol. ii, Torquay, Devonshire Press for the Society.

Dartmoor National Park, edited by W. G. Hoskins, HMSO; reprinted 1962 and later. Includes essays on 'Dartmoor from Roman times to the present day' and 'Places of special interest in the National Park', by W. G. Hoskins.

'The population of an English village 1086–1801, *TLAS*, xxxiii, 15–35; reprinted in *Provincial England*, 1963.

'The Englishman's house, I. The house in the town'; lvii, 953–5; II. 'Farmhouses and cottages'; III. The interior of the house; *The Listener*, lvii, 953–5, 995–7, 1035–6.

Reviews: *Bridgend: the Story of a Market Town* by H. J. Randall, *EHR*, lxxii, 161; *A Catalogue of Inclosure Maps in the Berkshire Record Office* by P. Walne, *EHR*, lxxii, 207; *Medieval York: a Topographical Survey based on Original Sources* by Angelo Raine, *EHR*, lxxii, 351; *Records of the Borough of Nottingham, IX, 1836–1900*, Nottingham Corporation, *EHR*, lxxii, 382–3; *The Records of the Corporation of Leicester*, ed. A. M. Woodcock, *EHR*, lxxii, 400; *The Victoria County History of Essex*, iv, ed. W. R. Powell, *EHR*, lxxii, 525–6; *Tudor and Stuart Lincoln* by J. W. F. Hill, *Econ.HR* (second ser.), x, 142–4; *People and Homes in Hampton-on-Thames in the Sixteenth and Seventeenth Centuries* by B. Garside, *Econ.HR* (second ser.), x, 297–8.

1958   *Royal Commission on Common Lands, Report*, Appendix II, History of Common Land and Common Rights, HMSO, pp. 149–66.

'The English landscape' in *Medieval England*, ed. A. L. Poole, Oxford University Press, pp. 1–36.

'Devon parish notes', *DCNQ*, xxvii, 37–8, 144–9.

'The finest travel-book in English', on Richard Ford and his handbook to Spain, *The Listener*, lx, 337–9.

Reviews: *The Victoria County History of Wiltshire*, v, ed. R. B. Pugh and Elizabeth Crittall, *EHR*, lxxiii, 133–4; *The Annals of West Coker* by Sir Mathew Nathan, ed. M. M. Postan, *EHR*, lxxiii, 342–3; *The First Ledger Book of High Wycombe*, ed. R. W. Greaves, *EHR*, lxxiii, 346; *Elizabethan Peterborough*, ed. W. T. Mellows, *EHR*, lxxiii, 350–1; *The Victorian County History of Oxfordshire*, v, ed. M. D. Lobel, *EHR*, lxxiii, 512–13; *Progress Notes of Warden Woodward, 1659–75*, ed. R. L. Rickard, Wiltshire Archaeological and Natural History Society, *EHR*, lxxiii, 528; *History on the Ground* by M. W. Beresford, *Econ.HR* (second ser.), xi, 160–1; *The Wealth of Five Northamptonshire Families, 1540–1640* by M. E. Finch (Northants. Record Society, xix, 1956), *Econ.HR* (second ser.), xi, 163–4; *A History of British Livestock Husbandry to 1700* by R. Trow-Smith. *Econ.HR* (second ser.), x, 480–2; *Devon Monastic Lands: calendar of particulars for grants, 1536–1558*, ed. Joyce Youings, Devon and Cornwall Record Society, *DCNQ*, xxvii, 26–7; *Medieval England: Aerial Survey* by M. W. Beresford and J. K. St Joseph, *The Listener*, lix, 466.

1959　*Local History in England*, Longmans; second revised edition, 1972.

Devon and its People, Exeter, A. Wheaton and Co; reprinted Newton Abbot, David & Charles, 1968.

Reviews: *The Local Collection Catalogue of Books and Maps relating to Berkshire*, Reading Central Public Library, *EHR*, lxxiv, 382–3; *Essex Homes, 1066–1850*, Essex Record Office, *EHR*, lxxiv, 759; *The Place Names of Derbyshire* by K. Cameron, *The Listener*, lxi, 942.

1960　*Two Thousand Years in Exeter*, Exeter, James Townsend & Sons; reprinted 1963, 1969.

Westward Expansion of Wessex, Leicester University Press; reprinted 1970, Department of English Local History, occasional papers, no. 13.

'Farmhouses and history', *HT*, May, 1960, 333–41.

Reviews: *A Guide to the Kent County Archives Office*, ed. F. Hull, *EHR*, lxxv, 378; *The Printed Maps of Warwickshire, 1576–1900*, ed. P. D. A. Harvey and Harry Thorpe, *EHR*, lxxv, 726; *Report on County Town Industries of South-West England* by T. Thomas and K. S. Woods, *Econ.HR* (second ser.), xiii, 300–1; *North England* by A. E. Smailes. *The Listener*, lxiii, 314; *The Buildings of England: Leicestershire and Rutland* by Nikolaus Pevsner, *The Listener*, lxiii, 854; *Buckinghamshire, ibid.*, 856.

1961　'Elizabethan merchants of Exeter', in *Elizabethan Government and Society*, eds. S. T. Bindoff, J. Hurstfield and C. H. Williams, Athlone Press, pp. 163–87; reprinted in *Old Devon*, 1966.

'George Oliver, D. D., 1781–1861', *Downside Review*, 334–48.

Reviews: *The Victoria County History of Essex*, Bibliography, ed. W. R. Powell, *EHR*, lxxvi, 189–90; *Rural England, 1086–1135: a Study of Social and Agrarian Conditions* by R. Lennard, *EHR*, lxxvi, 319–24;

The Ports of the Exe Estuary, 1660–1860 by E. A. G. Clark, *Econ.HR* (second ser.), xiv, 150–1; *Tradesmen in Early Stuart Wiltshire: a Miscellany*, ed. N. J. Williams, *Ag.HR*, ix, 68; *A History of Torquay and the Famous Anchorage of Torbay* by Percy Russell, *DCNQ*, xxviii, 295–7; *English Place-names* by Kenneth Cameron, *DCNQ*, xxviii, 330–1; *The Buildings of England: Suffolk* by Nikolaus Pevsner, *The Listener*, lxv, 708; *Joseph Ashby of Tysoe, 1859–1919* by M. K. Ashby, *The Listener*, lxv, 935.

1962   'Richard Thornton, 1776–1865. A Victorian millionaire', *HT*, August 1962, 574–9.

'The threatened countryside, VI beautiful Devon', *The Listener*, lxvii, 988–9.

Reviews: *St. Austell: Church: Town: Parish* by A. L. Rowse, *EHR*, lxxvii, 139; *A Tudor Book of Rates*, ed. T. S. Willan. *Econ.HR* (second ser.), xv, 373–5; *The Lake Counties, 1500–1830: a social and economic history* by C. M. L. Bouch and G. P. Jones, *The Listener*, lxvii, 652 and 655; *The Pattern of English Building*, by Alec Clifton-Taylor. *The Listener*, lxviii, 1057.

1963   *Provincial England: essays in social and economic history*, London, Macmillan; New York, St Martins Press; reprinted 1964, 1965; Papermac no. 140, 1965.

The Common Lands of England and Wales (with Sir Laurence Dudley Stamp), Collins, New Naturalist series.

Rutland, Faber, Shell Guide.

Reviews: *Guide to the Nottinghamshire County Records Office*, ed. P. A. Kennedy, *EHR*, lxxviii, 206–7; *The House and Home* by M. W. Barley, *The Listener*, lxix, 521–2; *The Place-names of the West Riding of Yorkshire*, ed. A. H. Smith. 8 vols, *The Listener*, lxix, 607; *The Domesday Geography of South-East England*, ed. H. C. Darby and E. M. J. Campbell, *The Listener*, lxx, 283–4; *The Domesday Geography of Northern England*, ed. H. C. Darby and I. S. Maxwell, *ibid*; *Victorian Cities* by Asa Briggs, *The Listener*, lxx, 572; *Industrial Archaeology*, by Kenneth Hudson, *The Listener*, lxx, 759.

1964   'Harvest fluctuations in English economic history, 1480–1619', *Ag.HR*, xii, 28–47; reprinted in W. E. Minchinton, ed. *Essays in Agrarian History*, i, Newton Abbot, David & Charles, pp. 93–115.

'Exeter today', *The Listener*, lxxii, 842–3.

'Harvest and hunger', *The Listener*, lxxii, 931–2.

'Epidemics in English history', *The Listener*, lxxii, 1044–6.

Reviews: *Elizabethan Winchester* by Tom Atkinson, *History* xlix, 69–70; *The Place-Names of Gloucestershire*, ed. A. H. Smith, 3 vols, *The Listener*, lxxii, 361.

1965   'An exploration of England', I. 'Devon farms without a village', *The Listener*, lxxiv, 82–5; II 'Evolving townscapes', ibid., 122–5.

Reviews: *The Railway Navvies* by Terry Coleman, *The Listener*, lxxiv, 314; *The Industrial Archaeology of Southern England* by Kenneth Hudson,

The Listener, lxxiv, 502.

1966 *Old Devon*, Newton Abbot, David & Charles.
English Local History, the Past and Future, an inaugural lecture delivered in the University of Leicester, 3 March 1966, Leicester University Press.
Reviews: *Field Studies in the British Isles* ed. J. A. Steers, *EHR*, lxxi, 221–2; *The Victoria County History of Gloucestershire,* vi, ed. C. R. Elrington, *History*, li, 394–5; *Georgian Lincoln* by Sir Francis Hill, *The Listener*, lxxvi, 360.

1967 *Fieldwork in Local History*, Faber; reprinted 1968.
Reviews: *Exeter Houses, 1400–1700* by D. Portman, *Econ.HR* (second ser.), xx, 389.

1968 *The Human Geography of the South West*, The George Johnstone Lecture, Newton Abbot, Seale-Hayne Agricultural College.
Human nature displayed in the 'History of Myddle' also known as 'Antiquities and memoirs of the Parish of Myddle, County of Salop' written by Richerd Gough, and newly introduced by W. G. Hoskins, reprint of first edition, Fontwell Centaur Press.
'Harvest fluctuations, and English economic history, 1620–1759', *Ag.HR*, xvi, 15–31.
Reviews: *The Domesday Geography of South West England*, ed. H. C. Darby and R. Weldon Finn, *Econ.HR* (second ser.), xxi, 383–4; *A History of the County of Leicester*, v, *Gartree Hundred*, ed. J. M. Lee and H. A. Mckinley. *Ag.HR*, xvi, 68–70; *New Towns of the Middle Ages* by Maurice Beresford, *The Listener*, lxxix, 215; *The Agrarian History of England and Wales*, iv, *1500–1640*, ed. Joan Thirsk, *The Listener*, lxxix, 478–9; *The Living Village* by Paul Jennings, and *The Departed Village* by R. E. Moreau, *The Listener*, lxxx, 832–3.

1969 Reviews: *Records of the Borough of Leicester*, vi, *The Chamberlain's Accounts, 1688–1835*, ed. G. A. Chinnery, *Econ.HR* (second ser.), xxii, 133–4; *Tuckers Hall, Exeter, the History of a Provincial City Company through five centuries* by Joyce Youings, *Econ.HR* (second ser.), xxii, 557.

1970 *Leicester*, Faber, Shell Guide.
History from the Farm, edited by W. G. Hoskins, Faber.
Review: *The Devonshire Lay Subsidy of 1332*, ed. Audrey M. Erskine, *DCNQ*, xxxi, 195–6.

1971 'Historical sources for hedge dating', in *Hedges and Local History*, London, Standing Conference for Local History, pp. 14–19.

1972 *Exeter Militia List, 1803*, edited with an introduction by W. G. Hoskins, London, Phillimore with the Devon and Cornwall Record Society.
'The homes of family names', *HT*, March, 189–94.
Reviews: *The Rural Landscapes of the Welsh Borderland* by Dorothy Sylvester, *Ag.HR*, xx, 77–8; *The Victoria County History of Shropshire*, viii, ed. A. T. Gaydon, *Ag.HR*, xx, 78–80; *Geographical Interpretations of Histori-*

cal Sources, ed. A. R. H. Baker, J. D. Hamshere and John Langton, and *An Agricultural Geography of Great Britain* by J. T. Coppock, *Ag.HR*, xx, 183.

1973   *English Landscapes*, London, BBC.

Index